Why Dominant Parties Lose

Why have dominant parties persisted in power for decades in countries spread across the globe? Why did most eventually lose? *Why Dominant Parties Lose* develops a theory of single-party dominance, its durability, and its breakdown into fully competitive democracy. Greene shows that dominant parties turn public resources into patronage goods to bias electoral competition in their favor and virtually win elections before election day without resorting to electoral fraud or bone-crushing repression. Opposition parties fail not because of limited voter demand or institutional constraints but because their resource disadvantages force them to form as niche parties with appeals that are out of step with the average voter. When the political economy of dominance – a large state and a politically quiescent public bureaucracy – erodes, the partisan playing field becomes fairer and opposition parties can expand into catchall competitors that threaten the dominant party at the polls. Greene uses this argument to show why Mexico transformed from a dominant party authoritarian regime under PRI rule to a fully competitive democracy. He also shows that this argument can account for single-party dominance in other countries where the surrounding regime is authoritarian (Malaysia and Taiwan) and where it is democratic (Japan and Italy). The findings have implications for Mexico's political future, the formation of new political parties, transitions to democracy, and the study of competitive authoritarianism.

Kenneth F. Greene is Assistant Professor of Government at the University of Texas at Austin. His research on regimes, political parties, and voting behavior has been published in the *American Journal of Political Science, Comparative Political Studies, PS: Political Science and Politics, Política y Gobierno, Foreign Affairs en Español*, and edited volumes. He has served as Co-Principal Investigator on two National Science Foundation grants for elite and voter survey research in Mexico, won a Fulbright-García Robles fellowship, and held visiting positions at the Center for Democracy and Civil Society at Georgetown University and the Kellogg Institute for International Studies at the University of Notre Dame. He received his PhD from the University of California, Berkeley in 2002.

Why Dominant Parties Lose

Mexico's Democratization in Comparative Perspective

KENNETH F. GREENE
University of Texas at Austin

CAMBRIDGE
UNIVERSITY PRESS

32 Avenue of the Americas, New York NY 10013-2473, USA

Cambridge University Press is part of the University of Cambridge.

It furthers the University's mission by disseminating knowledge in the pursuit of education, learning, and research at the highest international levels of excellence.

www.cambridge.org
Information on this title: www.cambridge.org/9780521139892

© Kenneth F. Greene 2007

This publication is in copyright. Subject to statutory exception and to the provisions of relevant collective licensing agreements, no reproduction of any part may take place without the written permission of Cambridge University Press.

First published 2007
Reprinted 2008, 2009
First paperback edition 2009
Reprinted 2010, 2011, 2013

A catalog record for this publication is available from the British Library.

Library of Congress Cataloging in Publication data
Greene, Kenneth F., 1969–
Why dominant parties lose : Mexico's democratization in comparative perspective / Kenneth F. Greene.
    p. cm.
Includes bibliographical references and index.
ISBN-13: 978-0-521-87719-0 (hardback)
ISBN-10: 0-521-87719-9 (hardback)
1. One party systems. 2. Opposition (Political science). 3. Democratization – Mexico. 4. Presidents – Mexico – Election – 2000. 5. Comparative government.
I. Title.
JF2051.G75 2007
324.2–dc22   2007018740

ISBN 978-0-521-87719-0 Hardback
ISBN 978-0-521-13989-2 Paperback

Cambridge University Press has no responsibility for the persistence or accuracy of URLs for external or third-party Internet Web sites referred to in this publication, and does not guarantee that any content on such Web sites is, or will remain, accurate or appropriate.

To my mother,
Penny

And to Stephanie

Contents

Figures and Tables		*page* ix
Acknowledgments		xiii
1	The Puzzle of Single-Party Dominance	1

PART I. THE MACRO-PERSPECTIVE

2	A Theory of Single-Party Dominance and Opposition Party Development	33
3	Dominant Party Advantages and Opposition Party Failure, 1930s–1990s	71

PART 2. THE MICRO-PERSPECTIVE

4	Why Participate? A Theory of Elite Activism in Dominant Party Systems	119
5	The Empirical Dynamics of Elite Activism	139

PART 3. IMPLICATIONS

6	Constrained to the Core: Opposition Party Organizations, 1980s–1990s	173
7	Dominance Defeated: Voting Behavior in the 2000 Elections	210
8	Extending the Argument to Italy, Japan, Malaysia, and Taiwan	255
9	Conclusions and Implications	297
References		311
Index		333

Figures and Tables

FIGURES

1.1	Lower House of Congress Election Results, Mexico, 1961–2000	*page* 2
2.1	Overview of the Argument: Opposition Party Formation and Success in Dominant Party Systems	36
2.2	Model Predictions: The Effects of Patronage on Equilibrium Party Strategies	57
3.1	Opportunities for Opposition Party Development due to Shifts in the PRI's Economic Policy Platform, 1934–2000	74
3.2	Freedom House Ratings, Mexico, 1972–2000	96
3.3	Economic Participation of State-Owned Enterprises (SOEs), 1970–2000	102
3.4	Number of Federal Government Employees (millions), 1983–1999	103
3.5	Television Coverage by Party, 1988–2000	110
3.6	Reported Revenue by Party (Public and Private), 1994–2000	112
4.1	Predicted Policy Preferences of Indifferent Elite Activists with Changing Costs of Participation	132
5.1	Party Elites' Mean Locations in the Competition Space	145
5.2	Party Elites' Economic Development Policy Preferences	146
5.3	Party Elites' Regime Preferences	147
5.4	Year of PAN Elite Affiliation from Sample Surveys	151
5.5	PRD Elite Recruitment Paths until 1988	153
5.6	Year/Period of PRD Elite Affiliation from Sample Surveys	154
5.7	Party Elites' Predicted Economic Policy Preferences, 1970–1999	163

x   *Figures and Tables*

5.8	Party Elites' Predicted Regime Preferences, 1970–1999	167
6.1	Trends in Voters' Economic Policy Preferences by Party Identification, 1982–1998	178
6.2	How Party Elites View their Core Constituencies	181
6.3	Party Elites' Party-Building Preferences	187
6.4	Party Elites' Nonparty Organizational Memberships	192
6.5	Party Membership and Geographic Concentration	193
7.1	Reported Campaign Spending by Party, 1994 and 2000	213
7.2	Location of Party Identifiers in the Competition Space, 1988–1999	216
7.3	National Party Leaders' Predicted Support for PAN-PRD Alliance in 2000	225
7.4	Effects of Issue Distance and Campaign Information on Candidate Choice	249
7.5	Probability of Defecting from Cárdenas	251

TABLES

3.1	Campaign Finance Regulations, 1929–2000	108
5.1	Mexico Party Personnel Surveys Sample Characteristics	141
5.2	Issue Position Questions and Party Elites' Mean Self-Placements	144
5.3	Regression Models of Party Elites' Economic Policy and Regime Preferences	161
6.1	Party Elites' Party-Building Preferences by Period of Affiliation	180
6.2	OLS Regression Models of Party Elites' Party-Building Preferences	186
6.3	Borough Case Study Information	197
7.1	Voter Types by Party Preference Orders, December 1998	218
7.2	Party Elites' and Voters' Support for the Opposition Alliance	220
7.3	Opposition Voters' Support for the Opposition Alliance	222
7.4	Party Elites' Support for the Opposition Alliance by National Priority	223
7.5	OLS Regression Models of National Party Leaders' Support for PAN-PRD Alliance in 2000	225
7.6	Party Identification in February and Vote Choice in July	233
7.7	Voters' Assessments of the Candidates' Probability of Winning	240
7.8	Mean Distance between Voter Self-Placement and Perception of Candidate Location on Key Campaign Issues	241

7.9	Mean Distance between Voter Self-Placement and Perception of Candidate Location on the Left-Right Scale	242
7.10	Multinomial Logistic Regression Model of Vote Choice, 2000	247
7.11	Predicted Probabilities of Vote Choice for an Undecided Voter (baseline model)	248
7.12	Predicted Effects of Explanatory Variables on Vote Choice (first differences)	248

Acknowledgments

Writing a book requires the involvement of a surprisingly large number of people, and I have had the good fortune to be surrounded by an exceptionally smart and giving crowd. The inspiration for this project began in Mexico City in 1990. Looking for a little adventure, and with the encouragement of Carmen and Pilar Ugalde, I began hanging around with members of a poor-people's movement called the Asamblea de Barrios, the leaders of which were also founders of the PRD. I was impressed with their level of commitment – intellectual, ethical, and physical – to political change and I was intrigued by the relationship between the social movement and the party. Later, I found this same level of commitment and deep sense of pride among members of the PAN. What drove these citizens to engage in the risky business of opposing the PRI? Why did they do it if everyone knew – themselves included – that the PRI was overwhelmingly likely to win the next election just as it had won the previous election and the one before that? Why did they dedicate their lives to political change when it seemed such a distant dream? These questions have captivated me for over a decade. They propelled me through years of painstaking research in the field and more than a few long nights in the office. My greatest debt is to the many hundreds of party leaders and activists in the PAN, PRD, and PRI – too many to name individually – who gave me invaluable access to information about their parties and took the time to teach me about their work, their lives, and their passion for politics.

This book would be much worse and may not have existed at all without the support and advice of numerous colleagues and friends. Ruth Berins Collier listened to countless versions of my ideas and pushed me to refine them theoretically and nail them down empirically. David Collier taught me a deep appreciation for methodological rigor in intellectual inquiry and precision in its application. Henry Brady provided precisely the kind of guidance and inspiration I needed at key points in the project. Pradeep Chhibber gave critical advice at various points. Bob Powell and Jim Robinson encouraged me to formalize my ideas using mathematical modeling and Harrison Wagner, Tse-min Lin, and Jim Adams helped me through essential steps along the way. Jay Seawright was exceptionally generous with his creative ideas. Andy Baker and Chappell Lawson read complete drafts of the manuscript and provided invaluable comments. Both have also been amazingly encouraging and patient friends. Gerry Munck gave plenty of helpful advice, mixed with motivational heckling. Herbert Kitschelt was inspirational both directly and indirectly through his wonderful work on political parties that set off a light bulb in my head.

My fantastic colleagues at the University of Texas at Austin, including Kurt Weyland, Wendy Hunter, Raul Madrid, Henry Deitz, Jason Brownlee, Daron Shaw, and Rob Moser, gave comments on various pieces of the manuscript and all manner of advice on issues great and small. Victoria Rodríguez and Peter Ward also gave guidance and support. Two anonymous reviewers for the press gave exactly the kind of comments I did not know that I needed by poking at the weak points and encouraging me to rethink areas where I may have been lazy.

I have also benefited from an extended network of generous and incredibly smart colleagues who have shared their insights and more than a little of their time over the years. Ethan Scheiner, Steve Levitsky, Julia Lynch, David Shirk, Marc Morjé Howard, Anna Grzymala-Busse, Meredith Weiss, Jay McCann, and Lucan Way read and commented on portions of the manuscript. Jay was also a resource beyond compare for statistical advice; Lucan spent hours discussing the issues with me as his dog walked us around Notre Dame's lakes; and Marc knew just when to tell me to "get on with it." John Sides, Rob Weiner, Scott Mainwaring, Michael Coppedge, Robert Fishman, Jorge Domínguez, Thad Dunning, Barbara Geddes, Steve Fish, Wayne Cornelius, Rod Camp, Kathleen Bruhn, Joe Klesner, Georgia Kernell, Bronwyn Leebaw, John Cioffi, Aaron Schneider, Lise Morjé Howard, Zack Elkins, Orit Kedar, and Steve Heydemann helped in myriad direct and indirect ways. Mark M. Williams also lent copious time to the project, especially when computers were involved. In Mexico, I benefited from affiliations with the Centro de Investigación y Docencia Económicas (CIDE) and the Instituto Tecnológico Autónoma de México (ITAM). I learned and continue to learn an amazing amount from my colleagues and generous hosts, including Andreas Schedler, Joy Langston, Benito Nacif, Alejandro Poiré, Guillermo Trejo, Yemile Mizrahi, Beatriz Magaloni, Denise Dresser, and Jeff Weldon. I especially thank Federico Estévez, mentor of many, who helped me develop as a scholar of Mexico and opened numerous doors for me along the way. I also thank Alan Zarembo for his hospitality and uncanny Scrabble abilities. I thank Senior Editor Lew Bateman for his confidence in the project and Editor Eric Crahan for patiently shepherding me and the manuscript through the publication process. So many colleagues and friends have given advice on themes directly or indirectly related to this project that I may have inadvertently forgotten to acknowledge their contribution. Sorry about that. The book undoubtedly contains errors, omissions, and poor-quality thinking, none of which is a reflection of the first-rate thinkers who have helped me along the way.

I had the privilege of presenting some of the arguments and empirical findings in this book at conferences and universities where I received helpful advice, including LASA (August 2000 and March 2003), APSA (August 2000, September 2004, September 2006), ECPR (September 2005), UCSD (February 2003), UT-Austin (March 2003), ITAM (July 2003), UC-Riverside (June 2004), University of Pennsylvania (November 2004), Georgetown (November 2004), CIDE (January 2005), and Notre Dame (October 2005). A small portion of Chapter 5 appeared as "Opposition Party Strategy and Spatial Competition in Dominant Party Regimes: A Theory and the Case of Mexico" *Comparative Political Studies 35*, 7 (September), 755–783.

The research for this book required collecting a large amount of new empirical data. I could not have conducted the Mexico Party Personnel Surveys without the financial support of a Dissertation Improvement Grant from the National Science Foundation (SBER #9819213), nor would they have been possible without the in-kind contributions and invaluable support of *Reforma* newspaper. I particularly thank Rosanna Fuentes-Berain, Alejandro Moreno, and Jogin Abreu, without whose trust and hard work the surveys never would have been accomplished. Alejandro Moreno and Dan Lund also generously gave me access to many other valuable sample survey data sets.

For financial support, I thank the National Science Foundation, Fulbright-Garcia Robles-Mexico, the Institute for International Studies at the University of California, Berkeley, the Institute for the Study of World Politics, UC-MEXUS, the Center for U.S.-Mexican Studies at the

University of California, San Diego, the Mellon Foundation, the Mexico Center and the Lozano Long Institute of Latin American Studies at the University of Texas at Austin, the Center for Democracy and the Third Sector at Georgetown University, the Helen Kellogg Institute for International Studies at the University of Notre Dame, and the Faculty Research Assignment, Summer Research Assignment, and Dean's Fellowship programs at the University of Texas at Austin.

My academic pursuits never would have been possible without the love and support of family and close friends. I thank Douglas Matlock for a lifetime of support. I thank Fredda, Scott, Polly, and Jack Johnson; Lael Rubin and David Rosenzweig; Chuck and Barbara Rubin; the Cohen family; Kay Zentall; and Michael and Stacey Greene for a variety of help, big and small. I thank my father, Charles Greene, and Susan Greene for teaching me to argue. Despite our differences, I am sure that my father would have been proud to see the completion of this book. I thank Pat Schandler and Marilyn Burns, who supported me and my educational pursuits materially and with encouragement. I thank Evan Nichols for his creativity and everlasting humor, and regulars in the Friday Night Dinner Crew (Amy, Marg, José, Kathie, Roger, Jeff, Cristen, Sean, and ever-growing population of munchkins) for their grounding influence.

I thank my mother, Penny Greene, for the immeasurable support that a parent gives and Stephanie Rubin for her love, ongoing encouragement, and level of kind-heartedness that never cease to amaze me.

1

The Puzzle of Single-Party Dominance

This book is about single-party dominance, its persistence, and its downfall. Dominant parties have maintained continuous executive and legislative rule for decades despite genuine partisan competition in countries spanning almost all world regions. In these systems, opposition parties compete but lose in open elections for such extended periods of time that we can speak of a "dominant party equilibrium." What sustains this equilibrium and what makes it break down is the subject of this book. Fashioning an adequate explanation is important partly because the current literature falls short and partly because explaining single-party dominance has profound implications for our understanding of the forces that encourage or stunt partisan competition, the process of opposition party building in inhospitable circumstances, the quality of political representation, and the dynamics of regime stability or breakdown in hybrid systems that combine authoritarian and democratic features.

This book focuses both on the question of single-party dominance in general and on the specific case of Mexico where the Institutional Revolutionary Party (PRI) maintained power for longer than any noncommunist party in modern history. The PRI and its predecessors won every presidential election from 1929 to 2000, held the majority in Congress until 1997, won every governorship until 1989, and controlled the vast majority of municipalities. It was so powerful and seemingly unshakable that leaders in other developing countries wanted their own PRI (Krauze, 1997: 549–550), and major political actors inside Mexico thought of it as virtually "the only game in town." Despite long-term equilibrium dominance, opposition parties began to expand in the 1980s, and by 1997 the PRI

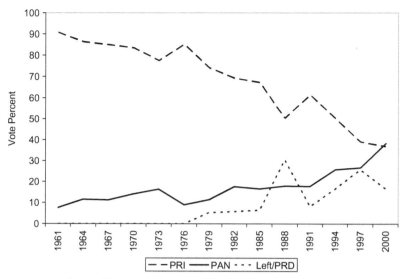

FIGURE 1.1. Lower House of Congress Election Results, Mexico, 1961–2000.

had lost its majority in Congress to the National Action Party (PAN) on the right and the Party of the Democratic Revolution (PRD) on the left. In 2000, Vicente Fox of the PAN won the presidency and became the first leader in Mexico's modern history to peacefully receive power from a rival political group.

The PRI's long-time dominance is surprising because it occurred in the context of regular elections with meaningful contestation, where opposition forces were allowed to register as parties and compete for all elected posts. The PRI's ultimate loss and Mexico's transformation into a fully competitive democracy is also intriguing because, as in other dominant party systems, change occurred without the breakdown of the incumbent regime, but rather through painstaking party-building efforts by opposition candidates and activists. Over decades these volunteers built challenger parties and fashioned increasingly powerful electoral challenges to the PRI. But for most of their existence, they remained small parties that made niche appeals to minority electoral constituencies and were thoroughly uncompetitive at the polls. It was not until the 1980s and 1990s that they expanded into major parties with a catchall character that could challenge PRI dominance. Figure 1.1 illustrates the long period of PRI dominance, its protracted decline, and the simultaneous rise of the opposition parties.

What accounts for equilibrium dominance and its eventual breakdown in Mexico and elsewhere? How do traditionally undercompetitive party systems transform into fully competitive democracies? What allows previously small and weak niche-oriented challenger parties to become larger and more powerful catchall competitors that can win elections? What accounts for the timing of dominant party decline in general and why, in the particular case of Mexico, did this change occur in the 1980s and 1990s rather than decades earlier or later?

THE PUZZLE

Current approaches cannot explain equilibrium dominance or its breakdown, and in fact, the alternative theories predict that dominance never exists or it never ends. Most existing theories about party system competitiveness were crafted to explain the dynamics of partisan competition in the fully competitive democracies, and they assume a level playing field where both incumbents and challengers have equal opportunities to appeal to voters in a fair electoral marketplace. In particular, they discount the effect of differential resource endowments by assuming that no party is advantaged with extra money, more canvassers, or the ability to communicate more often and more effectively with voters. The assumption that the electoral market is "neutral" or perfectly fair in which no party has a systematic advantage underlies existing work in the best-known approaches to party competition in the comparative-historical, institutional, and formal theory traditions. But I show empirically that dominant party systems have sufficient social cleavages, enough voter demand, and permissive enough electoral institutions for competitive opposition parties to emerge, even though they do not for long periods of time. Thus, these schools of thought overpredict opposition party competitiveness and therefore cannot explain why single-party dominance occurs at all.

The recognition that incumbency advantages matter has been incorporated into some theoretical statements about party competition, principally in more recent formal theory treatments. However, in their current form, these "non-neutral" models that assume an unfair electoral market for votes err in the other direction and cannot explain why a challenging party would ever enter competition. According to these models, opposition parties that are doomed to lose should not form in the presence of a systematically advantaged incumbent, and therefore dominant party

4 *Why Dominant Parties Lose*

systems should collapse into one-party regimes that endure indefinitely without challengers.[1]

If these approaches were correct, then, discounting the fully closed authoritarian regimes, the world should be populated with fully competitive democracies or one-party regimes where challengers are allowed to form but do not. Clearly, neither set of approaches explains the dominant party equilibrium that exists when opposition parties compete but persistently fail.

Specific work on Mexico largely echoes these two approaches from the party competition literature. In the 1950s and early 1960s, authors argued that Mexico under the PRI was a democracy, albeit an uncommon one where the incumbent continuously won reelection (Fitzgibbon, 1951: 519; Cline, 1962: 149–156, 173; Scott, 1964: 146). But if meaningful electoral competition were also fair, then we cannot account for the absence of at least one viable challenger. In the 1960s and 1970s, authors began to think of Mexico as a fully closed authoritarian regime, or what Mario Vargas Llosa called the "perfect dictatorship," that should be compared to the military regimes in South America (Brandenburg, 1964: 3–7; González Casanova, 1965; Kaufman Purcell, 1973: 29; Reyna and Weinert, 1977). But if elections were neither meaningful nor fair, and the PRI won consistently through outcome-changing electoral fraud and bone-crushing repression, then there would have been little reason to turn to parties and instead opposition forces should have formed revolutionary movements designed to overthrow the regime or social movements designed to reform it. To be sure, these movements did exist at times in Mexico and other dominant party systems, but opposition forces also consistently formed parties to compete in elections as their primary organizational expression.[2] Thus, existing conceptualizations of Mexico's political regime under the PRI either overemphasize its democratic characteristics, leading

---

[1] This approach argues that individually rational politicians who want to win elections should always join an incumbent party with a higher probability of victory than a challenger party that is expected to lose. Opposition parties may still form if they can attract personnel by offering a much higher probability of *nomination* than the incumbent party; however, because the incumbent's probability of *victory* is so much higher, assured nominations probably only attract those who have no future chance of winning nomination in the dominant party, such as failed presidential contenders (Epstein, 1967). I take up this issue in more detail in Chapter 4.

[2] Opposition forces sometimes form parties in fully closed authoritarian systems, but unlike in dominant party systems, they are not the main outlet for opposition activism. Throughout the book, "fully closed authoritarian" refers to regimes that are noncompetitive and nonresponsive.

to the puzzle of why opposition parties failed, or overemphasize its authoritarian characteristics, leading to the puzzle of why opposition parties formed at all.

THE ARGUMENT IN BRIEF

In this book, I develop a resource theory of single-party dominance and opposition party development that focuses on incumbency advantages. I argue that challenger party competitiveness is primarily determined by two types of dominant party advantages: the incumbent's resource advantages and its ability to raise the costs of participation in the opposition. Dramatic resource advantages allow the incumbent to outspend on campaigns, deploy legions of canvassers, and, most importantly, to supplement policy appeals with patronage goods that bias voters in their favor. Dominant parties also impose two types of costs on candidates and activists who decide to affiliate with a challenger. One type of cost is the opportunity cost of foregoing the material advantages that they would have received by joining the dominant party, such as a stipend, kickbacks, or access to an old boys' network of business contacts and favors. The other cost is the cost associated with targeted physical intimidation, beatings, or even killings of opposition activists that occur episodically in some (but not all) dominant party systems. Between these tools, resource advantages are more important. Though potentially harsh and almost always threatening, repression in these systems never rose to the level of purging or purifying the body politic as it did in fully closed authoritarian regimes. Incumbents' access to these competition-altering tools clearly varies across countries and over time, and taking stock of these variations plays a key role in this study.

By virtue of their incumbency advantages, dominant parties attract and retain virtually all careerist politicians who want to win office. So who forms opposition parties? Contrary to the purely instrumental assumptions about individual politicians in existing theory, in-depth interviews in Mexico and anecdotal evidence from other cases reveal that opposition party elites *also* value policy and partisan expression as a way of transforming voters' hearts and minds. But the only citizens willing to pay high costs and reap uncertain benefits are those who strongly disagree with the status quo policies offered by the incumbent. These ideologically oriented candidates and activists build opposition parties when existing theory suggests that they should not, but they end up creating niche parties that make specialized appeals to minority electoral constituencies. The challenger parties' appeals are then sufficiently out of step with the preference of the average voter that they remain too small to beat the dominant party at the polls. Only when the incumbent's advantages diminish can challengers attract the more moderate personnel that may transform niche challengers into electorally competitive catchall parties.

Dominant party resources primarily come from diverting public funds for partisan use. Unless access to these public resources is blocked by a professionalized public bureaucracy or their use for electoral purposes is prevented by an independent electoral management body with oversight and sanctioning authority, incumbents will skew competition in their favor by dramatically outspending competitors on campaigns and all aspects of party building. Where these institutional constraints do not operate, the magnitude of the incumbent's resource advantages rises and falls with the degree of state ownership over the economy.[3] In this context, state-owned enterprises are particularly important because they are prone to politicization. Their often-secretive budgets and lack of third-party oversight yield manifold opportunities to blur the line between public and partisan resources. Thus, the political economy of single-party dominance involves creating a large and politically controlled public sector. When privatization deprives incumbents of access to illicit public resources, dominant party rule is threatened. In short, economic and political monopolies are mutually reinforcing in the dominant party equilibrium.

IMPLICATIONS FOR MEXICAN POLITICS

This resource theory of single-party dominance helps understand key analytic problems in Mexico's politics. First, my argument accounts for opposition party existence but failure beginning with the initiation of the post-Revolutionary party system and single-party dominance in 1929. In the face of the PRI's advantages, challenger parties only existed because a hard core of ideologically committed citizens formed them to express their deeply anti-status quo beliefs. Citizens who wanted political careers overwhelmingly threw their lot in with the PRI. But opposition personnel were so anti-status quo that they made challenger parties into specialized tight-knit clubs that lacked broad appeal. From an electoral perspective, their organizations and campaign styles seemed designed to fail because they only brought out the faithful and never made a significant dent in the

---

[3] Threats to the size of the state may come from a variety of sources, including international pressure. Levitsky and Way (2006) provide a conceptualization of this relationship under the category of "Western linkage."

PRI's power. Commentators tended to explain their failure as the result of electoral fraud. There is compelling evidence that the PRI won several key elections, especially local contests, through fraud in the 1980s when opposition parties became more competitive (Eisenstadt, 2004). There is also speculation that the PRI stole the 1988 presidential election, and even though there is "abundant proof of electoral tampering...it has not been possible to unearth evidence – documentary, verbal, mathematical, or otherwise – to conclusively demonstrate that Salinas lost and Cárdenas won" (Castañeda, 2000: 233). As a result, we cannot know whether the PRI committed outcome-changing fraud or simply padded its victory (Castañeda, 2000: 232). In general, during its many decades in power, the PRI's politicization of public funds tilted the partisan playing field so much in its favor that it did not need to steal elections in the counting; it won them through unfair advantages before election day.

Second, my argument helps explain opposition parties' failure to coordinate against the incumbent. Opposition coordination failure helped sustain PRI dominance, especially during its final two decades in power as its resource advantages waned. It would seem natural for challengers to coalesce in a broad anti-PRI front, much like they eventually did in Chile against Augusto Pinochet or in Kenya against retiring President Daniel Arap Moi's KANU party (Howard and Roessler, 2006; Van de Walle, 2002). Despite their mutual interest in democracy, opposition elites did not coordinate because they were ideologically polarized on economic policy around a comparatively centrist PRI. These policy differences resulted from the very pattern of opposition party building that discouraged all but the most anti-status quo volunteers from joining them. Since elites refused to coordinate, mass-level coordination was greatly complicated and anti-PRI voters who prioritized democracy were left to gamble on which challenger party had the better chance of defeating the incumbent in a given election. Riker (1976) first characterized elite coordination failure as a key reason for dominant party persistence, but he did not specify why opposition parties would form on the extremes in the first place.[4] Unless the incumbent has tools to expel challengers from the most efficient position – typically at the center of the distribution of voter preferences – then, as neutral theories suggest, opposition parties should win

---

[4] Riker's argument was about unidimensional competition in India, a dominant party democratic regime. As I show below, competition in dominant party authoritarian regimes is typically two-dimensional and includes a cross-cutting regime dimension that gives challengers common cause against the incumbent. Thus, opposition coordination failure in these systems is even more puzzling.

with at least the same probability as the incumbent, thus ending single-party dominance.[5] My argument supplies Riker's missing mechanism by showing how the dominant party's advantages carve out a broad center for the incumbent.

Third, a focus on incumbency advantages also helps understand the opposition's ultimate victory. The economic crisis beginning in 1982 angered voters and increasingly turned them against the PRI. Yet the incumbent continued to win national elections until 1997. In fully competitive systems, when voters dislike the incumbent, they more or less automatically turn to the opposition by voting the incumbent out. This did not happen in Mexico in the 1980s in large part because the PRI still had access to the resources of massive state-owned enterprises, dominated the airwaves in campaigns, and outspent competitors by a factor of about ten. By the late 1990s, in contrast, state control over the economy had decreased dramatically and a leaner federal public bureaucracy yielded fewer patronage jobs. As a result, the PRI's national patronage system ran dry. The PRI increasingly favored legal public financing, but this new system included oversight mechanisms that benefited all parties and made partisan competition for votes much fairer. As resource asymmetries declined, opposition parties improved substantially at the polls; however, their expansion was not automatic since decades of niche-party building constrained their ability to take advantage of new opportunities. It was not until the late 1990s that opposition parties managed to overcome this inertia and overturn PRI majorities.

Finally, my argument about the origins and development of opposition parties among ideologically polarized political elites has relevance for two important aspects of post-transition politics in fully democratic Mexico after 2000. Despite Congress's increasing independence and importance as well as widespread agreement that Mexico's state needs reforming, major legislation has stalled and Congress remains plagued by gridlock. One reason is that the policy divisions that once hampered opposition coordination in elections now hamper legislative coordination (see Bruhn and Greene, 2007). In addition, unlike other authoritarian incumbents that were virtually destroyed after losing the executive branch, the PRI has remained competitive in federal elections (see Greene, 2008). This has occurred in part because persistent intra-party rigidities in the PAN and PRD have kept them from convincingly claiming the political center.

---

[5] See the section "Supply-Side Approaches" in this chapter for an expanded discussion.

The Puzzle of Single-Party Dominance

In developing my account of PRI rule and its breakdown, I describe opposition party development during much of 20th century Mexico. Yet my description differs from existing work. Excellent literature on the PAN (Mabry, 1973; Arriola, 1994; Loaeza, 1999; Chand, 2001; Mizrahi, 2003; Shirk, 2005) and the PRD as well as its forerunners (Carr, 1992; Bruhn, 1997; Sánchez, 1999; Borjas Benavente, 2003) draws out these parties' differences. To be sure, the PAN is a rightwing party with an upper- and middle-class core constituency and links to both 19th century economic liberalism as well as the Catholic Church. The PRD, on the other hand, is a leftwing party with deep roots in previous communist and socialist parties, urban poor people's movements, and radical intellectual cliques. But a closer look shows striking similarities. Both parties faced a common fate of long-time struggle as regime outsiders, and they both crafted quite similar party-building strategies and organizational profiles as a result. By theorizing the dynamics of single-party dominance, I account for these similarities.

In an excellent book that became available only after my book was completed, Beatriz Magaloni (2006) offers an analysis of PRI dominance and decline that runs parallel to my argument in several general ways.[6] Both books conceptualize single-party dominance as an equilibrium that was unsettled by economic conditions beginning in 1982; however, we have contrasting views about the causal importance of voters versus party elites in ending dominant party rule. Magaloni focuses on voter dissatisfaction in the face of economic crisis whereas I focus on the opposition parties' capacity to take advantage of this dissatisfaction. Voter dissatisfaction with the PRI is clearly important, but it alone cannot account for two key outcomes that my theory can explain. First, like other approaches that I discuss below, Magaloni's theory presumes that opposition parties were always viable alternatives for voters dissatisfied with the incumbent party. I show this is not the case and that the dynamics of dominance compelled opposition elites to build challenger parties that were out of step with the average voter's preferences and thus could not generate enough support to win national elections until the late 1990s. Second, we agree that opposition coordination failure was a major element in sustaining PRI dominance in its final decades, but Magaloni argues that

---

[6] I had earlier benefited greatly from Magaloni's (1997) doctoral dissertation which focused more specifically on voting behavior in Mexico but did not contain the extended argument about PRI dominance found in her book. I cite her dissertation (along with the corresponding citations of her book) numerous times throughout the present study.

10   *Why Dominant Parties Lose*

ideologically polarized voters produced this outcome. Although *opposition voters* were indeed polarized to the left and right, given that voters *in general* were quite moderate, opposition party elites' strategies were the cause rather than the consequence of their noncentrist support bases (Greene, 2002b). Thus, I argue that opposition party behavior was the binding constraint on transforming Mexico from a dominant party system into a fully competitive democracy. I craft a theory of opposition party building in dominant party settings that can explain why opposition parties remained undercompetitive and uncoordinated for decades as well as why they eventually expanded enough to win. I use this argument to explain the dominant party equilibrium and its breakdown in Mexico as well as in a number of the world's other dominant party systems.

BROADER IMPLICATIONS

Studying party dynamics in Mexico and other dominant party systems gives analytic leverage on four broader questions that are of interest for comparative politics. First, although work on single-party dominance goes back at least 50 years to Duverger (1954), Tucker (1961), Blondel (1972), Huntington and Moore (1970), Arian and Barnes (1974), Sartori (1976), Pempel (1990), Brooker (2000), and Cheng (2001), none of these studies actually supplies a viable theory of dominant party persistence or decline. These authors were mostly concerned with the creation of dominant party systems and as such they focused on the major periods of nation building that produced them (e.g., revolution, independence, reconstruction after defeat in war, or sustained struggles between rival political forces over modernization). Some argued that incumbents' initial legitimacy as harbingers of national transformation underwrote their long-term dominance. But it is unlikely that the mechanisms that *produce* dominant party rule also *reproduce* it over time, and leading authorities on dominance have recognized that founding projects have limited staying power. Levite and Tarrow argued that "subcultural dominance cannot be indefinitely sustained by dominant parties in societies undergoing change . . . regimes age and even epochal events pass into memory" (1983: 299). Tucker (1961) noted that dominant parties tend to lose their founding ideology quite early and transform from "revolutionary nationalist regimes" into "extinct revolutionary nationalist regimes" or what Huntington (1970: 23, 40–41) called "established one-party regimes." In the specific case of Mexico, analysts similarly referred to the PRI as a "pragmatic" dominant party that primarily sought to sustain itself in

The Puzzle of Single-Party Dominance 11

power. But to name something takes us only so far. Explaining the fate of "pragmatic" dominant parties long after their founding projects are abandoned requires not another theory of why dominance begins but one focused on the mechanisms that allow incumbents to win consistently against challengers in open elections.

Second, the transformation of dominant party authoritarian regimes into fully competitive democracies has received little scholarly attention, and researchers are just beginning to uncover the mechanisms that sustain competitive authoritarian regimes more generally (Levitsky and Way, 2006). Transitions to democracy in these systems do not occur through elite pacts or regime breakdown as they do in the fully closed authoritarian regimes (O'Donnell and Schmitter, 1986; Karl and Schmitter, 1991). Rather, since elections already involve open competition, transitions occur by building opposition party electoral capacity. As a result, we should focus on the four major tasks of opposition party building: recruiting candidates and activists, creating organizational capacity, generating resources, and shaping appeals that resonate with voters. This final task becomes more important as the market for votes transits from a biased one that favors the incumbent to a fair one in which parties engage in the type of issue-based competition that is one important component of elections in fully competitive democracies.

Third, since opposition parties in dominant party systems are built mainly by outsiders, this book also provides a novel argument about the development of externally mobilized parties that originate in society. Aldrich (1995) developed a theory of internally mobilized parties that emerge as coalitions of legislators who band together to solve social choice problems endemic to democratic policymaking. But externally mobilized parties emerge for different reasons (Shefter, 1977a) and with a different set of hurdles. One of the most important hurdles is that their resource poverty makes it difficult to attract candidates and activists. Current work tells us that aspiring politicians should not join a disadvantaged challenger party (see Schlesinger, 1966, 1991; Rohde, 1979; Aldrich and Bianco, 1992; Cox, 1997: Ch. 8). But on this basis, not only can we not account for challengers to dominant parties, we cannot account for an entire class of activism in organizations that are doomed to lose. For instance, the outsider parties described by Shefter (1977a, 1994) that challenge patronage-rich incumbents should never form. Third-party challengers to the Democrats and Republicans in the United States should not exist. The Green parties described by Kitschelt (1989a), radical rightwing parties described by Kitschelt (1995) and Givens (2005), and a substantial number of the 261 other new parties that formed in Western Europe between World War II and the 1990s (see Hug, 2001: 80) should never have organized. In general, all political parties that begin as "protest" parties or that attempt to lead public opinion by amassing support in the fashion of a social movement should not exist. The problem confronting prospective participants in the opposition is not unlike what Lichbach called the "rebel's dilemma" where "No potential dissent will become actual dissent" (1998: xii). Somewhat akin to rebellions that should not happen but do, disadvantaged parties form because ideologically charged citizens act on their principles over their interests to build parties from the ground up. I incorporate this notion into an individual-level theory of partisan affiliation that examines how prospective candidates and activists partition themselves between a dominant party and a challenger in the face of asymmetric resources and costs of participation.

DOMINANCE DEFINED AND THE COMPARISON SET

The final reason for studying dominant party systems is that they have been overlooked in recent research that classifies regimes as democracies or dictatorships. By eliminating the grey areas in between, these studies also erase dominant party systems from the world map (Przeworski et al., 2000; Boix, 2003). I define dominant party systems as hybrids that combine meaningful electoral competition with continuous executive and legislative rule by a single party for at least 20 years or at least four consecutive elections. The key feature of dominant party systems is that elections are meaningful but manifestly unfair. Meaningful elections induce opposition actors to form parties and compete for votes. Unfair elections mean that biases in partisan competition tilt the playing field so much in the incumbent party's favor that opposition parties are extremely unlikely to win.

Elections must be *both* meaningful and unfair to sustain the dominant party equilibrium. Meaningful elections distinguish dominant party systems from fully closed authoritarian regimes. If elections were less than meaningful and incumbents effectively annulled competition either by banning challengers outright or by making it too costly for opposition forces to form parties, then dominant party systems would collapse into one-party regimes without challengers. At the same time, unfair elections distinguish dominant party systems from fully competitive democracies.[7]

---

[7] For a similar definition of competitive authoritarian regimes, see Levitsky and Way (2006).

The Puzzle of Single-Party Dominance

If elections were fair and incumbents could not bias competition significantly in their favor, then the level playing field would make dominant party systems collapse into fully competitive democracies.

Meaningful electoral competition entails three procedural elements that I draw, in part, from Przeworski and colleagues (2000: 18–29). First, the "election rule" is that the chief executive and a legislature that cannot be dismissed by the executive are chosen in regular popular elections. Second, the "opposition party rule" – a more restrictive version of Przeworski and colleagues' (2000: 20) party rule – indicates that all opposition forces are allowed to form independent parties and compete in elections. This means that the incumbent does not ban challenger parties entirely or as they arise and opposition parties are not forced to join the dominant party or to endorse only the incumbent's candidates.[8] If this rule is violated, as it is in constitutional or *de facto* one-party regimes, then I score the system as a fully closed authoritarian regime. Consider Kenya, for instance, beginning with its independence from Britain in 1963. Until 1982, the dominant KANU banned opposition parties as they arose. From 1982 to 1991, it adopted a constitutional provision that declared Kenya a one-party state. Multiparty elections were later held in 1992 and 1997, but by some accounts, fraud overturned opposition victories that would have ended the incumbent's rule.[9] Like Kenya, Cameroon (1961–1983), Tunisia (1957–), Tanzania (1964–1995), Zambia (1964–1991), Indonesia (1965–), Côte d'Ivoire (1958–1990), Angola (1976–), Gabon (1968–1993), Guyana (1968–1985), Madagascar (1978–1984), Mozambique (1976–1994), and Egypt (1953–) are coded as fully closed authoritarian regimes rather than as dominant party systems.

Finally, an expanded version of the "consolidation rule" indicates that the incumbent may not re-write the rules in a way that permanently consolidates its rule and may not engage in outcome-changing electoral fraud, without which dominance would have ended. Fraud with certainty is incompatible with dominant party rule because it annuls competition and discourages opposition forces from forming parties that compete in elections. As a result, my concept of dominant party authoritarian regime

---

[8] The Mexican Communist Party (PCM) was not registered from 1949 to 1977. Many analysts state or imply that it was actively banned; however, as I detail in Chapter 3, it failed to meet the registration requirements at a time when other left parties and independent candidates were on the ballot (Molinar, 1991: 33–36; Rodríguez Araujo and Sirvent, 2005: 35–37).

[9] Even if fraud did not change the results of these elections, Kenya would not meet the longevity threshold for single-party dominance after 1992, as defined below.

(DPAR) differs from Sartori's (1976) conceptualization of "hegemonic party" system where "turnover is not even envisaged" (1976: 230) and fraud prohibits opposition victories with certainty (1976: 194–196).[10] Fraud on the margins to increase the incumbent's vote share when observers generally agree that it would have won anyway does not, in and of itself, qualify a regime as fully closed authoritarian because it still implies genuine electoral competition that may involve serious challenger parties.[11] As I argue in more detail in Chapter 2, dominant parties' pre-electoral advantages and in particular their virtual monopoly over patronage resources mean that they usually win elections before election day. As a result, fraud is typically unnecessary and is considered only when other pre-election mechanisms fail and elections are predicted to be close. Even when fraud is used, it is not always successful because it requires substantial resources and coordination among multiple regime supporters that can break down. Consequently, opposition actors never know whether fraud will be attempted or if it will be successful. Fraud with uncertainty is compatible with the dominant party equilibrium because it still provides a rationale for opposition forces to invest in parties and compete for votes.

In sum, meaningful competition means that the electoral arena is open and although authoritarian controls may bring competition below the threshold of "minimally free elections" that many take as a defining feature of democracy, the costs of forming an opposition party do not outweigh the expected benefits. As a result, opposition forces play the electoral game by recruiting candidates and activists, campaigning for partisan hearts and minds, and competing for votes.[12]

The primary focus of this book is dominant party authoritarian regimes (DPARs) which are a large and by some definitions the modal subset of what scholars have recently termed "competitive authoritarian," (Levitsky and Way, 2002, 2006) "electoral authoritarian" (Schedler, 2002, 2005) or "hybrid" regimes (Diamond, 2002; also see Carothers, 2002; Van de Walle, 2002).[13] In describing competitive authoritarian regimes,

---

[10] See Chapter 8 for an expanded discussion of the relationship between dominant party authoritarian regimes, hegemonic party systems, and predominant party systems.

[11] For a similar treatment of electoral fraud in competitive authoritarian regimes, see Levitsky and Way (2006).

[12] The criteria for meaningfulness set out above do satisfy the classic definitions of minimally free elections found in Schumpeter (1947) and Przeworski et al. (2000); however, I agree with Karl (1986) that such definitions suffer from an "electoralist" fallacy that ignores the surrounding freedoms that ensure the free operation of electoral institutions.

[13] Six of Diamond's (2002: 23) seven historical cases are DPARs. Three of Levitsky and Way's (2002: 51–52) 16 cases are DPARs, four are proto-dominant party systems where

The Puzzle of Single-Party Dominance 15

Levitsky and Way (2002, 2006) clearly distinguish them from fully closed authoritarian regimes, and even though they recognize the impact of authoritarian controls on opposition forces, they emphasize the existence of meaningful competition. They state that,

> Although elections are held and are generally free of massive fraud, incumbents routinely abuse state resources, deny the opposition adequate media coverage, [and] harass opposition candidates and their supporters ... [They] use bribery, co-optation, and more subtle forms of persecution, such as the use of tax authorities, compliant judiciaries, and other state agencies to 'legally' harass, persecute, or extort cooperative behavior from critics (2002: 53).

All DPARs are competitive authoritarian regimes, but not all competitive authoritarian regimes have dominant parties. To be considered dominant, incumbents must also surpass power and longevity thresholds. Regarding power, prior definitions offer widely varying criteria from a mere plurality of the vote up to 75% of legislative seats.[14] I argue that dominance means the ability to determine social choice. In presidentialist systems, this means that the incumbent controls the executive and at least an absolute majority of legislative seats.[15] In parliamentary and mixed systems, it means holding the premiership, at least a plurality of legislative seats, and the impossibility of forming a government without the dominant party.[16]

Existing analyses also disagree about the longevity threshold. The least restrictive measure stipulates a single election (Coleman, 1960: 286–293; Van de Walle and Butler, 1999), but this so dramatically widens the universe of cases that it makes the concept virtually useless. One of the most restrictive measures, on the other hand, sets the bar as high as 50 years (Cox, 1997: 238). But this criterion reduces the universe to just

the incumbent has not yet surpassed the longevity threshold, two are personalist regimes where the president's death might end dominance, and in five incumbents have not ruled through parties.

[14] Blondel's (1968) threshold is 40% of votes; Pempel (1990: 3) uses a plurality of seats; Sartori (1976: 195) uses a majority of seats, McDonald (1971: 220) uses 60% of seats; Coleman (1960: 295) uses 70% of seats, and Beck et al. (2001:170) use 75% of seats. Some of these differences derive from analysts' focus on either presidential or parliamentary systems.

[15] This falls short of the supermajority often needed to make constitutional amendments; however, in practice, the incumbent's control over the executive branch and ordinary legislation should induce enough opposition legislators to "bandwagon" (see Weiner, 2003).

[16] Following Laver and Schofield (1990), indispensability means that a party must occupy the median policy position between coalition partners that cannot form a government without it.

Mexico.[17] I argue that a useful longevity threshold should capture the notion that a dominant party system is a stable pattern of inter-party competition (i.e., a dominant party equilibrium),[18] but should not be so restrictive that it makes the category disappear. Consequently, I set the threshold at 20 years or four consecutive elections. This "one generation" requirement is one way to operationalize Duverger's vague but insightful definition that "A dominant party is that which public opinion *believes* to be dominant" (1954: 308–309).[19] Although it could be argued that a system that was dominant at anytime t was in fact dominant prior to t, to pursue this no-threshold argument, we would have to measure dominance by the mechanisms that sustain it. Treating potential explanatory variables as descriptive measures would succeed only in constructing a tautology.[20]

Clear examples of DPARs where incumbents permitted meaningful electoral competition and passed the power and longevity thresholds, even though they also employed, to varying degrees, authoritarian controls to help maintain their rule include Malaysia under UMNO/BN (1974–), Taiwan under the KMT (1987–2000), Singapore under the PAP (1981–), Mexico under the PRI (1929–1997), Gambia under the PPP (1963–1994),

---

[17] Other longevity thresholds vary. Przeworski et al. (2000: 27) set the bar at two elections; Sartori raises it to four in one passage (1976: 196) and three in another (1976: 199). Blondel (1968: 180–203) uses a minimum of 20 years; Cox stipulates 30 to 50 years (1997: 238); Ware (1996) argues that the dominant party should hold power "usually;" and Pempel states that a dominant party must hold power for "a substantial period of time" (1990: 4), amounting to "permanent or semi-permanent governance" (1990: 15).

[18] I agree with Arian and Barnes (1974: 592–593) that dominant party systems are *sui generis*, a unique category that is not merely a stage in transition from one type of party system to another.

[19] Despite these justifications, any longevity threshold is arbitrary and will cause classification controversies. Using the two decade or four election criteria narrowly admits Taiwan, for instance. After it lifted martial law in 1986, the KMT won in multiparty elections until 2000. It is below the threshold in years, but above in consecutive elections, having won five.

[20] If, nevertheless, the no-threshold argument were correct, then using any criterion t would artificially limit the universe of cases by dropping what I call proto-dominant party systems that failed before year t or have not yet reached year t. Fortunately, such a truncation will likely bias tests against my hypotheses (Geddes, 2003; King, Keohane, and Verba, 1994). When comparing dominant party systems to fully competitive democracies in the next section, some of the former would be incorrectly coded as the latter, making the two sets more homogenous. When examining the longevity of dominant party systems alone, variation on the dependent variable would be truncated because only cases of dominance longer than t will be included, and this selection bias would also work against my hypotheses.

The Puzzle of Single-Party Dominance 17

and Senegal under the PS (1977–2000).[21] I also include Botswana under the BDP (1965–) that is clearly a dominant party system although analysts disagree about its regime type.[22]

Most of this book deals with the case of Mexico; however, I extend my argument to Malaysia and Taiwan in Chapter 8. There, I also show how my approach can help account for dominance in the dominant party democracies of Italy and Japan where incumbents benefited from massive resource advantages but did not employ authoritarian controls. Finally, I do not deal with regionally dominant parties such as the Solid South under the Democrats (see Key, 1964a) because the dynamics of locally weak oppositions differ substantially from the dynamics of nationally weak ones.[23]

WHY EXISTING THEORIES FAIL TO EXPLAIN SINGLE-PARTY DOMINANCE

Existing theoretical work cannot explain the dominant party equilibrium or its breakdown. Having discussed the limitations of arguments that focus on electoral fraud and repression as well as Mexico-specific arguments, I now test hypotheses derived from the well-developed literature on the number of competitive parties. Applying this existing work to dominant party systems implies that opposition parties fail because there is inadequate voter demand, electoral institutions are insufficiently permissive, or there is not enough ideological "space" for opposition parties to occupy. The predictions of these theories should hold in dominant party systems because they permit meaningful electoral competition.

---

[21] Zimbabwe might be considered a DPAR from 1980 to 2002. Following the 1980 Lancaster Peace Accords, a hybrid regime emerged that included regular popular elections and did not ban opposition parties. (ZAPU merged with ZANU voluntarily although under some duress.) However, Mugabe disregarded the Constitution in ways that country experts argue consolidated his rule. Thus, I exclude it from my analysis.

[22] Przeworski et al. (2000: 23) classify Botswana as a (fully closed) authoritarian regime. Freedom House scores after 1973 just barely rate it as "free" based on the combination of "free" political rights and "partly free" civil liberties for most years. Africanists more clearly identify it as a democracy (see Osei-Hwedie, 2001; Van de Walle, 2004). Classifying Botswana as a dominant party democratic regime would not affect my argument because my approach examines the impact of potential authoritarian controls empirically.

[23] One important difference is that in regional dominance, nationally competitive party organizations can transfer resources to their regionally weak counterparts to increase their viability whereas challengers to nationally dominant parties have almost no access to outside funds.

18   *Why Dominant Parties Lose*

Nevertheless, dominant parties flourish and challengers fail even where these approaches predict that they should succeed. I test these arguments using data that compare dominant party systems to fully competitive democracies for selected years. I classified system type using the Przeworski and colleagues (2000) data set that distinguishes (fully competitive) democratic from (fully closed) authoritarian regimes. Since these authors do not have a category for dominant party systems, I identified them using the coding rules developed above.[24]

Demand-Side Theories: Social Cleavages, Voter Dealignment, and Economic Explanations

I first discuss the deficiencies of approaches that focus on voter demand for opposition parties, including social cleavages theory, voter dealignment theories based on retrospective evaluations of the incumbent's performance in office, and economic explanations related to the effects of socio-economic modernization and crisis conditions.

Social cleavage theory posits that parties emerge to represent the political demands of groups that crystallize around major social divisions (Lipset and Rokkan, 1967). Political scientists adapted this argument to account for the number of competing parties based on the number and strength of such cleavages. Thus, multiparty systems emerged in countries with several major social divisions whereas milder social cleavages produced political dualism in the United States (Charlesworth, 1948; Lipson, 1953; Hartz, 1955; Key, 1964b; Cox, 1997: 15).

If this argument makes sense for dominant party systems, then they must have less of the "raw materials" that motivate citizens to form political parties compared to multi-party systems. To examine its empirical plausibility, I compared ethno-linguistic fractionalization (ELF) as coded by Roeder (2001) – a common proxy for social cleavages – and the effective number of parties[25] in dominant party systems and fully competitive

---

[24] Unless otherwise noted, I include the available country-year or country-election-year data for Botswana under the BDP (1965–), Gambia under the PPP (1963–1994), Malaysia under UMNO/BN (1974–), Mexico under the PRI (1929–1997), Senegal under the PS (1977–2000), Singapore under the PAP (1981–), and Taiwan under the KMT (1987–2000). For this analysis, dominant party democratic regimes are not included in the category of fully competitive democracies. For tests that compare all dominant party systems (DPARs and DPDRs) to all fully competitive democracies, see Chapter 8.

[25] I use the standard measure of vote-weighted parties from Laakso and Taagepera (1979) where $N = \Sigma_1^x 1/v_i^2$. Data come from Przeworski et al. (2000) and the Beck et al. (2001).

democracies in 1961 and again in 1985. A simple difference of means test shows that ELF scores are statistically indistinguishable, indicating that dominant party systems have about the same amount of the raw materials for generating political parties as do fully competitive democracies. However, dominant party systems had, on average, 1.4 fewer effective parties in 1961 and 1.3 fewer in 1985. These differences were statistically significant at the .05 level.[26] In addition, among those systems that transited from dominant to nondominant status between 1961 and 1985, there was, on average, no change in ELF.

It is not surprising that dominant party systems have fewer competitive parties than do fully competitive democracies. The point is that social cleavages do not appear to be responsible for this difference and while objective social divisions may be a necessary condition for the formation and development of challengers to dominant parties, it is not a sufficient condition. The sociological approach fails because it is silent on the constraints to new party formation and development (Sartori, 1968), including but not limited to resource availability.

Another version of the voter availability thesis comes from research on partisan dealignment. When applied to dominant party systems, this approach presumes that voters are aligned with the dominant party and then asks what conditions promote sufficient dealignment to create opportunities for opposition party success. One of the main forces that promotes dealignment is negative retrospective evaluations of the incumbent's performance in office, particularly with respect to economic issues. In the United States and other established democracies, such negative evaluations typically translate into anti-incumbent voting in about equal measure (Abramson et al., 1994). But in dominant party systems, the effects are muted. The best data for testing this hypothesis come from Mexico and Taiwan where appropriate public opinion survey data were available. But contrary to the theory's empirical predictions, a majority of voters in these countries held negative retrospective evaluations of the incumbent, but still planned to vote for it. In Mexico, 76% of voters evaluated the PRI's economic performance negatively beginning more than a decade

---

[26] Specifically, ELF 1961 was .38 for fully competitive democracies with 2.92 effective parties and ELF 1961 was .56 for dominant party systems with 1.53 effective parties. ELF 1985 was .40 for fully competitive democracies with 2.75 effective parties and ELF 1985 was .52 for dominant party systems with 1.48 effective parties. N = 43 countries for 1961 and N = 46 for 1981. Effective number of parties data were not available for four dominant party systems in 1961 because they were not independent countries. I used the closest subsequent year, no later than 1965.

before it lost power;[27] however, during the 1990s, up to 57% of voters who were the *most* dissatisfied with the PRI's performance still planned to vote for it.[28] In the 1980s, the PRI presided over negative growth rates, record inflation, and dramatic dips in real wages. Although this performance debacle did affect voters, hardship translated into far fewer votes for the opposition than one might expect. In Taiwan, the results are just as striking. Fully 61% of voters surveyed thought that the KMT had done a poor job in dealing with China – a central partisan cleavage (Niou and Ordeshook, 1992). Nevertheless, 51% of those who held the *most* negative assessments still planned to vote for its candidate in the 1996 elections.[29]

Data and analyses from other dominant party systems echo the muted effects of negative retrospective evaluations on the incumbent's staying power. Diaw and Diouf reach a similar conclusion for Senegal, albeit without public opinion data, when they lament the "failure of the opposition to convert popular discontent into a program of action" (1998: 127). Olukoshi argues that in most African countries there is not "an effective and coherent political opposition that is seen by the generality of the populace as constituting a credible alternative to the discredited incumbents which they seek to replace" (1998: 12).

The retrospective voting thesis fails to account for single-party dominance because it treats voters' decisions as a plebiscite on the incumbent's performance alone (Key, 1966; Fiorina, 1981) without asking whether voters find the challengers attractive. Although a majority of Mexican and Taiwanese voters evaluated their incumbent's past performance

---

[27] Author's calculations based on data from the 1988 IMOP Gallup Poll cited in Domínguez and McCann (1996: 101). Other data suggest that voters disliked the PRI's performance earlier. The 1986 *New York Times* Poll shows that 59% of respondents thought that their household economic situation was bad or very bad, but 45% of these voters still identified with the PRI. In the same survey, a striking 89% thought that the national economy was bad or very bad.

[28] Buendía (2004: 126–128) shows that 57.2% of voters who held negative retrospective pocketbook evaluations still planned to vote for the PRI in 1991. In 1994 and 1997 these numbers remained high at 43.2% and 33.1%, respectively. Buendía also shows that sociotropic evaluations produce virtually the same findings. Magaloni (1997) generates an even higher PRI advantage in 1994 using different surveys and measurement techniques. Her data show that 49.7% of voters who assessed the PRI's performance negatively planned to vote for it (author's calculations based on 1997: 194; also see Magaloni, 2006: 202).

[29] Data come from Hsieh, Lacy, and Niou (1998: 397) and represent voters' evaluations of KMT performance on cross-strait relations with China prior to the 1996 presidential elections.

negatively, when making prospective evaluations, they overwhelmingly preferred the incumbent. Indeed, only 34% of voters in Mexico in 1994 and 13% of voters in Taiwan in 1996 thought the incumbent would perform worse than the opposition in the future.[30] In dominant party systems, negative *retrospective* evaluations of the incumbent may not automatically translate into more positive *prospective* evaluations of the challengers because, for other reasons, challenger parties may form as noncentrist niche parties that are not sufficiently attractive to dealigned voters. As a result, dealignment may not automatically produce realignment and although negative retrospective evaluations of the incumbent may be a necessary condition for opposition party success, it is clearly not sufficient. These data also show that voters truly supported the incumbent when compared to the opposition and therefore imply that challenger parties did not lose primarily due to electoral fraud.

These data go a long way toward showing that no matter what the incumbent's actual performance in office, voters did not hold it as accountable as existing theory predicts.[31] Nevertheless, Haggard and Kaufman (1995) argue that economic crisis contributes to the breakdown of authoritarian regimes. As a simple test of this argument, I examined the effects of change in election year GDP per capita in all DPARs on both the effective number of parties and the vote gap between the dominant party and the first challenger (models not shown). Consistent with Geddes (1999a: 135, 139–140), I find no support for the thesis that economic crisis in and of itself brings down DPARs.[32]

A final demand-side argument comes from modernization theory and suggests that democratization occurs not due to economic crisis but economic growth or development. Regarding growth, Przeworski and colleagues (2000) find limited evidence for what they call the "endogenous" argument that modernization within a country caused democratization

---

[30] Author's calculations based on Magaloni (1997: 194) and Hsieh, Lacy, and Niou (1998: 397).

[31] Magaloni's excellent dissertation (1997; also see her 2006 book) argued that a modified retrospective model of voting behavior better accounts for the PRI's protracted decline in the face of poor economic performance. In her model, older voters who experienced a longer period of good economic performance under the PRI update their vote intentions slower than younger voters.

[32] Data on the effective number of parties and GDP per capita until 1990 come from Przeworski et al. (2000). Data on GDP per capita after 1990 were coded by the author. I captured long-run, cross-case effects with a pooled OLS. An alternative test would use a time-series cross-sectional model to take account of the within-case over-time effects as well.

between 1950 and 1990.[33] Not only does their best empirical model fail in general, it fails spectacularly for dominant party systems where it incorrectly predicts the regime type of 71.4% of all DPARs as democracies compared to only 13.4% incorrect predictions for fully closed authoritarian regimes.[34] Regarding development, Boix (2003) and Boix and Stokes (2003) argue that income equality drives endogenous democratization. However, a simple pooled cross-sectional test of this argument using election-year data from Deininger and Squire (1996) shows no statistically significant effect of the GINI coefficient on the effective number of parties in DPARs.[35] Thus, even if economic crisis, growth, or development cause authoritarian breakdown in general, DPARs are outliers that appear surprisingly resilient to the democratizing effects of these variables (Haggard and Kaufman, 1995: 13; Smith, 2005: 427).

My argument for dominant party persistence and decline in fact shares many elements with the modernization theories just discussed. Both approaches recognize the underlying importance of income distribution for understanding why social actors would become politically active against the incumbent. In my approach, however, the economic role of the state is central. Where substantial portions of the economy are publicly controlled by an incumbent that politically dominates the bureaucracy, agents in the private sector have fewer resources, no matter how they are distributed, that they could use to support opposition parties. Thus, I argue in Chapter 2 that we should pay attention not only to the level of development and the distribution of income but also to the public-private balance of economic power. Public sector power allowed incumbent dominant parties to withstand economic crises and to "manage the political pressures that stem from economic success" (Haggard and Kaufman, 1995: 13).

Institutional Approaches: Electoral Rules and Barriers to Entry

Institutional theories argue that electoral rules regulate the number of parties. In a generalization of Duverger's Law (Duverger, 1954: 113),

---

[33] Boix and Stokes (2003) find more evidence for the endogenous argument with an expanded data set that begins in 1800; however, since Mexico is the only country where dominance began before 1950, these findings are less relevant for my purposes.

[34] Author's calculations from Przeworski et al., 2000: 59–76, 84–86. Note that Przeworski et al.'s model predicts that Singapore should have been a democracy with 98% probability, Mexico and Taiwan should have been democracies with 89% probability, Malaysia with 69% probability, and Botswana with 58% probability (2000: 84–85).

[35] As above, a time-series cross-sectional model may be a more appropriate test.

The Puzzle of Single-Party Dominance   23

Cox (1997) theorizes that the maximum number of competitors in a given district is M+1 where M is district magnitude.

This account only represents a promising avenue for explaining single-party dominance if district magnitude is lower in these systems than in fully competitive ones. To probe the theory's applicability, I compared the mean district magnitude for lower house elections (MDMH) and the effective number of parties across all fully competitive democracies and dominant party systems between 1975 and 1990 using data from Beck and colleagues (2001).[36] The difference in MDMH across system type was statistically indistinguishable, but dominant party systems had, on average, 1.65 fewer effective parties, and this difference was statistically significant at the .001 level. The same difference in the effective number of parties appeared between the 18 fully competitive democracies and five dominant party systems that used the most restrictive electoral formulas where $M = 1$ (i.e., single-member districts).

Duverger's Law actually provides a correct prediction, on average, for both fully competitive democracies and dominant party systems because it only theorizes an upper bound of $M + 1$ and the mean effective number of parties falls well below this mark. But the theory provides no leverage, nor does it claim to, in understanding why the effective number of parties falls below $M + 1$. Thus, it does not help explain the gap in the effective number of parties between dominant and fully competitive systems or in explaining single-party dominance itself.

A second institutional argument is that the electoral formula not only affects the number of parties but also the pattern of inter-party competition (Cox, 1990). Systems with plurality winner single-member districts should produce two catchall parties that are centrist with respect to voters' preferences whereas those that use multi-member districts create multipartism and often feature what Sartori (1976: 132–40) termed "polarized pluralism" with center-fleeing niche parties. However, in dominant party systems, polarization existed both in systems that used pure

---

[36] Scholars debate about the best way to calculate district magnitude in mixed systems. Beck at al. (2001) use a weighted average. For instance, Mexico after 1987 had 300 plurality winner single-member districts and five multi-member districts that each elect 40 seats using proportional representation, yielding $M = 16.6$. If instead we follow Cox (1997) and use the median district magnitude, then $M = 1$ for Mexico. Finally, if we follow Taagapera and Shugart (1991) and use the size of the legislature over the total number of districts, $M = 1.64$ for Mexico. Thus, using MDMH for the cross-national test in the main text could bias the result; however, using the same formula to calculate magnitude across dominant party and fully competitive democratic systems diminishes the likelihood that it would.

24   *Why Dominant Parties Lose*

single-member districts (e.g., Mexico before 1965, Malaysia) and in systems that used mixed systems (e.g., Mexico after 1965) or multi-member districts (e.g., Taiwan).

A final and less well-developed argument in the institutionalist tradition highlights the effects of thresholds of representation. Thresholds may weed out very small parties that cannot win the minimum vote share needed to gain a single seat in the legislature. But empirically it turns out that, using data from Beck and colleagues (2001), the mean threshold in dominant party systems is 0.2% (with 1.6 effective parties), while the mean threshold in fully competitive democracies is actually higher at 1.7% (with 3.2 effective parties). All differences are statistically significant at the .001 level. Overall then, dominant party systems are in fact more institutionally permissive than their fully democratic counterparts with substantially more competitive parties.

Institutional theories fail because they presume a neutral market for votes where competition is completely fair. As Cox (1997: 26) notes, in institutional theories, "No party ever fails to get voters because it is too poor to advertise its position; no would-be party ever fails to materialize because it does not have the organizational substrate (e.g. labor unions, churches) needed to launch a mass party. In an expanded view, of course, the creation of parties and the advertisement of their positions would be key points at which the reduction of the number of political players occurs." I take up Cox's call for an expanded approach by systematically theorizing the role of resource asymmetries in party success or failure.

Supply-Side Approaches: Is it Rational to Form Opposition Parties?

Rational choice models of party competition focus on the supply side and ask when it is rational to form a new party, given the constraints imposed by institutions and voter demand. But in their current form, neither the models that presume a neutral market for votes where competition is completely fair nor those that presume a non-neutral market that is biased in favor of one party can account for the dominant party equilibrium.

Existing neutral models with entry predict at least two competitive parties in equilibrium. A first class of neutral model assumes that the parties announce their policy positions simultaneously. Feddersen, Sened, and Wright (1990) provide a model where a party's expected utility of competing is given by the probability of winning times the benefit of winning minus the cost of competing, or $Eu = pb - c$. A party only enters competition if its expected utility is nonnegative (i.e., if $pb \geq c$). Since the model uses deterministic spatial voting and no party has a nonspatial advantage, no party can win if it locates away from the median voter. Therefore, if a party enters, it enters at the median and wins with probability $p = 1/n$, where n is the number of parties. As Cox (1997: Ch. 8) points out, this also gives the equilibrium number of parties as $n = b/c$. Thus, single-party dominance could only be sustained if benefits were equal to costs (i.e., if $b/c = 1$). But if benefits equal costs, it is not clear why any party would enter, including the putative dominant party. Osborne and Slivinski's (1996: 71) citizen-candidate model generates an even more restrictive outcome where dominance can only result when $b \geq 2c$ and the single entrant locates at the median.

It might be more realistic to assume a sequential entry model where, if opposition parties form, they announce positions after the dominant party. These models confer a sort of incumbency advantage because they allow established parties to anticipate the position of new entrants and move to cut-off their market share. Work by Prescott and Visscher (1977), Palfrey (1984), Greenberg and Shepsle (1987), and Shvetsova (1995) examines different numbers of exogenous parties and electoral arrangements. Yet none of these models can account for single-party dominance. First, these models only work if the number of eventual entrants is known *ex ante* so that the first-mover can use backward induction to determine its best strategy. But it is not clear, and none of these models specify, why the eventual number of entrants would be known. The dominant party could base its prediction on the upper bound supplied by the electoral system, but if the eventual number of parties falls below the upper bound – the incumbent party's goal – then the conjecture could yield disastrous results! Second, and more consequentially, existing sequential models that assume a neutral entry market yield at least two parties in equilibrium. For instance, in Prescott and Visscher's (1977) model, if a single established (dominant) party expects one other party to enter competition, it moves off the median, randomly choosing to move to the left or right, and produces two equally sized parties in equilibrium.

Empirically, dominant parties exist in multiparty systems with at least two challengers. Nevertheless, existing models that take the number of parties as fixed still cannot account for the dominant party equilibrium. If we assume deterministic spatial voting and unidimensional competition with complete party mobility where parties vie for a single seat, then Cox (1990: 930) shows that any equilibrium must be dispersed and symmetric; however, the interior party virtually always loses and the peripheral parties may tie.[37] If we maintain unidimensional competition and make the somewhat more realistic assumption of probabilistic voting, then de Palma et al. (1990) and Adams (1999) show that the equilibrium is convergent at the median and all parties win with the same probability. Clearly, neither type of neutral model can account for the dominant party equilibrium.

The models reviewed above assume that competition occurs over a single dimension such as left versus right. As I argue below, dominant party authoritarian regimes typically feature two-dimensional competition. But adding dimensions only gives opposition parties more opportunities to enter and deepens the puzzle of single-party dominance. Existing multidimensional models take the number of entrants as given and begin with a minimum of two; however, for any number of parties, these models predict that any competitor can win when best strategy policy locations are adopted. Neutral models with deterministic voting and two-party competition predict that the parties locate inside the "uncovered set" (McKelvey, 1986) that is typically positioned at the geometric center of voter ideal points (Hinich and Munger, 1997: 61, fn 3; Cox, 1987: 420). Neutral models with probabilistic voting and multiple parties predict convergence to the centrist minimum-sum point (Lin et al., 1999).[38] Without any systematic nonspatial advantages, these models imply that challengers have the same chance of winning as the incumbent. As a result, single-party dominance would not occur.

Thus, if the electoral market were neutral, then opposition parties could simply form and compete with the dominant party as viable catchall competitors. I argue that they instead form as niche parties that adopt less efficient policy locations precisely because the market for votes is non-neutral. But existing non-neutral models err in the opposite direction and cannot understand why challengers would ever enter competition. As described above, when one party (call it the incumbent) has an identifiable and long-term advantage, all rational careerists should join it, thus transforming dominant party systems into one-party regimes without

---

[37] The interior party typically loses because, despite the divergent equilibrium, the peripheral parties are sufficiently centrist to squeeze the interior party's vote share. Note that the interior party can tie but cannot win for certain strangely shaped trimodal voter preference distributions. One can also imagine dispersed bimodal distributions that permit one of the peripheral parties to win while the other parties lose; however, these distributions take such an odd shape that it is difficult to believe that they exist empirically.

[38] The convergent result obtains when the nonpolicy component is relatively large (but see Adams, 1999). Otherwise, no equilibrium exists. Nonconvergent equilibria are possible as well; however, Lin (2007) argues that the minimum-sum point is the focal equilibrium.

The Puzzle of Single-Party Dominance

challengers. As an alternative, I argue that we can account for the existence but failure of opposition parties by modifying non-neutral models to include policy goals and partisan expression. These expressive benefits are powerful enough to encourage citizens to join opposition parties in the attempt to transform dominant party systems into fully competitive democracies.

PLAN OF THE BOOK

This book combines formal modeling, quantitative analysis, and qualitative fieldwork to build an argument about single-party dominance in general and the specific dynamics of its persistence and decline in Mexico. I craft new formal models to generate testable hypotheses that discipline and guide the study, although I also make the presentation accessible for readers unfamiliar with such models. I test these hypotheses using a four-pronged strategy. First, I examine the historical development of party politics in Mexico over time. Second, I analyze the implications of my hypotheses at a lower level of analysis by examining data from 1,470 individual responses to the Mexico Party Personnel Surveys that I conducted with a team of researchers at party conventions and national council meetings in 1999.[39] Third, to draw out the specific meaning of the quantitative findings and provide rich stories about grassroots party building, I use local case studies and over 100 semi-structured interviews with candidates and activists at the national, state, and municipal levels. Finally, to extend the analysis beyond Mexico, I present detailed case studies of two other dominant party authoritarian regimes (Malaysia and Taiwan) and in an extension I show how my approach can help understand partisan dynamics in two dominant party democratic regimes (Italy and Japan). I also make briefer references to a host of other dominant party systems throughout the book. By testing the implications of my theory on multiple cases and at multiple levels of analysis, I conduct true out-of-sample tests to overcome the traditional problems associated with single-country studies.

In the following chapter, I develop a general theory of single-party dominance and opposition party development. I argue that incumbent dominant parties can sustain their rule when they create a large public

---

[39] All surveys were funded by the National Science Foundation (SES #9819213) with in-kind contributions from *Reforma* newspaper for the first four. I thank Alejandro Moreno, Jogin Abreu, and Rossana Fuentes-Berain without whom these surveys could not have been accomplished. Olivares-Plata Consultores conducted the last two surveys.

sector and politicize the public bureaucracy. This allows them monopolistic control over public resources that they can divert for partisan purposes. I develop a new formal model of party competition that shows how these resource advantages affect opposition parties by lowering their probability of victory and forcing them to form at the margins, far to the left or the right of the status quo policies offered by the incumbent where they attract minority electoral constituencies rather than closer to the center where they would appeal more broadly. I also show how authoritarian controls, including repression and the threat of electoral fraud, further reduce opposition party size and increase their extremism.

Chapter 3 introduces the case of Mexico and examines the sources of opposition party undercompetitiveness from the initiation of single-party dominance in 1929 until the 1990s. I show how my theory accounts for historical trends and processes with a substantial degree of precision and why existing theories that presume a neutral or fair market for votes fail. Specifically, I show how the PRI's advantages made left parties fail during three specific time periods when the PRI's move to the right theoretically opened enough "space" for the left to attract more support and win, and how these advantages made right parties fail during two periods when the PRI moved to the left.

Chapters 4 and 5 move from treating parties as unitary actors to examining the dynamics of political recruitment into the opposition. In Chapter 4, I develop a new formal model of individual-level party affiliation for candidates and activists – a group that I argue we should treat together as party elites – that incorporates key elements of the uneven partisan playing field. I take care to explain the model for less technically inclined readers. The model generates very specific hypotheses about the internal composition of opposition parties as the dominant party's advantages change. It also shows how opposition parties can attract candidates and activists even in the absence of splits inside the dominant party. Chapter 5 then uses the Mexico Party Personnel Surveys and in-depth interviews to test the behavioral predictions derived from the model. It also gives a portrait of political recruitment and party-building efforts over time, particularly highlighting the generational differences between comparatively extremist early joiners that rise to leadership positions and more moderate later joiners.

Chapter 6 examines the implications of my theory for opposition party organizations and argues that their initial design as niche parties by early joiners makes them particularly inadaptable to changing conditions. Organizational rigidities hampered expansion so much that even as the PRI's resources waned in the 1980s and early 1990s and it ceded increasing opportunities for the challengers to expand by attracting more centrist constituencies, the opposition parties remained too out of step with the average voter to win. I demonstrate the strikingly similar organizational profiles and modes of recruitment in the PAN and PRD and show that both were constrained to the core. This chapter draws on the Mexico Party Personnel Surveys, party documents, membership data, and in-depth studies of party building efforts in boroughs of Mexico City.

Chapter 7 shows how the PRI's long rule was finally brought to an end in the 2000 elections. First, I show that resource asymmetries between the PRI and challengers leveled enough to create a fair electoral market for votes. Second, I show how my theory helps explain the failure of the opposition alliance and how intra-party coordination problems constrained presidential candidates from making the most efficient appeals. I then show how Vicente Fox solved the coordination problem by making a successful end-run around the PAN using independent resources whereas Cuauhtémoc Cárdenas was limited to the PRD's party resources and thus constrained by its narrower appeals. As a result, Fox, not Cárdenas, brought 71 years of PRI rule to an end.

Chapter 8 extends the argument to other dominant party systems. I show that my focus on hyper-incumbency advantages helps understand the dynamics of dominant party longevity and failure in two DPARs (Malaysia and Taiwan). I also show that, more surprisingly, the theory travels well to dominant party democratic regimes (DPDRs) where incumbents did not supplement resource advantages with authoritarian controls (Japan and Italy). In this chapter, I also show how alternative electoral institutions and government formats can affect dominant party persistence as the incumbent's advantages decline.

The conclusion highlights the theoretical and empirical implications of the argument for the future of partisan politics in Mexico, the effects of resource disadvantages on the development of externally mobilized parties that emanate from society, and the study of regime stability and the transition to fully competitive democracy in competitive authoritarian regimes.

PART ONE

THE MACRO-PERSPECTIVE

2

A Theory of Single-Party Dominance and Opposition Party Development

In his influential study, T. J. Pempel wrote that successful dominant parties create a "virtuous cycle of dominance" to reinforce their rule (1990: 16). But, once established, how is this cycle sustained? What are the mechanisms that reproduce the dominant party equilibrium and how is the cycle eventually broken?

In this chapter, I develop a theory of dominant party persistence and failure. At root, this is a question about the transformation of under-competitive party systems into fully competitive democracies. Since the electoral arena remains open in dominant party systems, explaining equilibrium dominance requires a theory of party competition. Yet the standard theories assume an unbiased or fair electoral market for votes and are thus inappropriate for studying dominant party systems where the incumbent's advantages systematically bias electoral competition in its favor. I theorize how these advantages help dominant parties virtually win elections before election day by forcing opposition parties, if they form, to compete with policy appeals that are extremist relative to the preference of the average voter. As a result, challenger parties seek both personnel and votes from among the most anti-status quo constituencies.

A crucial question is not just how systematic disadvantages affect challengers, but also how the cycle of dominance is sustained. I argue that dominant parties rise and fall primarily with the state's control over the economy. As long as the federal public bureaucracy is politically controlled, incumbent dominant parties can divert resources from the public budget, especially from state-owned enterprises, to partisan coffers. Conversely, privatization weakens dominant parties because it limits their access to public funds, and without these funds, well-greased patronage networks run dry, the machinery of dominance seizes up, and the increasingly fair marketplace for votes allows opposition parties to expand. Authoritarian controls, including repression and electoral fraud, are less important but do play a secondary role in some but not all dominant party systems when vote buying fails.

The first part of this chapter details the overall theory that guides the book. It links the political economy of dominance and authoritarian tools to opposition party strategy and viability. In particular, I show how asymmetric resources create an unfair electoral market for votes that, perversely, forces challenger parties to form as noncentrist niche-oriented competitors that are more interested in making policy statements than in winning elections. After introducing the logic verbally, the second part of the chapter presents a new formal model of party competition that makes the assumptions, mechanics, and results of the theory explicit. Less technically inclined readers can skim this section without losing the argument's main points. My theory is one way to complete Riker's (1976) insightful but underspecified theory of dominance that challengers fail because they compete as relative extremists that flank the incumbent to the left and right, thus remaining too small to win outright and too opposed to each other on policy to coordinate. But Riker, like existing neutral theories that presume fair competition, did not specify why challengers would stick toward the extremes rather than become more competitive by squeezing toward the center. I show how hyper-incumbency advantages force challengers to abandon the center and militate against elite coordination, thus sustaining the dominant party equilibrium. The last section before the conclusion examines the implications of this argument for the dynamics of opposition party development. In particular, it draws out key problems of building resource-poor outsider parties: the problems of appealing to and communicating with voters based on program not patronage, the problem of recruiting volunteer candidates and activists despite the low probability of winning and high cost of participation, and the difficulty in overcoming both intra- and inter-party coordination problems that are inevitably built into challenger parties due to their development path.

A THEORY OF DOMINANT PARTY PERSISTENCE AND FAILURE

A theory of single-party dominance should account for both equilibrium dominance and its breakdown. In other words, it should be able to explain challenger party formation but persistent failure during extended periods

A Theory of Single-Party Dominance

as well as the conditions under which opposition parties expand enough to best the incumbent and transform dominant party systems into fully competitive democracies. I argue that these outcomes can be explained primarily by the incumbent's access to patronage resources and secondarily by its use of authoritarian controls, including repression and electoral fraud. Together, these tools force opposition party failure because they affect who joins the opposition. The incumbent's resource advantages reduce the likelihood of challenger party victory and repression raises the costs of participation. Knowing that the competitive game is rigged against them, the only citizens willing to actively oppose the incumbent are those with the most anti-status quo policy preferences. In other words, citizens would have to despise the dominant party's policies to find it worthwhile to join a costly cause with a low chance of success. These relative extremists then form niche-oriented challenger parties that make specialized appeals to minority (i.e., nonmajority) electoral constituencies. Challengers do not transform into more moderate and competitive catchall parties until the incumbent's advantages decline. The argument is presented schematically in Figure 2.1 and discussed step-by-step below.

The Outcome to be Explained

The primary outcome of interest for this study is opposition party success or failure at the polls. This outcome is, of course, linked to the character of the broader political system. If opposition parties form but fail over an extended period, dominant party rule is in equilibrium. If opposition parties do not form at all and instead opposition forces turn to alternative forms of mobilization such as revolutionary and social movements, then dominant party rule collapses into one-party rule. Finally, if opposition parties expand enough to win, then dominant party rule transforms into fully competitive democracy.

To distinguish between smaller opposition parties that fail and larger ones that can attract majorities, I differentiate between "niche" and "catchall" parties by looking at the content of electoral appeals, the size of electoral constituencies, and organizational profiles. Niche parties are limited to core constituencies in the electorate that may be defined geographically, programmatically, or based on ethnic identification. Niche parties draw candidates and activists from their core constituencies; they make programmatic appeals that are directed toward these core constituencies by focusing on noncentral partisan cleavages or by making relatively

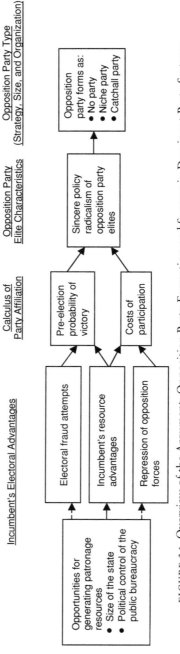

FIGURE 2.1. Overview of the Argument: Opposition Party Formation and Success in Dominant Party Systems

extreme appeals on central cleavages; and they create closed membership structures with high barriers to new activist affiliation in order to strictly distinguish their identity from competitors. Niche parties have a strong presence among specific groups in the electorate, but they are too small to win national elections.

Catchall parties, on the other hand, are open organizations that expand beyond their initial core constituencies and draw voters as well as candidates and activists from multiple electoral groups; they make moderate appeals on central partisan cleavages; and they lower the barriers to new activist entry in order to expand. In Kirchheimer's (1966) catchall parties, like in Panebianco's (1988) electoral-professional parties, what Kitschelt (1990) calls a "logic of electoral competition" dominates a "logic of constituency representation."

Mexico's dominant party equilibrium consisted of a relatively centrist PRI flanked by niche independent opposition parties that were polarized to the right and left. From the 1940s to the 1970s, the PAN adopted rightwing positions associated with a small socially conservative Catholic confessional constituency. Because it appealed to voters largely on the noncentral Church-State cleavage, the PAN effectively "wandered in the electoral wilderness for 40 years" (Loaeza, 1999). In the 1970s, it began to compete on the central partisan cleavage of economic development policy by adding market-oriented appeals to its program. Yet it quickly became identified with a big business minority and this noncentrist position repelled substantial portions of the national electorate. The PRD and its predecessors staked out positions on the opposite pole associated with dissident communist and socialist labor groups and segments of the urban lower class. In many ways the mirror image of the PAN, the left's significantly statist position attracted only a fraction of the national vote. The opposition parties were sufficiently noncentrist that they failed to attract enough votes to win individually and they were sufficiently ideologically polarized that they refused to coordinate with each other. As a result, the PRI remained dominant for some seven decades.

Similar stories can be told about opposition parties in other dominant party authoritarian regimes. In Senegal, the opposition fragmented to the right and left of the PS that remained dominant for 23 years (Coulon, 1990: 424–25; Diaw and Diouf, 1998: 128–130, 135). The four main challengers to Malaysia's dominant party were out of step with the average voter and "to succeed, must contest UMNO for the moderate political discursive space" (Chua, 2001: 142–143). In Botswana, the opposition BNF used "populist Marxist appeals" that appealed to minority constituencies

(Lipset, 1998: 48), the opposition BCP generated narrow, regional, and group-specific support (Osei-Hwedie, 2001: 71; Holm, 1987: 139), and the two challengers waged a "bitter rivalry" that precluded coordination (Osei-Hwedie, 2001: 71), thus allowing the BDP to dominate continuously for 39 years by 2000. In Taiwan, the opposition DPP experienced "sluggish growth in partisan support" due to "ideological rigidity and organizational weakness" (Chu, 2001: 277) and was unable to beat the incumbent KMT for 13 years and five elections after electoral competition became meaningful in 1987.

By definition, when opposition parties expand into catchall competitors with broader appeals, the incumbent is threatened and the dominant party equilibrium breaks down. In Mexico, both the PRD and the PAN moderated and expanded during the 1990s. The PRD oversaw the final phase of a two-decade transformation of the socialist and communist left into a democratic one that eventually accepted the major tenets of free trade. As a result, the left grew from about 5% of the congressional vote until the early 1980s to 25.7% in 1997, just 13.4% below the PRI. The left also won four governorships during the 1990s and greatly expanded its presence in municipal elections. The PAN was even more successful. Until the 1980s it won only about 10% of the congressional vote. But by the 1990s, it carved out a moderate image that drew on centrist slogans, cultivated broader support among the middle class and workers, and even made timid forays into the urban lower class. This moderation redounded in expansion: the PAN won six governorships beginning in the late-1980s, greatly expanded its presence in Congress, conquered areas beyond its stronghold in the North, and propelled Vicente Fox to the presidency in 2000.

A similar process of transformation occurred in other dominant party systems where challengers eventually beat incumbents at the polls. In Taiwan, the DPP expanded from a niche-oriented party with minority appeals into a broader organization that could attract plurality support and eventually beat the KMT in 2000 (Rigger, 2001a), although this transformation remains incomplete (Chu, 2001: 286–289). In Malaysia, the opposition came the closest to winning against the dominant UMNO/BN when the DAP and PAS moderated and formed a temporary coalition in 1990 (Singh, 2000: 34–35) and another in 1999 (Chua, 2001: 142–143). In general, when opposition parties expand into catchall competitors, they seriously challenge and eventually defeat dominant parties. Where opposition parties fail to expand and instead remain niche-oriented challengers, they are undercompetitive alone and fail to coordinate, thus allowing incumbent dominant parties to remain in power.

A Theory of Single-Party Dominance

How do we explain the dominant party equilibrium and its breakdown? What are the mechanisms that prohibit challengers from making the most efficient electoral appeals at the center as catchall parties and instead force them to form as niche parties with noncentrist appeals that inevitably lose? What thwarts opposition party coordination against the incumbent? What conditions ultimately diminish the effects of these competition-altering mechanisms and allow challenger parties to expand into catchall competitors that transform dominant party systems into fully competitive democracies?

Resource Asymmetries

Resource endowments deeply affect political parties and their ability to compete. Resource-rich parties attract better candidates (Green and Krasno, 1988; Miller and Stokes, 1963; Zaller, 1998, Stone, Maisel, and Maestas, 2004; Banks and Kiewit, 1989). They can communicate more often and more effectively with voters by hiring huge numbers of party workers and buying large amounts of time in the mass media, effectively speaking to voters with a megaphone while poor challengers speak in a whisper. Perhaps most importantly, they may be able to buy electoral support by distributing public resources to specific constituencies.

Individual incumbents in fully competitive democracies typically enjoy resource advantages, including extra fundraising capacity (Jacobson, 1980; Jacobson and Kernell, 1981; Goodliffe, 2001) and the perquisites of office that afford some material benefits (Cain et al., 1987; Cover and Brumberg, 1982; Mayhew, 1974; Levitt and Wolfram, 1997). Even these relatively small advantages are sufficient to create strikingly high rates of reelection. Resource advantages in dominant party systems are party-specific rather than candidate-specific and are so much larger that they should be considered *hyper-incumbency advantages*.

Once established, dominance persists when incumbents can use their control over the government to generate these hyper-incumbency advantages. In general, these advantages fall into two categories. Like advantage-seeking politicians in all competitive systems, dominant parties use legal policy mechanisms for partisan advantage, including targeted legislation and pork-barrel projects as well as deeper attempts to manipulate the long-run political economy to grow their core constituencies in the electorate (Przeworski and Sprague, 1986; Esping-Andersen, 1985, 1990: 48–55; Boix, 1998). In most competitive systems, divided government or limited tenure in office usually limits the impact of these distortions, but dominant parties control the government fully, do not suffer substantial checks by opposition parties, and expect to maintain power over the long term. As a result, dominant parties' budgetary decisions follow a more clearly political logic and often produce deep biases in the distribution of resources to benefit particular regions or constituencies (see Díaz-Cayeros, 1997 on Mexico; Gomez, 1994 on Malaysia; also see Golden, 2004; Scheiner, 2006).

What sets dominant parties apart from incumbents in fully competitive systems is that the former also have monopolistic access to public resources that they can transform into patronage goods. I define patronage as a vote-buying strategy that involves office-holders' targeted and partisan distribution of public resources for electoral support (see Mainwaring, 1999; Kitschelt and Wilkinson, 2007; Stokes, 2007). Note that patronage is not limited to public sector jobs in this definition, but includes public resources, broadly defined.[1]

In particular, dominant parties have access to five types of *illicit* public resources that they politicize for partisan purposes. First, they can divert funds from the budgets of state-owned enterprises (SOEs). These often massive companies have budgets ranging up to billions of dollars and typically include holdings in sectors such as energy, manufacturing, telecommunications, banking, and transportation. More importantly, they are usually run by high-level political appointees, their finances are generally hidden from public scrutiny, and they engage in multiple and difficult-to-track financial transfers with the federal government that yield manifold opportunities for the incumbent to divert public funds for partisan use. In a few countries (Taiwan, Malaysia), dominant parties are also permitted to own businesses, and these ventures typically operate in sectors that are protected by the state. Second, money may also be funneled to party coffers directly from the public budget through secret line items controlled by the executive branch and hidden legislative allocations reserved for legislators from the dominant party. Third, a large public sector allows the incumbent to dole out huge numbers of patronage jobs to supporters and withhold them from opponents. Fourth, the economic importance of the state encourages domestic businesses to exchange kickbacks and sometimes illicit campaign contributions for economic protection. Finally, dominant parties use the "administrative resources of the state," including

---

[1] Patronage differs from clientelism in that the latter may involve the use of private resources for political gain (Stokes, 2007). In dominant party systems there is an inevitable overlap since systems with political monopolies over public resources often induce private actors to collaborate. I develop this theme below.

office supplies, phones, postage, vehicles, and public employees themselves to help inform, persuade, and mobilize voters. These go far beyond the limited perquisites of office typical in fully competitive democracies and extend to the virtual transformation of public agencies into campaign headquarters.

The expectation of rotation in power usually deters incumbents in fully competitive democracies from using the fiscal power of the state to systematically skew competition significantly in their favor because they fear reprisals while out of power.[2] Dominant party systems clearly lack such rotation, and thus the incumbent's interest in creating quasi-permanent resource advantages over outsiders may go unchecked. If the incumbent can *access* and *use* public resources for partisan gain, then it has an almost bottomless war chest for party building and perennial campaigning while the opposition spends like a pauper.

Dominant parties can *access* public funds when the public bureaucracy is politically controlled. Where hiring, firing, and career advancement are based on political connections rather than merit, bureaucrats are less likely to act as gatekeepers to the public budget and more likely to allow the incumbent to divert resources for partisan political purposes (Shefter, 1977a, 1977b, 1994; Epstein, 1967: 110–111; Geddes, 1994). Dominant parties can *use* public funds for their partisan advantage where campaign finance laws do not exist or cannot be enforced because the electoral authority is controlled by the incumbent. Oversight by an independent body in charge of elections administration may restrain incumbents from overspending on campaigns and from distributing massive amounts of patronage to voters. Abuses may still exist on the margins, but they are unlikely to cause the massive distortions in the market for votes that sustain dominant party power.

Dominant parties' control over the government also discourages private donors from funding challenger parties. Where rotation is expected, as in the United States, it is often strategically wise for major donors to hedge their bets by contributing some amount to the party they like less (Jacobson, 1980; Jacobson and Kernell, 1981; Goodliffe, 2001). Even where a donor's preferred party has virtually no chance of winning, she may contribute if costs are low. Such donors helped launch third parties in the United States (Rosenstone, Behr, and Lazarus, 1984) and Green parties in West Europe (Kitschelt, 1989a). But the lack of rotation and the threat

---

[2] This statement may not hold if incumbents in fully competitive democracies create cartel-like agreements with challengers.

of economic or physical retribution in some dominant party systems make it strategically foolish for major donors to support an opposition party to any significant extent.[3] Instead, they are likely to give to the dominant party only, in exchange for political favors.

In sum, dominant parties are able to use their control over the government to monopolize the legal and illicit use of public resources as well as contributions from private donors. These resource advantages give dominant parties a competitive advantage over resource-poor challengers. As I show below with a formal model, resource asymmetries mean that challengers win with a lower probability no matter what their strategy and, perversely, the opposition parties that do form are forced to compete as losing niche parties with noncentrist policy appeals.

Authoritarian Tools: Electoral Fraud and Repression

Resource advantages are not the only arrow in the dominant party's quiver that can render challengers less effective. Incumbents in dominant party authoritarian regimes also reserve the ability to engage in electoral fraud or repression. However, the effects of these authoritarian tools are not as straightforward as they might initially appear. In this section, I show why they are secondary to resource advantages in sustaining the dominant party equilibrium.

Electoral fraud affects the probability that a challenger party will win and thus affects the character of the opposition parties that form. Yet unlike other analyses, including Sartori's (1976) influential work, I do not believe that fraud attempts reduce this probability to zero for four reasons. First, if prospective opposition candidates and activists believed that fraud would always deny them electoral victories with absolute certainty, then there would be little reason for them to form opposition parties and instead we should see opposition forces forming revolutionary movements designed to overthrow the dominant party or social movements designed to reform it. Outcome-changing fraud with certainty is incompatible with dominant party rule because the absence of opposition parties would make the system degenerate into a one-party regime. Second, as the prior section implies and the model presented below makes clear, when dominant parties have resource advantages that they can use to bribe

---

[3] Private donations to opposition parties would almost certainly be secret if they existed. Still, we would expect country experts to uncover some evidence of such donations if they occur, yet the case literature almost never mentions them.

A Theory of Single-Party Dominance   43

voters, they do not typically need to resort to heavy-handed fraud. As long as the electoral market is sufficiently biased in their favor, dominant parties virtually win elections before election day, making fraud unnecessary in most circumstances. Third, dominant parties typically win elections with such high margins, that, again, they do not often need to resort to fraud. Probably for that reason and not because of successful mass conspiracy, there is little evidence of outcome-changing election fraud in Mexico and other dominant party systems during most of their rule. More generally, an expert on both electoral fraud and Mexican politics argues that "ballot rigging does not appear to be decisive most of the time. The colorful history of vote fabrication probably exaggerates its role in determining election outcomes" (Lehoucq, 2003: 251). To the extent that incumbents use fraud, we should expect to observe it more frequently when resource advantages decline and the incumbent is threatened by the prospect of fair competition in elections that it might actually lose.

Finally, even when the incumbent does resort to fraud, we cannot take its effects on the outcome for granted. Committing successful fraud requires several elements, including (a) large amounts of resources to fund the machinery of fraud, including pay for ballot-box stuffers and thugs, (b) a large network of reliable co-conspirators who are efficient and quiet, and (c) reliable forecasting about the minimum number of votes that need to be stolen to fix the outcome. Clearly, fraud is easier to perpetrate when election oversight mechanisms are weak, the judiciary is not independent, the media are controlled, and when elections can be stolen more in the counting than in the voting; nevertheless, the incumbent must still be threatened with electoral loss to turn to fraud and needs resources and a well-oiled machine to make fraud successful.

In sum, opposition forces do not know *ex ante* whether fraud will be attempted and, if it is, neither the incumbent nor the challenger know whether it will be successful. Thus, from the perspective of political actors, fraud affects election outcomes probabilistically rather than with certainty.

The other authoritarian tool that dominant parties may use is repression. Repression may be directed at voters – and in some systems incumbents physically coerce voters or threaten them with economic sanctions – but analytically, imposing an extra cost on voters for choosing the opposition (repression) functions just like adding extra benefits for choosing the incumbent (patronage). The threat of repression has a different effect when it is directed at opposition parties. It raises the costs of joining a challenger above the cost of joining the dominant party. These costs will not directly affect the challenger party's chances of winning, but it will force them to become more policy oriented and thus draw them away from the status quo offered by the dominant party. This occurs because a prospective candidate or activist would have to be that much more opposed to the incumbent on policy to be willing to pay the higher costs of working for the opposition. If incumbents raise costs to a sufficiently high level, then no citizens will find it worthwhile to oppose the incumbent and, as in the case of fraud with certainty, opposition parties would not form at all and dominant party rule would break down. As repression falls, challenger parties should attract candidates and activists who are more moderate and this should result in expansion, allowing challengers to develop from niche parties into catchall ones.

The use of repression against opposition forces varies substantially across dominant party systems and over time. Dominant party authoritarian regimes (DPARs), including Mexico, Taiwan, Malaysia, and Senegal impose some level of repression against opposition forces. To be clear, these systems permit regular and meaningful elections. If they did not, they would be classified as fully closed authoritarian regimes. DPARs are headed by civilians, but by virtue of the incumbent's control over both the executive and the legislature it may deploy the military and any aspect of law enforcement against regime outsiders. DPARs also typically have a well-developed internal security apparatus that may include a Ministry of the Interior for domestic surveillance, a secret police, a preventive or judicial police, and a regular police force, as well as flexible laws governing the domestic use of the military (Brooker, 2000).

Despite the ability to coerce, DPARs typically use targeted repression against opposition forces on an episodic basis that falls far short of the "ban on all pluralism" (Féher, Heller, and Markus, 1983: 159–165) that describes constitutionally one-party regimes. For instance, in the Soviet Union, the state destroyed "horizontal links between individuals and groups of individuals" (Fish, 1995: 22) in an attempt to purge or purify the body politic (Tucker, 1965; Jowitt, 1992; also see Alves, 1985 on Brazil; Garretón, 1989 on Chile). Extra-legal jailings, beatings, and assassinations are not unheard of in DPARs, but they are comparatively rare. Opposition forces typically know that they have some room to organize, even though they realize that they may be under surveillance and never know exactly how far they can push the regime at any given time. Differences between DPARs and one-party regimes are reflected in their Freedom House civil rights scores. The average score for DPARs is

A Theory of Single-Party Dominance

3.75, whereas the one-party fully closed authoritarian regimes score much worse at 5.66.

Repression is more moderate in DPARs than in one-party regimes because the former generate legitimacy through consent that is expressed in regular elections whereas the latter derive legitimacy – to the extent that they do – almost exclusively from founding projects (Jowitt, 1992). Dissidents in one-party regimes are thus viewed as threats to the nation that must be repressed. In DPARs, some version of national unity – either from a revolution in the case of Mexico or from a struggle for independence in almost all of the cases in Africa and the Caribbean – underlies the regime's initial legitimacy (Zolberg, 1966; Tucker, 1961; Huntington, 1970; Bartra, 1987, 1989; Crouch, 1996; Cheng, 2001), but it seeks to reproduce this legitimacy through regular consultations at the polls. Only when political conditions become uncontrollable and cooptation fails do DPARs repress opposition forces (Hellman, 1983; Schedler, 2005; Solinger, 2001; Reyna and Weinert, 1977). Thus, in DPARs there is a hierarchy of tactics for controlling the opposition that has been neatly summarized as "two carrots, then a stick."

The Role of the Dominant Party's Policy Appeals

Dominant party advantages are significant, but they are not absolute. Opposition forces can exploit poorly designed electoral strategies that leave large groups of voters available. In order to translate their advantages into the highest probability of victory, dominant parties should use their policy offers as one element in carving out a broad center. For many configurations of party competition, this means that the dominant party should offer a policy that appeals to the average (i.e., median) voter, conditional on the magnitude of the party's nonpolicy advantages and how efficiently its patronage machine operates. In other words, the median voter should like the incumbent's policy plus patronage more than the challenger's policy offer. If the dominant party shifts its policy offer over time, these shifts should occur within a relatively restricted range.

Work on dominant party systems in Africa (Zolberg, 1966), Mexico (Padgett, 1976; Collier and Collier, 1991; Cheng, 2001), and Taiwan (Chu, 2001: 281; Cheng, 2001) suggests that dominant parties are typically centrist with respect to the distribution of voters' policy preferences. Through their centrism, they often seek to incorporate broad social groups to become what Collier (1992) called a "coalition of the whole."

Dominant parties often view their mandate as the implementation of a "national project" such as economic modernization that involves the cooperation of all major actors in society. By positioning themselves near the center of the policy space, they can mitigate social conflict and remain flexible in distributing benefits to one or another sector of society. Arian and Barnes write,

The dominant party assures its continued success by effectively spreading out among many social strata rather than concentrating in only one; it mobilizes support from all sectors of society by mobilizing issues and groups from a broad spectrum. It finds its firmest base of support among the modal types in society and spreads out widely from these to consolidate its power (1974: 603).

Sticking near the center of the political space also helps enhance the dominant party's legitimacy. Incumbent dominant parties often attempt to deflect the criticism that they rule through fully authoritarian means by increasing turnout (Ames, 1970; Gómez and Bailey, 1990). Incumbents can increase turnout through a number of mechanisms, including patronage and coercion; however, they may also use policy appeals as one lower cost mechanism. While dominant parties can do little to reduce abstention due to indifference through their policy offers (since voters expect the incumbent to win re-election), they can reduce abstention due to alienation that occurs when voters feel too distant on policy from the closest viable party to make voting worthwhile. If a dominant party moves off the median, it enhances the probability of abstention due to alienation on its opposite flank.

Despite the advantages to centrism, dominant parties are sometimes less "pragmatic" and instead hold policy preferences that inform their platforms. If the incumbent wanders too far off the median on policy, then its patronage advantages will not be large enough to compensate the median voter for the lost utility on policy, and its chances of winning the election will fall. However, patronage is such a powerful advantage that, as the model below shows, incumbents can move surprisingly far from the median and still win even if the challenger pursues the best strategy available to it.

The main point is clear: whether dominant parties are pragmatic or policy oriented, they need advantages over the opposition in the form of asymmetric resources or costs of participation to maintain power. In the absence of such hyper-incumbency advantages (i.e., in fair or "neutral" competition), as shown in Chapter 1, opposition parties could form as catchall competitors that win with the same or better probability as the dominant party. The particular mix of patronage and repression in a given country year is a question of dominant party capacity, the budget constraint that governs patronage outlays, and the actors' willingness to tolerate repression. The combination of a shrinking public sector and the decreased availability of authoritarian controls constitute the "perfect storm" for dominant party longevity, and when these tools are no longer available, dominant parties are not long for this Earth.

Modeling Single-Party Dominance

How do the incumbent's resource advantages make challenger parties undercompetitive and sustain the dominant party equilibrium? I first show that when the incumbent uses resource advantages to buy voter support, challengers have a lower probability of victory, no matter what strategy they pursue. Then I show that, if challengers form, these disadvantages force them to form as niche parties that make noncentrist appeals, even when the most efficient appeals are centrist.[4] As a result, opposition parties are undercompetitive individually and too ideologically opposed to each other to coordinate against the incumbent, thus maintaining the dominant party equilibrium. To develop this resource theory of single-party dominance, I present a formal model of biased or non-neutral electoral competition where the incumbent has exclusive access to patronage goods that it can use to bribe voters but where the effect of patronage on voters' decisions is uncertain due to unknown efficiency in the incumbent's patronage machine. In an extension, I also show that authoritarian tools (asymmetric costs of participation and electoral fraud attempts) have the same effects on competitive dynamics as asymmetric resources. I take care to make the presentation accessible to less technically inclined readers; however, those who prefer to skim the mathematical elements can still get the main points from the text.

The Incumbent's Advantages Reduce the Probability of Opposition Victory

In competition for a single seat between an incumbent party with patronage resources that it uses to buy electoral support and a challenger without patronage, the incumbent always wins with a higher probability than the

---

[4] This model can extend to dominant party systems where competition is based on ethnic identities as long as ethnicity maps onto programmatic cleavages. For an example, see the section on Malaysia in Chapter 8.

48 *Why Dominant Parties Lose*

challenger. To see why, first imagine a baseline model of what Downs (1957: 12) called "perfect democratic competition" or Cox (1997) calls a "neutral entry model" that is completely fair so that no party has a resource advantage and the parties compete exclusively with their policy appeals. The appeals, although potentially on multiple issues, package on a single dimension that we can call left versus right. If the parties want to maximize their chances of winning, then they both adopt the policy preferred by the median voter – typically at the center of the electorate's policy preferences – and each will win the election with 50% probability (Downs, 1957; Davis, Hinich, and Ordeshook, 1970; Feddersen, Sened, and Wright, 1990).

This well-known result breaks down when competition is unfair or non-neutral as it is in dominant party systems. Imagine an electoral marketplace where voters respond not just to policy appeals but also to material benefits that they might receive. Dominant parties have a virtual monopoly over these extra material benefits because their exclusive or quasi-exclusive access to public resources yields substantial patronage goods. For all the reasons developed above, challenger parties do not have access to public resources or private donations that they could use as patronage. Nor can challengers make credible commitments to distribute patronage after the election if they win. Since they have never been in power, voters steeply discount their offers to the point of making them unproductive.

To see how this biased model of voter choice works and its effects on challenger party chances, assume that the parties simultaneously announce policy positions to the voters on a single left to right dimension and that they are constrained to implement these policies if they win.[5] Voters have preferences over policy that are arrayed on this dimension, represented for convenience by [−1,1]. A dominant party (D) makes a strategically chosen policy appeal on this dimension (x_d) but also offers voters some amount of patronage (g).[6] A challenger party (C) similarly

---

[5] Many models assume that candidates cannot lie strategically because voters would deeply discount their strategically announced policies. This may not be true when candidates run as independents or are linked to weak party organizations (Stokes, 2001; Levitsky, 2003), but where parties have more established positions as they do in most dominant party systems, credible commitment becomes a more reasonable assumption.

[6] Note that, in the model, the dominant party gives the same amount of patronage (g) to each voter. This is obviously inefficient. If the incumbent has technology to identify the voters who (1) will choose it on policy (core voters), (2) would be very expensive to buy (opposition voters), and (3) could be biased in favor of the incumbent for a reasonable price (marginal voters), then it would target the latter. These voters should be located on

A Theory of Single-Party Dominance

makes a strategically chosen policy appeal (x_c) but cannot offer patronage, nor can it make credible commitments to distribute patronage after the election. For simplicity, assume that x_c is always to the right of or the same as x_d (although their positions could be reversed). To win the election, a party has to win the median voter (m) and, without loss of generality, we can say that m is centrist and prefers the policy associated with zero.[7] As a party's policy appeal gets further from m's preference, she likes it less. Following standard practice, I model voter policy utility as a declining quadratic function. Thus, m has the following utility for D and C, respectively:

$$U_m(D) = -(m - x_d)^2 + g + z \qquad (1)$$

$$U_m(C) = -(m - x_c)^2 \qquad (2)$$

What are the chances that m votes for D or C? To determine this, z will be defined momentarily, but first note that m votes for D when it gets more from D's policy offer plus its patronage offer than from C's policy offer alone. Substituting in (1) and (2) above with $m = 0$, this is the same as saying:

$$\text{Choose D if } x_c^2 - x_d^2 + g + z > 0 \qquad (3)$$

The one element that is still undefined in this biased model of voting behavior is z which represents patronage-related uncertainty. Although the incumbent has a monopoly over patronage goods, the effects of this advantage on voters' decisions might be uncertain for three reasons. First, how voters respond to bribes is private information that the incumbent cannot always observe. It will try to enforce outcomes by monitoring voters' choices, but it never knows how hard voters will work to maintain the secret ballot or how effective its local operatives will be in discerning their choices.

Second, dominant parties create distribution networks to funnel patronage to voters and these networks introduce uncertainty into the effect of patronage goods on voting decisions. Examples of these delivery

---

the policy dimension between the incumbent and challenger. However, once the incumbent concentrates patronage on marginal voters, the challenger may benefit from moving, thus inducing the incumbent to change its patronage distribution. Thus, a more nuanced model might force a mixed-strategy equilibrium.

[7] Since the model assumes two-party competition for a single seat, the party that wins the median voter also wins all voters on its long market side, opposite its rival. Since 50% of the voters are to one side of m, winning m is sufficient to win the election.

systems include the Mexican PRI's sectoral organizations among laborers, peasants, and the urban middle class including public employees (Cornelius and Craig, 1991) and dense local networks that played similar roles in Malaysia's UMNO (Crouch, 1996: 62). These networks will operate less efficiently if local agents have incentives to divert resources to their favored constituencies or keep it for themselves. This implies that uncertainty rises as the magnitude of patronage flushed through the system falls because operatives might conclude that the dominant party will soon lose power. Uncertainty will also increase as the incumbent tries to target voters outside its traditional networks. These networks typically rely to a large extent on public sector unions, so as privatization and/or growth of the informal sector decrease the relative size of the public sector, the patronage delivery system should become less efficient and its effects more uncertain.[8]

Finally, the effects of patronage on vote choice are likely to vary across constituencies and over time. Patronage is typically more effective among poorer voters because the marginal utility of extra income is greater for them than for voters with more means (Eisenstadt and Roniger, 1981; Kitschelt, 2000). As a result, socio-economic modernization over time should make the effect of patronage less certain as increasingly affluent citizens resist bribery.

There are several ways to model patronage-related uncertainty (see Enelow and Hinich, 1982; Wittman, 1983; Groseclose, 2001). I follow Adams, Merrill, and Grofman (2005: 189) in assuming that the parties benefit or suffer from a random draw from a nonpolicy variable z that follows a normal distribution (i.e., bell-shaped) with mean zero and standard deviation σ_g where σ_g represents the level of patronage-related uncertainty (also see Londregan and Romer, 1993). When σ_g is very small, the patronage advantage is known to all competitors. When it is very large, there is a lot of uncertainty about how much patronage will affect the election. Appendix A discusses the plausible size of g and σ_g.

Returning to (3), we can find the probability that m chooses D, which can be written as

$$P_m(D) = \Phi\left[\frac{x_c^2 - x_d^2 + g}{\sigma_g}\right] \tag{4}$$

---

[8] The valence-related uncertainty parameter z is very flexible. It could also relate to the effects of candidate characteristics, weather, exogenous economic events, or any variable that has a distribution that is known to the competitors but has an unknown realization.

A Theory of Single-Party Dominance 51

where Φ is the standard cumulative normal distribution. To see how this function works, first note that $\Phi[0] = 0.5$ so that any value inside the brackets bigger than zero gives D a greater than 50% chance of winning.

Suppose both parties are exclusively interested in winning office. Then the problem for D is to pick a policy x_d that maximizes (4) while C chooses a policy x_c that tries to minimize it. In other terms, the utility functions for D and C respectively are

$$U_D(x_d, x_c) = P_m(D) \tag{5}$$

$$U_C(x_d, x_c) = 1 - P_m(D) \tag{6}$$

These utility functions amount to saying that D wants to make the number inside the brackets in (4) large and C wants to make it small. Both D and C know the location of the median voter m and the size of the dominant party's patronage advantage (g) but not how well the patronage machine will operate (σ_g) before they make their strategically chosen policy announcements $(x_c$ and $x_d)$ to the public. Both parties will quickly realize that the best each can do is to adopt a centrist policy associated with m's location at zero.[9] (Note that this is true because if D sets $x_d = 0$ and C adopts $x_c > 0$, then the number inside the brackets increases in the numerator and D's chance of winning improve above 50%.)

When both parties adopt the same policy, then $x_c^2 - x_d^2 = 0$ and the election rests entirely on the magnitude of patronage and its uncertainty (i.e., $\Phi[g/\sigma_g]$). The opposition's chance of winning only reaches parity with the incumbent at 50% when competition is perfectly fair $(g = 0)$. When competition is unfair $(g > 0)$, the challenger's chance falls below 50% even when the challenger makes the most strategically efficient policy announcement at the median. How much it falls for a given increase in patronage depends on the amount of uncertainty. When uncertainty is very small $(\sigma_g = 0.01)$ – illustrating a situation where the incumbent's patronage machine delivers payoffs and monitors voting with almost perfect precision – the opposition's chance of winning is approximately zero if the dominant party benefits from just 0.05 units of patronage, or less

---

[9] The result is somewhat different if the location of m is unknown. Groseclose (2001) argues that the disadvantaged party would then try to differentiate itself from the advantaged party in order to give some voters higher utility for it over the advantaged party and with the hope of happening upon the median voter. In contrast, the advantaged party wants to mimic its competitor's location because this will give m higher utility for it, no matter where m is located.

than 3% of what I argue is a reasonable maximum value for patronage volume (see Appendix A). When uncertainty is small ($\sigma_g = 0.5$), then the challenger always has some positive chance of winning, but it drops all the way to 2.3% when patronage is at its largest. Under medium uncertainty ($\sigma_g = 1$) maximum patronage decreases the opposition's chances to 15.9%, and under high uncertainty ($\sigma_g = 2$), it decreases its chances to 30.9%. The main finding is now clear: under any level of uncertainty, patronage-disadvantaged parties are always at a competitive disadvantage no matter what their strategy.

The Incumbent's Advantages Force Opposition Parties to Adopt Noncentrist Policies

The results of the pure office-seeking model above where the parties' utility functions are (5) and (6) illustrate a central problem for challengers to dominant parties. If resource disadvantages mean that a challenger will, despite following the best possible strategy, always have a lower probability of winning, then it cannot exist as a pure office-seeking party! Identifiable imbalances in the expected chance of winning should encourage rational politicians who want to win to join the incumbent rather than form a challenger party. Cox writes that when a dominant party is firmly established, "there is no (current seat-maximizing) reason to run under any other than the dominant label. Would-be career politicians will either enter the dominant party's endorsement process, or not at all" (1997: 166). Epstein (1986: 129) makes a similar theoretical point with reference to the Solid South in the United States under Democratic Party rule: "Those who seek office [in dominant-party states] may perceive the primary of the dominant party as a more advantageous vehicle for success than entry, however easy, as candidates of a minority party. Protests, along with ambition, talent, and interest, are thus attracted to a single party" (cited in Cox 1997: 169). It seems reasonable that parties in fully competitive democracies could exist as office-seeking parties even if they suffer a temporary valence disadvantage.[10] The situation is markedly different for challengers to dominant parties that are at a long-term systematic disadvantage. All major forces understand that the incumbent party offers the best chance for career advancement, and thus careerists who want to win office should join the dominant party instead of creating a new party.

---

[10] For instance, Adams, Merrill, and Grofman (2005) argue that valence advantages shift between the Democrats and Republicans in the United States from election to election, yet we do not see a constant back-and-forth movement of personnel between the parties.

A Theory of Single-Party Dominance

53

If the population of prospective politicians contained only pure careerists, then opposition parties would not exist and dominant party systems would collapse into one-party regimes. Since opposition parties clearly do exist in these systems, these parties must value something other than winning. Here I focus on the value of fighting for a policy that the party would like to institute if it wins. We can imagine other possible motivations, but policy represents the most promising avenue. Adding policy motivations to the parties' utility function has two important effects. First, policy motivations give a rationale for potential founders to create an opposition party despite systematic disadvantages, although they also force founders to hold sincere policy preferences that are extreme relative to the status quo. Modeling the founder's problem is a necessary element of the puzzle, but because it draws attention away from the dynamics of partisan competition, I present the details in Appendix B. Second, policy motivations affect the dynamics of competition such that (1) the disadvantaged challenger party's strategically chosen policy announcement is pulled away from the preference of the median voter and toward the sincere preference of its members and (2) the advantaged dominant party's strategy is drawn toward the median voter regardless of its sincerely preferred policy. I now show why these results occur.

To incorporate policy-seeking into the purely office-seeking party utility functions in (5) and (6), we can specify more complex utility functions. To build these functions, first assume that the dominant party D and challenger C have sincerely preferred policies D and C, respectively. Then assume that each party's utility for policy declines quadratically as the policies they announce (x_d and x_c) become more distant from the policies they like (D and C). If D wins, it gets the utility associated with $-(x_d - D)^2$ because it institutes its strategically chosen policy announcement x_d. If D loses, it receives the utility associated with $-(x_c - D)^2$ because C gets to institute its strategically chosen policy announcement x_c. Similarly, if C wins, it gets $-(x_c - C)^2$ and if it loses, it gets $-(x_d - C)^2$. Since we also know that D wins with probability $P_m(D)$ and C wins with probability $1 - P_m(D)$, we can say that each party's expected payoffs for policy alone are:

Expected policy payoff for D:
$$-(x_d - D)^2 P_m(D) - (x_c - D)^2 (1 - P_m(D)) \tag{7}$$

Expected policy payoff for C:
$$-(x_c - C)^2 (1 - P_m(D)) - (x_d - C)^2 P_m(D) \tag{8}$$

54   *Why Dominant Parties Lose*

Now assume that D cares both about winning and about policy outcomes, but that it weights the importance of winning in (5) by λ_d and the importance of policy in (7) by $1 - \lambda_d$ where λ_d can take on any value between 0 and 1. For instance, if D cares only about winning, then $\lambda_d = 1$ and $1 - \lambda_d = 0$. If D cares only about policy then $\lambda_d = 0$ and $1 - \lambda_d = 1$. Similarly, C cares both about winning and about policy, and it weights the importance of winning in (6) by λ_c and the importance of policy in (8) by $1 - \lambda_c$.[11]

With these elements in hand, we can specify the mixed office-seeking and policy-seeking utility functions for each party by combining (5) and (7) for D and (6) and (8) for C, yielding the following:[12]

$$U_D(x_d, x_c) = \lambda_d P_m(D) - (1 - \lambda_d)(x_d - D)^2 P_m(D)$$
$$- (1 - \lambda_d)(x_c - D)^2 [1 - P_m(D)] \qquad (9)$$

$$U_C(x_d, x_c) = \lambda_c[1 - P_m(D)] - (1 - \lambda_c)(x_c - C)^2 [1 - P_m(D)]$$
$$- (1 - \lambda_c)(x_d - C)^2 P_m(D) \qquad (10)$$

The function in (9) states that D's utility U_D for strategic policy announcements x_d and x_c is given by (1) how much it wants to win the election (λ_d) times the probability that it does win ($P_m(D)$); (2) how much it wants to institute policy ($1 - \lambda_d$) times the probability that it wins and the difference between its sincere policy preference and its strategic policy announcement ($x_d - D)^2$; and (3) how much it wants policy times the probability that the challenger wins ($1 - P_m(D)$) and the difference between its sincere policy preference and the challenger's announced policy ($x_c - D)^2$. The utility function for C shown in (10) is similar.[13] Note that if both parties want to maximize their chances of winning only,

---

[11] In (9) and (10), the λs and $1 - \lambda$s weight the importance of maximizing the probability of winning versus maximizing policy goals. Clearly, probability units and policy units are not the same and we cannot know how to compare them. I interpret λ_d and λ_c to include some conversion constant b that determines the marginal rate of substitution of probability for policy units. No matter what b is, the results shown in Figure 2.2 will have the same basic shape, thus permitting the qualitative interpretation that I give below for the model's findings.

[12] I adapt a similar model developed by Adams, Merrill, and Grofman (2005: Ch. 11).

[13] This model, like many models in the spatial theory tradition, assumes that the parties are constrained to implement their pre-election promises (i.e., their prospective policy offers are credible commitments).

A Theory of Single-Party Dominance

then $\lambda_d = \lambda_c = 1$ and the second and third components of (9) and (10) drop out, giving the pure office-seeking model in (5) and (6).

If the parties have some degree of policy-seeking preference (i.e., if $\lambda < 1$), then they will be drawn away from the median voter and toward their sincerely preferred policies.[14] How far they diverge from the center depends on their degree of policy-motivation and the location of their sincerely preferred policy. Appendix B shows why the challenger's sincere preference C must be extreme. I also assume that the dominant party prefers the opposite extreme, so that $C = 1$, and $D = -1$. Beginning with extreme parties is useful to show the substantial effects of changing λ in pulling the dominant party's strategically chosen policy announcement toward the center even when its sincere preference is extreme and in drawing the challenger away from the center even when the probability maximizing strategy is centrist.[15]

My model has one unique element. Following the insight above that disadvantaged parties cannot logically exist if they only seek to win office, I depart from all existing models that specify the parties' motivations *ex ante*. Instead, I allow the parties' relative emphasis on office-seeking and policy-seeking motivations to emerge from their expectations about their probability of winning. It seems likely that as a party's chance of winning rises, its internal coalition will choose to increase the party's emphasis on winning office at the expense of policy. This could occur, for example, for a challenger party as the dominant party's patronage advantage declines or the amount of patronage-related uncertainty increases. Thus, in the model, the parties become more office-seeking (i.e., λ_c and λ_d increase) as their chance of winning increases to one-half, after which they are pure office-seekers.[16] The intuition here is that a disadvantaged

---

[14] The equilibrium result would change if the parties did not know the location of m. See footnote 9.

[15] If D were sincerely centrist – as dominant parties probably are in the aggregate – then there would be no conflict between sincere and strategic preferences and D would choose $x_d = 0$, just as my model predicts even assuming sincere extremism.

[16] Specifically, $\lambda_d = 2[P_m(D)]$ for $P_m(D) < 0.5$ and $\lambda_d = 1$ for $P_m(D) \geq 0.5$. Also, $\lambda_c = 2[1 - P_m(D)]$ for $[1 - P_m(D)] < 0.5$ and $\lambda_c = 1$ for $[1 - P_m(D)] \geq 0.5$. We could generate a result where the dominant party diverges from the median if we continue to assume that D is extreme and specify different expressions for λ. For instance, $\lambda_d = P_m(D)$ and $\lambda_c = 1 - P_m(D)$ generates a divergent but asymmetric equilibrium where x_c is more non-centrist than x_d. Specifying a curvilinear relationship such as $\lambda_d = -4(P_m(D) - .5)^2 + 1$ and $\lambda_c = -4(1 - P_m(D) - .5)^2 + 1$ so that the parties are willing to trade off a higher chance of winning for policy they like more, yields the equilibrium $x_c = 0$ and $x_d < 0$.

56 *Why Dominant Parties Lose*

challenger party that expects to win with a low probability would only find it worthwhile to compete if it could win with a policy position it prefers more.

I solve the model computationally.[17] Figure 2.2 shows predictions for the parties' strategically chosen policy announcements (x_d and x_c) given the amount of patronage (g) with medium patronage-related uncertainty ($\sigma_g = 1$). Note that if competition is fair ($g = 0$), then both parties are pure office-seekers ($\lambda_d = \lambda_c = 1$), their best location to adopt is 0 at the preference of the median voter, and they each win with 50% probability, just as the standard Downsian model implies. But as competition becomes less fair, the challenger's chances decrease and its interest in pursuing policy goals correspondingly increases ($\lambda \rightarrow 0$). When the dominant party has a small amount of patronage, say, 0.2 units, the challenger locates at 0.19 away from the median and wins with 40.7% probability. As patronage increases to 0.5 units, the challenger positions itself further from the median at 0.34 and wins with 26.9% probability. If patronage is at its maximum, then the challenger goes to 0.46 and wins with just 11.3% probability.

In sum, as the dominant party's advantages (g) increase, the median voter (m) becomes more biased against the challenger. As this occurs, the dominant party remains a centrist or pragmatic office-seeker, but the challenger becomes a niche-oriented party that prioritizes policy, locates away from the center, attracts minority constituencies, and wins with a much lower probability.[18] However, the magnitude of the movement away from the median in Figure 2.2 should be interpreted qualitatively rather than quantitatively. The challenger's curve is one of many possible realizations of its strategically chosen policy announcement. The particular realization depends on the size of g and σ_g (see Appendix A) and on the location of C (see Appendix B); however, under all reasonable assumptions about these parameters, the challenger's curve will have the same basic shape. Thus, the model shows us that an advantaged (dominant) party is ineluctably drawn to the location of the median voter no matter how much it cares

---

However, both of these results rely on the assumption that D is sincerely extremist, an assumption that I argue against in the main text but use to motivate the model above to show the substantial effects of changing λ. (Also see footnote 15.)

[17] Given the model's complexity and the fact that I am interested in illustrating the results, it seems sensible to focus on computational simulations rather than an analytical solution.

[18] This argument is in direct contrast to Wittman (1983) who theorizes that incumbency advantages force challengers to converge on the median voter in order to outweigh the incumbent's nonpolicy advantage with a better policy offer.

A Theory of Single-Party Dominance 57

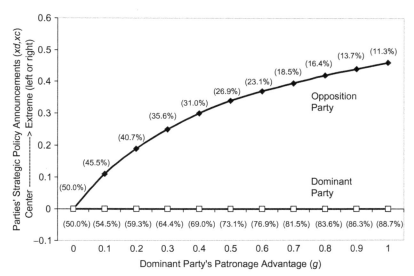

FIGURE 2.2. Model Predictions: The Effects of Patronage on Equilibrium Party Strategies (with probability of victory in parentheses; $\sigma = 1$).

about policy and a disadvantaged (challenger) party is drawn away from the median as its disadvantages make it care more about policy.

These results show how resource advantages can maintain the dominant party equilibrium. The model provides one way to complete Riker's (1976) underspecified argument that dominant parties occupy the center while challengers stay at the extremes. I show both why advantaged incumbents seek the center and why a disadvantaged challenger remains at the extreme.[19] At the same time, the model is flexible enough to also supply a logic for dominance from the left or right. Challengers will be expelled from the location of the dominant party's policy appeals by a distance associated with the size of its resource advantages and patronage-related uncertainty. As long as those advantages are large enough to make the incumbent more attractive than the challengers for a seat-winning proportion of voters, then a noncentrist incumbent can remain dominant.

Adding Authoritarian Tools

The version of the model above represents a highly stylized account in which the incumbent benefits from resource advantages but not from the

---

[19] Groseclose offers a model (2001) that also shows what he calls the "moderating frontrunner" and "extremist underdog" effects. While consistent with my model, these results rely on the assumption that both parties are policy-seekers in equal measure.

ability to perpetrate electoral fraud or impose extra costs on opposition forces for forming parties. In DPARs, repression raises the costs of participation in the opposition steeply and the possibility of electoral fraud further lowers the likelihood of winning. As we might expect, adding the effects of these authoritarian controls intensifies the model's results by pushing opposition parties even further toward the extreme.

Electoral fraud attempts artificially reduce the challenger's chance of winning; however, as developed above, they do so with some probability rather than with absolute certainty. Thus, fraud has exactly the same analytic effect as increasing patronage. Therefore, as fraud attempts increase but patronage remains constant, we would expect challengers to become more policy seeking with even more extreme strategically chosen policy announcements that are further from the median. The reader can easily imagine a steeper curve for the location of the opposition party in Figure 2.2. Empirically, though, it may be rare to observe instances of increased fraud without also seeing decreased patronage because dominant parties are unlikely to need the former when they can rely on the latter. Since the predicted level of opposition extremism results from the joint effect of incumbency advantages, periods of increased fraud may not automatically produce increased opposition radicalism if they are also accompanied by falling patronage.

Asymmetric costs also push challengers toward the extremes, but they do so indirectly. As I show in detail in Chapter 4, high costs for participation push the challenger party's sincere policy preferences toward the extreme. This occurs because as candidates and activists have to pay more personal costs for joining the opposition – costs such as foregoing material benefits or risking physical repression – they must be more opposed to the status quo policy offered by the dominant party to make participating in the opposition worthwhile. If the challenger's sincere preferences were more extreme, then its strategic policy announcements would become more extreme more quickly as its disadvantages increase. This again implies that as costs become more asymmetric, the curve represented in Figure 2.2 would be steeper.

Overall, as we add more advantages for the incumbent, challenger parties become less competitive and dominant party rule becomes more stable. Nevertheless, dominant party stability can breakdown quickly if incumbents leverage their advantages too much. At a certain point, the costs of participation become extremely high and the probability of winning approaches zero, thus encouraging opposition forces to abandon parties altogether. On the other side, if incumbents leverage their advantages

A Theory of Single-Party Dominance

too little, they stand to lose against expanded catchall challengers. Thus, incumbency advantages must be managed so that they are neither too weak and risk allowing the system to breakdown into a fully competitive democracy nor too strong and risk breakdown into a one-party regime.

IMPLICATIONS FOR OPPOSITION PARTY ENTRY
AND DEVELOPMENT

Dominant parties' advantages create four party-building problems for challengers: the problem of appeals, the problem of voter communication, the problem of personnel recruitment, and the twin problems of intra- and inter-party coordination. First, while the incumbent can use traditional appeals plus patronage to buy voter support, challengers attract voters with programmatic appeals and candidate qualities alone. Since voters are biased against challengers even when they make the most efficient policy appeals, they suffer an unavoidable deficit at the polls, as described with the biased model of party competition above.

Second, challengers suffer problems in communicating with voters. Opposition parties are capital poor because they cannot access the resources of the state and because their lack of political power discourages private donors from funding them. Consequently, they are priced out of the media market and suffer an unavoidable information deficit with voters. To communicate with voters at all, they must become labor-intensive organizations that rely on volunteers to run as candidates and staff all levels of the party organization. These volunteers disseminate information to voters and thus help reduce, even if to a small extent, the severe asymmetries that may push voters to choose the incumbent simply because they know less about the challenger.[20] Volunteers can also diminish the effectiveness of vote buying by encouraging voters to accept "gifts" but vote their true preference, and they can help mobilize public support in post-electoral conflicts (Eisenstadt, 2004). Finally, they can help diminish the cognitive and, potentially, the coercive costs of voting against the incumbent, somewhat akin to social movements in fully closed authoritarian regimes.

Unlike in parties in fully democratic systems where candidates and elite activists play very different roles, in challengers to dominant parties, the two groups are quite similar. Very few opposition candidates win when

---

[20] A well-known saying in Mexico that has been applied to political competition in the last two decades is "Better the devil you know than the angel you don't."

the dominant party has substantial advantages, making them much more like elite activists whose primary role is to expand the party's base. At the same time, activists are an important pool of potential candidates for parties that cannot attract experienced and high-quality candidates. Due to these similarities, I depart from the standard literature and refer to candidates and elite activists together as "party elites."

Third, the dominant party's advantages make it difficult for challenger parties to recruit party elites. Whereas competitive parties can use their viability as an incentive for affiliation, challengers to dominant parties cannot promise office benefits in the current round or in the foreseeable future. As a result, pure office-seekers are more likely to enter the dominant party's nomination process than the challengers' even if the latter offers a substantially higher probability of winning the nomination (Epstein, 1986). Those who seek club benefits by becoming party insiders are also more likely to profit in the dominant party than in the opposition because challenger parties typically pay only a handful of top administrators if anyone at all. Other potential party elites may be discouraged by the high opportunity costs of joining the challenger instead of the incumbent and they may be scared off by the real threat of coercion.

Due to the low instrumental benefits and high costs of participation in the opposition, challengers have to rely heavily on alternative incentives to attract and retain party elites. As one substitute, they offer the opportunity to express a deeply held programmatic or ideological belief that diverges from the status quo. This has important effects on intra-party relations and on party strategy. Relying on conviction as the currency that attracts and retains volunteer personnel means that advancement tends to be conditioned on "moral authority" that is gained through longevity of activism, commitment to the cause, and maintaining tight links to the party's core constituency. Moral authority is so powerful in opposition parties that it is often more important than electability in selecting candidates for office and more important than efficiency in choosing party executives. By turning inward, opposition parties risk becoming forums for expressing dissident views in the style of intellectual clubs rather than vehicles for ambitious politicians to win office and institute policies.

Recruiting citizens who are relatively extreme on policy also has strategy implications. Anti-status quo party elites create noncentrist niche-oriented parties in their own image. They establish tight links to core constituencies and create closed organizational structures that only recruit ideologically pure "good types." Since their parties are populated by

A Theory of Single-Party Dominance 61

personnel that are committed to deep political change, they are robust against cooptation by the dominant party; however, for the same reason, their parties are programmatically distant from the center and therefore out of step with what the average voter wants. As a result, they are unable to win plurality elections because voters view them as relative extremists, crazies, and even as quasi-revolutionaries who do not have the overall national interest in mind. Niche parties' relative extremism thus plays into the dominant party's strategy: the incumbent portrays itself as the centrist option against the minority and sectarian interests represented by its challengers.

In addition, when it is not profitable for electable high-quality candidates to join the opposition, incumbent elites are much less likely to defect to a challenger and opposition parties are likely to form from the bottom-up by outsiders in society. This is especially true in winner-take-all style presidentialist or mixed systems with first-past-the-post district races. In these systems, challengers cannot easily affect government policy at low levels of the vote (Linz and Valenzuela, 1994). Thus, there are fewer incentives for incumbents to buy-off small challenger parties and therefore fewer incentives for ambitious elites to form them. Elites may eventually defect from the incumbent to join an opposition party, but only when the incumbent's advantages erode sufficiently that challengers have a chance to win. Even then, insiders who are the most distant from the status quo position and therefore the most likely to lose nomination battles are more likely to defect to the opposition. Thus, in the five DPARs that use such systems, we should see more bottom-up opposition party building among outsiders.

Defection from the dominant party and a strong role for top-down opposition party building is more likely in parliamentary systems with proportional representation electoral systems or in systems that use the single nontransferable vote (SNTV). These rules allow small parties to win more easily and produce dominant parties with lower percentages of the vote. Since small parties have a voice in parliament and can be useful allies for dominant parties that hover around the 50% mark, incumbents have an interest in buying their support and challengers have incentives to bandwagon (Weiner, 2003). As a result, it should be profitable for candidates to launch opposition parties because they may be able to gain a seat and access to pork (Scheiner, 2006). Defections should be even more likely where central party organizations exert less control over individual politicians such as in those with SNTV (see Carey and Shugart, 1995). Thus, in all of the DPDRs that use parliamentary systems and in Taiwan and Japan that used SNTV, we should see a stronger role for elite defections and top-down opposition party building.

Defections should also play a more important role in fully closed authoritarian one-party regimes like Egypt and Iran – cases that do not feature meaningful elections and thus are not dominant party systems. Repression is so severe in these cases that opposition parties typically cannot exist without elite sponsors (Brownlee, 2005). Since opposition parties are legally banned, opposition forces turn to social movements or revolutionary organizations and do not appear as challenger parties until elites defect from the regime and allow them to operate in the open.

Finally, dominant party advantages create coordination problems both within and between opposition parties that prolong dominant party rule even after its advantages erode. Since resource and cost asymmetries affect the policy extremism of citizens who join challenger parties, the opposition is rife with generational conflicts. If the dominant party's advantages erode more or less linearly over time – as occurred in Mexico and other dominant party systems that underwent transitions from state-led to market-led economic development – then early joiners end up being quite extreme on policy while later joiners endorse much more moderate policies.

These generational conflicts can make opposition parties strategically sluggish and inadaptable to new circumstances. In particular, early joiners who design niche-oriented parties with tight links to core constituencies may constrain later joiners from opening these parties into broader catchall organizations, even at the cost of continuing to lose against the incumbent. The very process of opposition party building in dominant party systems thus creates path-dependent rigidities in challenger party organizations that are difficult to overcome. As a result, dominant party rule may be prolonged for some period even after the mechanisms that support dominance have eroded. In particular, I will deploy this argument to help account for the continuation of PRI rule following the 1982 economic crisis but before it lost its majority in Congress in 1997.

Intra-party generational conflicts can also block opposition party coordination against the incumbent. Opposition coordination failure has been considered a major reason for continued dominance (Riker, 1976; Laver and Schofield, 1990; Cox, 1997; Magaloni, 1996, also see 2006; Howard and Roessler, 2006; Van de Walle, 2006). When challengers unite against the incumbent, they can create a broad opposition front and potentially amass enough votes to win. However, niche-oriented early joiners are likely to hold highly anti-status quo policy preferences that are also distant from each other across opposition parties. This ideological distance will doom inter-party coordination and allow the incumbent to win even when challengers together would hold the majority.[21]

My argument links the incumbent's advantages and the costs it imposes on the opposition to the character of challenger parties. In this account, opposition parties' profiles are strongly conditioned by their environment. I pay much less attention to their proactive strategies to transform the system because these strategies are likely to be effective only on the margins. Opposition parties can attempt to publicize the dominant party's illicit use of public funds, but their access to the media is limited due to resource constraints and, in some cases, by the incumbent's cooptation or even outright control of the major outlets. Opposition parties can engage in local-level canvassing designed to wean voters off of patronage, but voters may feel that the material benefits of receiving bribes are too lucrative to forego. Finally, opposition parties can cultivate support among constituencies that do not receive patronage, but these groups are likely to be small. Thus, I argue that the forces that regulate the incumbent's advantages are of primary importance and I focus on how these advantages cause opposition failure.

CONCLUSION

In this chapter I crafted a theory of single-party dominance that focuses on the origin and effects of hyper-incumbency advantages. Advantages derive first and foremost from the incumbent's monopolistic or near monopolistic control over the resources of the state. When the public sector is large and the federal public bureaucracy is politically controlled, dominant parties can transform public resources into partisan ones that allow them to dramatically outspend challengers on all aspects of campaigning and party building. They also allow incumbents to bribe voters with patronage goods, thus making elections so unfair that the dominant party typically wins before election day. In DPARs, incumbents may supplement resource advantages with targeted and episodic repression of opposition forces and electoral fraud.

Working for the opposition is a high cost and low benefit activity. Thus, careerists who only seek elected office will join the dominant party and, as

---

[21] In the absence of a cross-cutting cleavage that gives incentives for challengers to unite against the incumbent, the opposition parties will be very distant from each other on policy and will fail to coordinate. As a result, the incumbent may continue to win even though opposition parties together win a majority of the vote.

a result, opposition parties will be undersupplied relative to the number of social cleavages, voters' dissatisfaction with the incumbent, and the permissiveness of electoral institutions. However, challenger parties may still emerge if some citizens are motivated by policy concerns. Yet only the most anti-status quo will find it worthwhile to participate in the opposition, conditional on the magnitude of the incumbent's advantages. This dynamic of political recruitment creates niche-oriented opposition parties that cultivate support from minority electoral constituencies. These parties are sufficiently noncentrist that they would be unrecognizable to those who expect meaningful elections to automatically produce fully competitive systems.

The model presented in this chapter leaves one important element underspecified. It treated parties as if they were unitary actors by assigning utility functions that stand for the parties' revealed preferences. It seems reasonable that dominant parties might have an internal party dictator, such as the president of the country, who could impose his preference as the party preference. It also seems reasonable that the preference of newly created opposition parties would be informed by their founders. Over the longer run, however, any utility function attributed to an opposition party would have to be some function of the sincere preferences of its members. While members' influence on overall party utility is a complicated question of internal organization and varies across parties and over time, the more basic assumption that members' preferences matter is enough to motivate an inquiry into the dynamics of party affiliation among prospective candidates and activists. I present a detailed analysis of the decision to join an already established opposition party in Chapter 4. The next chapter, however, keeps the analysis at the level of the parties as unitary actors and examines the PRI's advantages and opposition party failure in Mexico from the 1930s to the 1990s.

APPENDIX A: THE MAGNITUDE OF PATRONAGE AND PATRONAGE-RELATED UNCERTAINTY

Since voters value both patronage and the distance between the parties' policy offers and their personal policy preference, patronage needs to be expressed in policy units. Although this notion sounds highly artificial, it simply implies that a voter is willing to trade some policy distance for a patronage payoff. For present purposes, figuring out an upper bound for the magnitude of g and an approximate range for σ_g will suffice.

A Theory of Single-Party Dominance

Following a similar valence model due to Adams, Merrill, and Grofman (AMG), (2005: 289–91) note that the expected value in (1) in the main text of $g + z$ is g since z is a random variable with mean zero. Now, using (1) and (2) in the main text with $m = 0$ and $z = 0$, we can find the voter who is just indifferent between choosing D and choosing C (call her v^*). When $g = 0$, v^* is at the midpoint between D and C on policy, or at $(x_c + x_d)/2$. As g increases, v^* shifts away from D by $g/2(x_c - x_d)$. This expression yields two ways to estimate the size of g.

First, AMG argue that the effect of g is usually felt toward the center of the policy space. Thus, they examine the empirical size of the center of the voter density function for the country cases they study. I followed their estimation technique by conducting a factor analysis of issue items using both World Values 2000 and LatinoBarometer 1999 data for Mexico. I then constructed histograms of the voter preference curves and found that in both distributions, 40% of voters were in the AMG-defined center. Now, note that the size of the patronage advantage should equal at least the incumbent-challenger vote gap which peaked at 70% in Mexico in the 1976 elections. Also note that we can approximate the parties' positions on the dimensions $[-1,1]$ by assuming that the PRI was generally close to the median at about zero while the challengers were at a maximum distance from the median at 1. Thus, using AMG's formula, we have a maximum estimate for g with $0.7 = 0.4g/2(1 - 0)$, yielding $g = 3.5$. This estimate seems unnaturally high because it implies that maximum patronage was more than enough to sway any voter in the $[-1,1]$ competition space.

To use a second method for estimating g, note that v^* is located at $\frac{x_c+x_d}{2} + \frac{g}{2(x_c-x_d)}$. Some algebra shows that the patronage-disadvantaged party maximizes its vote share at $\pm \sqrt{g}$. If the dominant party again locates at 0 and the challenger locates at 1, then $g = 1$. This seems like a more reasonable estimate since it implies that, at maximum, a voter that is halfway across the total policy space from the dominant party could be bought. It is probably quite a conservative estimate since AMG (2005: 290) estimate that valence advantages in the United States and France due to candidate characteristics alone are as high as 42% of the total policy space. Surely, patronage advantages in a dominant party system should substantially outstrip candidate qualities alone.

Estimating patronage-related uncertainty (σ_g) presents a tougher problem. AMG estimate valence-related uncertainty due to candidate characteristics with average polling uncertainty, and place it at 0.5 to 1.5. When valence is patronage, this approach makes less sense because pre-election polls probably already register the effects of ongoing patronage disbursements. Data are not available to measure the predicted effectiveness of the incumbent's patronage machine or the expected amount of voter resistance; however, my case knowledge of Mexico and readings about other cases suggests that patronage-related uncertainty varies substantially over time, implying wider bounds than in AMG. I cautiously estimate the range of σ_g as 0 to 2.0 and assume $\sigma_g = 1$ in all model estimations in the book.

APPENDIX B: THE FOUNDER'S PROBLEM: WHO FORMS OPPOSITION PARTIES?

The biased model of party competition presented in the main text shows that an incumbent party that benefits from a probabilistic patronage advantage competing with a challenger without patronage for a single seat with endogenous preferences over office-seeking and policy-seeking behavior produces (1) a pure office-seeking incumbent party that announces a policy at the median, and (2) a challenger party that becomes more policy-seeking and less centrist as its disadvantages increase and its probability of victory correspondingly decreases.

The degree of the opposition party's center-fleeing behavior depends, in part, on our assumption about the party's sincere policy preference (C). In the model in the main text, I assumed extremism at 1 on the dimension [–1,1]. I now justify this assumption and show why opposition party founders are likely to be extremists relative to the status quo policy offered by the incumbent.

I model potential founders' utility much like the parties' utility functions in the main text. They value five things: (1) winning their party's nomination for office (s), (2) the ego rents associated with winning office itself ($u(o)$), (3) a social choice outcome that is close to their sincere policy preference (x), (4) the probability of winning (p), and (5) minimizing the costs that they pay for participating in politics (c).

Potential opposition party founders face a decision between joining the dominant party D, forming a challenger party C that does not exist unless they form it, or abstaining. I refer to these alternative possible actions as a_d, a_c, and a_0, respectively. I assume that founders' actions can be modeled as a decision-theoretic process, implying that the parties do not impose barriers to affiliation. This assumption makes sense for challenger parties that do not exist without the founders' choice to start one. Empirical research on dominant parties shows that they typically operate as "big

A Theory of Single-Party Dominance 67

tents" that try to maximize membership and thus do not impose barriers to affiliation.

The utility of abstaining is the utility for the social choice outcome that all citizens receive. Since abstainers do not participate, they pay no participation costs. Thus,

$$Eu(a_0) = -p_d(x_d - x_i)^2 - (1 - p_d)(x_c - x_i)^2 \tag{B.1}$$

We know that $p_d = 1$ because if the potential founder abstains, the opposition does not form and wins with zero probability. We also know, from the argument in the main text, that even though the absence of a competitor theoretically allows D to announce any policy position, it will most likely announce the policy preferred by the median voter in order to reduce abstention due to alienation. Without loss of generality we can say that $m = 0$ and therefore $x_d = 0$ in the competition space $[-1,1]$. Thus, the utility of abstaining reduces to

$$Eu(a_0) = -x_i^2 \tag{B.2}$$

The utility for joining D is similar but brings in the likelihood of winning the nomination, the value of office, and the cost of participation.

$$Eu(a_d) = p_d[s_d u(o) - (x_d - x_i)^2] - (1 - p_d)(x_c - x_i)^2 - c_d \tag{B.3}$$

Again, we know that $p_d = 1$ because no challenger party forms. I assume that the utility of winning office itself is a constant $u(o) = 1$. Thus, we now have:

$$Eu(a_d) = s_d - x_i^2 - c_d \tag{B.4}$$

This implies that the utility of joining the dominant party is governed by the chance of winning the nomination (which ensures winning office), the distance between the potential founder's sincere policy preference and the status quo at the median, and the costs of participation.

The utility of forming a challenger party is similar such that

$$Eu(a_c) = (1 - p_d)[s_c u(o) - (x_c - x_i)^2] - p_d(x_d - x_i)^2 - c_c \tag{B.5}$$

If an opposition party forms, then $p_d < 1$, although we do not know its exact value. The incumbent party's policy announcement remains $x_d = 0$ and the value of office $u(o)$ remains 1. In addition, we can assume that the founder wins nomination in his own party with certainty, so $s_c = 1$. Thus,

$$Eu(a_c) = (1 - p_d)[1 - (x_c - x_i)^2] - p_d x_i^2 - c_c \tag{B.6}$$

We can now determine the characteristics of potential founders who will not abstain and will choose to form a challenger party rather than join the incumbent.

A potential founder will abstain from politics entirely unless $Eu(a_d) > Eu(a_0)$ or $Eu(a_c) > Eu(a_0)$. Using (B.2) and (B.4) above and some algebra shows that

$$Eu(a_d) > Eu(a_0) \text{ if } s_d > c_d \tag{B.7}$$

Thus, a potential founder's decision to join the incumbent versus abstaining is not governed by their personal policy preferences, but by the relationship between her chance of winning the nomination and the costs of participation. We could import some notion to relate the probability of nomination to the distance between an individual's policy preference and the party median; however, in this simpler version, it is clear that when costs are low, the threshold for entering the dominant party is low and abstention among potential founders of the opposition should be low. In other words, the dominant party provides a big tent that encourages potential politicians to be active.

The threshold for joining the challenger instead of abstaining is much higher. Using (B.2) and (B.6) above, some algebra yields

$$Eu(a_c) > Eu(a_0) \text{ if } x_i > \frac{-1 + c_c + p_d + x_c^2 - p_d x_c^2}{2x_c - 2p_d x_c} \tag{B.8}$$

Note as $p_d \to 1$, the denominator becomes very small, and $x_i \to \infty$, such that no potential founder would be extreme enough on policy relative to the status quo to found a challenger instead of abstain. x_i also rises in c_c. Thus, when p_d and/or c_c are large, only potential founders with sincere policy preferences distant from the status quo would join the challenger instead of abstaining. Although there is no clear way to compare the threshold for joining the incumbent or challenger instead of abstaining, it seems likely that the binding constraint is governed by the dominant party.

We can now ask what the sincere policy preference x_i is of a potential founder who would find it worthwhile to become an actual opposition party founder. To do this, set $Eu(a_d) = Eu(a_c)$ and solve for x_i. Some algebra produces the following (note that for clarity I substitute p_c for $1 - p_d$):

$$x_i = \frac{c_c + s_d - p_c + p_c x_c^2}{2 p_c x_c} \tag{B.9}$$

A Theory of Single-Party Dominance
69

Increasing x_i means that the founder's sincere preference becomes further from the status quo position x_d and more extreme. Note first that as x_c decreases, x_i increases dramatically. This implies that the new challenger's strategically chosen policy announcement x_c cannot be close to the status quo position x_d because it would not be worthwhile to form a challenger party so close to the dominant party given the costs of doing so. We also know that it would make very little sense to form a new party where the strategic policy announcement is more extreme than the founder's sincere preference because doing so would produce a challenger that the founder may like less than the dominant party and has a lower probability of winning. Thus, we can assume that $x_i > x_c$. These two points together imply that the founder's sincere preference must be extreme relative to x_d. That is, if $x_i > x_c$ and $x_c > x_d$, then $x_i > x_d$. Since x_c is much larger than x_d, x_i must be much larger than x_d.

For further confirmation that x_i must be extreme, we can do a simulation. In the main text, I show that with medium levels of patronage-related uncertainty and maximum patronage, the best that a pure office-seeking party could do is to win with $p_c = .159$. Thus, we know that $p_c < .159$ if a challenger is founded when patronage is at its maximum (more on this below). We can also make conditions fantastically (and unrealistically) encouraging for an opposition party to form by setting $c_c = 0$ and $s_d = 0$ so that forming a new party is costless and the potential founder is certain to lose the nomination in the dominant party. Thus,

$$x_i = \frac{-.159 + .159x_c^2}{.318x_c} \tag{B.10}$$

Under these incredibly permissive circumstances, an opposition party would be founded by a citizen with a policy preference of $x_i \geq .9$. This is very close to my assumption that the sincere preference of a challenger party is 1.

Two questions remain. First, why would an opposition party form when patronage is at its maximum value of $g = 1$? (See Appendix A for a justification of why maximum patronage is set at 1.) We should expect a challenger to form when $Eu(a_d) < Eu(a_c)$ for some potential founder. This will occur whenever patronage, in conjunction with the probability of nomination in the dominant party, is low enough to produce a challenger. If patronage starts high and decreases, then a challenger party will form whenever patronage is at its maximum since beyond this theoretical maximum, no opposition parties will form and dominance breaks down into single-party rule.

Second, why should we expect only one opposition party to form? For instance, if $Eu(a_d) < Eu(a_c)$ for a citizen with a policy preference of $x_i \geq .9$, then multiple founders could start different opposition parties with sincere preferences $.9 \leq x_i \leq 1$. In addition, as patronage decreases, the dominant party moves, or the probability of nomination in the dominant party declines, citizens with $x_i < .9$ will find it worthwhile to form parties as well. I do not have an iron-clad answer here; however, the number of eventual parties should be limited by the institutional maximum of M+1, where M is district magnitude (see Cox, 1997). In addition, the most moderate challenger party that forms at time t will probably be the most competitive and could then beat out the others. At time $t+1$, the challenger that formed at time t will likely moderate, up to the amount shown in the model in the main text. As a result, it will likely "crowd" out more moderate challengers that would form, pushing the number of entrants down to the M+1 threshold.

3

Dominant Party Advantages and Opposition Party Failure, 1930s–1990s

Mexico's PRI and its forerunners dominated electoral politics from 1929 until it lost its majority in Congress in 1997 and lost the presidency in 2000; however, single-party dominance did not mean the absence of opposition parties. Opposition forces were allowed to register as parties and compete for all elected offices in regular elections.[1] Although these elections clearly fell below the minimum standards of democracy, they were more than hollow rituals. Yet despite meaningful competition, challengers remained undercompetitive until the 1990s because they made niche-oriented appeals to minority electoral constituencies. As a result, challengers ceded the broad center and electoral majorities to the incumbent, thus allowing dominant party rule to remain in equilibrium for most of the 20th century.

Equilibrium dominance – the long-term continuous rule of a single party with existing but ineffective challenger parties – should not have occurred in Mexico according to existing theory. Mexico had a sufficiently permissive electoral formula, enough social cleavages, a high enough level of economic development, and enough voters disapproved of the PRI's performance in office that at least one other party should have been fully competitive. The spatial dynamics of party position-taking in models that assume no incumbency advantage (i.e., so-called neutral theories) also

---

[1] The Mexican Communist Party (PCM) was not registered from 1949 to 1977. Many analysts state or imply that it was actively banned; however, as I detail below, experts on the subject document that it failed to meet the registration requirements (Schmitt, 1970: 33, 61; Rodríguez Araujo and Sirvent, 2005: 35) at a time when other left parties and independent candidates were registered (see, among others, Rodríguez Araujo and Sirvent, 2005; Molinar, 1991: 30–36).

predict at least two competitive parties.[2] A more specific version of this spatial theory that was crafted for Mexico logically implies the same conclusion. The "pendulum" theory argues that the PRI moved its policy appeals from left to right to satisfy voters' demands with policy responses (Needler, 1971: 46–49; Smith, 1989: 396; Cornelius and Craig, 1991: 40). But, all things equal, when the PRI moved to the right on policy, the left should have had expanded space to organize and when the PRI moved left, the right should have been able to form a viable catchall party with significant support. Thus, the incumbent's policy appeals alone are insufficient to explain dominance. More generally, if the market for votes were fair as the institutional, sociological, voting behavior, and most spatial theory approaches assume, then PRI dominance could not have been sustained.

The recognition that opposition parties were severely disadvantaged and its operatives episodically repressed has led some to argue that the PRI ruled through fully authoritarian means (Reyna and Weinert, 1977) or won consistently by outcome-changing electoral fraud that reduced the opposition's chances of winning to zero. But like the more abstract formal models that build in incumbency advantages (i.e., non-neutral theories), these approaches predict that opposition parties should not form at all since they know they would lose with absolute certainty. Although repression and fraud deeply affected opposition parties in Mexico by limiting their scope, these authoritarian controls were never so heavy handed as to make the electoral option futile. Instead, with the partial exception of the mid-1970s that I discuss below, opposition forces consistently turned to parties as their main vehicles for opposing the PRI. Thus, from the 1930s to the 1990s, Mexico experienced more opposition party development than predicted by theories that characterize Mexico as fully authoritarian but less opposition success than predicted by theories that assume a perfectly fair electoral playing field.

This chapter accounts for equilibrium dominance by arguing that the opposition failed despite periodic opportunities because the PRI benefited from dramatic resource advantages. When these advantages failed, the incumbent could deploy the repressive apparatus of the state against opposition personnel or attempt electoral fraud. The first section identifies five episodes from the 1930s to the 1990s when the PRI's policy shifts to the left or right should have, according to neutral theories that presume

---

[2] This holds true for neutral models whether entry is simultaneous or sequential. See Chapter 2 for details.

Dominant Party Advantages and Opposition Party Failure   73

a fair market for votes, created opportunities for challenger party success on its opposite flank. The second section develops an analytic narrative that tells the macro-story of opposition party failure during most of the 20th century and accounts for the specific mix of PRI policy, patronage, and repression that sustained its dominance. Outcome-changing electoral fraud was a much less important tool until the 1980s when the ruling party overturned voters' intentions in some races; however, there is insufficient evidence to determine whether single-party dominance would have ended without fraud. The rest of the chapter takes a thematic turn and draws out the variables emphasized in the analytic narrative.

THE INCUMBENT'S POLICY APPEALS AND OPPORTUNITIES FOR OPPOSITION PARTY DEVELOPMENT

The PRI traditionally used its control over public policy to appease electoral constituencies and undercut the appeal of potential dissidents. This "firefighting" strategy directed collective goods through public policy to specific groups as they mobilized for political change. In effect, then, the PRI tacked back-and-forth between the left and the right over time, although not as regularly or mechanically as the "pendulum" theory implies. Many analysts beginning perhaps with Huntington (1970) have thus referred to the PRI as a "pragmatic" party that quickly abandoned the left-leaning redistributive ideals of the Mexican Revolution and instead focused on maintaining power.

The historical record indicates a dominant PRI that has ranged across the political space. Sometimes it favored state intervention in the economy and sometimes it preferred the rule of market forces; however, it typically moved within a range that was relatively centrist. Figure 3.1 shows the PRI's economic policy platform from 1934 to 2000. Data for 1946–2000 come from Bruhn's (2001) content analysis of the PRI's published platforms.[3] Estimates for 1934 and 1940 were made by the author with reference to Bruhn's scores. Since the data represent the PRI's published platform rather than its actual policies in government, they are skewed systematically to the left. Partly as cover for its rightward shift beginning in the 1940s, the PRI always used the symbols and the language of the "revolutionary nationalism" to justify its rule (Bartra, 1989).

---

[3] Bruhn (2001) performed a content analysis of party platforms using the European Manifestos Project coding techniques and used exploratory factor analysis that extracted an economic policy dimension (the more salient of the two) and a regime dimension that separated pro-democracy and pro-human rights platforms from more authoritarian ones.

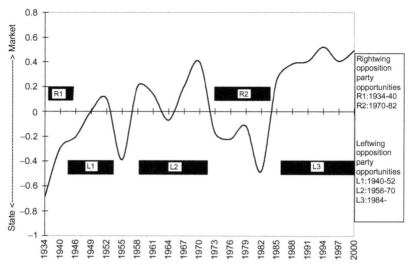

FIGURE 3.1. Opportunities for Opposition Party Development due to Shifts in the PRI's Economic Policy Platform, 1934–2000.
Sources: Scores for 1946–2000 from the author's calculations using Bruhn's (2001) data. Scores for 1934 and 1940 were estimated by the author with reference to Bruhn's scores.

Once this leftward skew is taken into account, the PRI's policy appeals show the amount of "space" available to challengers on the left and right over time. If the market for votes were fair as neutral theories imply and competition took place over policy offers alone, then challengers on the left should have had expanded opportunities to develop a successful political party during three periods: (1) when Presidents Manuel Avila Camacho (1940–1946) and Miguel Alemán (1946–1952) moved away from the populist development policy of the earlier Cárdenas Administration; (2) the period from about 1958 to 1970 when successive administrations favored capital interests and diminished labor's influence; and (3) beginning in 1982 when the debt crisis hit and the government made aggressive moves toward free market development policies. Similarly, fair competition should have allowed a party on the right to enter and develop substantial support during two other periods: (1) when President Cárdenas (1934–1940) adopted labor-friendly policies and a populist economic agenda; and (2) from 1970 to about 1982 when Presidents Echeverría and López Portillo re-initiated populist style spending and nationalized the banks.

HYPER-INCUMBENCY ADVANTAGES AND NEARLY A CENTURY OF OPPOSITION PARTY FAILURE

Why did opposition parties fail to expand into viable competitors when programmatic space was open to them? Why did they fail to occupy this space as neutral theories predict? I argue that they did not develop precisely because the market for votes was not fair; rather, it was biased in favor of the incumbent, even though it was not fully rigged by persistent outcome-changing fraud or crushing repression. When challenger parties had opportunities to develop, the PRI sought to undercut their appeal first by firefighting with its own policy appeals; second, by buying support with patronage goods; and, as a last resort, by repressing opposition activists (Hellman, 1983: Ch. 5; Middlebrook, 1986; 125). This section develops an analytic narrative by describing the combinations of policy, patronage, and repression that were employed during these five key historical episodes to stunt opposition party development and maintain PRI dominance.

Populism and Opportunities for Opposition Party Development on the Right in the late 1930s

From 1934 to 1940, President Lázaro Cárdenas created the opportunity for a viable rightwing opposition party by instituting a significantly statist political economy with socialist overtones. His administration nationalized the oil industry, engaged in substantial land redistribution and the collectivization of agriculture, armed and organized worker and peasant militias, instituted socialist public education, and prohibited priests from political activities including voting. He also used the state to mobilize labor and peasant unions, eventually reorganizing the existing elite-oriented National Revolutionary Party (PNR) into the mass-oriented Mexican Revolutionary Party (PRM). The PRM – the direct predecessor to the PRI – incorporated labor unions through a single peak-level association called the Confederation of Mexican Workers (CTM) and incorporated peasant producers through a parallel corporatist organization called the National Campesino Confederation (CNC). Both sectors were sanctioned and subsidized by the state and membership in them was compulsory for workers in a wide range of occupations. By cementing a durable organizational alliance with the working class, Cárdenas signaled his desire to extend the state-led development model with broad political

76 *Why Dominant Parties Lose*

participation beyond his presidential term. Collier and Collier thus refer to his presidency as a "'complete' instance of radical populism" (1991: 202).

For rightwing forces, the Cárdenas Administration amounted to a socialist project (Mabry, 1973). Opposition came from multiple groups (Collier and Collier, 1991: 247), but primarily included social conservatives and economic liberals. Social conservatives were outraged over state-mandated socialist public education and attacks on the Church. They viewed Cárdenas as one of the most aggressive in a long line of anticlerical presidents since the Constitution of 1857 circumscribed the Church's economic power and political participation. When the post-Revolutionary Constitution of 1917 maintained these anticlerical elements, Church-aligned forces attempted to overthrow the government in the Cristero Rebellion (1926–1929). Their defeat closed off the revolutionary avenue to political change for the right and social conservatives instead entered electoral politics by forming the Mexican Democratic Party (PDM). But the party's appeals, based almost exclusively on the question of Church-State relations, earned it few votes.

For their part, economic liberals criticized Cárdenas' populist development policy as too redistributive (Scott, 1964: 182–185). These forces had supported the liberal elements of the Mexican Revolution of 1910 such as the principle of no reelection that was designed to ensure the circulation of political elites (Brandenburg, 1956). But they were skeptical of the broader social agenda and economic powers of the state that were written into the Constitution, they were scandalized by the expropriation of the oil industry, and they feared an organized and mobilized labor movement, especially given the rising specter of communism on the world scene.

In September 1939, economic liberals and social conservatives together formed the PAN in the Bank of London and Mexico in Mexico City. The incumbent party was not particularly threatened by the electoral opposition of social conservatives because they had failed to generate significant support previously through the PDM,[4] but the opposition of capital-holders was another matter. A PAN that challenged the dominant party on economic policy – the main partisan cleavage in industrializing Mexico – could win the support of the business sector and would at least have the capacity to destabilize Mexico's political economy. At most, such

---

[4] Many other rightwing groups mobilized during this period as well, including formal (Gold Shirts) and informal anti-worker militias, the short-lived Revolutionary Anti-Communist Party and the Party of Mexican Nationalism.

Dominant Party Advantages and Opposition Party Failure 77

a party might also gain middle-class support and thus pose a real electoral challenge.

This significant pressure from the right led to an almost immediate policy response. Cárdenas gave assurances that he would not expropriate other businesses and, in late 1938, he "began to call for industrial peace, struck notes of class harmony, and sent the army to put down strikes" (Collier and Collier, 1991: 407). In the rural sector, the rate of land reform diminished from an average of 3.35 million hectares per year to less than 882,000 hectares per year.[5] Yet the most significant element of Cárdenas' shift to the right was his decision to use "el dedazo" – the outgoing president's right to choose the subsequent PRI candidate – to select Manuel Avila Camacho. Avila Camacho (1940–1946) was known to be significantly less progressive than his patron, and once in office he took quick steps to appease rightwing forces. He stopped promoting strike activity and instead pursued a policy of "national unity." Labor was purged of communists and socialists, including the Secretary-General of the CTM, Lombardo Toledano. The much more conservative Fidel Velázquez took charge in 1941 (and led the confederation until his death in 1997). Velázquez immediately pledged to end strike activity for the duration of World War II. Although many unions throughout Latin America also followed the Comintern's "Popular Front" policy of temporary unity with capitalists to defeat fascism, the suspension of labor militancy in Mexico came during a period of growing rightwing power and thus allowed capital interests to expand their influence within the ruling party's multiclass alliance.

As the PRI conservatized and rolled back the most progressive elements of the Cárdenas Administration, economic liberals abandoned the PAN. After all, there was little reason to engage in the expensive, risky, and uncertain task of opposing the PRI when it was willing to "do business." As this shift occurred, the PAN was increasingly left with social conservatives as its core constituency. According to Mabry, "Catholicism was more important than property interests for recruitment and party activity" (1973: 38). Conservatives' doctrine of "Catholic humanism" took a vague position on markets and, as a result, from the 1940s to the late 1970s, the party essentially abandoned consistent position-taking on economic policy matters. The PAN now defined itself as a confessional party. According to Loaeza, until 1978, "the PAN's evolution in large part reflected the doctrine, positions, and strategies of the Vatican" (1999: 182). After

---

[5] Author's calculations based on Fischer, Gerken, and Hiemenz (1982: 13).

78   *Why Dominant Parties Lose*

1940, the party also solidified links to Catholic organizations and even proposed an alliance with the quasi-fascist and ultra-conservative Union for National Order (UNS)[6] that grew directly out of the failed 1926–1929 Cristero Rebellion. Mabry calls this the period of "Catholic militancy," Loaeza (1999) refers to it a time of "Catholic hegemony," and Mizrahi (2003) calls the PAN a "sectarian" party during this period. The party's campaigns became "so pro-clerical that the Church disavowed its connections with the PAN" (Johnson, 1978: 169) since religious organizations were not allowed to participate in politics. Although the Church-State cleavage was salient enough to sustain the party, it did not have the capacity to attract majoritarian electoral constituencies (Martínez Valle, 1995: 77). Thus, the PAN remained a niche-oriented challenger that could not beat the PRI at the polls.

While the PRI's conservatization and its ability to reincorporate economic liberals goes a long way toward accounting for the PAN's limited electoral success after 1940, episodes of physical repression also limited the party's size. In the presidential election of 1940, the PAN supported General Juan Andreu Almazán, a breakaway candidate who opposed Cárdenas' progressive economic policies. Post-electoral conflicts became sufficiently violent that federal troops occupied several areas in the North and Almazán was forced to flee the country. Repression came more often in local electoral contests. For instance, the PAN had some appeal in León, Guanajuato in the center of Mexico's Bible Belt where core elements of the Cristero Rebellion arose. This appeal apparently ruffled the PRI because post-electoral protests in 1946 were met with a hail of bullets. Shirk (2005: 63–69) reports that 50 pro-PAN protesters were killed and some were even shot in the back while fleeing what is now known as the Plaza of the Martyrs. The PAN also found some success in Tijuana, Baja California, where social conservatives opposed the city's reputation for vice and the shady dealings of its governor and first lady. In a series of escalating confrontations with police surrounding the 1958 gubernatorial election, many PANistas were arrested and some wounded. In that same year, PANistas fought with police and were shot at in Michoacán, a PAN district chief was murdered in Ciudad Juárez, three party members were killed and 300 jailed in Mérida, and the party's presidential candidate was briefly jailed (Mabry, 1973: 57; Johnson, 1965: 660). In post-electoral protests in 1958, rail workers associated with the left were

---

[6] The name Unión Nacional Sinarquista (UNS) derives from "sin anarquía" (without anarchy).

Dominant Party Advantages and Opposition Party Failure   79

brutally repressed, but the government also used the opportunity to harass PANistas and disperse their meetings by force in Mexico City, Zacatecas, Campeche, Veracruz, and Chihuahua. One party leader reported that 20 PANistas were killed in the first four months of 1958 (Mabry, 1973: 59–60). More generally, Shirk writes that "nearly all the old guard PANistas interviewed [expressed] fear of persecution and violence to themselves and their loved ones" (2005: 90; fn 62). Thus, although state-sponsored repression never hit the forces of the right the way they hammered the left, widely known incidents of harassment, jailings, and some murders put prospective PAN activists on notice that there were potentially high costs to be paid for their participation.

In sum, the PRI's policy shift to the right beginning in the last years of the Cárdenas presidency and accelerating after 1940 undercut the PAN's appeal to economic liberals and broader segments of society. At the same time, selective and targeted repression raised the costs of participation. These twin tools worked so effectively for the dominant party that during the next nearly 40 years, the PAN wandered in the electoral wilderness and was unable to attract enough voters, activists, or candidates to compete effectively in national elections.

The End of Populism and Opportunities for Opposition Party Development on the Left in the 1940s and 1950s

As part of the post-Cárdenas conservatization, Presidents Avila Camacho (1940–1946) and Alemán (1946–1952) diminished the role of the state in agriculture promotion, reduced support for labor, and opened Mexico to more foreign investment. New agrarian legislation cut land redistribution by 80% per year, limited government credit for communal *ejido* lands, expanded the permissible size of private holdings, and created legal mechanisms for medium and large-holders to avoid expropriation. New labor legislation limited the right to strike and controlled wages more tightly to spur rapid industrialization (despite three peso devaluations). Arbitration boards that had been a powerful tool for workers under Cárdenas now increasingly ruled in favor of business. The government also used its legal right to replace union leaders to impose collaborationist or *charro* leaders on recalcitrant organizations (Middlebrook, 1995). In addition, known communists were purged from the federal bureaucracy, state-owned enterprises, and from the PRI itself (Carr, 1992: 143, 147).

Although the 1940s and 1950s saw a conservatization that trimmed the most progressive elements of the Cárdenas Administration, Mexico's

80   *Why Dominant Parties Lose*

development policies remained substantially state-centered. The most important shift was in the reach and class balance of the incumbent party's support organizations. In 1946, Alemán transformed the PRM into the PRI and established the National Confederation of Popular Organizations (CNOP) to give government employees, the nonlabor urban poor, and the growing urban middle class a voice inside the party. Subsequently, the PRI drew an increasing proportion of the party's legislative candidates from this more conservative sector rather than from either the labor or peasant sectors. In the 1940s, the CNOP accounted for about 30% of seats in the Chamber of Deputies and about one-third of PRI membership. By the 1970s, it held about 60% of seats and accounted for one-quarter of party members, and by 1991 it claimed 71% of seats but only about 15% of membership (Bailey, 1988: 100; Garrido, 1987: 75; Langston, 2001).

The move to the right put the incumbent's multi-class coalition under stress and theoretically opened space for a leftwing party to gain public support. Importantly, the PRI's control over labor unions was significant but incomplete by this time (Collier and Collier, 1991). Thus, according to Carr, "The early years of the Alemán presidency provided a golden opportunity for the Mexican left to deepen its links with the organized labor movement at a moment when the most militant and independently minded workers and *ejiditarios* [workers on collective farms] were questioning their relationship to the status quo" (1992: 165).

Yet the left failed to establish a viable party despite the increased space available to it. Schmitt writes that the Communist line "put all issues in terms of black and white" (1970: 227) and was thus "ineffective in terms of persuading Mexican interest groups or the populace at large to support its general program or specific aspects thereof" (1970: 34). The PCM was so out of step with the voters that it "suffered from widespread ridicule and opprobrium" (1970: 34, 52–53). Although the PCM gained temporary registration for the 1946 election with 10,315 registered activists in 19 states (Molinar, 1991: 33), it was unable or unwilling to meet the higher requirement of 30,000 members with at least 1,000 in 19 of 31 states and the Federal District for permanent registration status and thus lost access to the ballot in 1949.[7] Although the PCM may have been unwilling to pay the high costs for running openly against the PRI in this

---

[7] It is not clear whether the PCM was unable to recruit enough members (Schmitt, 1970: 33, 61) to remain on the ballot in 1949, or if, with the beginning of the Cold War, its decision to enhance ties to the Soviet Union made it correspondingly less interested in competing for votes. The available histories do not specifically address this latter issue.

Dominant Party Advantages and Opposition Party Failure   81

period, it was not specifically banned nor was the permanent registration requirement prohibitively high in a country with approximately 19 million adults at the time.[8] Indeed, other small leftwing parties remained on the ballot during this period (Molinar, 1991: 33–36; Bruhn, 1997). Thus, we need another way to account for the left's failure at the polls.

The PRI diminished the left's viability in part by distributing ample patronage to leftwing constituencies. The labor and peasant sectoral organizations now proved valuable tools not for encouraging worker militancy but for controlling it by funneling patronage to union leaders (Middlebrook, 1995). The urban popular sector was also used to control the growing group of government employees and urban poor (Hellman, 1983: 135–146; 166–167). According to Cornelius and Craig, the PRI "benefited from a vast network of government patronage, through which small-scale benefits could be delivered to large segments of the population" (1991: 61). In a very concrete way, then, the sectors became economizing devices that allowed the dominant party to buy the support of a handful of leaders and thereby control the much broader union movement. At the same time, the PCM was "chronically short of funds" and "unable to offer hope of real benefits to the lower class" (Schmitt, 1970: 34, 249).

But where patronage was insufficient to reduce worker militancy and the possibility of a broad-based leftwing opposition party, the government used force. In his inaugural speech, Alemán announced the end of tolerance for labor mobilization and work stoppages. He then unleashed a wave of repression. Carr writes that "Within the first six months of the new presidency police and army units had begun to attack leftwing personalities and organizations with growing frequency and boldness" (1992: 147). For instance, in October of 1948, the government staged an attack on the Mexican Rail Workers' Union (STFRM) headquarters and subsequently began a series of purges that sought to rid unions of leftists, including pro-socialist and communist forces (Carr, 1992: 145–156). The miner's strike of 1950, the May Day parade of 1952, the 1956 strikes at the National Polytechnic Institute, and the primary school teachers' strike of 1957 were all violently put down by police or the army (Semo, 2003: 72–73). A series of work stoppages by rail workers in 1958 met with what Carr (1992: 207) called a "massive attack" that included soldiers, police, and secret servicemen. Railway installations and two suburbs of Mexico

---

[8] The 1946 electoral code also prohibited parties that subordinated themselves to international organizations; however, the PCM officially disavowed such a connection (Schmitt, 1970: 204).

82   *Why Dominant Parties Lose*

City were occupied by the army and thousands of workers were arrested and several killed.

The spike in repression radicalized, fragmented, and reduced the size of leftwing opposition forces. According to Carr, "The violence was sufficiently unexpected and worrying that in May and June 1947 the Communist party leadership began to consider reactivating its underground structures and routines" (1992: 147). The most durable groups were also the most radical and therefore failed to attract broader groups to their cause. When this round of repression began the PCM counted 418 cells operating in 22 of 32 states and 5,559 registered members. By the end of the 1950s, its membership was down to "a couple of hundred" (Carr, 1992: 181, 223). The radicalization of the left extended beyond the PCM as well. The Mexican Worker-Peasant Party (POCM), founded in 1950, "was indistinguishable from the orthodox party" (Schmitt, 1970: 25) and, beginning in 1962, the Popular Socialist Party (PPS) founded by labor leader Lombardo Toledano dropped its traditional collaborationist stance and adopted a Marxist-Leninist profile (Schmitt, 1970: 24).

In sum, in the 1940s and 1950s, the Mexican left had a golden opportunity to create a viable independent party. Labor unions were organized but not yet fully incorporated into the PRI. In addition, Cárdenas had created rising expectations among broad segments of the population, suggesting that labor might have found willing allies. Yet the incumbent's effective use of patronage to buy off moderates and targeted repression to harass radicals trimmed the left's sails and reduced activism to those willing to pay high personal costs for political involvement while reaping uncertain rewards.

The Crisis of 1968 and Further Opportunities for Opposition Party Development on the Left in the 1970s

The PRI's platform continued to drift toward the right until 1970. Although the prior round of repression had cemented official control over formal labor unions, as the government backed away from social redistribution, unincorporated constituencies began to demand benefits. The situation was aggravated by a slowdown in economic expansion, creeping inflation, and the declining ability of the labor market to absorb new workers. Since the 1930s, the economically active population had developed at a rate at least equal to the population over 12 years of age, but from 1960 to 1970 this trend reversed (Rivera Ríos, 1986: 71–72). Against this backdrop, young people and unincorporated segments of the

Dominant Party Advantages and Opposition Party Failure   83

urban poor began to mobilize for benefits. The government became concerned not so much about student protest, but about the possibility that they would spark opposition activity among broader social segments that were not controlled by the PRI's sectoral organizations. As Middlebrook states, the student movement

did not immediately challenge the regime's labor and peasant bases, but it did pose a serious potential threat to the regime in its effort to link a radical middle class [student] leadership with opposition elements in the organized labor movement and among urban marginals (1986: 126).

Existing patronage networks helped constrain the potential for student protest to expand to labor unions, and this goes a long way in accounting for the limited assault on the PRI in the late 1960s. But the protests of 1968 still threatened to spread to other unincorporated groups and their high visibility embarrassed a government hosting the Olympics that year. Patronage was a less useful tool for quelling the students in part because the PRI lacked the capacity to distribute goods to groups not tied to its sectoral organizations. In addition, the students resisted the allure of patronage by rotating the strike leadership among the schools and faculties represented (Hellman, 1983: 176).

Without other means of undercutting opposition mobilization and fearing the potential rise of a partisan challenger with broad support, the government once again turned to repression. In October 1968, government forces massacred at least 300 students at the Plaza de Tlatelolco, and again repressed mostly student demonstrators in 1971. Subsequently, a wave of repression was unleashed against the left that rose to the level of state-sponsored violence in fully closed authoritarian regimes. Johnson (1978: 163) stated that "In the 1970s Mexico appeared on the verge of replacing Argentina as Latin America's most violence-prone nation." Leftwing activists were hunted, and according to the limited files made available by the Secretary of the Interior following the 2000 elections, some 532 people disappeared (Zarembo, 2001).

As in the 1940s and 1950s, increased repression reduced the size of opposition movements and radicalized them. Significant elements of the left turned away from parties and instead formed clandestine organizations. Radical intellectual cliques formed, including Punto Crítico at the National University (UNAM) in 1971 and the Revolutionary National Civic Association (ACNR) in the state of Guerrero. Guerrilla movements that were inspired by Ché's revolutionary *foquismo* and Mao's strategy of encircling cities formed in the states of Guerrero, Chihuahua, and on

84   *Why Dominant Parties Lose*

the outskirts of Mexico City. Other groups inspired by Liberation Theology and recently justified by Vatican II mobilized in the states of Chiapas and Oaxaca. During the 1970s the effect of these groups was palpable. According to Johnson (1978: 161), "A reading of Mexico's underground press gave the distinct impression that President Echeverría arrived at the midpoint of his presidency facing the threat of a nation risen to arms. Public evidence of turmoil and violence suggested this." Obviously, none of these movements sparked the revolutions they sought to bring about; however, all of them had an important effect in molding the mentality of the Mexican left that increasingly saw itself as under threat, on the run, armed, and determined to overthrow the PRI.

New left parties also formed during the mid-1970s, but due to the high costs and uncertain benefits of activism, these were small organizations with visions of radical social transformation. The People's Front Party (FEP) spearheaded by leaders of the PCM formed in advance of the 1964 elections; however, despite a concerted national effort to recruit enough activists to register as a party, it failed to get on the ballot (Schmitt, 1970: 238–241). The Mexican Workers Party (PMT) was founded in 1974 and included Demetrio Vallejo, the leader of the militant rail workers union who had spearheaded the strikes of 1958 and been jailed for 11 years, socialist leader Heberto Castillo, and released political prisoners that had been jailed following the 1968 student movement. The Revolutionary Workers Party (PRT), which formed in 1976, had its philosophical roots in Trotskyism and the Fourth International, and ardently called for a new revolution in Mexico. The parties also failed to gain access to the ballot. All three new parties made social justice concerns their main cause and theoretically could have attracted substantial support, but they were sufficiently extremist that they attracted few activists and little social support.

Neopopulism and Opportunities for Opposition Party Development on the Right, 1970–1982

Although repression radicalized and reduced the size of the left, the economic slowdown that gave rise to student protest lingered and anti-PRI sentiment threatened to spread to moderate left groups. PRI insiders knew that repression was not a viable long-term solution for a party that based its legitimacy, in large part, on regular consultations at the polls. Thus, in order to woo the more moderate left and stem the possibility of a broader opposition movement, President Luis Echeverría (1970–1976) shifted policy from the center-right to the center-left and changed the

Dominant Party Advantages and Opposition Party Failure   85

government's slogan from "stabilizing development" to "shared development." Under this new plan, he expanded the state's role in the economy and in redistributing the fruits of development. From the 1970 to 1980, the number of state-owned enterprises increased from 391 to over 1,000 (Lustig, 1992: 104) and income from these companies grew by 2.1% of GDP. Overall public sector income increased much more, from 19.8% in 1970 to 31.5% of GDP in 1983 (Bailey, 1988: 129). The federal public bureaucracy expanded as well, from 532 units in 1974 (including all federal level secretariats, departments, subsecretariats, general directorates, and parastatals) to 1,693 units in 1982 (Bailey, 1988: 99).

Echeverría also engaged in populist style redistribution reminiscent of the Cárdenas Administration. According to Kessler (1999: 22), "Echeverría's solution was to neutralize social mobilization by throwing all the state's resources into social redistribution and development." In an effort to stay ahead of inflation, he raised wages four times during his six-year administration, doubling nominal pay between 1970 and 1975. Public sector expenditures grew from 21.7% of GDP in 1970 to 48.8% by 1982 (Bailey, 1988: 129). Social security coverage expanded by a third and added 10 million more workers. The education budget increased by five times and by 1976 the number of technical institutes alone rose from 281 to 1,301 (Hellman, 1983: 191). The National Workers Housing Fund built 100,000 units of affordable housing and spent 3.5 million pesos (Hellman, 1983: 207). Just days after taking office, Echeverría expropriated 100,000 hectares in northwest Mexico for redistribution.

The policy shift succeeded in undermining the potential for a broader leftwing movement against the PRI and isolated the radical left. Rebel cells continued to operate and radical elements of the independent labor movement engaged in what Carr called a "labor insurgency." Although less willing to repress the moderate opposition, the government continued to use violence selectively against certain groups. Student protests met with massive police and army presences in June 1971, May 1973, and August 1974, and the government continued to hunt urban and rural guerrillas. It even invited 63 specialists in urban counterinsurgency from Brazil's Superior War College to train the Mexican army (Hellman, 1983: 208).

By the end of the Echeverría presidency, opposition forces had come to question the usefulness of challenging the PRI through elections. The PCM still lacked enough activists to register as a party during this period (Schmitt, 1970: 61), and the left remained thoroughly radicalized and largely underground. At the same time, fights between social conservatives and economic liberals in the PAN, in part over the question of participation in elections, conspired to keep it from running a presidential candidate in 1976. Thus, the PRI's José López Portillo ran unopposed and, for the first time, Mexico's dominant party system was transformed, if only temporarily, into a one-party regime. This signaled a severe crisis of legitimacy for a dominant party that had always based its claim to legitimacy in large part on popular consent given through regular elections.

In order to enhance the presence of the opposition and encourage increasingly anti-regime movements to channel their grievances through the electoral process, the government implemented an important electoral reform in 1977. Its architect, Secretary of the Interior Jesús Reyes Heroles, argued that by lowering the barriers to new party entry, radical elements particularly on the left would moderate. To smooth the way to form new political parties, the reform created a new category called "political associations" defined as organizations that are "susceptible to transforming themselves into political parties."[9] As a result of this latter reform that permitted registration conditional on subsequent electoral performance, the PCM obtained legal registration for the first time since 1949. In addition, four political associations on the left were registered as well as the Democratic Mexican Party (PDM) on the right. The PMT and the PRT, however, failed to meet the minimum requirements (Rodríguez Araujo and Sirvent, 2005: 50). Not only did the reforms succeed in encouraging opposition forces to work through parties, they also "denied [the PRI] some aspects of their reliance on fraud and coercion" (Klesner, 1997), thus forcing it to compete somewhat more with policy appeals and rely somewhat less on patronage and repression.

The combination of electoral reform, a significant commitment to state-centered development policies, and repression of the most radical elements, encouraged the left to moderate. By the late 1970s, most rebel cells were either destroyed or voluntarily demobilized. Both the PCM and the PRT gave up on the goal of revolution and in 1981 parties and intellectual cliques of the independent left formed the Unified Mexican Socialist Party (PSUM), which Bruhn (1997: 323) called "the first significant attempt to unify the left in one electoral party." The Trotskyist PRT was the only significant left party that did not join formally, but Carr (1985: 2) says that it entered into a tacit alliance with the PCM and its leader Arnoldo Martínez Verdugo who dominated the PSUM. The new party represented a significant moderation of leftwing forces not only because it channeled

---

[9] To qualify, a "political association" required a national directorship, two years of activity, and at least 5,000 members spread over 10 states.

Dominant Party Advantages and Opposition Party Failure 87

opposition efforts through the electoral process rather than armed rebellion, but also because it increasingly invited middle-class allies to join including businessmen, students, and progressive forces broadly defined (Carr, 1985: 1–2).

Yet the government's aggressive moves to contain the left sparked serious discontent among economic liberals on the right for the first time since the 1930s. To finance his dramatic expansion of the state, Echeverría imposed new income and luxury consumption taxes on wealthy Mexicans, new employer taxes were instituted (Hellman, 1983: 192), and new public sector borrowing increased eleven-fold from US$443 million in 1970 to US$5.1 billion in 1976 (Kessler, 1999: 26). Loaeza summarizes the extent of liberals' concerns:

The reanimation of many of the components of Mexican populism awakened a strong reaction among broad sectors of opinion, fundamentally among businessmen and urban middle class groups who feared that the government's political discourse would translate into a real political radicalization that would push the country toward the kind of socialism that Chile experienced under the presidency of Salvador Allende (1999: 303).

Given the government's shift to the left, why did a viable party fail to emerge on the right? In the 1970s, the PAN seemed to be in a good position to take advantage of increasing discontent on the right. Under party president Christlieb Ibarrola (1962–1968), the PAN took initial steps to open itself to broader segments of society (Martínez Valle, 1995: 81). Conchello (1972–1975) further courted economic liberals and the middle class by vocally opposing Echeverría's neopopulist policies (Shirk, 2005: 77–80). As a result, Arriola writes that in the 1970s,

[The PAN] appeared as the only national opposition party capable of creating a vigorous anti-Echeverría campaign that would have been able to articulate the fears and concerns of businessmen, the middle class, and other groups on the right (1994: 30).

The PAN did expand in the late 1960s and early 1970s and it established important footholds in urban centers, but it was unable to attract broad enough constituencies to win outside of limited areas. Its electoral failure during this period owes in part to the party's confessional sensibilities over the prior 30 years and to divisions within the right between social conservatives and economic liberals. As Echeverría's neopopulist economics reinvigorated opposition sentiment among business elites and elements of the middle class, leaders like Conchello increasingly attempted to transform the PAN from a confessional party into a pro-market Christian

Democratic one with broader reach. But his plan met with stiff resistance from the party's social conservatives, known as *doctrinarios*. After serving only one three-year term, Conchello was defeated by González Morfín from the doctrinaire group in a very tight election that required six rounds to generate a majority (Reveles Vazquez, 1996: 24; Shirk, 2005: 80–83). González Morfín criticized the outgoing president as an "opportunistic pragmatist" for his interest in expanding the party, and in an amazing statement that belied his position, he argued that party politics should not be "reduced to a game of force, won by he who has the most power;" rather, it should be used as a way to "redeem society" (Loaeza, 1999: 307).

Social conservatives' ideology of Catholic humanism also conflicted with elements of the business community over human rights. The PAN vigorously criticized the government's repression of students in 1968, and in its 20th National Convention held in February of 1969, it seemed to reflect the progressive sentiments of the 1962–1965 Vatican II Council when it called for "revolutionary actions to transform the political, economic, and social structures of the country" (Martínez Valle, 1995: 89–90). Many business groups, on the other hand, feared socialist revolution and supported the repression (Basañez, 1996: 209). Thus, questions of party expansion, human rights, and party identity put a wedge between what might have been a natural alliance among social and fiscal conservatives during the 1970s. In this period, the party remained closely tied to its smaller confessional base and was unable to draw supporters on the economic policy issues of the day.

Even if the PAN was unable to rally massive discontent on the right, why did a new rightwing party fail to organize in the 1970s? A high-profile business leader in the state of Sonora even called for the creation of the Liberal Mexican Party to fill this space, but he abandoned the idea by 1978 (Arriola, 1988: 153). The available literature does not offer a clear argument as to why a new rightwing party did not emerge in this period, but two reasons seem plausible. First, Echeverría mollified the most important businessmen through key concessions. Basañez (1996: 210) writes that the president of the major business association in Mexico (COPARMEX) was "ferociously" opposed to the government's populist rhetoric and expansion of the state, and the association's members reacted by engaging in massive capital flight that reached an estimated US$3.7 billion. Echeverría responded by creating the Business Coordinating Council (CCE) that gave businessmen, particularly members of the Monterrey elite, a forum for expressing their policy preferences and communicating with the government. By 1975 the CCE had generated enough power that it influenced

Dominant Party Advantages and Opposition Party Failure 89

the selection of López Portillo as the PRI's candidate for the presidency in 1976 and it now actively opposed the creation of a new opposition party (Arriola, 1988: 153). Influencing policy from behind the scenes rather than direct political activism was a more comfortable role for big business in any case (Zermeño, 1982: 7). Thus, entrepreneurs' natural inclinations against direct political action and Echeverría's willingness to open special channels for their influence may have been the deciding factors in dissuading capital-holders from joining the PAN or forming another rightwing opposition party.[10]

The second reason that a new rightwing party may not have emerged is that it probably would have found limited support from its most natural and important constituency: the middle class. First, Echeverría responded to concerns over upward mobility voiced by students in 1968 by expanding higher education to broader segments of society and by lowering both the voting age and the minimum age for holding office (Basañez, 1983: 41–43). Second, he expanded social security and provided subsidies for electricity and oil. Although these programs primarily benefited working-class groups, they also helped the urban middle class. They were paid for, in large part, by increasing foreign loans. During his term from 1971 to 1977, public external debt in Mexico increased from US\$7 billion to US\$23 billion. Although the middle class would feel the effects of this borrowing acutely in the 1980s, during the 1970s it was a painless way to buy political support. Third, Echeverría expanded the state's role in industry and raised import tariffs to encourage domestic production of inputs. Growing the state opened up thousands of new jobs in the bureaucracy that middle-class citizens could fill. Doing so behind tariff barriers helped spur small industry, especially in capital goods and metalworking (Shadlen, 2004: 67–69). Fourth, small industry that was either owned or managed by middle-class groups was thoroughly organized and incorporated into the small business chamber CANACINTRA. Shadlen (2004) shows that the chamber adopted an accommodationist strategy with the government during this period and, as a result, wielded

---

[10] There are at least two other plausible reasons why economic liberals did not start their own party. First, aside from small groups like the CCE, liberals were dispersed and had limited mechanisms for coordination. In a 1980 survey, 80% of the business chamber confederation's (CONCAMIN) members responded that industrialists rarely act as a unified political force (Zermeño, 1982: 8). Thus, an existing party would have served as a focal organization and the PAN would have been the only logical choice. Second, startup costs could have been a deterrent since the electoral code required registering 30,000 activists in 21 states.

90   *Why Dominant Parties Lose*

more policy influence than it might have. Finally, the CNOP continued to incorporate elements of the urban middle class. Thus, even if the PAN had been willing to accept disgruntled entrepreneurs in the early to mid-1970s or if entrepreneurs had spearheaded a new rightwing party on their own, it is doubtful that such a party would have generated much middle-class support, without which it could not have won.

As it turned out, economic liberals who had helped select José López Portillo (1976–1982) as the next president for his pro-market credentials were sorely disappointed. The discovery of major oil deposits in 1976 led the president to proclaim "an end to Mexico's underdevelopment" and encouraged a continuation of the international borrowing and spending habits of the prior administration. The role of the state in the economy expanded, and in particular, PEMEX grew dramatically to extract and refine the new reserves. Despite early optimism, by 1982 the economy had not taken off, the debt was rising, and inflation was soaring. Amidst a major episode of capital flight, López Portillo announced the nationalization of the banks in that year. Business leaders naturally viewed this as a huge assault (Arriola, 1994) and, at that point, many abandoned their prior aversion for direct action and turned to the PAN.

By 1982, the PAN was in a much better position to accommodate economic liberals in its ranks. The showdown between social conservatives and economic liberals in 1976 had cost the party dearly. In one estimate, it lost a decade of growth (Mizrahi, 2003). Thus, by 1982, it was significantly more willing to accept new activists.

The *neopanistas* who entered the party in the early 1980s brought a clear agenda for shifting Mexico's political economy away from state-led development and toward free market capitalism (Arriola, 1994; Mizrahi, 2003). Their influence had the important effect of changing the party's focus from Church-State relations and associated moral issues that had limited resonance with voters to economic development policy that constituted the main partisan cleavage. As a result, the party made impressive electoral gains over the next decade in state and federal elections (Lujambio, 2000). However, these gains fell short of toppling the PRI for nearly 20 years.

Three factors help account for why the PAN expanded more slowly than would be predicted by theories that presume a fair market for votes. First, the economic liberals that helped the party expand also staked out a position that was relatively extreme compared to the average voter and constrained it from further expansion until it moderated. Second, the PAN recruited comparatively noncentrist party elites in part because the PRI still had access to huge amounts of illicit public funds until the latter half of the 1980s and thus could bribe voters with patronage goods. Finally, the PRI also lowered the PAN's chances of winning by attempting electoral fraud in some of the most competitive races. Lujambio (2001: 55–56) reports 16 "unrecognized wins" in municipal elections where the PAN ran 5,353 candidates from 1980 to 1995. It is also well accepted that the PRI stole the gubernatorial election in Chihuahua in 1986. Although undeniably important, the evidence points to too few stolen elections to conclude that the PRI maintained single-party dominance purely or even primarily through the false counting of votes.

Debt Crisis, Neoliberalism, and Opportunities for Opposition Party Development on the Left in the 1980s

It was in this atmosphere of rising political mobilization of the right that the debt crisis hit in 1982. The breakup of the Organization of Petroleum Exporting Countries (OPEC) led to a sudden constriction of credit on the international market, and interest rates on the existing foreign debt skyrocketed. Mexico, which had financed its neopopulist policies and the extraction of oil deposits during the 1970s through extensive international borrowing, now found itself in a credit crunch. By late 1982, the government was no longer able to make its debt payment, and its default led off a crisis throughout Latin America. The de la Madrid Administration (1982–1988) initially responded with a series of short-term orthodox shocks designed to reduce public spending and re-ignite investment. When by 1984 these policies failed to control inflation, the government switched to a longer-term strategy broadly in accordance with free market ideology (Collier, 1992).

The reason for the government's move to the right by adopting free market economic policies after 1984 has been the source of some debate. But whether the cause was political or economic, domestic or international, the policy shift nonetheless opened space for the potential entry of a leftwing opposition party. From 1983 to 1988, GDP grew by an average of only 0.2% and total social spending, including health and education, fell by 40%. Real wages also fell by 40% and job creation stagnated. Deaths caused by nutritional deficiencies among preschool age children rose from 1.5% in 1980 to an alarming 9.1% in 1988 (Lustig, 1992: Ch. 3). Overall, the social conditions for a strong left party were more present during the 1980s than at any time since the Great Depression of the 1930s. Yet the left failed to expand its vote share before 1988. In the

92   *Why Dominant Parties Lose*

1982 elections the main independent left party, the PSUM, reached only 4.6% of the vote, while the PRT got 1.3%. In the 1985 elections, the PRT remained at 1.3% and the PSUM dropped to 3.4%. According to Semo, "These parties could not generate enough support to cause the PRI concern at the local or national level" (2003: 83). What accounts for the left's failure during this period?

Unlike in the 1970s, there is little evidence of repression against opposition activists during the *early* 1980s. The government had just instituted an electoral reform specifically to encourage the left to participate in electoral politics, and although it did not want left parties to expand substantially, neither did it want them to disappear and re-initiate guerrilla activities. I agree with Semo's assessment that "In these years it was clear that repression and fraud were not the only causes for the independent left's stalled electoral development" (2003: 83). Two other reasons account for the left's very slow progress in party politics until after 1985.

First, the political effects of the economic crash were to some extent softened by the state's large role in the economy until mid-decade. Due to the nationalization of the banks in 1982 and the fall in private-sector income, the relative size of the public sector actually expanded until 1984. As a result, the government retained a large number of jobs that it could distribute as patronage through its sectoral organizations. It also kept public money flowing to the PRI that the party could use to purchase voter support. But the economic crash was severe enough that patronage alone was only a temporary analgesic for the PRI's headache. The party's sectoral organizations strained under economic austerity and increasing numbers of citizens turned to informal sector activities to make ends meet. At the same time, a rapidly growing number of urban and rural poor people's movements demanded resources from the state and, in some cases, mobilized public sentiment against the PRI (Ramírez Saiz, 1986). Thus, the PRI's use of patronage resources to buy voter support remained an important albeit much less effective tool during this period.

Second, the PSUM failed to take advantage of new opportunities to attract voters due in part to internal organizational rigidities. Although it, along with its leading voice, the PCM, gave up on the goal of revolution and armed struggle, the PSUM was distant from becoming a moderate left party and remained out of step with the average voter. It even struggled to gain the support of urban and rural social movements that were headed by like-minded socialists and progressives. Although these movements were sympathetic to the left, they were more focused on securing short-term

Dominant Party Advantages and Opposition Party Failure   93

material gains from the government such as housing and services than they were on radical leftwing politics. In some cases, aligning with the independent left decreased their success (Hellman, 1994). Socialist ideologues in the PSUM were also skeptical that these civic movements could or should be main protagonists in the left's historical project of change. As a result, social movements and the left failed to strike an alliance in the early and mid-1980s that could have generated broader support for a leftwing opposition party.

As social conditions worsened, actors on the left began to see more benefits to unification. In 1987 most of the member organizations of the PSUM joined with an expanded group of small leftwing groups, unregistered parties, and a few key players from now extensive leftwing social movements to form the Mexican Socialist Party (PMS) (see Bruhn, 1997: 324). With this expanded coalition, the PMS had greater potential than any prior left party. Nevertheless, it retained the basic ideals of socialism and only begrudgingly accepted the tenets of democracy. Whether it would have done well in the 1988 elections on its own will never be known because it lasted less than a year as an independent organization. In 1988 it voluntarily dissolved to transfer its legal registration to the PRD that was founded the following year. Nevertheless, the PMS represented another key step in the moderation of leftwing forces, and its affiliates became the backbone of the PRD.

On parallel tracks, the government's new free market policies led to tensions inside the PRI between economically liberal technocrats and a statist faction that prioritized distribution over growth. The statist faction was led by Cuauhtémoc Cárdenas, the former Governor of the state of Michoacán and son of President Lázaro Cárdenas, and by Porfirio Muñoz Ledo, the former President of the PRI. In 1986, they formed the Democratic Current (CD) inside the PRI to support Cárdenas' nomination for the presidency. When Cárdenas was passed over for Carlos Salinas de Gortari in 1987, the CD left the PRI. Its members joined with previously organized forces of the independent left, including the PCM, PSUM, PMS, PRT, several small parties that had traditionally collaborated with the PRI, and independent social movements that had previously engaged in electoral politics only on the margins. Together these forces formed the National Democratic Front (FDN) and participated in the 1988 elections with Cárdenas as their candidate. Cárdenas won 38.1% of the official vote in an election marred by widespread accusations of fraud. Despite general agreement that fraud occurred, the available evidence makes it impossible to determine whether that fraud reversed a Cárdenas victory or padded the PRI's plurality up to a slim majority (Castañeda, 2000: 232–239), as discussed earlier.

The government's free market solution to the 1982 economic crisis had led to a massive and quasi-spontaneous anti-incumbent vote that favored the left. It now seemed that the left could gain the broad-based support that has eluded it in the past. With the expectation of quickly winning majoritarian support at the polls, FDN member organizations minus the parties that had traditionally collaborated with the PRI, formed the PRD in 1989 (Bruhn, 1997).[11]

By several measures, the PRD should have been able to develop into a catchall party and win substantial support in the early 1990s. After 1988, international observers and the press found no credible evidence of systematic fraud large enough that it could have changed national election results; social conditions supported leftwing politics more than anytime since the 1930s; and the emergence of a free and somewhat investigative press progressively limited the government's ability to repress opposition forces (Lawson, 2002). Nevertheless, the left's support behind the PRD plummeted during the early 1990s. In the 1991 midterm elections, it won just 11% of the vote, and in the 1994 presidential elections it garnered 16%. In both elections, the PAN on the right replaced it as the second-largest opposition party.

Four factors discouraged the PRD from making moderate appeals that would attract the average voter and thus help account for its electoral difficulties in the 1990s. First, despite economic crisis and the purposive slimming of the state under free market policies, the Salinas Administration generated one-time resources through privatization revenues. It used part of these funds to buy electoral support from leftwing constituencies through a massive poverty-alleviation program called the National Solidarity Program (PRONASOL). As a result, the PRD continued to have a lower chance of winning than it would have had the market for votes been fair. This program and the PRI's resource advantages in the 1990s are discussed further below.

Second, although the PRD was a new party with a relatively moderate presidential candidate, the majority of its top leadership continued to hold comparatively extreme policy preferences. Most of the leaders came from prior independent left parties and had been recruited into the opposition when joining was such a high cost and low benefit activity that only relative extremists found it worthwhile to do so. Thus, despite these parties'

---

[11] The PPS, PFCRN, and PARM participated in the FDN but did not join the PRD.

long-term process of moderation beginning in the late 1970s, their core members still held significantly statist policy ideals that translated into comparatively radical platforms and constrained expansion. Chapter 5 explains the preferences of party personnel in detail.

Third, the attractiveness of the left was limited by the renewed use of repression that temporarily raised the costs of participation until the mid-1990s. Activists in the PRD complained of harassment during almost every state and federal election in this period, including day-to-day repression that involved shutting off access to urban services, making threats, and jailing them on trumped up charges. They also complained about episodes of physical violence that the PRD claims included the murder of more than 300 of its activists (Eisenstadt, 1999). By the mid-1990s, the spike in repression had simmered, but under the Salinas Administration it was a real disincentive for moderate leftists to flock to the PRD.

Finally, as the reduction in the PRI's advantages made the opposition more competitive, the incumbent attempted electoral fraud in some races. The most notable fraud against the left was in the 1988 presidential elections when Salinas defeated Cárdenas. As discussed in detail earlier, while there is clear evidence of fraud, it is impossible to know if Cárdenas actually won in the balloting or if the PRI padded its victory (see Castañeda, 2000: 232–233). However, the use of fraud put prospective PRD activists on notice that they would suffer a lower probability of winning with the left. Domínguez and McCann (1996) showed that, perversely, the more the left campaigned against fraud, the more its own partisans discounted the possibility of a PRD victory and stayed home. Thus, predicting less opportunity with the left, only politicians who deeply opposed the PRI on policy chose to join the PRD during this period.

Overall, despite opportunities for opposition party development on the left and the right during five specific episodes in the twentieth century, viable challengers did not emerge. The PRI's attempts to "firefight" opposition mobilization on one of its flanks by shifting its policy appeals opened ideological space for a challenger on its opposite flank. If the market for votes had been fair or neutral as most party competition theories and the Mexico-specific "pendulum" theory imply, then challengers should have become viable and single-party dominance should not have been sustainable. But the market for votes was not neutral, and opposition parties failed because the PRI was able to buttress its policy appeals with patronage and repression that made opposition parties less attractive options. By virtue of their lower probability of winning and the higher costs of joining, challenger parties were reduced in size and forced to take positions

Why Dominant Parties Lose

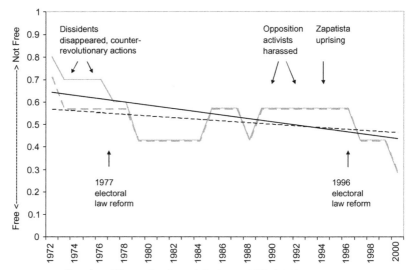

FIGURE 3.2. Freedom House Ratings, Mexico, 1972–2000.
Note: Dashed lines represent original Freedom House scores (rescaled from 0 to 1) and their best fit trend line. Solid lines represent modified Freedom House scores that take into account new information about the 1970s revealed after 2000 (described in text). Scores were modified for 1972–1978 only, thus the solid and dashed lines run together after 1979.

on the issues that either focused on noncentral partisan cleavages (e.g., the Church-State divide) or relatively extremist positions on the central cleavage, economic development policy.

The remainder of the chapter focuses on variations in the PRI's use of repression and access to patronage over time. It introduces measures that are used in the rest of the book.

SINGLE-PARTY DOMINANCE AND REPRESSION

The analytic narrative above described an overall reduction in the level of repression between about 1968 and 2000, with an important increase between 1988 and 1993. One way to capture this trend is to use Freedom House civil liberties scores. In Figure 3.2, I rescaled the original scores to run from 0 to 1 where 0 is the complete absence of political repression and 1 corresponds to maximum repression. Only the most repressive fully closed authoritarian regimes around the world earn a 1, including Soviet bloc countries, North Korea, and the worst dictatorships in Africa and the Middle East. By this measure, Mexico in the early 1970s, shown

Dominant Party Advantages and Opposition Party Failure   97

with a dashed line, was a significantly repressive regime. Nevertheless, these scores probably under-represent the true amount of repression. The full extent of officially sanctioned torture and disappearances during the 1970s, as described above, was not known until after the 2000 elections when President Fox permitted limited access to files from the Secretary of the Interior.

To take this new and important information into account, I raised scores from 1972 to 1976 to reflect the more repressive environment, and I added scores for 1970 and 1971 that are equal to the modified 1972 score.[12] These modified scores are also shown in Figure 3.2 with a solid line. The new measure has significantly increased face validity over the original scores that erroneously show repression in the mid-1980s when opposition activists were harassed as equal to repression in the 1970s when opposition forces were hunted. The modified scores square with assessments by country experts and correctly portray the 1970s as a period of greater repression, correctly portray the opening following the electoral reforms of 1977 as much more significant, and correctly show a sharper overall trend of falling repression from 1972 to 2000. Nevertheless, when I employ these scores in quantitative tests in Chapter 5, I also show results with the original scores as a robustness check.

The analytic narrative also made it clear that repression principally targeted the leftwing opposition. The right was harassed, especially in the 1940s and 1950s, and in a few instances its operatives were murdered. Yet the left suffered more brutal and more regular repression. Even the modified Freedom House scores cannot take this asymmetry into account. Nevertheless, they are useful for giving a summary sense of variation in the use of repression over time, and they are the best available quantitative measures for the statistical analyses that appear in later chapters.[13]

SINGLE-PARTY DOMINANCE AND RESOURCE ASYMMETRIES

The analytic narrative emphasized the PRI's resource advantages over challengers as a major reason for its continued dominance despite periodic opportunities for opposition party development on its right and left.

---

[12] Freedom House's policy leaves scores "as is" regardless of new information. Inquiries as to how they would have scored 1970–76 with the updated information went unanswered.

[13] I also consulted Gibney and Dalton's Political Terror Scales. However, data were only available beginning in 1980 and scores for Mexico show almost no variation. There is a small shift toward greater repression beginning in 1994 that likely reflects the conflict in Chiapas.

But where did the incumbent party's resources come from and why were they available? The PRI funded what Cornelius and Craig (1991) called a "national patronage system" by diverting money from the public budget and especially from the revenues of state-owned enterprises, by doling out jobs in the bureaucracy to loyal supporters and obliging them to contribute to the party with their wages and their labor, by generating kickbacks from government contracts, and by using government infrastructure and employees to mount massive campaigns in the media and in the streets. According to Preston and Dillon,

> Although it wasn't a secret that the PRI lived off the public till, the party had by and large been careful to conceal the transfer of resources. Local party headquarters were housed in municipal buildings without paying rent; full-time party staffers were paid by local government treasuries; the PRI took its cut of fees and union dues (2004: 290).

The party also operated by "assigning public officials – at tax-payer expense – to coordinate party election campaigns, loaning government cars and trucks to move supporters to rallies and polling places, and other methods" (Dillon, 2000: 6). In one case where the PRI president of the state of Nuevo León was indicted for misuse of public funds, he admitted that "The PRI received economic support from the state treasury throughout my presidency to support party operations, following an established procedure [that was] historical practice, rooted in the traditions of our country for many years" (Dillon, 2000: 6).

The PRI was able to use public funds for partisan purposes because lack of rotation in government – and the expectation that the PRI would continue to win – allowed it to raid the resources of the state with virtual impunity. The incumbent's power also allowed it to design electoral codes that locked in its resource advantages over challengers. In fully competitive democracies with at least two viable parties, the incumbent party is typically deterred from raiding the public budget because it fears reprisals while out of power. Similarly, party finance regulations and civil service reforms (Geddes, 1994) are typically adopted when competing parties have a mutual interest in blocking each other's unbridled access to resources. The absence of rotation in Mexico and other dominant party systems leaves the incumbent party free to generate and spend resources with impunity and creates what I called hyper-incumbency advantages.

In a speech given to party stalwarts in 1994, President Zedillo essentially admitted that the PRI had "appropriated the government" for its political gain. Nevertheless, it is difficult to measure the source of

Dominant Party Advantages and Opposition Party Failure   99

the incumbent's resource advantages, and this question has never been adequately addressed in the literature. I argue that opportunities for generating patronage are regulated by the size of the public sector and the degree of political control over the bureaucracy. When the state is heavily involved in the economy, the incumbent simply has more resources and jobs at its disposal. Yet even when the state is large, a professional and nonpartisan federal bureaucracy may act as a gatekeeper and constrain the dominant party's ability to access public funds (Shefter, 1977a). By the same token, a public bureaucracy that is politically beholden to the dominant party is more likely to ignore or even aid the incumbent in plundering public resources for partisan advantage. My argument is not that all public sector resources become patronage for the dominant party, but that such resources rise and fall with the magnitude of the state's control over the economy. I describe each condition in turn.

Accessing Resources: Political Control of the Public Bureaucracy

Mexico's public bureaucracy has always been politically controlled, and a professional civil service did not develop until 2001 after the PRI lost the presidency. During its entire period of electoral dominance, PRI governments controlled hiring, firing, and advancement either directly through political appointments or indirectly through control of public sector unions. Cabinet members and general directors of public agencies were given complete control over the appointment of subsecretaries, department heads, and managers, collectively known as "workers of confidence." These posts would be distributed to loyal members of one's political support network called a *camarilla* with the expectation that they support the political goals of the group's leader (Grindle, 1977; Smith, 1979; Camp, 1995). According to Moctezuma Barragán and Roemer,

> The appointment and termination of public servants has been carried out in our country by means of a system of vertical designation (spoils system) . . . Posts inside the public administration have been the prizes and rewards (or punishments) for those who have shown 'loyalty' to the boss or leader of his political group (2001: 122).

The federal public bureaucracy, a system that Preston and Dillon (2004: 220) refer to as "a stalagmite of accumulated patronage" was especially tightly controlled. As late as 1997, Arrellano and Guerrero (2000: fn 12) estimated that about 20,000 federal public employees were direct political appointments who could be hired and fired without reason. By that time of course over 80% of state-owned enterprises had been privatized and the federal public bureaucracy had been downsized dramatically, suggesting that the number of "workers of confidence" was substantially higher in earlier years.

Where managing appointments directly was not practical, the PRI exercised control through the federal public employees union (FSTSE) which is integrated into the party's labor sector (CTM). Since the 1963 Federal Public Servants Act, the FSTSE controlled hiring and firing of lower level federal employees, and with the exception of a small number of employees in two of nine federal agencies, there was no tenure system (Moctezuma Barragán and Roemer, 2001: 118, 127). Thus, Arrellano and Guerrero conclude, "A civil service career does not exist in Mexico at any level of government" (2000: 16).

The incumbent's control over the federal bureaucracy was so important for its ability to generate and distribute patronage resources that no changes were made even when the Treasury (SHCP) pushed for reforms to reduce demands on the public budget following the economic crises of 1982 and 1994. Arrellano and Guerrero argue that,

> The public administration system was a strategic tool for political control... It is not surprising that administrative reform has been largely postponed. Simply speaking, to generate a transparent, accountable, honest, and externally controlled public apparatus would jeopardize the political control that the dominant political group has enjoyed during past decades (2000: 6).

As a result of this political control, public employees were less likely to act as gatekeepers of public goods. Since they did not enjoy legal protections and advancement was based on loyalty rather than merit (Merino, 1996: 9), whistle-blowing was discouraged. The PRI's control over the bureaucracy was so complete that as early as 1945, Ebenstein argued that "plundering" would not likely diminish until electoral competition involved two or more parties (1945: 111).

By subordinating the bureaucracy, the PRI gained access to five types of resources. First, it could transfer funds from the public budget via state-owned enterprises, secret line items controlled by the executive, and stealth legislation in Congress. Second, it could use the economic power of the state to generate corporate kickbacks and contributions for government contracts and economic protection. Third, it could dole out a vast number of jobs to loyal political operatives who would in turn continue to prove their loyalty by working for the party. Fourth, bureaucrats themselves created a revenue stream because they were automatically enrolled

Dominant Party Advantages and Opposition Party Failure   101

in the PRI and encouraged to make "voluntary" contributions to the party with a suggested sliding scale according to job description. Finally, without bureaucratic constraints, the administrative resources of the state were available for recruiting, campaigning, and mobilizing voters on election day.

Generating Resources: The Size of the State

Since the politicized bureaucracy would not block the PRI's access to public funds, the availability of patronage goods rose and fell with the state's control of the economy. From the 1930s until the start of economic restructuring in 1984, Mexico's political economy was based on a labor-intensive import-substitution industrialization (ISI) model that created a large public sector and a massive federal bureaucracy. At their height, state-owned enterprises accounted for over 22.3% of GDP (Aspe, 1993: 182–183), and included holdings in energy, transportation, and communications. Among the largest and best-known companies was Petróleos Mexicanos (PEMEX) in oil, the Compañía Federal de Electricidad in electricity, Teléfonos de México (TELMEX) in telecommunications, the Compañía Minera de Cananea in copper mining, SICARSTA in steel, and Ferrocarriles Nacionales and Aeroméxico in train and air transport. The government also had extensive marketing and technical assistance boards in agriculture such as CONASUPO that included price supports for millions of farmers, especially in sugar, corn, bean, and coffee production (Sanderson, 1981; Snyder, 2001). During the 1980s, government holdings also included the country's entire banking system. To administer these companies, the federal bureaucracy grew to about 3 million employees and accounted for nearly 10% of the entire labor force. Including subnational governments and decentralized agencies brings this number to almost 5 million employees and 16.5% of the labor force.

The fiscal relationships between public companies, the government, and the PRI's campaigns were fluid. They involved huge and complicated transfers between agencies and a bewildering array of budget line items that permitted obfuscation and the creative sourcing of finances.[14] With virtually no oversight by opposition forces, the media, or international financial agencies, the government treated the public budget as the party's

---

[14] SOEs were formally incorporated into the federal budget in 1965. Before them, individual ministers, though they reported to the President, controlled SOE budgets (Centeno, 1994; MacLeod, 2004).

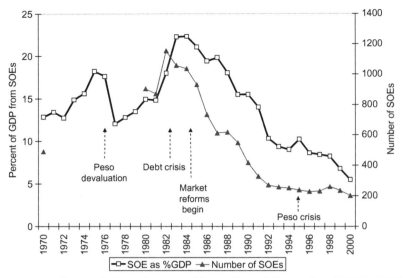

FIGURE 3.3. Economic Participation of State-Owned Enterprises (SOEs), 1970–2000.
Sources: Lustig, 1992; Aspe, 1993; MacLeod, 2004.

piggy bank and, as a result, "The official party enjoys almost unlimited access to government funds to finance its campaigns" (Cornelius and Craig, 1991: 61). The PRI had armies of campaign workers, financed a dense infrastructure that reached down to the block level in major cities, occupied huge amounts of media time, and plastered its slogan on every imaginable surface until the national territory appeared thoroughly branded. Meanwhile, opposition parties operated on shoestring budgets, relied on volunteers, and campaigned sporadically using face-to-face contacts and underground newspapers.

The PRI's huge resource advantages lasted for decades, but the economic crisis and subsequent restructuring "sharply reduced the resources that could be pumped through [the PRI's] national patronage system" (Cornelius and Craig, 1991: 61). Austerity and free market economics wreaked havoc on the party's access to patronage in three ways.

First, the participation of state-owned enterprises in the economy diminished. Figure 3.3 shows that both the number and economic participation of SOEs varied over time but generally increased until the economic crisis and then reduced. The government held as many as 1,155 enterprises in 1982 with a majority share in 755. By 1990, only eight years after the debt crisis hit and six years after a major commitment to

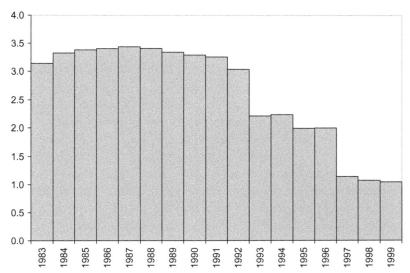

FIGURE 3.4. Number of Federal Government Employees (millions), 1983–1999.
Note: Includes central government and state-owned enterprise employees.
Source: 1983–1989 from Salinas (1994); 1990–1999 from Centro Latinoamericano de la Administración para el Desarrollo (CLAD), http://www.clad.org.ve/siare/tamano/estadistica.html, accessed August 10, 2001.

free market development policies was made, the government held some interest in only 280 enterprises and a majority interest in 147. By 2000 the total had shrunk to 202 (MacLeod, 2004: 39, 72; Lustig, 1992). As a result, the percent of GDP generated by public enterprises decreased from 22.3% in 1983 to just 5.5% in 2000.[15] Equally telling is the changing balance between the public and private sectors. In 1984, state-owned firms accounted for 72% of all revenue from Mexico's 50 largest companies. In 1999, it had dropped to just 21% (MacLeod, 2004: 98). This dramatic decrease in public control over the economy meant that the PRI had access to fewer public resources from which it could generate patronage goods to buy voter support.

Second, economic restructuring meant slimming down the size of the federal public bureaucracy and especially employment in state-owned enterprises. Figure 3.4 shows that the federal government employed well over 3 million people in the 1980s, shrinking to just 1.05 million by 2000. At its height, the federal government accounted for 10.6% of the total

[15] Data come from Lustig, 1992; Aspe, 1993; MacLeod, 2004; and INEGI at http://dgcnesyp.inegi.gob.mx/cgi-win/bdieinsti.exe/NIVH100010001#ARBOL.

104 *Why Dominant Parties Lose*

economically active population and this declined to just 2.6% by 2000. As a result, about 2.4 million workers that would have been in government-controlled unions were instead less likely to contribute their time and money to the PRI. If federal employees were beholden to the incumbent, none were more so than workers in state-owned enterprises whose unions were major contributors to the party. But from 1980 to 2000, privatization meant that the SOE workforce fell from 1.06 million at its height to just over 476,000 by 2000 (MacLeod, 2004). This reduction far outpaced the cuts in national administration made by other Latin American countries during the same period. By 1999, Mexico's SOE workforce was 79% below its 1991 total. Venezuela ranked second in cuts, but its workforce dropped by only 28%. At the same time, the number of SOE jobs in Brazil rose by 92%, and even in Chile, often held out as a model of market reform, the workforce increased by 12%.[16] In Mexico, slimming the federal public bureaucracy reduced the number of jobs available for the PRI to distribute as patronage. Even though an important portion of the decrease came from transferring public teachers to state governments, since the PRI had begun to lose control of state houses and legislatures, these employees were decreasingly available either as patronage appointments or as PRI supporters and financiers.

Finally, the move from the relatively closed ISI development model to a more open economy reduced the reach and organizational capacity of the PRI's sectoral organizations (CTM, CNC, and CNOP) that previously distributed massive quantities of patronage to voters. Rising unemployment and crisis conditions pushed workers into the informal sector, and by the 1990s, informal workers outnumbered formal ones (Cross, 1998). At the same time, formal sector jobs in services grew faster than manufacturing or agriculture. By 1991, services accounted for half of all employment, double what it had been a decade earlier, while other sectors remained about the same.[17] Both informal sector and service sector workers are comparatively difficult to organize because they tend to be more geographically dispersed than workers in other formal sectors and often have area-specific rather than collective interests. Finally, as is obvious from Figure 3.4, the government employees union (FSTSE) suffered dramatic losses. Since workers in newly created jobs were often not incorporated into formal sector unions associated with the PRI, they were also outside the party's patronage network. Declining resources also

---

[16] Data available at http://www.clad.org.ve/.
[17] See the World Bank's World Development Indicators at www.worldbank.org.

Dominant Party Advantages and Opposition Party Failure 105

contributed to splits in the unions traditionally associated with the PRI. In the 1980s and 1990s, the CTM lost unions to alternative independent confederations such as the National Workers' Union (UNT) that claimed as many members as the CTM by 1997.[18]

All three processes came to a head by the late 1980s. The resources that the incumbent used to run its national reward and punishment system were drying up. The federal bureaucracy was smaller and there were fewer state-owned enterprises whose budgets could be manipulated for partisan purposes. The PRI was running out of public money and the effects were palpable. The party's sectors were sclerotic, unable to reach increasingly large blocs of voters, and even had difficulty maintaining monopoly control over its traditional constituencies. Local PRI organizations became anemic, poorly staffed, and had virtually no operating budget (author interviews, 1999). In response, President Salinas (1988–1994) initiated a three-pronged strategy.

First, he increasingly turned to the private sector to fund the party. Investigative journalist Andrés Oppenheimer reported that Finance Minister Pedro Aspe sent a memo to the president of the PRI in 1992 informing him that the central government could no longer finance the party and, as a result, the party would have to make up for the "estimated $1 billion in government funds that was wire transferred every year to the party's headquarters" (1996: 83–110). A few months later, on February 23, 1993, President Salinas invited the 30 richest businessmen in Mexico to a secret banquet where they contributed an average of US$25 million each to the upcoming presidential campaign, for a total of about US$750 million. Many of these billionaires had built massive fortunes from the government's privatization program and so were willing to bankroll the PRI into the future.

Second, Salinas tried to reorganize the party to reach voters outside its traditional sectoral organizations. Together with PRI President Luis Donaldo Colosio, he attempted to transform the party's sectoral structure that defines citizens by their economic identities as producers into a geographically defined structure that would link to citizens in their neighborhoods.

---

[18] Oppenheimer also argues that the move to a free market system meant that international financial institutions and independent research firms conducting economic analyses would want access to financial records, thus increasing pressure for public accounts to be square. This could have limited access to secret funds used for clientelism. Though plausible, I was unable to confirm this argument for Mexico through other sources; however, Geddes (1999: 139) makes a similar argument about personalist authoritarian regimes. See Oppenheimer's comments at http://www.pbs.org/wgbh/pages/frontline/shows/mexico/interviews/oppenheimer.html

However, entrenched sector bosses rallied their troops and blocked the initiative. Later, Salinas tried to expand the amorphous urban popular sector (CNOP) to include service sector workers, the informal sector, and community organizations among the urban poor; however, lack of resources doomed the re-organization effort (author interviews, 1999).[19] In another attempt, the party created the national Territorial Movement (MT), but it was quickly captured by local political strongmen who distributed its resources to their own loyal constituencies and failed to generate substantial new support (author interviews, 1999).

Finally, Salinas used temporary privatization revenues to fund PRONASOL, a poverty-alleviation program with substantial partisan bias. Privatization yielded an average of US$4.1 billion per year during the Salinas presidency (MacLeod, 2004: 73), over US$12 billion of which came from reprivatizing the banking system in 1991 and 1992 (Kessler, 1999: 96). Although 80% of these revenues were locked-in for debt repayment (Rogozinski, 1993; MacLeod, 2004), much of the remainder funded PRONASOL (Kessler, 1999; *Wall Street Journal* 1/8/1993) which ranged from 0.2% of GDP in 1988 to a height of 0.6% of GDP in 1994, or US$2.5 billion.

Ostensibly, PRONASOL was supposed to alleviate the short-term hardships caused by the transition to free market economics. But research by Dresser (1991), Molinar and Weldon (1994), Bruhn (1996), and Díaz-Cayeros, Estévez, and Magaloni (2001) show that the pattern of program funding was designed to enhance the PRI's vote share. Centeno (1994: 65–66) argues that PRONASOL was "the core element of the Salinas Administration's formula for maintaining control ... it was a perfect example of classic PRI tactics, whereby opposition and discontent could be coopted through patronage." Case studies also show that the program helped diminish the attractiveness of opposition parties. For instance, Haber (1997) argues that PRONASOL funds essentially convinced the powerful Popular Defense Committee (CDP) in Durango not to join the PRD and instead create a new center-left opposition party called the Workers Party (PT).

Although effective, the targeted use of poverty-alleviation programs to sustain PRI electoral dominance was limited to the Salinas Administration. The privatization revenues that funded PRONASOL were one-time

---

[19] Interviewees reported that Salinas worried that CNOP strongmen would not target resources to disaffected voters and decided to reroute funds to his PRONASOL program instead.

resources that had mostly dried up by the end of 1994. The incoming Zedillo Administration (1994–2000) generated just US$750 million per year from privatization (MacLeod, 2004: 73), less than one-third of PRONASOL's budget at its height. Subsequent poverty-alleviation programs have been more formula-driven and researchers generally agree that they have not been manipulated to enhance the PRI's vote share (Trejo and Jones, 1998; Rocha Menocal, 2001).

By the 1994 elections, the PRI was in a state of disrepair. The bloated state sector that had supported it was increasingly in private hands; the leaner bureaucracy afforded fewer patronage appointments and only a trickling revenue stream for party coffers; and the once tendril-like reach of the party's affiliated organizations was now shaky and arthritic. Even the stop-gap patronage from privatization revenues had dissipated. By the mid-1990s, both urban and rural constituencies were defecting from the PRI in record numbers and, in the estimation of several analysts, the electorate became consequentially dealigned (Klesner, 1994; Bruhn, 1997). In its search for new revenues, the PRI increasingly consented to campaign finance reform that included increased public funding. But public party finance meant more monitoring and oversight, and these requirements made it more difficult – although not impossible – to generate and spend illicit public funds for partisan benefit.

Manipulating the Rules: Party Finance Regulations and Campaign Spending

Beyond diverting state resources for partisan use, dominant parties such as the PRI can cement their privileges by creating a favorable electoral code. Since dominant parties do not fear reprisals when out of power, they resist campaign finance regulation, and only when their revenue stream is threatened will they endorse public funding and stricter oversight.

Party financing in Mexico was intrinsically tied to the question of electoral competitiveness. Molinar explains that,

In general, countries that have regulated party finances and elections have tried to control the economic power that social agents can exert over politics . . . In Mexico, the goal of regulating party finances is different and in a certain sense prior. What was sought was not so much to isolate the political system from economic influence, but to create the conditions for competitive elections (2001: 8).

But before 1996, the playing field was anything but level. The PRI used its dominant position to lock in advantages either by omitting finance regulations or by designing them in its favor. Table 3.1 summarizes the

TABLE 3.1. *Campaign Finance Regulations, 1929–2000*

Period	Reporting Required	Private Financing Cap	Government Contributions Prohibited	Public Financing	Public Funds Distribution Formula	Estimated PRI Share of Public Funding*	Public Funds for Advertising
1929–1976	No	No	No	No	—	—	None (–1972); 20 min. radio and TV per month (1973)
1977–1986	No	No	No	Yes	Decided by incumbent	Unknown	"Equitable free access" as determined by the govt.
1987–1989	No	No	No	Yes	50% by vote share 50% by seat share	82.2% (1988)	15 min. radio and TV per month
1990–1992	No	No	No	Yes	90% by vote share 10% equally	55.3% (1991)	Proportional to vote share
1993–1995	Yes	Yes	Yes	Yes	90% by vote share 10% equally	65.3% (1994)	Proportional to vote share
1996–2000	Yes	Yes	Yes	Yes	70% by vote share 30% equally	65.2% (1997) 57.4% (2000)	70% by vote share 30% equally

* Author's calculations using the electoral formula and PRI vote and seat shares. Note that financial records are not available before 1994, so the 1988 and 1991 estimates should be taken with caution.

Source: Electoral formulas, various years and Schedler (2005).

Dominant Party Advantages and Opposition Party Failure 109

most important features of campaign finance laws from 1929 to 2000. Until 1962 there was no public campaign funding, no regulation of private donations, no reporting requirements, no oversight of party financing, and, amazingly, no prohibition against government agencies contributing to political campaigns. Thus, in the 33 years following the initiation of single-party dominance, the PRI's advantages were absolute. Beginning in 1963, parties were permitted tax exemptions on stamps, rent, and for funds raised through raffles, carnivals, and the sale of party newspapers; however, as one can readily imagine, these minor changes did virtually nothing to diminish the PRI's massive resource advantages.

The 1977 reform was designed to encourage opposition forces to rededicate their efforts to partisan competition. As a result, it included language that seemed to support a level playing field by stating that "In federal electoral processes, national political parties should have equitable access to the minimum needed to sustain activities directed at obtaining votes" (Constitution of the United States of Mexico, Article 41, paragraph 5). But "equitable" and "minimum" were not defined in the law, and it fell to the Secretary of the Interior – a presidential appointee and always a close ally – to decide the amount and distribution of public funds. It is likely that the opposition saw little benefit from the reform; however, because there were no reporting requirements, we cannot know. More importantly, there were still no limits on private or governmental financing.

By the late 1980s, opportunities for generating money from state-owned enterprises and the federal public bureaucracy had fallen substantially. In order to wean itself from the diminishing flow of illicit public dollars, the PRI instituted a reform in 1987 that mandated increased public campaign funding. But the formula advantaged the incumbent. Half the funds were distributed based on party vote share in the previous election and the other half was dispersed based on the share of seats won in either the plurality district races or in the multimember districts. The Secretary of the Interior decided which method to use for the latter half. When this formula was employed in the 1988 elections, the PRI came away with 82.2% of all public funding because it won 68.1% of the votes and 96.3% of the plurality seats in the previous election.[20] Against this backdrop, the increase to 15 minutes of free radio and television time was insignificant and, as shown in Figure 3.5, the PRI came away with 86% of all television

---

[20] Author's calculations based on the relevant electoral formula summarized in Table 3.1. Financial records are not available so this estimate should be taken with some caution.

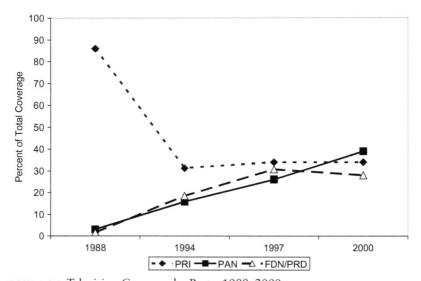

FIGURE 3.5. Television Coverage by Party, 1988–2000.
Note: Data reported for "FDN/PRD" refer to the FDN for 1988 and to the PRD for 1994–2000.
Sources: Data for 1988 come from Arredondo et al., 1991: 62–64 and Martínez, 2002. Other estimates appear in Trejo Delabre, 2000. Data were not available for 1991; however, media financed by IFE resulted in 31% of the spots for the PRI, 22.4% for the PAN, and 13.8% for the PRD (Magar and Molinar: 1995: 134). Data for 1994 are from the Federal Elections Institute (IFE), calculated from Magar and Molinar, 1995: 134–135. Other estimates come from the Mexican Academy of Human Rights (AMDH). Data for 1997 come from Lawson, 2002: 161 and Trejo Delabre, 2000. Other estimates appear in Martínez, 2002: 2. Data for 2000 are candidate coverage in the two main news shows from IFE (see Lawson 2004: 189). Other estimates by *Reforma* newspaper and Lawson's MIT study appear in Lawson, 2004: 189; additional estimates come from the AMDH.

coverage that year. In addition, there were still no reporting requirements and no limits on private or government contributions to campaigns.

The 1990 law that was in place for the 1991 midterm elections maintained all of the PRI's advantages from the previous code; however it changed the distribution formula so that 90% of public funds were doled out by previous vote share and 10% was given equally to all registered parties. This yielded 53.3% of public funds for the PRI, a minor concession since it would have taken 64.5% under the prior formula.[21] Free media time was now also proportional to the vote and when combined with the

---

[21] Ibid.

Dominant Party Advantages and Opposition Party Failure   111

opposition's increase in resources, yielded 31% of all media coverage for the PRI, compared to 22.4% for the PAN and 13.8% for the PRD.[22] Yet again, the lack of reporting requirements or regulations for private or government financing of campaigns suggests that the PRI simply added the new public funds to its still comparatively large albeit falling advantages from other sources.

The 1993 law that was used for the 1994 presidential elections included the first restrictions on private and governmental financing as well as the first reporting requirements. Now cash and in-kind donations were prohibited from government agencies, mercantile businesses, foreign businesses or individuals, or from churches or sects with a religious character. By this time, of course, those contributions would have been worth less anyway because the state-owned enterprises that had served as cash cows for the PRI's campaigns accounted for just 9% of GDP, down from 22.3% a decade earlier. Private contributions from individuals were also limited to 1% of total party financing and business contributions to 5% (up to 10% of donations could be anonymous). Parties were now also required to report their total income and expenditures, but not specific information on how they spent their resources. As a result, we know that the PRI had 65.3% of public financing, but more importantly, 72% of total financing (see Figure 3.6). The PAN came away with 14% of the total, and the PRD with just 3%. In addition, the PRI also still occupied more media time at 33.4% of the total compared to the PAN's 21.9% and the PRD's 15.8%. Clearly, party financing still favored the PRI and put opposition parties at a severe disadvantage in the electoral competition game.

These figures, however, under-represent the PRI's true advantages in 1994. Even though the new campaign finance regulations helped trim the PRI's use of public funds for its partisan gain, it still benefited from hidden resources. In 1996, the nonprofit Civic Alliance helped uncover the president's use of an obscure element in the Constitution (Art. 74, 4, paragraph 3) to create a secret budget inside the line item "Branch 23" that yielded an average of US$180.4 million per year from 1988 to 1994. It is not known for certain how the money was spent, although Cornelius (2004: 61) states that it "was a major source of campaign financing for state-level PRI organizations." Also, 60% of the substantially larger budget of Branch 23 rewarded loyal bureaucrats with lavish bonuses.[23] Thus,

---

[22] Ibid.

[23] See Secretary of the Treasury (SHCP) Press Release, 10/22/02, at http://www.shcp.gob.mx/estruct/uctov/discurso/2000/ace4200.html.

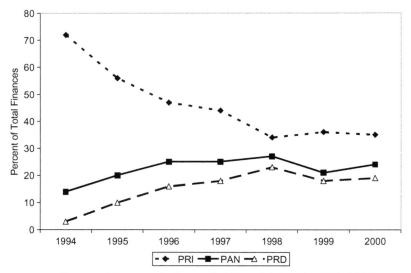

FIGURE 3.6. Reported Revenue by Party (Public and Private), 1994–2000. *Source:* Lujambio, 2001.

the secret budget was a standard part of the PRI's patronage system. The PRI also continued to search for private funding and there is evidence that it accepted contributions far above the legal limit. In July 1993, one year before the presidential elections, the PRI accepted US$15.1 million in counter checks from Union Bank owner Carlos Cabal Peniche.[24] The contribution was essentially a kickback. A portion of Cabal Peniche's huge fortune – a fortune that inexplicably went from almost nothing to an estimated US$1.1 billion in six years – was acquired through bad loans that were converted into public debt in the FOBAPROA banking scandal.[25]

The 1996 reforms that were used in both the 1997 midterm elections and the 2000 presidential elections made significant advances and consequentially leveled the playing field. Now 70% of public funds were distributed by vote share and 30% was given equally among all registered parties. Public financing in 1997 was 12 times its 1994 nominal peso value

---

[24] Some believe that Cabal Peniche contributed more for a longer period. See Juan Ramón Jiménez, "Cabal, la historia secreta" in *La Crisis* at http://www.lacrisis.com.mx/especial011203.htm.

[25] Following the 1994 economic crisis, the banking sector collapsed. The banks were reprivatized in 1991–1992, but many became overextended due to mismanagement and bad loans made by private owners to their friends, family, and business partners. By mid-1999, US$65 billion (13.5% of GDP) had been transferred to the government bank insurance program (FOBAPROA). Over the PRD's objections, the PAN and PRI voted to transfer most of this debt to the public debt. For details, see Kessler, 1999.

Dominant Party Advantages and Opposition Party Failure 113

or 4.4 times larger as a proportion of GDP, making Mexico's elections among the most expensive per capita in the world. Private financing was severely limited to 0.05% of each party's total funding, a 120-fold reduction over the previous law. Perhaps most importantly, detailed reporting requirements were now put in place and the Federal Elections Institute was endowed with investigative and sanctioning powers. As a result, even though the PRI retained 65.2% of public funding in 1997, it accounted for a reported 44% of total party financing. The PAN took 25% and the PRD took 14%. Media coverage was similar, with the PRI taking up 34% of all air time and the challengers each taking 20%. In reality, the PRI had a somewhat larger advantage because the president's secret budget still contained an average of US$61 million per year from 1994 to 1997. Nevertheless, spending was much more equitable and, as a result, the opposition parties together improved their vote share enough to strip the PRI of its majority in Congress for the first time.

Finally, the 2000 elections used the same electoral code and official records show that the PRI took 57.4% of public funding, but accounted for only 35% of total campaign revenue compared to the PAN's 24% and the PRD's 19%. In the media, all three parties had roughly the same amount of coverage, but the PRI fell below the PAN for the first time. In television airtime alone, the PAN took 29% of the total, the PRI got just over 26%, and the PRD got 21%.

Yet these numbers again fall short of a full representation of total spending. Where it could, the PRI continued to squeeze funds out of the now greatly diminished public sector. In 2002, it was revealed that the director of the state-run oil company PEMEX and his top aides transferred US$147.2 million through the Union of Mexican Petroleum Workers (STPRM) to the PRI's presidential campaign. As Mexico's largest state-owned enterprise that contributed about one-third of all government revenues in the 1980s and 1990s, PEMEX was the crown jewel of what Denise Dresser called "the party's piggy bank, its own personal checkbook" (*Proceso*, 2/17/02). When the details of the case were confirmed by the Attorney General, *La Jornada* newspaper editorialized that "for the first time there is precise documentation of an operation in which public funds were used to support the PRI. The practice was an open secret, everyone knew, but it could not be proven as long as the PRI remained in power."[26]

---

[26] "PEMEX: Frentes del escándolo" *La Jornada*, January 24, 2002. http://www.jornada. unam.mx/2002/01/24/edito.html

114 *Why Dominant Parties Lose*

What was new in 2000 is that the opposition also cheated. With the help of long-time business associates, Fox created a support organization called Amigos de Fox to raise money and recruit campaign workers. In a post-electoral investigation conducted by the Federal Elections Institute (IFE), it was found that Amigos helped the Fox campaign spend more than the allowed limit and receive illegal funds from foreign donors. Although Amigos' budget has never been revealed publicly, the electoral court (TEPJF) levied a fine of US$56.4 million against the PAN and its coalition ally the Green Party (PVEM). If we take this as the actual amount of overspending – although it was probably more – then it represents about 40% of what the PRI received through the PEMEX scandal. Yet despite these illicit sources of campaign funding, the overall distribution in 2000, like in 1997, was much more equitable than before. In Chapter 7, I discuss financing in the 2000 elections in more detail and show how the level playing field contributed to the PRI's loss of the presidency in 2000, thus ending single-party dominance.

In sum, during the 1990s, the dramatic resource asymmetries that separated the incumbent and challengers were reduced by the privatization of public enterprises, increases in public campaign financing, reporting requirements, spending limits, prohibitions against government contributions to parties, and the regulation of private financing. By 1997 the playing field was quite level and Mexico came as close to many established democracies to a fair or neutral market for votes where no party held an outright pre-electoral advantage. As a result, opposition parties had greater access to the voters.

CONCLUSION

Despite predictions from Mexico-specific theories and abstract models about party competition that PRI dominance should have been unsustainable, equilibrium dominance persisted from 1929 until the PRI lost its majority control of Congress in 1997 and lost the presidency in 2000. Challenger parties failed despite periodic opportunities because the PRI was able to "firefight" opposition mobilization on one flank by changing its policy appeals and simultaneously demobilize forces on its other flank with patronage and repression. Among the available tools, patronage was the preferred option. The PRI generated clientelistic benefits that it could use to buy voter support by transforming public resources into partisan goods and subordinating the federal public bureaucracy. The party's access to illicit public goods was substantial for much of the 20th century because the state played a major role in the economy. However, the government's free market response to the 1982 debt crisis sapped the PRI's resource base and forced its massive patronage machine to grind toward a halt. The party was forced to turn to legal public campaign financing as well as private donations. Despite some illicit funding in the 1994 and 2000 elections, the smaller public sector, leaner federal bureaucracy, and stricter campaign finance oversight substantially leveled the playing field and allowed opposition parties to compete for votes in an increasingly fair political marketplace.

The macro-level analysis presented in this chapter helps understand how the PRI's advantages allowed it to maintain power by limiting opposition party expansion. To complete this argument, we need to see how the PRI's advantages affected opposition party development at the micro-level. In this context, we need to ask two questions. Why would any prospective candidates and activists join the opposition if they know that the PRI's advantages will force them to lose and possibility expose them and their families to physical harm? Provided that there will be some citizens who are willing to forego winning and risk harm to oppose the dominant party, what kind of citizens will they be? In Chapter 4, I provide a theory of elite activism in dominant party systems that generates predictions about who joins the opposition as the incumbent's resource advantages and use of repression change. Chapter 5 then uses in-depth data from candidates and activists to test these predictions. Together, Chapters 4 and 5 provide an individual-level argument about opposition party development that is consistent with and expands upon the party-level findings in this chapter.

PART TWO

THE MICRO-PERSPECTIVE

4

Why Participate?

A Theory of Elite Activism in Dominant Party Systems

All political parties rely on citizens to serve as candidates that run for office and activists that mobilize voters; however, because opposition parties in dominant party systems are resource-poor, they rise or fall based on their ability to attract volunteers to fill these posts. But if prospective candidates and national-level activists (a group I refer to collectively as party elites or elite activists)[1] know that challenger parties are at a competitive disadvantage, why would they join them instead of joining the dominant party or simply abstaining? How do changes in the competitive environment, such as decreases in the dominant party's resource advantages and its use of repression, affect the profile of citizens willing to join a challenger?

This brief chapter addresses these questions by supplying a theory of elite activist party affiliation that is appropriate for studying dominant party systems. My concern here is not with the visionaries or charismatics that form parties, but with the candidates and activists who decide to support them and thus provide fuel for the entrepreneur's spark. The affiliation model takes for granted that a founder has formed an opposition party[2] and that prospective party elites know that the dominant party benefits from hyper-incumbency advantages, thus distorting competitive dynamics as depicted in Chapter 2. The payoff for constructing a separate model of party affiliation is that it allows us to generate very specific hypotheses about the sincere policy preferences of party elites that

---

[1] In Chapter 2, I argue that candidates and national-level activists are very similar types in challengers to dominant parties.
[2] See "The Founder's Problem" in Chapter 2, Appendix B.

119

120   *Why Dominant Parties Lose*

the challenger can attract as political conditions change. The model also shows how opposition parties can grow in dominant party systems even without elite splits from the incumbent party, often considered a necessary condition to get viable challengers in such systems (Geddes, 1999b).

Theories of party affiliation for candidates and activists are not new, but existing models were developed to study partisan dynamics in fully competitive democracies. Due to this focus, they assume a neutral or perfectly competitive electoral market in which no party has an outright advantage and the costs of participation are equal across parties. Although these theories may illuminate important aspects of party competition in many of the established democracies, they gloss over the very things that make dominant parties dominant. Once we take unfair competition into account, the standard assumption of purely instrumental incentives for affiliation in existing models leads to the prediction that all ambitious politicians should join the dominant party and no one should join a challenger party. Even more broadly, the standard assumption cannot account for the affiliation of any party elites to an entire class of parties even in fully competitive democracies when the probability of victory is low and/or the costs of participation are high. Based on in-depth interviews with candidates and activists in Mexico's PAN and PRD, I argue that prospective party elites are motivated not only by the instrumental benefits of holding office, but also by the selective expressive benefits of campaigning for a partisan cause in which they believe.

Once expressive benefits are taken into account, the model shows that as the incumbent's resource advantages drive the challenger's probability of victory down, only prospective party elites who are increasingly distant from the status quo on policy are willing to join the opposition. Similarly, as the cost of joining the opposition rises relative to the dominant party – either due to unequal opportunity costs or direct repression – those willing to join the opposition are more extreme on policy. Simply put, one has to be a true believer to join a losing and potentially dangerous cause. The model also shows that two different types of party elites that I call office-seekers and message-seekers react differently to changes in the competitive environment and that, paradoxically, office-seekers who join the opposition are more extreme on policy when the chances of winning are the lowest.

The chapter proceeds as follows. First, I discuss the importance of selective expressive incentives for elite activism in challengers to dominant parties. Second, I introduce office-seekers and message-seekers as two types of party elites that place different importance on winning elections versus

Why Participate? 121

expressing policy goals. Third, I present the formal model of party elite affiliation. Before concluding, I use the model to generate six hypotheses about the characteristics of candidates and activists who join the opposition under various levels of incumbency advantage.

WHY JOIN? INSTRUMENTAL AND EXPRESSIVE INCENTIVES FOR ELITE ACTIVISM

To understand why citizens become candidates and activists in dominant party systems and when they choose to affiliate with the dominant party or with an opposition party, I build a formal decision-theoretic model of party affiliation. The model adapts work by Aldrich and Bianco (1992) to dominant party settings by allowing the costs of activism to vary according to insider versus outsider status, giving the incumbent an electoral advantage due to its patronage resources, and allowing elite activists to value partisan expression for its own sake.[3]

Most current models view party elites as pure instrumentalists.[4] In Schlesinger's words, "Parties are the product of democratic elections and, therefore, destined to be primarily vehicles for allowing individuals ambitious for public office to compete for office effectively" (1991: vii). Schlesinger's participants as well as those in work by Rohde (1979), Aldrich and Bianco (1992), and Cox (1997: Ch. 8) are exclusively interested in winning, from which they derive ego rents associated with the prestige, power, and notoriety of public office. But this leads us to a dead end. As I showed in Chapter 2 using party utility functions, if challengers were pure instrumentalists and directed toward winning the next election, then they would have no reason to exist in dominant party systems. The asymmetric probability of victory would discourage potential founders from forming a challenger party if they only value winning. The same logic applies to potential party elites deciding whether to join an existing opposition party (Epstein, 1986; Cox, 1997: 166). Consequently, opposition parties would not exist and dominant party systems would transform into one-party regimes that are in equilibrium without the possibility of endogenous change.

---

[3] In making the model decision-theoretic, I assume that there are no barriers to affiliation. That is, existing party members do not prohibit any prospective elite activist from joining.

[4] Analogous models for lower-level rank-and-file activists treat them as highly policy-motivated (see Aldrich, 1983: 976). However, analytically here and empirically in the next chapter I deal exclusively with high-level participants who form their party's power structure.

Employing a purely instrumental calculus of participation thus fails to account for an entire class of activism in organizations that are doomed to lose. For instance, on a purely instrumental basis, third parties in the United States would never form, the reformist outsider parties described by Shefter (1977a, 1977b, 1994) would not exist, the Green parties in Western Europe described by Kitschelt (1989a) would not have emerged, and the radical rightwing parties described by Kitschelt (1995), and Givens (2005) would never organize. More broadly, all disadvantaged "protest," outsider, and social movement parties would simply fail to form or quickly collapse as instrumentally rational politicians abandon them. Thus, challengers to advantaged parties face a collective action problem not unlike what Lichbach calls the "rebel's dilemma" where "Rational dissidents will not voluntarily contribute... No potential dissent will become actual dissent; none will assist in either overturning the state or forcing the state to redress grievances" (1998: xii).

How do challengers to dominant parties overcome the collective action problem and give prospective party elites a reason to join? More specifically, how do opposition party founders generate selective incentives to recruit elite activists? A number of solutions have been offered for the collective action problem confronting prospective groups that are unlikely to fulfill their goals in their first attempt (for surveys, see Aldrich, 1993; Lichbach, 1996; Chong, 2000). Two stand out as plausible ways to inspire partisan activism: material side-payments and expressive motivations.

Olson (1971) argued that large groups that seek infinitely divisible collective benefits, such as the policy promises in a typical political party's platform, will often fail to form because individuals perceive the costs of contributing as greater than the benefit of receiving the good without participating. One of the ways to circumvent this free-rider problem is to make selective benefits exclusively available to participants. Olson (1971) and Tullock (1971) focused on material side-payments such as stipends and in-kind goods. However, this argument makes little sense for resource-poor opposition parties. In the case of Mexico, challengers scarcely had sufficient funds to establish national party headquarters. Until the 1990s, they had skeletal paid staffs that numbered in the single digits, they ran sparse campaigns that were largely financed by the candidates themselves if at all, and they barely had enough money to keep the lights on. Work on challengers in Taiwan (Chu 2001; Solinger 2001; Cotton 1997; Ferdinand, 1998), Singapore (Rahim, 2001), and Malaysia (Gomez, 1994) also points to opposition parties' persistent resource poverty and reliance on volunteer activists. It is possible that opposition parties in these systems make material side payments to their members that were hidden from researchers, but to have escaped detection, these benefits were probably too small to outweigh the substantial costs of joining the opposition.

Instead of modifying baseline models by adding material side payments, I concentrate on what Chong refers to as "narrowly rational expressive" benefits (1991: 73). These benefits accrue to self-interested activists when they are able to "effectively express their anger or disapproval over a policy or existing state of affairs" (1991: 88). Such a benefit comes whether or not the party wins the next election, but rather from the sheer act of participation. It is thus what Clark and Wilson (1961) call a *purposive selective benefit*. The benefit is purposive because the outcomes sought, such as changing economic policy or affecting the openness of the political system, are collective goods tied to the group's purpose (Clark and Wilson, 1961: 135 and fn 7). At the same time, the benefit is selective because, according to Moe, "If group policies reflect [a participant's] ideological, religious, or moral principles, he may feel a responsibility to 'do his part' in support of these policies... It is not the actual provision of these collective goods that represents the source of purposive benefits in this case, but the support and pursuit of worthwhile collective goods" (1980: 118). Thus, nonparticipants cannot, by definition, access these selective goods.

Expressive benefits can be powerful enough to overcome high costs of participation and other disadvantages that groups with a low probability of success might experience. Clark and Wilson state "If organizational purposes constitute the primary incentive, then low prestige, unpleasant working conditions, and other material and solidary advantages will be outweighed – in the mind of the contributor – by the 'good' ends which the organization may eventually achieve" (1961: 136). Chong further implies that expression is a more salient incentive when the balance of power tilts substantially against the out group, as it clearly does when opposition parties challenge a dominant party. He writes, "We are able to transform society and 'make history' by way of collective action only when there is a worthy opponent that must be subdued" (1991: 88). Moe echoes this idea when he states that "Collective goods can actually generate their own selective incentives" (1980: 118). For some citizens, the allure of expression is powerful enough to motivate participation even when they know that their individual contribution will not appreciably improve the chances of achieving their organization's goals (Moe, 1980: 118).

Opposition party founders act as political entrepreneurs who facilitate the selective expressive benefits enjoyed by elite activists. The potential for these expressive benefits exist in society, but the founder makes them accessible by creating a focal organization through which participants can express their dissatisfaction with the incumbent. Without such entrepreneurial activity, the will to oppose the dominant party might exist as a latent force in society, but actual opposition will fail to materialize.

Expressive benefits already play a prominent role in studies of social movements (Tarrow, 1994; Hechter, 1987; Chong, 1991) and interest groups (Moe, 1980). Most likely they have been excluded from studies of parties because unlike nonpartisan organizations that are not expected to achieve their goals over the short-term, parties are typically predicted not to form when they cannot win. In dominant party systems, challenger parties, like social movements, are oriented toward changing the organization and distribution of power in society by transforming public hearts and minds or, in Schattschneider's (1942) words, by "mobilizing bias." Since challengers to dominant parties are also unlikely to win over the short-term, their collective goals also generate expressive incentives for their activists that function as selective purposive benefits. But expressive benefits alone give no rationale for the existence of opposition parties in place of social movements. Challenger parties are also clearly interested in winning elections just like their counterparts in fully competitive democracies. Therefore, I argue that modeling participation in opposition parties in dominant party systems requires us to include both instrumental and expressive benefits.[5]

On-the-ground fieldwork in Mexico confirms that opposition party elites thought about their participation in terms of both expressive and instrumental benefits. For instance, past party presidents felt a tension between winning votes and maintaining ideological purity. PRD President Andrés Manuel López Obrador (1996–1999) stated, "The strategy should be to win votes by winning society" (Saldierna, 1999: 3). In a remarkably similar statement, PAN President Felipe Calderón Hinojosa (1996–1999) declared that "The challenge is to win elections without losing the party" (cited in Mizrahi, 1998: 95). Leaders of Schlesinger's purely instrumental parties would never put limits on their parties' expansion. Alternatively, leaders of purely expressive organizations such as communist

---

[5] Some work on European parties and small parties gets conceptually closer to the research on social movements (see, for instance, Panebianco, 1988; Pomper, 1992). However, this work does not deal with incentives for participation directly.

office. Message-seekers prioritize expressive benefits and prefer to operate behind the scenes, crafting the party's message, expanding its base, and winning elections from society, one heart and mind at a time. They were no less committed to political change but preferred to play a role inside the party bureaucracy or in their home communities without running for office. While office-seekers were interested in affecting political change from the top-down through the use of the bully pulpit, message-seekers were committed to political change from the bottom-up.

Some typical quotes from author interviews with office-seekers in Mexico's opposition parties help bring them to life:

- "You can't really influence policy unless you first win the election. I want to change a lot of things in Mexico, but we can't do any of that unless we win."
- "I joined the party to become a Federal Deputy. I put in my time working in the party, but now I'm ready to run for office."
- "From the very beginning, the idea was to win office. We didn't have the resources to get anyone elected, and we had to convince friends and family to run as candidates, but we always wanted to get our people elected."
- "If I don't run for office, then who will get rid of the PRI?"

Some typical quotes from message-seekers help show their distinctiveness:

- "We need to transform society before we can change politics."
- "I want our party to win, but not at the risk of becoming just like the PRI."
- "I support our candidates, but my role is to work here in the neighborhood, helping people improve their lives and teaching them what our party stands for."
- "If we win without changing people's minds, then what have we won? First, we need to be a party of civic education."
- "Consciousness-raising is the most important thing we do. We are building a strong organization in these working class neighborhoods. Neither the PAN nor the PRI can say they have the kind of base organization that we have."

In the remainder of the chapter, I supply utility functions that formalize how each party elite type values instrumental and expressive incentives for participation. In conjunction with findings from Chapter 2, these

Why Participate?

expressions then allow us to derive hypotheses about the characteristics of party elites who should affiliate with challenger parties as the incumbent's resource advantages and the costs of participation change.

Office-Seekers

When deciding whether to affiliate with the dominant party or a challenger, office-seekers take account of three incentives. First, they examine the pre-election probability of victory, preferring to join the party that offers the higher likelihood of election and thus the better chance that they will win office. Second, they examine the difficulty of winning a nomination in each of the parties, preferring more permeable parties that offer new joiners the quickest access to the ballot (Cox, 1997). Finally, they prefer to work for a party with which they agree on policy because this will maximize their ability to express support for a cause that they admire. Thus, the expected utility to a prospective office-seeker i of action k, defined as affiliating with a dominant party (d) or a challenger (c), can be specified as

$$Eu_i(a_k) = p_k[s_k u(o) + u(e_k)] - c_k \tag{1}$$

This function states that the expected utility of each possible affiliation decision (a_k) is given by the probability of winning the election as a candidate with party k (p_k), the probability of nomination in party k (s_k), the benefit of holding office regardless of party affiliation ($u(o)$), the selective benefit of expressing the partisan message of party k ($u(e_k)$), and the cost of affiliating with party k (c_k).

What makes the utility function in (1) representative of an office-seeker's incentive structure is that the probability of victory tempers the value of all other sources of positive utility. An office-seeker likes to get more of the purposive benefit that comes from working for a cause in which he believes, but he is less interested in working for a good cause if it has a lower probability of victory. As a result, he may work for a party whose cause he perceives to be less worthwhile but offers a higher chance of victory. Office-seekers are principled but their first goal is to win.

The $u(o)$ term captures the utility of office for its own sake and includes the ego rents associated with holding public office as well as the "thrill of competing." Since this benefit is the same for successful office-seekers whether they win with the dominant party or the challenger, it is a constant and not consequential in choosing between the parties. The cost term c_k

is party specific to capture the asymmetric costs of participation in the dominant party compared to the opposition. The nomination term s_k is also party specific since it may be easier for newcomers to secure a nomination in a smaller challenger party than in a larger dominant party, and this could plausibly outweigh the other disincentives for joining the opposition.

Prospective participants assess the selective benefit derived from partisan expression $u(e_k)$ through their evaluations of the parties' identities that they experience in two ways. First, they know the parties' strategically chosen policy announcement in the prior election (x_c and x_d). Since these announcements (i.e., platforms) are linked to the probability of winning, they enter into prospective joiners' utility functions through p_c and p_d from the model of party competition presented in Chapter 2. Second, prospective joiners experience the parties' identities not only through their highly distilled platforms, but also through the broader set of relationships that existing party operatives establish with voters, including speeches, campaign advertising, and local canvassing. Thus, if the platform represents the party's focalized message, then its operatives' actions represent the broader band of information that the party transmits to society. If prospective joiners want to express the message of a party they agree with, then they will want to join a party whose existing participants' sincere preferences are much like their own.

I capture the value of these expressive incentives for elite activism through the congruence between existing members' sincere preferences and the sincere preference of the prospective joiner. Thus,

$$u(e_k) = -(\omega_k - x_i)^2 \tag{2}$$

where x_i represents the prospective elite activists' sincere policy preference and ω_k represents the mean existing opinion within each party. Specifically,

$$\omega_k = \left(\frac{\sum x_{io} + \sum x_{im}}{n_k} \right) \tag{3}$$

where x_{io} is the policy preference of each office-seeker i in party k, x_{im} is the preference of each message-seeker i in party k, and n is the total number of elite activists in party k. I use the mean rather than the median because the mean captures the amount of noise in the band of messages that the party communicates to the voters. In addition to the average existing preference, prospective joiners should be concerned with intra-party

Why Participate? 125

parties as classically conceived would likely show no willingness to water down their parties' purposes to win votes because their goals are imbued with what Clark and Wilson (1961: 147) call a "moral or sacrosanct quality." Instead, leaders of Mexico's opposition parties tried to run a middle ground between loyalty to policy goals and expansion designed to beat the incumbent at the polls.

Elite activists also revealed a mix of motivations that included expressive and instrumental elements. In more than 100 in-depth interviews, I found some participants who felt as though they were involved in an historical and ideological crusade for social transformation against the incumbent PRI and their rival opposition party. Some on the left yearned for a socialist utopia and some on the right dreamed of redressing the historical evil done to the cause of 19th-century liberalism by the PRI's interpretation of the Mexican Revolution. Others, however, preferred to take stock of public opinion and make the most electorally efficient appeals. The Mexico Party Personnel Surveys show an almost even split between those who prized expressive or instrumental benefits. When asked whether they preferred their party to maintain a firm ideological line regardless of public opinion or instead make more flexible appeals at the risk of a less coherent program, just over half of PAN and PRD respondents chose ideological purity. How should we model these mixed motivations for elite activism?

TYPES OF PARTY ELITES: OFFICE-SEEKERS AND MESSAGE-SEEKERS

Although elite activists may hold a mix of motivations that range between the purely instrumental and the purely expressive, in in-depth interviews, I most often encountered two modal types of participants in the opposition that I call office-seekers and message-seekers.[6] Office-seekers value instrumental benefits over expressive ones and thus dedicate their energies toward helping the party win. They typically promoted themselves as effective community leaders who enjoyed public speaking and wanted to pursue particular policies in government by winning elected

---

[6] An alternative way to model activist types would allow mixing over motivations. Activists would be chosen from a distribution of motivations that range from pure office-seeking to pure message-seeking through some stochastic process. Instead, I simplified the modeling exercise by specifying two activist types. It is important to note, however, that, as developed below, I make no *ex ante* assumptions about the underlying distribution of office-seekers and message-seekers in the population or their policy preferences.

Why Participate? 129

variability because expressing the message of a more unified party will enhance their individual contribution.

Message-Seekers

Another type of elite activist enters politics to pursue programmatic goals through partisan political pressure, the dissemination of information, and the construction of a broad-based movement. These citizens want to transform politics from society by winning hearts and minds, pressuring the incumbent to change policy, and ultimately by creating a groundswell of support that will naturally sweep them into power. Whether on the left or the right, they believe they are engaged in a Gramscian war of position. Rather than just campaigning for a particular candidate, they campaign for an historical cause such as the realization of a free, just, pious, socialist, or liberal society.

While office-seekers are interested in winning office in order to change politics, message-seekers want to change political interests in society in order to win elections. Winning converts is more important than winning votes, and to accomplish this task they invest substantial time and personal pride. If office-seekers seek change, message-seekers seek transformation. They tend to prefer to work inside the party to grow the movement's core constituency, and they are typically more interested in creating new activists rather than attracting sympathizers who are less deeply committed to the cause.

Yet message-seekers are not necessarily programmatic radicals. They are party elites for whom political change from the bottom-up is more important than winning office. Since message-seekers derive less utility than do office-seekers from winning, they may be more willing to join an opposition party over the dominant party at lower levels of policy disagreement with the incumbent. In other words, message-seekers may be passionate centrists rather than rabid radicals, and this makes them different from Kitschelt's (1989a) "ideologues" and Panebianco's (1988) "believers" that are defined as extremists. Message-seekers, like office-seekers, are defined by what they value, not what they advocate. Taking this approach means that we can see how participants react in the aggregate to changes in the competitive environment.[7]

---

[7] Similarly, message-seekers are not the programmatically extreme activists in nonformal (Hirschman, 1970; May, 1973) and formal (Aldrich, 1983; Jackson, 1999) models of intra-party dynamics.

Combining the expressive and instrumental incentives for participation, and applying a functional form appropriate for message-seekers yields the following expected utility function:

$$Eu_i(a_k) = u(e_k)[\alpha + p_k] - c_k \qquad (4)$$

This function states that the expected utility of action k (a_k) is given by the utility of expressing the party's message $(u(e_k))$, the probability of victory (p_k), minus a cost for participating (c_k). Unlike office-seekers, message-seekers do not care about the utility of office or the probability of winning nomination. In the function, α is constant across all message-seekers and indicates that, unlike office-seekers, message-seekers value partisan expression partly for its own sake without discounting it by the probability of victory. At the same time, the functional form captures the idea that message-seekers also naturally prefer to voice their perspective with a larger party that has a better chance of winning.[8]

A key assumption for the model concerns the origin of party elites' policy preferences (the x_is). All citizens are potential party elites, so the overall distribution of preferences should be like the aggregate distribution of policy preferences in the electorate itself. I assume that office-seekers, message-seekers, and voters are all uniformly distributed over a single dimension that we can represent on the interval $[-1,1]$ with a density of $\frac{1}{2}$. This assumption is important mostly for what it does not do. It does not make any *ex ante* assumptions about policy-related differences between voters and party elites. As alluded to earlier, models of intraparty dynamics in the nonformal (Hirschman, 1970; May, 1973) and formal (Jackson, 1999) tradition assume that activists are more extreme than voters. This builds one of the main conclusions into the assumptions rather than deriving it from the dynamics of affiliation. In my model, the only difference between voters and the two types of party elites is that they have different utility functions (i.e., they value different incentives).[9]

---

[8] In a future extension, message-seekers' utility might be modeled with a curvilinear relationship to the probability of victory. When the party is very small and has a low probability of victory, message-seekers may see little use in voicing their position to a miniscule movement that has little chance of swaying public opinion. When the movement is very large, participants may find diminished value in preaching to the converted. Thus, the expressive utility of activism might be modeled as a logit curve.

[9] These assumptions are similar to those of the citizen-candidate model proposed by Osborne and Slivinski (1996) and Besley and Coate (1997).

Why Participate?

RESULTS OF THE MODEL

We can now combine the elements of the model to generate hypotheses about the sincere policy preferences of elite activists who join the opposition as the competitive environment changes. Specifically, we want to know how office-seekers and message-seekers partition themselves between the incumbent and the challenger as the incumbent's probability of winning changes with asymmetric resources and costs of participation. I assume that $x_d < x_c$, so that the opposition party is always to the left of the dominant party (i.e., no leapfrogging is allowed, although the two parties may be minimally differentiated on policy).[10] The model produces analogous results when the challenger is on the right.

The key finding that I want to highlight is the policy preference of the pivotal office-seeker (call her x_o^*) and message-seeker (call her x_m^*), who are just indifferent between affiliating with the dominant party and the challenger. Finding these hypothetical participants' policy preferences will tell us about all party elites' affiliation decisions because all those to the right of the indifferent participant will choose the incumbent and all those to the left will choose the challenger.

To find x_o^* and x_m^*, I solve the simultaneous equations given by (1), (2), (3), and (4). In Figure 4.1A, I show how office-seekers and message-seekers partition themselves between the incumbent and challenger when the costs of participation are equal (i.e., there is no repression and no asymmetry in opportunity costs).[11] To understand this figure, imagine that, given the incumbent's resource advantages and the relative policy offers of the two parties, the challenger has a 25% chance of winning the election. If this were true, then the model predicts that all office-seekers whose sincere policy preference is to the left of −.45 will join the challenger. In other words, one would have to be this far to the left of the status quo to want to join a party with only a 25% chance of winning rather than join one with a 75% chance. Correspondingly, all office-seekers whose policy preferences are to the right of −.45 − the commanding majority − are

---

[10] Since dominant parties typically compete in all districts while opposition parties often have regional support, it makes sense to examine the case of competition between the incumbent and a single challenger. Competition between two challengers in the absence of the dominant party occurs rarely if at all.

[11] In order to make the presentation possible in two dimensions and to highlight the effect of changes in the probability of victory and the costs of participation, I assume that the probability of nomination is equal and certain for office-seekers in both parties. We could change this assumption, but the new results would follow a very similar pattern.

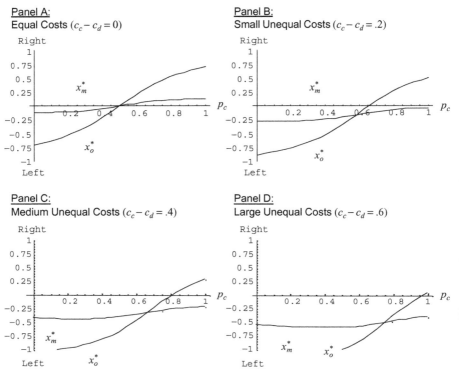

FIGURE 4.1. Predicted Policy Preferences of Indifferent Elite Activists with Changing Costs of Participation

predicted to join the incumbent because they are insufficiently opposed to it on policy to forego the substantially higher chance of winning that it offers. At the same time, when the challenger has a 25% chance of winning, all message-seekers who are further to the left than −.10 are predicted to join the opposition while the rest join the incumbent. As above, since message-seekers care less about winning, they are willing to join a losing challenger at a lower level of policy disagreement with the incumbent.

If we think about opposition party development as occurring over multiple elections where the challenger slowly chips away at the incumbent, then the panels in Figure 4.1 provide an aggregate picture of opposition party building. Elite activists join the incumbent in overwhelming numbers when the challenger is unlikely to win, but some are so far from the status quo on policy that they join the challenger. They do not partition themselves equally between the parties until there is an equal chance of

Why Participate? 133

winning with either. Perhaps most interesting is the different dynamic of aggregate change among new office-seekers and new message-seekers. As the probability of challenger victory rises, new office-seekers are willing to join the opposition at lower levels of policy disagreement with the incumbent than are new message-seekers. This finding appears obvious once we consider how each activist type values the various incentives for participation, but before thinking of affiliation in this way, office-seeker extremism would have been highly counter-intuitive.

Modeling Unequal Costs and Abstention due to Alienation

The perfectly equal costs represented in Figure 4.1A are an overly generous representation of partisan dynamics in dominant party systems. Costs will always be asymmetric and are largely controlled by the incumbent. Privileged access to an old boys' network of favors raises the opportunity cost of joining a challenger. Costs are of course highly unequal when the incumbent can threaten to repress opposition activists by bringing the force of the state down upon them or by stripping them of public protection in the face of extra-governmental aggression.

To understand the effects of asymmetric costs, we first need to tackle a scaling problem not encountered in standard affiliation models developed for the study of the United States (see Aldrich and Bianco, 1992; Cox, 1997). In these models, costs simply drop out because they do not affect affiliation decisions. When costs are unequal, they need to be scaled relative to policy preference units that I have expressed on the interval $[-1,1]$. If cost units are too large relative to location units, then they dominate the calculation faced by each activist and drive the model. If they are too small then it is as if costs are almost unimportant. The two issues to consider are the *magnitude* of cost units and the *difference* in costs across the parties.[12]

It seems reasonable that costs should be bound by the magnitude of benefits. Thus, I assume that costs are less than the instrumental benefits of activism and that expressive benefits should never be more than instrumental benefits. If either of these conditions did not hold, then all activism would be expressive. The magnitude of costs and benefits that satisfies these assumptions sets $u(o) = 1$ and maximum costs at one.[13]

---

[12] The magnitude problem (but not the difference problem) also applies to the utility of office $u(o)$ since $u(o)$'s size is arbitrary with respect to location units as well.

[13] This maximum derives from the fact that the largest possible distance between an activist and either party in the two-party model is one.

134 *Why Dominant Parties Lose*

If repression were so severe that joining the opposition would cost an activist her life, then no real number could capture the difference. Although this may have been true of the most repressive eras in fully closed authoritarian regimes such as the Soviet Union under Stalin, Cambodia under the Khmer Rouge, and Chile under Pinochet, it is difficult to imagine such high levels of repression in dominant party systems where meaningful elections allow opposition forces to form parties and compete. As detailed in Chapter 2, repression was quite real in dominant party systems, but it was substantially milder than in fully closed authoritarian regimes.

Figure 4.1B-D show the policy preference of the indifferent office-seeker and message-seeker as the cost of joining the opposition party increases compared to the costs of joining the incumbent. In general, as costs increase, the indifferent elite activist becomes more extreme on policy. Beginning with a differential of 0.4 cost units in Panel C, the indifferent office-seeker is out of bounds until the opposition's probability of victory reaches about 12%. When the costs are slightly more than double for joining the opposition, as shown in Panel D, no office-seekers join until the challenger has a 50% chance of victory. The indifferent message-seeker also becomes more programmatically extreme as the cost of affiliating with the opposition increases; however, some message-seekers are almost always willing to join unless the cost differential is incredibly high.

I interpret these findings as relevant to the question of abstention. Abstention in the model will be entirely due to alienation. If we assume that abstainers receive none of the selective benefits available to participants and pay no costs, then they receive a benefit of zero. Thus, the binding constraint on activism concerns the magnitude of costs. Based on (1), prospective office-seekers will join some party if $Eu_i(a_k) > 0$, which is the same as employing the decision rule, become active if $p_k[s_k u(o) + u(e_k)] > c_k$. If we assume the least inviting situation for a prospective office-seeker so that he is sure to lose the nomination and pay maximum costs for joining, then the decision rule becomes, join if $p_k u(e_k) > 1$. Similarly, at maximum costs, a message-seeker would join if $u(e_k) + p_k u(e_k) > 1$. For both types, if the dominant party is nearly certain to win, then only a prospective office-seeker who gets virtually no expressive benefit will abstain, and this will only occur when his sincere policy preference is very far from those of the existing stock of members in the dominant party. He could still join the opposition, but because its probability of winning will be small, he only does so if he gets a large expressive benefit. As he gets further from the preferences of the existing stock of elite activists in the opposition, his expressive benefit will also decline. Thus, in general, only extremists abstain, and they do so out of alienation from the policy message of the two parties. As costs rise, it will be harder for expressive benefits to overcome the disincentives for activism. As a result, when costs are very large, no prospective elite activists join parties. Or, more realistically, as costs become highly asymmetric against the opposition, no prospective elite activists join the opposition and the binding constraint is exclusively about whether it is worthwhile to join the incumbent.

These findings imply that repression is a delicate tool for dominant parties that use it in places like Mexico, Taiwan, Senegal, and Malaysia. Such incumbents may diminish the likelihood that a strong challenger emerges because only a limited number of comparatively radical elite activists will seek to join one, but they also run the risk of going too far and pushing opposition forces away from party politics and toward either social movements or revolutionary activities. Dominant parties may then find themselves in the uncomfortable position, as Mexico's PRI did in 1976, of running elections in which only the dominant party competes.

HYPOTHESES FOR THE CHARACTERISTICS OF OPPOSITION PARTY ELITES

The formal model developed here yields at least six hypotheses that can be derived from Figure 4.1. First, despite the low instrumental benefits of activism, citizens actually do sacrifice time and effort to join opposition parties. Sometimes these citizens run great financial, physical, and psychological risks to do so, but they are driven by the desire to express support for political goals in which they believe deeply. Second, opposition parties are built by relative policy extremists. This finding conflicts with existing approaches in which policy preferences simply play no role in partitioning the set of potential party elites. It also implies what we know from Chapter 2, that challenger parties are built on the extremes first rather than beginning as catchall parties. This brings a sense of party *building* into the dynamics of opposition party development and serves as a corrective to the neutral theories discussed in Chapter 1 where challenger parties are predicted to form easily as catchall competitors toward the center of the space.

Third, I show that opposition parties only attract moderates as the incumbent's resources and use of repression decline. In the model, there are no endogenous sources of opposition party development. Instead, challengers only recruit more broadly as moderate prospective participants find that the combined benefits of joining a challenger party outweigh those of affiliating with the incumbent.

Fourth, office-seekers in particular are very sensitive to changes in the political environment. As the incumbent's advantages decrease, new office-seekers should be increasingly moderate. If we could measure dominant party power against office-seekers' policy extremism, we should observe a sharp negative slope. Message-seekers react less to changes in the political environment, so their slope in analogous tests should be much flatter.

Fifth, since early joiners are more likely to rise to leadership positions by virtue of their long tenure in opposition parties, leaders are more likely to be extreme on policy than activists. This is exactly the opposite of what party theory from the fully competitive democracies would predict. Work by May (1973), Aldrich (1983), and Kitschelt (1989a, 1989b) all predict that lower-level activists are more radical on policy than party elites who hold preferences that are centrist with respect to the voters in order to maximize votes and win elections. But challengers in dominant party systems grow up differently and their path of development produces relatively radical leaders and more moderate lower-level activists.

Finally, these predictions imply that there will be intra-party coordination problems in the opposition between a coalition for niche appeals and a coalition for catchall appeals. The niche coalition will be led by early joiners and especially by those who rise to leadership positions. The catchall coalition will be led instead by later joiners, and especially by later-joining office-seekers. We should observe conflicts between these groups over key aspects of party building, including the party's policy profile, the openness of its recruitment procedures for candidates and activists, the degree of leadership control over the party, and the interest in targeting core versus noncore constituencies for expanding the party. These coordination problems derive from the very path of opposition party development in dominant party systems.

Since the leaders who spearhead the niche coalition join opposition parties early on, they form the party institutions within which both niche and catchall players operate. These leaders will likely create relatively closed party structures with high barriers to new activist affiliation, hierarchical leadership control, and tight links to core constituencies. Once established, such niche-oriented parties will be very difficult for catchall players to pry open. Consequently, opposition parties are effectively constrained by their origins. The rigidities built into challenger parties as the result of their development path may make them strategically sluggish and unable to take advantage of major opportunities, even when the incumbent makes a policy blunder that should theoretically turn voters against it. As a result, dominant parties may remain in power for some time even after their advantages erode.

CONCLUSION

This chapter built a formal decision-theoretic model of party elite affiliation in which prospective candidates and activists choose whether to join a dominant party, a challenger, or abstain. The model adapts standard participation models that were developed for studying the fully competitive democracies to dominant party systems by making three changes. First, the model incorporates the dominant party's advantages in the electoral competition game. Dominant parties have exclusive access to illicit public resources and thus can use patronage goods to attract voters. As a result, prospective party elites know that they will reap instrumental rewards with much lower probability as part of the challenger party.

Second, my approach adds expressive elements to party elites' utility functions. Specifying a model that includes only instrumental motivations naturally predicts that no activists will join a challenger to an incumbent dominant party. Adding partisan expression helps account for the opposition activism that actually exists in these systems. Partisan expression has long been accepted as an important selective benefit for participants in social movements and interest groups. Since opposition parties in dominant party systems face similarly high barriers to success, it seems plausible to add expression to participants' utility functions. Interviews with party elites in Mexico lent empirical validity to this modeling decision.

Third, the model allows the costs of participation to vary by party. Costs might vary by insider versus outsider status if the dominant party engages in repression designed to raise the costs of participation in the opposition. Costs might also vary if the dominant party uses its substantial resources to diminish the opportunity costs of affiliating with the incumbent. Raising the relative costs of participation in the opposition either indirectly through resources or directly through repression makes challenger parties less attractive to prospective joiners and thus moves the location of the indifferent elite activist toward the extremes on policy. As a result, raising costs also keeps opposition parties small and diminishes their electoral viability.

The next two chapters supply evidence in favor of the model developed here. Chapter 5 uses sample survey data from party elites to test the behavioral hypotheses generated from the formal model. Chapter 6 then looks at intra-party dynamics and the organizational rigidities built into opposition parties due to the process of political recruitment.

5

The Empirical Dynamics of Elite Activism

During long decades of PRI dominance, opposition parties labored and failed to generate substantial electoral support. They were outspent by an incumbent with a virtually bottomless war chest derived largely from public funds, their programmatic appeals were outflanked by the PRI's vote buying machine, and they were occasionally repressed by a regime that was not unwilling to use threats and violence as a last resort. These mechanisms minimized opposition parties' electoral fortunes because they affected the type of party elites they were able to attract. The PRI's advantages discouraged all but the most anti-status quo citizens from serving as candidates and activists in the opposition. These comparatively extremist party elites endorsed building niche parties that appealed to smaller electoral constituencies. It was only as economic restructuring reduced the incumbent's resource advantages and leveled the partisan playing field that moderates who supported centrist catchall strategies were willing to join the opposition.

This chapter tests the predictions about recruitment dynamics that were generated from the formal model of elite activist affiliation developed in Chapter 4. Using individual-level data from the Mexico Party Personnel Surveys, I demonstrate that opposition party elites' policy extremism with respect to the status quo increases with the dominant party's resource advantages and use of repression. However, office-seekers and message-seekers respond differently to changes in the political environment. Office-seekers who join when the probability of opposition victory is low will be more extreme than message-seekers who join at the same time. But as the partisan playing field levels, new opposition office-seekers will be more moderate than new message-seekers because the latter group is less

139

140   *Why Dominant Parties Lose*

interested in winning than in building a movement to transform society. Demonstrating this pattern of political recruitment is key to understanding the intra- and inter-party coordination problems that hamper opposition party development and help dominant incumbents divide and conquer the opposition.

After introducing the survey data used in this chapter, I operationalize the dependent variable – the policy preferences of individual party elites – and describe the dynamics of party affiliation. The next brief section introduces five specific hypotheses for party elite behavior. Then I provide measures of the key independent variables: the incumbent's resource advantages, the regime's use of repression, and whether party elites are office-seekers or message-seekers. The final section before the conclusion presents statistical models to show the effects of the explanatory variables on party elites' sincere policy preferences.

THE DATA: MEXICO PARTY PERSONNEL SURVEYS

The primary data for this chapter come from the Mexico Party Personnel Surveys that I conducted with a team of interviewers between March and November 1999.[1] We administered six separate but parallel sample surveys, two each for the PAN, PRI, and PRD. One set of surveys was directed to members of the National Political Council of each party that are made up of distinguished party leaders, including some current office-holders at the national, state, and local levels. Councilors are high-level party personnel that oversee the smaller National Executive Committee, make important decisions about budgeting and the distribution of intra-party power, and, in some cases, select candidates as well as the party president. The other set of surveys was directed to activists who attended national party conventions. For the PAN and the PRD, respondents were delegates with voting privileges in forums that ratified statutory changes proposed by the National Executive Committees. The PRI did not hold a pre-election convention in 1999. Because it had recently instituted an open primary for selecting its presidential candidate, leadership opted for a national event that included a candidate launch. This event gave activists less direct influence than a convention would have, but it was still widely viewed as the key opportunity for activists from all over the country to lobby, network, and secure positions in the administration should their candidate win. We conducted our interviews there. When referring to

---

[1] See Chapter 1 footnote 39 for acknowledgments.

The Empirical Dynamics of Elite Activism 141

TABLE 5.1. *Mexico Party Personnel Surveys Sample Characteristics*

Group Interviewed	Party	Sample Size	Population	Population Share in the Sample
	PAN	174	267	65.2%
Leaders	PRD	177	300	59.0%
	PRI	192	353	54.4%
	PAN	477	Approx. 3,000	Approx. 15.9%
Activists	PRD	180	Approx. 3,000	Approx. 6.0%
	PRI	270	Approx. 6,000	Approx. 4.5%

party leaders, I mean members of a party's National Political Council. When referring to activists, I mean official delegates to national party meetings, including the PAN's National Assembly, the PRD's National Convention, and invitees to the PRI's candidate launch. To refer to both leaders and activists together, I use the term party elites, elite activists or, occasionally, for the sake of fluidity, I call them party personnel.

The goal was to construct representative samples of the parties' power structures, not their overall membership. The sample sizes are shown in Table 5.1. The overall database contains 1,470 responses, with 543 coming from national party leaders and 927 coming from activists. By party, there were 651 respondents from the PAN, 462 from the PRI, and 357 from the PRD. All interviews were face-to-face, lasted approximately 35 to 40 minutes, and consisted of over 100 questions.

In the case of the National Political Councils, I wanted to include a high proportion of overall membership since Councilors remain powerful at the national level whether or not they attended the particular meetings where the surveys were conducted. Our team accomplished this goal by interviewing a very large proportion – at least half – of Councilors in each party. In the case of activists, I wanted samples that were representative of convention attendees. Activists who do not attend conventions have virtually no voice at the national level, so excluding them from the samples was of less concern. Attendance at the conventions ranged between about 3,000 and about 6,000, but lists of attendees were not available. In each case, teams of no fewer than 30 interviewers were used to cover all major access points to the conventions and areas of congregation. Interviews were conducted throughout the day to ensure that personnel arriving at different times were included in the samples. No data are available on the response rate; however, my own observation and reports from team supervisors as well as the interviewers themselves indicate that

142 *Why Dominant Parties Lose*

respondents were highly enthusiastic. Thus, although representativeness cannot be ensured, the care in survey administration and the large number of responses suggest that there are no major systematic biases.

It bears remembering that these data represent the current stock of party elites at party meetings in 1999. There was no way to measure the policy preferences of personnel who belonged to a party at an earlier date but then became inactive. By not measuring the elite activist outflow, my findings could be biased; however, the bias would favor my hypotheses only if departing members in the 1970s, when the PRI's resources and use of repression were high, were all more moderate than those who remained or, if the outflow in the 1990s, when the incumbent's resources and use of repression were low, were all more radical than those who stayed. This particular make-up of departing members is unlikely for two reasons. First, it runs counter to logical theory about the costs and benefits of party affiliation presented in Chapter 4. Second, the Mexico Party Personnel Surveys did ask respondents' if they had been a member of another party previously, and this gives a measure of the outflow for personnel who remained active in party politics. To challenge my findings, these data would have to show that departing members of the independent left/PRD and the PAN in the 1970s and 1980s who wound up in the PRI were more moderate on policy than those who remained in the opposition parties. However, the data show no such evidence. Further, members who left the opposition parties in the 1990s would have to be more radical on policy and end up in new parties to the left of the PRD and to the right of the PAN. There are no such new parties or organized political groups (i.e., groups seeking party status). All those that registered through 2000 were tiny and equally or more centrist than either the PAN or the PRD of the 1990s. Thus, although measuring the stock of continuing personnel in 1999 rather than also tapping the preferences of the elite activist outflow could bias findings in favor of my hypothesis, logic and the available evidence suggest that this is not the case.

THE DEPENDENT VARIABLE: PARTY ELITES' POLICY PREFERENCES

In order to understand the policy preferences of party elites and voters, we need to determine what issues structured partisan competition and party-voter alignments. Before the 2000 elections, competition in Mexico was two-dimensional. The parties competed over an economic policy dimension that pitted liberals who favored market-led development against those who preferred state-led development. Although this

The Empirical Dynamics of Elite Activism

single standard cleavage is sufficient to explain the patterns of competition in many countries, studying partisan alignments in Mexico before 2000 requires also taking account of a cross-cutting regime cleavage that separated democratizers from authoritarians. Democratizers are those who favored a rapid and complete transition to fully democratic competition and the decentralization of political power. Comparatively more authoritarian actors instead preferred to slow or completely stall the rise of intense partisan competition and maintain the extremely centralized power of the presidency.

These two dimensions structured opinion at both the elite and mass levels.[2] Domínguez and McCann (1996), Magaloni (1997), and Moreno (1999) show evidence that the economic policy and regime dimensions structured vote choice. I use new data from the Mexico Party Personnel Surveys to show that party elites had the same cognitive map of the partisan competition space (also see Greene, 2002a). The surveys included issue questions related to economic development policy, the transition to full and open democratic competition, and social policy. Question wording and party mean scores are reported in Table 5.2. The mean issue scores are similar across parties, but once the items are grouped into issue areas, they show substantial variation within and across the parties.

In order to recover the relevant dimensions of partisan competition, I used Principal-Components factor analysis. The goal was to measure the partisan competition space as it was perceived by personnel from all three parties. Therefore, all respondents from the PAN, PRI, and PRD were included, but the responses were weighted by party so that no party was over-represented. Varimax rotation was then applied to make the factor dimensions orthogonal.

The analysis recovered the two expected dimensions of partisan competition. The economic policy cleavage included the items related to the control of cross-border capital flows, the role of the state in providing basic social welfare, and the role of the state versus private enterprise in business. This dimension accounted for 26.8% of the variance in the sample. The regime divide included questions related to the pace of transition to fully free and fair competition and the degree of political decentralization. It accounted for 22.4% of the variance in the sample.[3]

---

[2] For a discussion of theoretical models that demonstrate advantages to centrism for two-dimensional competition, see Chapter 1, "Supply-Side Approaches."

[3] The eigenvalues for the economic policy and regime factors were 1.61 and 1.34, respectively.

144   *Why Dominant Parties Lose*

TABLE 5.2. *Issue Position Questions and Party Elites' Mean Self-Placements*

Question		Mean Self-Placement		
Phrase 1	Phrase 2	PRD	PRI	PAN
Mexico's government should impose controls on foreign capital flows (1)	Mexico's government should permit the free flow of foreign capital (5)	1.93	2.82	3.06
The state should provide for citizens' welfare (1)	Individuals should provide for their own welfare (5)	1.85	2.77	3.31
Government property in business and industry should increase (1)	Private property in business and industry should increase (5)	2.47	3.17	3.91
The political reform has not advanced far enough (1)	The political reform has advanced far enough (5)	1.41	2.52	1.92
Mexico requires real federalism (1)	Mexico requires a strong president (5)	1.50	2.58	1.86
The death penalty should never be applied under any circumstances (1)	The death penalty should be applied in some cases (5)	2.20	3.46	2.42
Abortion should be a woman's right to choose (1)	Abortion should never be permitted (5)	1.78	2.44	3.65

Minimum N = 398 for PRI, 637 for PAN, and 330 for PRD.
Source: Mexico Party Personnel Surveys.

While the factor analysis technique was exploratory, it should be stressed that the underlying issue items were selected for inclusion in the sample surveys only after reviewing the literature on partisan attitudes in Mexico and consultation with experts in the field. Prominent studies of Mexico treat the competition space as two dimensional (see Molinar, 1991; Domínguez and McCann, 1996; Magaloni, 1997, also see 2006). Bruhn (2001) also recovered the same two dimensions in her content analysis of party platforms using the European Manifestos Project methodology. Thus, strong priors about the structure of partisan competition informed the analysis of party elite attitudes presented here.

The analysis found little evidence that a socio-religious dimension structured party elites' perception of the partisan competition space. The abortion and death penalty issues did not load together as a unique dimension, suggesting that party personnel did not conceptualize their partisan preferences in these terms. Given its traditionally close relationship to the Church, one would expect the PAN to pursue social issues in partisan competition more than the other parties; however, even among the PAN elites, social issues did not form a separate dimension. This was true

The Empirical Dynamics of Elite Activism 145

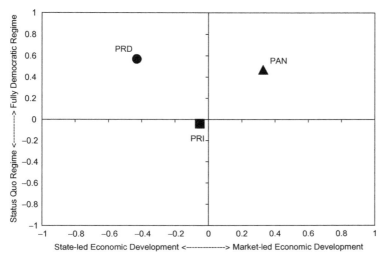

FIGURE 5.1. Party Elites' Mean Locations in the Competition Space.
Source: Mexico Party Personnel Surveys.

for the pooled sample of all party elites for just the abortion and death penalty questions, and it remained true in models (not shown) for a subset of activists who were also asked about the role of the Church in public education.

In the absence of a salient socio-religious cleavage, economic policy and regime issues framed partisan political competition in Mexico and served as the main issues around which candidates and activists were recruited into the competing parties. Figure 5.1 shows the sincere policy stand of each party as measured by the mean preference of its elites on each dimension. Note that the origin was scaled to represent the true center in Mexico's politics, as perceived by the sample survey respondents.[4] As a result, distances from the graph's origin can be interpreted as deviations from the center of the partisan competition space.

As expected, PRD elites preferred a larger role for the state in economic development and favored democracy. PAN elites similarly supported democracy but disagreed sharply on economic policy and preferred market-led development. In the aggregate, PRI elites were close to the center. Although PRI administrations may have promoted market-oriented

---

[4] To do this, from each respondent's factor score, I subtracted the factor score associated with the respondent who chose the middle point "3" on the scale of "1" to "5" for all issue questions.

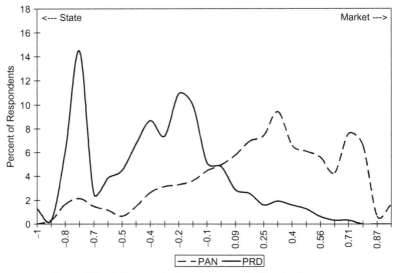

FIGURE 5.2. Party Elites' Economic Development Policy Preferences.
Source: Mexico Party Personnel Surveys.

economic policies while in office since the mid-1980s, the average party elite was in fact quite centrist and located between the PAN and PRD. On regime issues, PRI elites as measured in 1999 were not fully authoritarian, but compared to their counterparts in the opposition they were substantially more in favor of the centralization of political authority and slowing the transition to fully competitive democracy. Differences between the parties were statistically significant at the .01 level for all comparisons except PAN versus PRD personnel on the question of democracy.

The same pattern emerges at the individual level. In logistic regressions of party affiliation choice (not shown), economic policy and regime preferences correctly sort almost 80% of all personnel into their chosen parties. Economic policy distinguishes between all three parties, with the PRD on the left, the PRI in the center, and the PAN on the right. Regime preferences distinguish between the PRI and the challengers, but not between the PAN and PRD. Demographic variables contribute a small amount to the explanation, principally by distinguishing between the PAN and PRD on individual-level religiosity.

To examine intra-party differences, Figures 5.2 and 5.3 show the distributions of opposition party personnel preferences over the economic policy and regime dimensions, respectively. Again, there was substantial agreement between PAN and PRD elites on the need for a fast and thorough transition to democracy. Divisions over economic policy were more

The Empirical Dynamics of Elite Activism

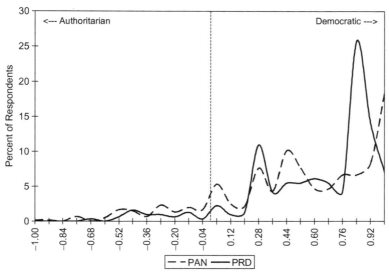

FIGURE 5.3. Party Elites' Regime Preferences.
Source: Mexico Party Personnel Surveys.

marked. PAN personnel were clearly on the right and favored market-led development policies, while those in the PRD were on the left and favored an active role for the state in development. It is equally clear that elites in each party conflicted over the best policy appeals, with one group supporting more extreme positions and another endorsing more moderate positions toward the center of the space. What explains these policy disagreements within and between the opposition parties?

HYPOTHESES: DOMINANCE AND THE DYNAMICS OF RECRUITMENT INTO OPPOSITION PARTIES

The formal theory of party affiliation presented in Chapter 4 generated predictions about how elite activists sort themselves into the dominant party or the opposition. By specifying the partition or location of the prospective elite activist who is just indifferent between joining one party or the other, the formal theory yields five behavioral hypotheses.

Hypothesis 1: *Resource Asymmetries*: Opposition party elites' policy extremism rises with the dominant party's resource advantages. As resource asymmetries increase, the probability of opposition victory decreases, implying that a prospective participant would have to be more distant from the status quo to join the opposition.

148 *Why Dominant Parties Lose*

Conversely, as resources become more symmetric, more moderate personnel find it worthwhile to join the opposition.

Hypothesis 2: *Asymmetric Costs of Participation*: Opposition party elites' policy extremism rises with the costs of participation. As opportunity costs or repression increase, a prospective participant would have to be more distant from the status quo policy to join the challenger. As costs become more symmetric, more moderate personnel join the opposition.

Hypothesis 3: *Party Elite Type*: Since office-seekers prioritize winning, they are more sensitive to changes in the incumbent's resource advantages. In the aggregate, they will be more extreme than message-seekers when resources are highly asymmetric and less extreme when they are more symmetric. The aggregate differences among message-seeker cohorts should be small and may not be statistically distinguishable from zero.

Hypothesis 4: *Proportion of Office-Seekers*. Since office-seekers who join the opposition are more extreme when the dominant party's advantages are high, there should be fewer of them than message-seekers. As advantages decline, the proportion of office-seekers should rise and the proportion of message-seekers should fall.

Hypothesis 5: *Dominant Party Personnel*. The mean preference of elite activists who join the PRI should be centrist under all conditions; however, as the challengers attract more moderates, new PRI joiners should be more centrist and the standard deviation of PRI elites' preferences should shrink.

EXPLANATORY VARIABLES: RESOURCE ADVANTAGES, REPRESSION, AND PARTY ELITE TYPE

In order to measure the variables highlighted in the hypotheses above, we need information on the political conditions experienced by citizens at the time they decided to affiliate with an opposition party. I argue that these initial conditions informed the psychology of partisan activism and thus had durable effects on party elites' policy preferences, even as conditions changed.[5]

---

[5] On socialization effects among party activists, see May's (1973) theoretical statement and Miller and Jennings' (1986: Ch. 7) empirical finding that Democrats' preferences were relatively invariant over time, especially for the cohort that was socialized during the tumultuous 1960s.

The quantitative analysis in this chapter is designed to provide two types of tests for the behavioral predictions above. First, the hypotheses imply a selection effect where the existing political environment at a given point in time discourages prospective opposition party elites from actually joining a challenger party unless they have a certain characteristic – in this case a minimum level of ideological extremism relative to the status quo. Second, although the argument is longitudinal in nature, the dependent variables – respondents' policy preferences – were measured at one point in time in 1999 only. This faux longitudinal analysis is appropriate for testing the durability of elite activists' initial socialization into politics because it ignores the learning process. We would assume that party personnel learn over time and update their preferences as they do. Yet if everyone updated in a similar way by taking into account new political conditions as they emerged, then interviewees in 1999 would hold very similar preferences. Thus, not taking the learning process into account actually biases the results against Hypotheses 1 and 2 and nicely tests for the psychological durability of initial socialization. If the data in fact show that political conditions at the time of initial party affiliation still affected party personnel in 1999, then we can be confident that these findings are robust.

Measuring Dominant Party Resource Advantages

Resource asymmetries between competing parties are difficult to measure under any circumstances, but particularly difficult in a dominant party setting. Incumbent dominant parties that win votes in part by bribing voters using illicit public resources have incentives to hide the amount and source of their finances. Probably for this reason, data on campaign finance are not available for Mexico until 1994. As a result, we need an indirect longitudinal measure of the PRI's resource advantages. I have argued that dominant parties can raise more partisan funds when the state's participation in the economy is large. Incumbents appropriate the state's economic power in a number of ways ranging from the direct use of public funds and administrative resources, to the provision of public sector jobs, the use of highly targeted spending bills, and awarding contracts and public protection for corporate kickbacks. The precise mix of instruments varies by country and can also vary over time, so in-depth case knowledge helps determine the best measurement strategy. For Mexico, I capture variation in the PRI's resource advantages by scoring the contribution made by state-owned enterprise (SOE) investment and production to the gross domestic product for each party member's year of initial party affiliation. As shown in Chapter 3, SOE participation in the economy averaged 15% of GDP in the 1970s and 18% in the 1980s, reaching a high of 22.3% in 1983 and then declining continually over the next two decades to a low of 5.5% in 2000. I argue that this decline progressively decreased the PRI's ability to generate resources for patronage goods because it limited the size of the pie from which it could take partisan slices, and this affected the political environment experienced by each prospective party elite in a given year.

As the incumbent became poorer, political competition for votes was waged on a more level playing field. Regardless of other changes in or between the parties, the challengers should have experienced increasing access to the voters and thus an exogenous increase in their probability of victory. As winning became more likely, the challengers should have attracted more moderate personnel intent on pursuing catchall strategies. To assess the relevant hypotheses above, we need to match the PRI's resource advantages by year with party elites' initial year of party affiliation.

Determining the year of initial affiliation with a rightwing opposition party is straightforward. Since the PAN dominated politics on the right from its founding in 1939, the first year of activism in the PAN is closely correlated with the first year of activism for any rightwing partisan political organization. Figure 5.4 shows the affiliation of PAN personnel in the sample by year.

The 649 PAN respondents include some number of new members every year from 1939 to 1999. Even though the party expanded rapidly in the late 1990s, the affiliation year of the party elites surveyed reaches its peak in 1995 and then falls off. This distribution draws attention to the type of members included in the samples. Becoming a National Councilor required at least five years of service. Convention delegates also needed time in the party to gain enough recognition to be elected locally or selected by a national body. Thus, even though the surveys were not representative of all party personnel in 1999, they were representative of the party's power structure.

Initial year of affiliation with the left is much less straightforward due to the unfortunate fact that the Mexico Party Personnel Surveys did not ask PRD personnel when they became active in the left prior to their involvement in the PRD. The party was founded in 1989 and a substantial proportion of party elites in the sample said that they became active in that year. However, both in-depth interviews and responses to other questions

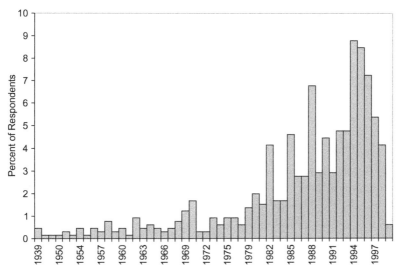

FIGURE 5.4. Year of PAN Elite Affiliation from Sample Surveys.
Source: Mexico Party Personnel Surveys.

in the survey make it clear that many belonged to leftwing parties and organizations before becoming founding members of the PRD.

I estimate the missing affiliation year data by using each respondent's prior organizational affiliations captured in the detailed biographies that were collected as part of the Mexico Party Personnel Surveys.[6] This strategy is reasonable because most of the primary organizations on the left existed under a specific name for less than a decade. As a result, information on organizational affiliations can be used to impute the decade of initial activism in the left. For instance, a PRD elite who reports prior membership in the PST almost certainly joined it during the 1970s since this party was founded in 1973 and absorbed into the PSUM in 1981.

Unlike the right, the Mexican left also created a series of organizations that were not legally registered as political parties, but nonetheless acted as partisan political associations. The relationship between leftwing movements and parties was so tight that PRD elites barely distinguished the two forms. When asked about their prior participation in leftwing political groups and, separately, about their prior participation in leftwing

---

[6] Existing missing data fixes such as Amelia and MICE are not appropriate because the variable in question is truncated.

152 *Why Dominant Parties Lose*

parties, party elites gave responses that mixed the two types of organizations. This was not true for the right where party personnel participated in fewer politicized nonparty movements and also carefully distinguished between the two types.

To show the recruitment path of leftwing activists that became PRD elites, I reconstructed the genealogy of the Mexican left using secondary sources (see, primarily, Martínez Verdugo, 1985; Carr, 1992; and Bruhn, 1997). An abridged version of the PRD's family tree appears in Figure 5.5. It lists only the organizations that PRD elites reported having belonged to; however, these groups do represent the left's most important organizations before the PRD formed in 1989.

Overall, the Mexico Party Personnel Surveys included 357 responses from PRD elites. Of these, 162 or just over 45% joined the partisan left before 1989, and for these members, decade of affiliation was imputed based on prior organizational experience. In the 1960s, the primary feeder organizations included the Mexican Communist Party (PCM), the Revolutionary Teacher's Movement (MRM), and independent labor movements that sparked significant mobilizations in 1958. Together, these groups accounted for 10.4% of all PRD elites surveyed.[7] During the 1970s, three parties and five organizations accounted for most of the left's partisan political mobilization. Together, 11.5% of PRD elites had participated in these groups with most coming from the Trotskyist Mexican Workers Party (PMT) and the Maoist Revolutionary Leftist Organization-Proletarian Line (OIR-LM).[8] From 1980 to 1987, the left made two major attempts to unify and moderate. This consolidation along with an overall increase in activism is noticeable in Figure 5.5. Organizations that existed during this period accounted for 17.6% of PRD elites surveyed. The Mexican Unified Socialist Party (PSUM) and the Mexican Socialist Party (PMS) account for the lion's share, while various organizations of the urban popular movement (MUP) and the People's Revolutionary Movement (MRP) account for comparatively less.

These data also show that the PRD is definitively not dominated by defectors from the PRI. As described in detail in Chapter 3, the dissident

---

[7] Interestingly, PRD respondents did not mention having belonged to other leftwing organizations that played important roles in the 1960s, including the Mexican Worker-Peasant Party (POCM) and the National Liberation Movement (MLN).

[8] OIR-LM plays almost no role in histories of the Mexican left by Carr (1992) and Martínez Verdugo (1985), perhaps because it was Maoist and both authors were mainly concerned with orthodox communism. Other organizations that were important in the 1970s were conspicuously absent from PRD responses, including the Popular Socialist Party (PPS).

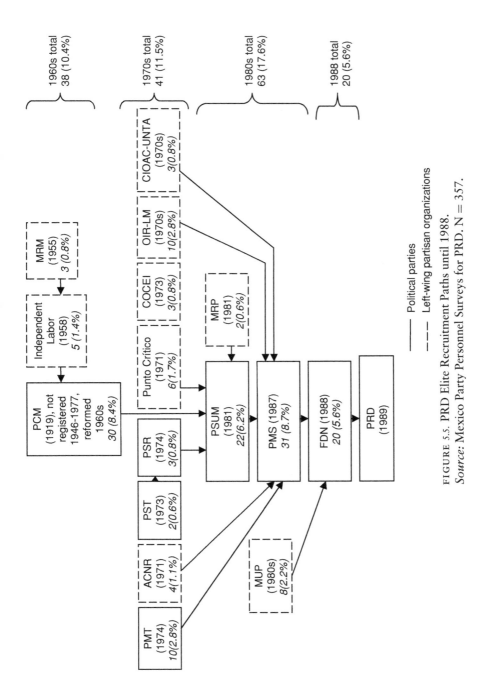

FIGURE 5.5. PRD Elite Recruitment Paths until 1988.
Source: Mexico Party Personnel Surveys for PRD. N = 357.

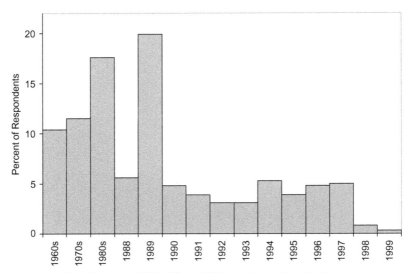

FIGURE 5.6. Year/Period of PRD Elite Affiliation from Sample Surveys.
Note: PRD elites before 1989 refer to those who joined a party or partisan organization of the independent left and remained active in the PRD once it formed. See the text for details.
Source: Mexico Party Personnel Surveys.

Democratic Current (CD) led by Cuauhtémoc Cárdenas and Porfirio Muñoz Ledo split from the PRI in 1987 and, together with several small leftwing parties, formed the National Democratic Front (FDN) to support Cárdenas' presidential bid in 1988. The CD was then folded into the PRD when it formed in 1989. Amazingly, only one party elite said he or she was a member of the CD before joining the PRD. Twenty respondents, or 5.6% of the total, said they had belonged to the FDN. Some portion of those 20 undoubtedly came from the CD, but even if all of them did, this represents a strikingly small proportion of PRD elites, especially given the emphasis on PRI defectors in existing work on the PRD (see Bruhn, 1997; Borjas Benavente, 2003).[9]

Figure 5.6 shows the distribution of respondents by year or period of initial affiliation, using information on participants' prior memberships to extend the time series backward. It shows that more than 45% of PRD elites in the samples joined a leftwing party or political organization before 1989 while 55% entered the PRD after it formed in 1989, including 20% who joined in the party's founding year. This latter number still

---

[9] I do not believe that these results were aberrant. The overall distribution of prior party membership in my surveys is close to that found in a March 1998 survey of 200 delegates to the PRD's IV National Congress by the Centro Mexiquense de Estudios de Opinión.

The Empirical Dynamics of Elite Activism 155

may be an overestimate given some missing data on prior organizational affiliations; however, since the prediction is that the incumbent's resource advantages during the year of initial affiliation with the opposition is correlated with policy extremism, incorrectly scoring affiliation as 1989 for those who joined the left earlier would bias the results against my hypotheses. The figure also shows that after 1989, the number of new members falls off significantly. As with the PAN, this does not necessarily reflect a decrease in recruitment; rather, it again draws attention to the fact that respondents were either National Political Councilors, a post that required at least three years of prior service, or they were convention delegates that needed some standing in the party to be selected as such. In the rest of the chapter, I use these data to refer to each activist's year of initial affiliation with the opposition.

The Costs of Activism: Opportunity Costs and the Repression of Opposition Forces

The costs of political activism in dominant party systems are largely controlled by the incumbent. The dominant party may lower the opportunity cost of participation for its members by providing stipends, in-kind goods, insider favors, transportation, and meals. Since opposition parties are typically resource-poor, they cannot provide these types of goods for their members, thus raising the opportunity cost of participation in the opposition. In addition, dominant parties may target repression against opposition personnel. They may cut off access to basic services such as water and power, threaten their livelihood, or harass, jail, or physically abuse them or their families. As developed above, when the costs of joining the opposition rise relative to participation in the dominant party, those who nevertheless choose the challenger are likely to have sincere policy preferences that are distant from the status quo.

Despite the clear asymmetry in opportunity costs, there is no straightforward way to measure the value of access to the PRI's old boy network. Repression, however, is easier to measure. As described in detail in Chapter 3, the PRI's use of repression varied over time, but generally declined over the century's last three decades. Repression reached its height following the 1968 massacre of students in Mexico City. During the 1970s, protests were violently suppressed and leftwing forces, some operating as guerrilla fighters, were hunted and disappeared. Repression dipped significantly after 1976 when the PRI was embarrassed by its presidential candidate running unopposed. To encourage partisan movements to compete as parties, the government instituted a major electoral reform in

1977 and curtailed its use of repression. During the Salinas Administration (1988–1994) activists complained of renewed harassment. Repression seemed particularly targeted against the left and designed to limit the PRD's appeal in the context of economic crisis and deteriorating social conditions.

One way to measure the level of repression in Mexico over time is to use Freedom House civil liberties scores. I modified these scores slightly for the early 1970s using information that only became available after the 2000 political watershed. A detailed description of these modifications appears in Chapter 3 along with a much richer historical narrative of the PRI's use of repression over time. The modified Freedom House scores are much more consistent with this narrative than the originals, and they represent the best available quantitative scores for use in the statistical analysis.[10]

Types of Party Elites: Office-Seekers and Message-Seekers

Citizens' reasons for getting involved in politics is an important intervening variable that conditions the relationship between dominant party advantages and the individual policy preferences of those willing to join the opposition. Office-seekers' emphasis on winning makes them very sensitive to changes in the incumbent's advantages. In contrast, message-seekers pay less attention to the incumbent's advantages since they focus on their party's social movement-like characteristics and work to craft the partisan message, train the next generation of activists, and design the outreach strategy to grow their party.

I identify office-seekers as those who prefer to run for elected office whereas message-seekers prefer to hold positions inside the party bureaucracy. To tap these differences, the survey asked respondents to choose their preferred post, regardless of the position they held at the time of the interview. Overall, both the PAN and the PRD have more office-seekers than message-seekers. In 1999, 54% of PAN and 65% of PRD elites self-identified as office-seekers while the remainder were message-seekers. For comparative purposes it is interesting but not surprising to note that the PRI contained the highest proportion of office-seekers at 73.8%.

The formal theory of party affiliation presented in Chapter 4 assumed that office-seekers and message-seekers are equally represented in society.

---

[10] As noted in Chapter 3, I also consulted Gibney and Dalton's Political Terror Scales. However, data were only available beginning in 1980 and scores for Mexico show almost no variation over time.

The Empirical Dynamics of Elite Activism 157

This implies that there should be no major ideological or demographic differences between them; rather, their distinct preferences derive from different personal goals in the political arena. To test this assumption, I constructed logistic regression models (not shown) for each party with party elite type as the dependent variable. Explanatory variables included policy preferences, demographics, position in the party, longevity of activism, and six questions about reasons for activism. For the PAN and PRD, the best model correctly sorted only 61% and 63% of respondents into the office-seeker and message-seeker categories, respectively. In other words, the models do scarcely better than a coin toss would, implying that office-seeking versus message-seeking orientation does not result from particular demographic characteristics, position in the party hierarchy, radical or moderate policy preferences, or reasons for becoming an activist; rather, these orientations derive from deeper unmeasured differences in tastes.

As shown above, both the PAN and the PRD contain somewhat more office-seekers than message-seekers, as one would expect for any political party. Nevertheless, as Hypothesis 4 indicates, the ratio of the two types should change with shifting political conditions. Since office-seekers emphasize winning, there should be fewer of them in the opposition when the incumbent holds substantial advantages. But as these advantages erode, the proportion of office-seekers in the opposition should rise faster than message-seekers because the latter care less about winning. Since we know from Chapter 3 that the PRI's resource advantages and use of repression declined over time, Hypothesis 4 implies that office-seekers should become an increasing proportion of new recruits and therefore of overall membership from 1970 to 2000. Data bear this out. Among party elites who affiliated with the PAN in the 1970s, 33% were office-seekers but by the late 1990s, they accounted for nearly 60% of party elites. The same trend is evident in the PRD. In the 1970s, 38% of party elites were office-seekers but by the late 1990s, office-seekers accounted for nearly 70% of all party elites.

QUANTITATIVE TESTS OF THE FORMAL MODEL OF PARTY
ELITE AFFILIATION

In this section, I test the remaining hypotheses generated by the formal model of party affiliation by estimating OLS regression models where the dependent variables are respondents' preferences over economic policy and regime issues in 1999. The primary explanatory variables of interest, as operationalized above, match measures of the PRI's resource

158 *Why Dominant Parties Lose*

advantages and use of repression by year to each respondent's initial year of affiliation with the opposition.[11] The main goal is to assess whether the resource advantages and repression variables remain important predictors of policy preferences when controlling for a host of other variables (discussed below). The most encouraging results would show that the expected relationships remain statistically significant for office-seekers. Expectations for message-seekers from statistical estimation are less clear cut. The formal model predicts only a small change in message-seekers' policy preferences due to variation in the explanatory variables. Since statistical models have trouble distinguishing small significant effects from insignificant ones without a very large number of observations, statistically insignificant results with the coefficient in the right direction for message-seekers would generally correspond to the formal theory's predictions.

The models also include variables associated with alternative hypotheses and controls, including the level of national economic development, respondents' position in their party's hierarchy, the PRI's policy appeals, and a host of individual-level demographic variables, including age, gender, education, and religiosity. I discuss them before moving on.

Socio-economic development might affect the policy preferences of those willing to join the opposition in three ways. First, development could distribute resources throughout society, creating more independent sources of opposition party funding and leveling the partisan playing field. Second, development could reduce inequality and increase the size of the middle class[12] – a group that is less susceptible to patronage politics.[13] Based on either mechanism, since socio-economic development could increase the challengers' likelihood of winning, it would encourage more moderates to join the opposition. Following the cross-national analysis presented in Chapter 1 and recent work by Przeworski and colleagues (2000), I include real GDP per capita matched to each respondent's initial year of affiliation to test for these effects.[14] Finally, economic development

---

[11] Note that for left party joiners before 1989, I imputed the decade of affiliation and thus match the appropriate decade-long average of PRI resource advantages and use of repression. For the 1980s, I use 1980–1988 averages. This procedure necessarily biases the tests against my hypotheses because it flattens out the secular decrease over time that would have appeared if I had data on the year of initial affiliation.

[12] Boix (2003) argues that inequality and not development hinders democratization.

[13] See Eisenstadt and Roniger (1981) and Kitschelt (2000). Shefter (1977) disagrees.

[14] Following Przeworski et al. (2000), GDP data come from the chain rule series in Penn World Table 6.1.

The Empirical Dynamics of Elite Activism 159

might affect opposition party viability through shorter-term changes in economic prosperity. Dramatic economic downturns such as Mexico's crises of 1982 and 1994 might quickly generate negative evaluations of the incumbent's performance, leading voters to choose opposition parties and thus increasing the challengers' chances of winning.[15] As a result, contemporaneous economic indicators may be associated with the policy preferences of personnel who joined challenger parties in a given year. To test for this possibility, I included the annual percentage change in GDP, again matched to each respondent's initial year of affiliation.

Position in the party hierarchy may also condition party elites' policy preferences. One of the best known theories about intraparty policy differences argues that candidates and party leaders tend to hold moderate policy preferences to mirror the median voter, whereas lower level activists tend to be more radical (see May, 1973; Aldrich, 1983). To test for this, I add a dummy variable that measures whether a respondent was a national leader or an activist.

The model also controls for the PRI's policy appeals, matched to each respondent's initial year of affiliation with the opposition. In Chapter 3, I showed that the PRI's policy shifts over time were part of a "firefighting" strategy designed to undercut opposition parties' support bases. In a similar vein, the PRI's appeals could have affected the preferences of individual activists willing to join the opposition. For example, as the PRI moved further right, moderate rightwingers would have found their interests more represented in the dominant party, leaving only the more radical rightwingers to oppose it. At the same time, the PRI's move to the right would also encourage more moderate leftwingers to join the leftwing opposition. If the PRI moved to the left instead, it would have had a similar effect on the opposite side of the spectrum.

Finally, demographic variables may affect individual's policy preferences. As discussed above, my analysis uses cross-sectional data to make a longitudinal argument. We also already know that the PRI's resource advantages and the regime's use of repression declined over time. As a result, age in 1999 could be a confounding variable. Yet advancing age is generally thought to decrease rather than increase radicalism. Thus, if the explanatory variables remain significant when controlling for age, the hypothesis should be seen as significantly strengthened. Education in 1999 could also be a confound; however, public opinion surveys typically

---

[15] This argument is consistent with Haggard and Kaufman's (1995) finding that economic crisis leads to authoritarian breakdown.

160 *Why Dominant Parties Lose*

find that higher levels of education are associated with more support for free trade,[16] and party personnel may follow the same pattern as the general public. Thus, education could account for the predicted relationships for both parties only if less educated personnel entered the PAN in recent years and more educated personnel affiliated with the PRD. This turns out to be empirically false. Both religiosity and gender could be confounds, but there is no *a priori* reason to believe that either variable is associated with a preference for more or less moderate policies.

I constructed two OLS regression models for each party where economic policy and regime preferences are the dependent variables. Both outcome variables are factor scores generated through the procedures described above. On economic policy preferences, negative values indicate a preference for state-led economic development, positive values indicate a preference for market-led development, and zero is associated with a centrist position. Thus, movement toward the center is represented by negative coefficients for PAN and positive coefficients for PRD personnel. On regime issues, positive values are associated with a preference for a faster and more complete transition to democracy and the decentralization of political power, negative scores are associated with authoritarian positions, and zero is the substantive center. Thus, negative coefficients for both PAN and PRD personnel indicate moderation on regime issues.

Results are shown in Table 5.3. I parsed the resources and repression variables between office-seekers and message-seekers to show their effects separately. Resources*Office represents state-owned enterprises as a percent of GDP for office-seekers' initial year of affiliation only and Resources*Message represents the same but for message-seekers only. Repression*Office is a proxy for the costs of participation and represents the modified Freedom House score that corresponds to each office-seeker's year of affiliation. Repression*Message measures the same for message-seekers alone. Type is a dummy variable coded 0 for message-seekers who prefer to work inside the party bureaucracy and 1 for office-seekers who aspire to hold elected office. PRI's Economic Position and PRI's Regime Position are factor scores representing the incumbent's policy platform derived from Bruhn's (2001) content analysis and rescaled from −1 to 1 to make them correspond to the partisan space constructed with data from

---

[16] Domínguez and McCann (1996: 66) show that education increased support for neoliberalism using 1988 IMOP-Gallup poll data for Mexico. I corroborated this with Latino-Barometer 1998 data for Mexico.

Independent Variable	PRD				PAN			
	Dependent Variable				Dependent Variable			
	Economic Policy (+ = free market)		Regime Issues (+ = democracy)		Economic Policy (+ = free market)		Regime Issues (+ = democracy)	
	Coeff	Std Err	Coeff	Std Err	Coeff	Std Err	Coeff	Std Err
Resources*Office	−0.013**	0.006	0.012*	0.007	0.020**	0.008	0.002	0.005
Resources*Message	−0.008	0.011	0.020*	0.011	0.006	0.009	0.010*	0.006
Repression*Office	−0.229**	0.110	1.093**	0.501	0.225**	0.111	0.321*	0.181
Repression*Message	0.289	0.707	0.730	0.709	0.159	0.356	0.213	0.228
Type (0 = message; 1 = office)	0.373	0.511	−0.180	0.544	−0.216	0.273	0.042	0.056
Position (0 = activist; 1 = leader)	−0.088*	0.053	0.079	0.057	0.045*	0.027	0.115**	0.058
Age	−0.002	0.002	−0.001	0.002	0.003*	0.002	0.000	0.002
Religiosity	−0.023**	0.012	0.010	0.013	−0.009	0.012	−0.022*	0.012
Gender (0 = male; 1 = female)	−0.026	0.047	0.000	0.052	−0.014	0.044	−0.131**	0.044
Education	0.042**	0.021	0.040*	0.023	0.071***	0.019	0.092***	0.019
PRI's Economic Position	0.400	0.641			0.172*	0.098		
PRI's Regime Position			0.173	0.249			−0.128	0.155
GDP per capita	0.000	0.000			0.000	0.000		
Change in GDP (annual)	−0.009	0.009			0.004	0.005		
Constant	−0.148	0.631	−0.344	0.497	−0.383	0.366	−0.056	0.173
r^2	.11		.12		.10		.10	
Number of cases	249		249		513		525	

Coefficients are unstandardized.

*** p < .01; ** p < .05; * p < .1

Source: Mexico Party Personnel Surveys.

162   *Why Dominant Parties Lose*

the party personnel. Age in 1999 is self-reported. Education in 1999 measures the highest level of schooling completed on a seven-point increasing scale ranging from no education to doctorate. Religion in 1999 measures Church attendance with a seven-point increasing scale. Gender is coded 0 for male and 1 for female.

The most important result evident in Table 5.3 is that the coefficients for resources and repression for office-seekers are in the expected direction and remain statistically significant in all models except one. The coefficients for message-seekers are only significant for repression and only when regime preference is the dependent variable. However, as noted above, the hypotheses predicted only very small effects for message-seekers, so failure to reach statistical significance is not unexpected.

Resources and repression remain important predictors of the policy preferences of opposition party personnel even when controlling for demographic variables and indicators of macro-economic health. Advancing age is typically associated with policy moderation, but it fails to reach statistical significance in three of the four models and the sign is in the wrong direction where it is significant. Among personnel in both parties, education is associated with a greater preference for market-led economic development, but even when we control for these effects, resources and repression remain significant. It is even more impressive that GDP per capita and annual change in GDP have no effect on policy preferences, indicating that socio-economic development did not breed moderation and economic crisis did not quickly produce centrist parties that could take advantage of the PRI's performance blunders.

Discussion: Thirty Years of Challenger Party Recruitment

The effects of resources and repression on individual policy preferences are substantively large. The most accessible way to appreciate the results is to look at the predicted preferences of joiners by year of affiliation. To create these simulations, I generated predictions from the model while using the real values of the resources and repression variables to reproduce the political conditions that a prospective party elite would have encountered in a given year. I held all other variables at their mean or mode. Results for economic policy preference appear in Figure 5.7. I also added the preferences of PRI personnel as predicted by regression models (not shown) that are analogous to those run on opposition party personnel; however, I did not distinguish PRI respondents by party elite type. (The

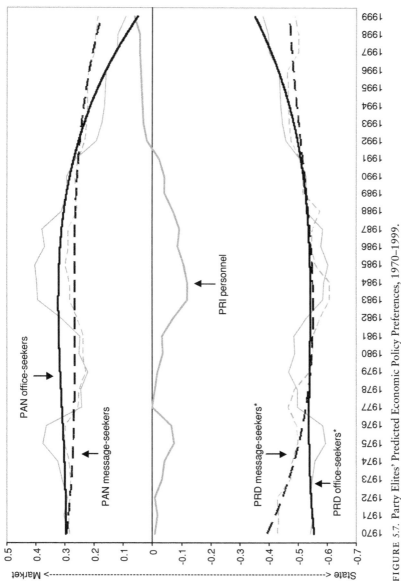

FIGURE 5.7. Party Elites' Predicted Economic Policy Preferences, 1970–1999.

Note: Solid lines represent office-seekers; dashed lines represent message-seekers; thin lines are predicted values; heavy lines are cubic trends. The line for PRI represents predicted values for all PRI personnel.

* PRD elites before 1989 refer to those who joined a party or partisan organization of the independent left and remained active in the PRD once it formed. See the text for details.

163

164   *Why Dominant Parties Lose*

great majority of PRI members are office-seekers and being a message-seeker in an incumbent dominant party means something different than it does in a long-time challenger.)

In Figure 5.7, the solid trend lines for office-seekers and the dashed trend lines for message-seekers show that those who joined the leftwing and rightwing opposition in the 1970s were less centrist on economic policy than those who joined in the late 1990s. The overall impression is of challenger parties polarized around a centrist PRI when the incumbent party's resource advantages were high and its use of repression extensive, and increasingly centrist challenger parties as those advantages declined. This figure clearly shows the trends predicted by Hypotheses 1 and 2.

There are, however, apparent differences between personnel according to their goals in politics. Just as predicted in Hypothesis 3, office-seekers who joined earlier and faced a lower chance of winning held more extreme preferences than did message-seekers who joined at the same time. As the promise of achieving office through a challenger party increased, new office-seekers who joined were more moderate than new message-seekers who did. Indeed, as a group, message-seekers, who perceive benefits simply in working for an esteemed partisan cause, responded much less to changes in the partisan competitive environment as evidenced by their substantially flatter dashed trend line. Overall, the trended results of the empirical model look strikingly similar to the theoretical predictions of the formal model in Figure 4.1 in Chapter 4.

The underlying predicted values, represented by the thinner solid grey line for office-seekers and the dashed grey line for message-seekers, show much more nuance than the trend lines. These predictions also square with what we know from the richer histories of opposition party development presented in Chapter 3. Those who joined the left in the early and mid-1970s and remained active once the PRD was founded were quite far to the left. This period of radicalism responded to the PRI's substantial resource advantages and its reliance on repression. State-sponsored violence was leveled against student protests in 1968 and 1971 and then spread to a complete crackdown on the left during the mid-1970s. As a result, the independent left shrank in size, radicalized in posture, and fragmented. This period saw the rise of small radical leftwing parties touting Maoist, Trotskyist, or mainline Marxist brands of revolution as well as guerrilla cells and radical intellectual cliques.

While the left's radicalization in the 1970s is well known, the PAN's move to the right on economic policy during this period is less well

The Empirical Dynamics of Elite Activism 165

documented. Typically, analysts think of the early 1980s as the beginning of business influence in the PAN, and indeed model predictions bear this out. But there is also evidence of an earlier shift to pro-market sensibilities. Much like fiscal conservatives' reaction to economic populism in the 1930s, business interests reacted to the Echeverría Administration's attempt to finance the PRI's patronage system through international borrowing and massive investment in social programs by moving into the opposition. Once in the PAN, these pro-market forces helped elect José Angel Conchello to the party presidency, a man Shirk (2005: 79) describes as a "caustic antileftist" with "close connections to the business sector." However, fiscal conservatives' triumph was by no means secure. They conflicted so severely with social conservatives' "Catholic humanism" and skepticism of the market's effect on social organization that the party was immobilized and unable to field a candidate for Mexico's presidency in 1976.

Beginning in 1977, new joiners in both the PAN and the left were much more moderate than those who had joined just a few years earlier. This quick shift was a response to important changes in the way the PRI engaged the opposition. The left's radicalization and the right's nonparticipation threatened to create a crisis of legitimacy for the PRI. The incumbent party had always maintained an open electoral arena and ruled with a public mandate, even if that mandate was the result of unfair elections. The increasing irrelevance of elections in the 1970s signaled to PRI powerbrokers that the uneven playing field had tipped too far off balance and needed to be recalibrated. To encourage opposition groups to re-enter partisan politics, the PRI engineered an electoral reform in 1977 that was accompanied by a substantial reduction in repression.

In response, much of the revolutionary left that had not been physically eliminated laid down arms and radical left parties gave up on the goal of revolution. As they moderated, they coalesced behind the Mexican Socialist Party (PMS). On the right, the PAN formed a special commission to promote unity and struck what Shirk calls a "careful balance between pragmatism and principle," without which "it is doubtful that the party would have survived" (2005: 85). Figure 5.7 echoes these developments by showing that new elites on both the left and the right joined an opposition party at lower levels of policy extremism than they had before. Thus, 1977 represents a key turning point in the opposition's evolution.

This trend toward moderation did not last, however. Office-seekers who joined the PAN after 1981 were much more to the right than those who joined in the late 1970s. This jump likely responded to a major increase in the state's ownership over the economy. After a tense squabble with domestic capital-holders, President López Portillo nationalized the banks in 1981. This attack politicized entrepreneurs and many joined the PAN in the early 1980s (Arriola, 1988; Loaeza, 1999; Shirk, 2005). These so-called *neopanistas* once again conflicted with "doctrinaire" social conservatives over the party's identity and the desirability of unbridled free-market capitalism. As Mizrahi (2003) shows, the two groups struck a *de facto* accord where *neopanistas* more often stood for elected office and left the party bureaucracy to the PAN's traditional members. Figure 5.7 reflects this by showing that new PAN office-seekers were more extreme on economic policy issues through the late 1980s but message-seekers stayed at about the same average policy position. New joiners in the left after 1982 were also somewhat more extreme on economic policy than those who joined in the late 1970s.

The increased policy extremism of new personnel in both parties after 1982 runs counter to the common argument that the debt crisis caused the PRI to lose. Although the crisis undoubtedly turned some voters against the PRI, wholesale rejection of the incumbent was tempered by the party's continuing ability to deliver patronage. During the mid-1980s, the state's role in economic development actually expanded as a percent of GDP, thus allowing the PRI to maintain cash flow and outspend competitors. As a result, prospective party personnel did not have a greatly expanded probability of winning office by joining the opposition, leaving only the more policy motivated prospective participants in the population to affiliate with the PAN and the left. This meant that opposition parties did not moderate enough in the early and mid-1980s to take advantage of increasing anti-PRI sentiment.

It is not until after 1985 when the de la Madrid and Salinas Administrations dramatically downsized the state and privatized state-owned enterprises that new joiners in the PAN and the left were truly more centrist. On both sides of the political spectrum, there is an almost 15-year moderating trend beginning in the 1980s and continuing through century's end. As the PRI's resource advantages diminished, the electoral market for votes leveled and the equalizing probability of victory among the parties encouraged more moderates to join the challenger parties.

Figure 5.8 presents the results of simulations for elite activists' sincere preferences over regime issues. As above, I used real yearly data for the PRI's resource advantages and use of repression while holding all other variables at their mean or mode to generate predictions from the model.

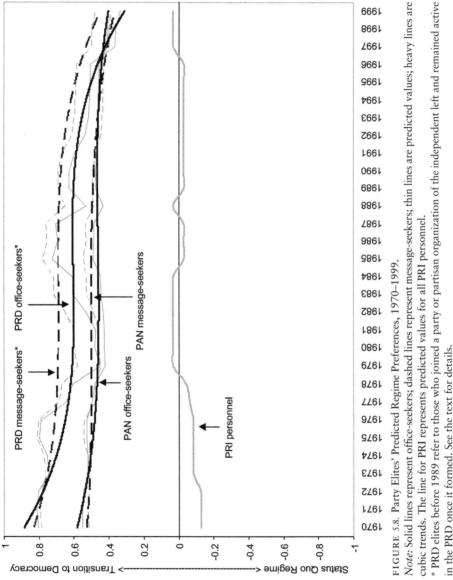

FIGURE 5.8. Party Elites' Predicted Regime Preferences, 1970–1999.
Note: Solid lines represent office-seekers; dashed lines represent message-seekers; thin lines are cubic trends. The line for PRI represents predicted values for all PRI personnel.
* PRD elites before 1989 refer to those who joined a party or partisan organization of the independent left and remained active in the PRD once it formed. See the text for details.

Like the simulations for economic policy preferences, the general trend shows increasing centrism on both ends of the political spectrum. A party elite who joined the opposition in the 1970s when the PRI's advantages were massive remained more in favor of a full and speedy transition to democracy than one who joined in the 1990s. At first glance, this trend may appear unsurprising since, by the 1990s, elections were increasingly fair, the opposition held more elected and appointed offices, and repression had declined substantially. However, it is important to remember that all surveys were conducted in 1999. Thus, early joiners lived in the same contemporary political conditions as later joiners when they responded to the surveys. What conditioned their different preferences were the political conditions that existed when they first decided to join an opposition party.

The underlying predicted regime preferences again tell a more nuanced story. New personnel who joined the left after 1977 and remained active in the PRD once it was founded responded to the political opening by holding more moderate positions on regime issues. When PRI resources and the use of repression increased again in the 1980s, new left party personnel were on average more extreme once again. PAN elites' regime preferences responded less to changes in the incumbent's advantages. As Table 5.3 shows, most of this difference is accounted for by the large coefficients for repression for PRD personnel and the smaller coefficients for PAN personnel. This is consistent with what we know from the more detailed discussion in Chapter 3: partisans on the left suffered disproportionately under the yoke of repression.

The trends also show the expected differences between office-seekers and message-seekers. Although the differences are not large, office-seekers who joined early were on average more extreme on regime issues than their message-seeking counterparts. But with a decrease in PRI advantages, new office-seekers were more moderate than their new message-seeker co-partisans.

Overall, the multivariate results supply strong evidence in favor of the hypotheses generated by the formal model of party affiliation. The effects found here are especially impressive since the formal model predicted that the *indifferent* elite activist's preference would moderate as the dominant party's resource advantages and use of repression decline. The results above refer to the *mean* elite preference, which necessarily becomes moderate more slowly than the indifferent elite does. Consequently, the results should be taken as especially significant findings in favor of the hypotheses.

CONCLUSION

Dominant party advantages force opposition parties to form as undercompetitive organizations that cannot win. Elections need not be completely fraudulent nor must challengers be harassed into submission to maintain single-party dominance. Rather, incumbent dominant parties can create resource and cost asymmetries to make otherwise meaningful elections so unfair that they distort the type of opposition parties that do form.

This chapter showed strong empirical support for the theory of party elite affiliation. When the PRI's competition-altering instruments were at their zenith, challenger parties were only able to recruit very anti-status quo elite activists. No other citizens were willing to engage in activism that was very costly and unlikely to yield electoral victory. But the PRI's advantages did not only have contemporaneous effects on opposition party elite behavior; rather, they socialized generations of opposition personnel so thoroughly that leaders and activists' policy preferences decades later were still informed by the political conditions that existed at the time they joined the opposition. Due to these recruitment dynamics, early joiners in the opposition were policy radicals who built parties that focused on smaller core constituencies and these niche parties inevitably failed to generate broad support.

When the PAN and PRD finally did expand, it was not due primarily to their own successful strategies or to a watershed event that suddenly transformed Mexico's political system; rather it was the cumulative process of opposition party building as the PRI's advantages declined. The events of the 1980s loom large in this story. Economic crisis beginning in 1982 and austerity under free-market restructuring turned voters against the PRI but did not immediately result in support for the opposition. Voters continued to view the challengers as too far to the left or to the right. Only when the free market policy response to the crisis created a leaner public bureaucracy and reduced the overall size of the state's resources did the PRI's access to illicit public funds fall. As they did, the partisan playing field leveled and more moderates were willing to join the opposition. However, these catchall-oriented later joiners conflicted with niche-oriented early joiners. Chapter 6 examines the resulting intra-party coordination problems.

PART THREE

IMPLICATIONS

6

Constrained to the Core

Opposition Party Organizations, 1980s–1990s

By the mid-1980s, the PRI should have experienced a double threat. First, economic crisis beginning in 1982 caused declining real wages, increasing poverty, and faltering growth. As a result, voters increasingly lost faith in the PRI's "performance legitimacy." In a 1986 poll, 89% of respondents rated the national economy as bad or very bad and in a 1988 poll, fully 76% said that the opposition would handle the economy as well or better than the PRI.[1] Second, the government's response to the economic crisis deepened the PRI's predicament by instituting market-oriented reforms that included downsizing the public bureaucracy and selling off state-owned enterprises (SOEs). Using the previous presidential election in 1982 as a benchmark, SOEs accounted for 20% less of the economy by the 1988 presidential election, 37% less by the 1991 midterms, and 60% less by the 1994 presidential race. Thus, not only did voters begin to lose faith in the PRI's ability to direct the economy, but privatization increasingly deprived the PRI of the resources it might have used to buy back their loyalty.

As a result of these pressures, voters began to turn away from the PRI. Its solid support among identified voters fell from 60% of the electorate in 1983 to just 32% in the late 1990s; however, voters did not turn entirely toward the opposition and instead the proportion of independents soared to over 35%.[2] More tellingly, surveys conducted between 1988 and 1994

---

[1] Data for 1986 come from the *New York Times* Poll. Data for May 1988 are the author's calculations based on data from the IMOP (Gallup) Poll in Domínguez and McCann (1996: 101).

[2] PAN and PRD identifiers rose to about 20% and 10% of the electorate, respectively. Data for 1983 are from the Basañez Poll and for 1988 from the IMOP (Gallup) Poll, both cited

174   *Why Dominant Parties Lose*

show that up to 57% of the respondents who expressed the *most* dissatisfaction with the PRI's performance still planned to vote for it (see Buendía, 2004: 126–128; Domínguez and McCann, 1996: 101; Magaloni, 1997: 192–193; also see, 2006: 201). Thus, even if voters were increasingly dissatisfied with the PRI, they did not like the opposition parties enough to turn the PRI out of power. As a result, the PRI won four more national elections between 1985 and 1994.

Performance debacles usually make incumbents lose much more quickly in fully competitive party systems (Key, 1966; Fiorina, 1981; Abramson et al., 1994) and economic crises are associated with the breakdown of fully closed authoritarian regimes (Haggard and Kaufman, 1995). Why not in Mexico? Why did the challenger parties fail to gain support among dissatisfied voters and generate more stable winning coalitions until the late 1990s? Why did voters dislike the PRI but dislike the opposition even more? In sum, why did the challengers remain losing niche-oriented competitors when they had the opportunity to become broader catchall parties that could win?

The standard explanation offered by journalists and some academics is that electoral fraud deprived opposition parties of earned victories at the polls. There is no doubt that fraud played a role in some elections during this period; however, this argument cannot account for voters' negative assessments of the PAN and PRD in opinion surveys.[3] As an alternative, Magaloni (1997; also see, 2006) argues that challengers failed despite voter distaste for the PRI because evaluations of dominant party performance are mediated by voters' accumulated life experiences. Thus, older voters who experienced a longer period of economic success under the PRI should turn away from it more slowly than younger voters who lived a larger proportion of their lives under economic crisis. However, this ingenious argument does not account for why voters would also dislike the opposition parties' prospective policy offers.[4] Thus, we need an explanation that also looks at the failures of the opposition parties themselves.

in Domínguez and McCann (1996: 88). Data for 1986 are from the *New York Times* Poll, and data for 2000 report the mean of all nine polls that year reported in Moreno (2003: 32–33, 41).

[3] Fear could have led voters to hide their true opinions from pollsters as occurred in the Soviet Union (Kuran, 1991); however, Mexico under the PRI was so much less repressive that this seems unlikely.

[4] Magaloni (1997; also see 2006) adds a separate (and entirely plausible) argument that voters discount the challengers' prospective policy offers because they have no retrospective information on their credibility. But if voters also discount the PRI's prospective offer based on its prior performance, then the advantage of being "known" may disappear or even become negative.

I argue that opposition parties were less appealing to voters despite increasing dissatisfaction with the PRI because they were constrained by their origins. Challenger parties were initially designed to survive under difficult conditions where success was unlikely but paying high personal costs, including the risk of repression, was expected. As a result, early joiners in the opposition created niche parties that featured tight links to core constituencies, high barriers to new activist recruitment, localized and mostly in-person communication with voters, and specialized policy appeals. But this largely self-protective posture did not help the challengers grow and it even constrained them from drawing in broader support once new opportunities for expansion arose after the 1982 economic crisis. What worked in one period ceased to be effective in another.

Opposition parties demonstrated such rigidity because early joiners created and continuously supported niche organizations with a "bunker" mentality. These almost club-like organizations were initially imbued with an identity of sacrifice, moral authority, and idealism that fostered deep attachments among their adherents and encouraged early joiners to participate despite the multiple costs of activism. Later joiners who entered politics in an era of more open and intense partisan competition instead preferred to open their parties to broader constituencies. However, they were stifled by hierarchical organizations that limited their advancement during the 1980s and 1990s. As a result of these internal conflicts between generational cohorts, opposition party elites were unable to coordinate on the most efficient strategy and their organizations demonstrated tremendous path-dependency.

This chapter shows a particularly insidious and subtle effect of single-party dominance on partisan competition: The dynamics of individual-level recruitment into the opposition create rigid challenger party organizations that are slow to innovate in the face of new opportunities. Thus, challengers may fail in part due to the weight of the past rather than the more blatant aspects of dominant party power. This argument amounts to a challenge to rational choice accounts of party competition that predict strategic flexibility and discount the role of legacies in the party-building process. In a similar vein, it challenges retrospective voting theory that assumes that challenger parties automatically take advantage of the incumbent's performance failure. I develop my argument in three steps. The first section shows that the 1980s opened opportunities for opposition party expansion, but only if challengers could offer more centrist policies. The second section accounts for early joining elite activists' seemingly perverse preferences for niche party organizations with noncentrist appeals, even as such organizations proved unable to expand support

176 *Why Dominant Parties Lose*

from the 1980s to the mid-1990s. The final section before the conclusion moves from preferences to practices and uses elite activists' biographies, party membership data, and case studies of party-building efforts in two boroughs in Mexico City to show how niche organizations constrained growth.

THE ELECTORAL DISCONNECTION: CENTRIST VOTERS AND NONCENTRIST OPPOSITION PARTIES

Since at least the 1980s when public opinion polls on partisan attitudes first became available, Mexican voters have been moderate on the issues. In the 1986 *New York Times* Poll, 53% identified themselves as centrists (Domínguez and McCann, 1996: 57). Respondents to the 1988 IMOP (Gallup) Poll were divided, often almost equally, on major economic issues such as privatization and restricting foreign investment and imports (Domínguez and McCann, 1996: 59, 61, 63). Using the Mexico portion of the World Values Survey for 1990, 1996–1997, and 2000, Moreno (2003: 116) finds that voters' preferences were close to normally distributed (i.e., bell-shaped) and centered on the middle of the left-right dimension. Finally, using the 1998 LatinoBarometer-Mexico Poll, I found that voters' issue preferences (not their left-right self-placements) were also close to normally distributed and centered on the middle. These various data sources and indicators show that the average voter in Mexico (whether taken as the median or the mean) was located near the substantive center of politics from at least 1986 to 2000.

As a result, the opposition parties would have done well to moderate their appeals.[5] During earlier periods, the PRI's advantages expelled challengers from the center, as shown in Chapter 2; however, as the PRI's ability to buy voter loyalty fell, opportunities opened for expansion through moderation. Although the theoretical predictions from neutral or unbiased models of competition (i.e., where no party has a patronage advantage) with three parties vary in strength according to their underlying assumptions, they consistently point to advantages to centrism.[6]

[5] Elections in Mexico are not fought over issues alone. Voting behavior studies find effects due to candidate characteristics, the media (Lawson, 2002), and incumbent performance (Poiré, 1999). Even though some studies find that voters have limited issue consistency (Domínguez and McCann, 1996; Magaloni and Poiré, 2004a), others find ideological structure in the parties' electoral bases (Moreno, 1999; Magaloni, 1997, also see 2006; Klesner, 2004).

[6] As I showed in detail in Chapter 1, if competition is unidimensional and voting is deterministic then the equilibrium is dispersed but the peripheral parties can adopt sufficiently

Yet the PAN and PRD did not move far enough toward the center from the 1980s to the mid-1990s to take significant advantage of the new opportunities. Bruhn's (2001) content analysis of party platforms shows that on economic policy the PAN adopted rightwing pro-market positions and the PRD took leftwing pro-state positions such that neither party could be considered centrist until the mid-1990s. The parties' profiles were also apparent not just in what they tried to portray to the voters, but also in the characteristics of the voters they actually attracted. Figure 6.1 shows trends in the mean economic policy preference of party identifiers from 1982 to 1998. PRI identifiers are in the center, despite a rightward drift from the early 1980s to the mid-1990s. (This movement is not unexpected given the government's shift to a market-led development model and support for NAFTA in this period.) PAN identifiers remain to the right in favor of the market until the mid-1990s, after which they become much more centrist and in fact look very similar to PRI supporters. Identifiers with the PRD and the parties of the independent left before it are consistently to the left and in support of state-centered development. The left's support broadened after the 1982 crisis, but the average PRD identifier could not be called centrist until the mid-1990s. The overall picture thus shows a comparatively centrist incumbent flanked by parties with support coalitions to the left and right until the mid-1990s.[7]

Existing theory about party strategy in the rational choice tradition generally predicts that parties will adapt immediately to changing conditions, thus making the incumbent's losses into the opposition's gains. Even adaptive party theory that was designed to bring the learning process back into spatial analysis finds that parties achieve near-optimal strategies

---

centrist positions to make the interior party lose (Cox, 1990), thus implying an important level of "squeezing." If voting is probabilistic, then the most likely equilibrium is convergent at the minimum-sum point which is the median in one dimension (de Palma et al., 1990) and centrist in two dimensions (Lin et al., 1999). Finally, following Domínguez and McCann (1997), if competition were two-dimensional but voters chose first on the regime dimension and then, if they preferred democracy, on the economic policy dimension, then the challengers would have strong incentives for centrism on economic policy for reasons explained in Chapter 7. Note that these predictions hold for single-member district races with plurality rule, including Mexico's presidential race, 300 of the 500 Chamber of Deputies seats, and 96 of the 128 Senate seats. I am unaware of models designed for mixed electoral systems and although the presence of multi-member district proportional representation seats could alter the predictions above, plurality rule seats clearly dominate in Mexico's system.

[7] Even though most public opinion surveys find modest evidence of issue voting, if one imposes a normal distribution of voters' preferences on the trends in party identification in Figure 6.1 and then calculates the PRI's vote share based on simple proximity voting, the results are strikingly similar to actual vote outcomes from 1982 to 1997 with a correlation of .82.

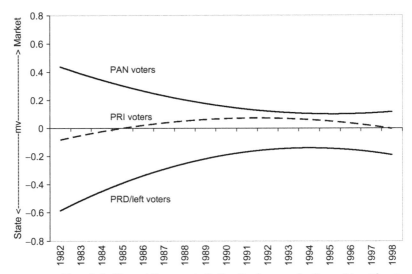

FIGURE 6.1. Trends in Voters' Economic Policy Preferences by Party Identification, 1982–1998.
Note: Data represent Z scores that show the relative position of each party's identifiers at each cross section; "mv" represents the location of the mean voter at each cross-section.
Sources: Office of the President, 1982, 1993; *New York Times*, 1986; Gallup/IMOP-BIMSA, 1988; *Los Angeles Times*, 1996; LatinoBarometer, 1998.

over several elections, or fewer if campaigns are long as they are in Mexico (Kollman, Miller, and Page, 1992). These models predict such fast updating in part because they assume that parties act like unified teams (Downs, 1957) or are led by a party dictator (Snyder, 1994) that is dedicated to winning elections. As a result, party organizations and the way they distribute power among their members are assumed to be unimportant.

But the PAN and PRD were not unified around the goal of winning with centrist strategies. Instead, they were groups of elite activists with differing preferences that derived in part from the different political experiences of elite activist cohorts. Early joiners' initial socialization into politics made them more extreme on policy over the long term than later joiners. Thus, the sequencing of party affiliation created a perverse outcome: early joining party elites created niche parties in their own image that were constrained to the core.[8]

---

[8] Even if there were a party dictator, he likely would have held noncentrist preferences. For a model that shows why, see Chapter 2, Appendix B.

IN THEIR OWN IMAGE: PARTY ELITES' PREFERENCES AND PARTY ORGANIZATIONS

Elite activists who joined opposition parties at an earlier stage, when the incumbent's resource advantages and use of repression were high, endorsed the creation of closed organizations that functioned as tight-knit clubs with deep links to core constituencies. Later joiners generally disagreed with this isolationist mindset and instead wanted to open their parties to the broader society. But not all party elites reacted similarly to changes in the political environment. As the PRI's power declined and elections became fairer, new office-seekers that joined the opposition were more interested in opening affiliation structures to create catchall parties that could propel them into office. New message-seekers, in contrast, continued to prefer relatively closed structures because they prioritized their party's identity and ideology over winning.

The Mexico Party Personnel Surveys tapped niche versus catchall organizational preferences by asking elite activists to rate the importance of four trade-offs in party-building strategy: whether it is more important to appeal to new voters (catchall) or core constituencies (niche), open recruitment to maximize the number of activists (catchall) or restrict it to higher quality recruits (niche), create campaigns in the mass media (catchall) or focus on local campaigning (niche), and adopt centrist appeals at the risk of converging with other parties (catchall) or differentiate appeals from competitors (niche). Mean values for office-seekers and message-seekers that affiliated during various periods are presented in Table 6.1 along with the Party Building Index that averages across all categories.

Office-seekers in the PAN who joined earlier generally preferred more niche-oriented party-building strategies while those who joined later endorsed catchall strategies. Reading the values in Panel A across shows that office-seekers (listed first in each cell) who joined in the 1971 to 1976 period scored 4.0 out of 5.0 on the Party Building Index and landed substantially on the niche side. Those who joined between 1995 and 1999 were at 3.3, and this difference represents a 17.5% shift toward catchall orientations. Although the change is small, it is consistent across all categories. By contrast, note that the mean values for message-seekers bounce around over time, and overall the latest joining message-seekers endorsed even more niche strategies than did early joiners.

Data for the PRD in Panel B echo the findings for the PAN. Office-seekers who affiliated with parties of the independent left between 1972 and 1979 scored higher (i.e., more niche oriented) on each item and on the

TABLE 6.1. *Party Elites' Party-Building Preferences by Period of Affiliation*

Panel A. PAN

In your opinion, the party should... (1 = first phrase, 5 = second phrase)	Period of Initial Affiliation with the PAN (Office-Seekers/Message-Seekers)				
	1971–1976	1977–1982	1983–1988	1989–1994	1995–1999
Base: Appeal to new voters or core constituencies	3.5/2.3	2.7/2.6	2.7/2.6	2.9/3.2	2.6/3.1
Recruitment: Open or restrict activist affiliation	3.6/3.3	3.5/3.2	3.5/2.9	3.4/3.1	3.3/3.7
Communication: Media or grassroots campaigns	4.4/3.6	3.8/4.0	3.8/3.7	3.9/3.8	3.7/4.2
Appeal: Centrism or differentiate from competitors	4.4/3.6	4.2/4.0	3.9/3.8	3.8/3.8	3.6/3.5
Party Building Index (+ = niche)	4.0/3.2	3.6/3.4	3.5/3.3	3.5/3.5	3.3/3.6

Panel B. PRD

In your opinion, the party should... (1 = first phrase, 5 = second phrase)	Period of Initial Affiliation with the left/PRD (Office-Seekers/Message-Seekers)			
	1972–1979	1980–1987	1988–1994	1995–1999
Base: Appeal to new voters or core constituencies	2.2/2.0	1.9/2.5	1.8/2.2	1.7/2.5
Recruitment: Open or restrict activist affiliation	2.6/1.8	2.4/2.2	2.3/2.6	2.0/2.8
Communication: Media or grassroots campaigns	4.3/4.2	3.8/3.3	3.8/4.1	3.5/4.2
Appeal: Centrism or differentiate from competitors	3.6/3.5	3.3/3.1	3.0/3.6	2.8/3.9
Party Building Index (+ = niche)	3.2/2.9	2.9/2.8	2.7/3.1	2.4/3.4

Cells show mean values; first entry is for office-seekers, second entry is for message-seekers. Lower values indicate a preference for catchall-party characteristics; higher values indicate a preference for niche-party characteristics.

Note: PRD elites before 1989 refers to those who joined a party or partisan organization of the independent left and remained active in the PRD once it formed. See the text for details.

Source: Mexico Party Personnel Surveys.

Number of PAN respondents: Office-Seekers = 329; Message-Seekers = 211

Number of PRD respondents: Office-Seekers = 208; Message-Seekers = 110

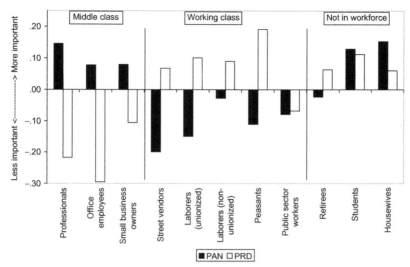

FIGURE 6.2. How Party Elites View their Core Constituencies.
Source: Mexico Party Personnel Surveys.

Party Building Index than did those who joined from 1995 to 1999. The overall difference made the latest joiners 20% more interested in catchall party-building strategies than in niche ones. By contrast, newer message-seekers in the PRD actually endorsed more niche-oriented strategies over time.

What accounts for these seemingly perverse preferences, especially among office-seekers? Why would early joiners endorse party-building strategies that limit their party's size and constrain its potential for expansion? I first show why the logic of opposition party building in dominant party systems generates such counter-intuitive preferences by discussing party elites' attachment to core constituencies, recruitment practices, and techniques for communicating with voters. Then I build a statistical model to show how the PRI's resource advantages at the time each elite activist decided to join the opposition had long-lasting effects on their party-building preferences.

Base: Core Constituencies as the Lifeblood of the Opposition

The PAN and the PRD (as well as the parties of the independent left before it) were built on the support of specific core constituencies in the electorate. One way to appreciate these differences is to examine how party elites perceived their party's base. Figure 6.2 shows ratings for the relative importance of eleven social groups in each party's core support. Positive scores indicate more importance and negative scores indicate less (but since the ratings are relative, negative scores do not mean lack of importance). Elites in both parties thought that groups not in the workforce such as retirees, students, and housewives were important core supporters. These groups aside, PAN and PRD support coalitions diverge. PAN personnel thought of their party as a middle-class one, particularly linked to professionals, office workers, and small business owners. In contrast, PRD elites perceived their party as tied to working-class groups such as peasants, urban laborers, and street vendors, but not to public sector employees who were tightly linked to the incumbent PRI through its control over state-owned enterprises. The problem, however, is that neither the middle class nor the nonaligned working class was large enough to carry national elections by itself.

Why would early joiners continue to endorse niche party-building strategies focused on smaller core constituencies as shown in Table 6.1, even when this was a losing strategy? Core constituencies played such a strong role in both the PAN and the PRD because long-serving party elites had built political careers on the support of these voters. Core voters were the opposition's lifeblood during the lean years when its chances of winning were very low. Without these loyalists who voted their beliefs over their interests, opposition parties may not have survived. Early joiners were acutely aware of the role core supporters played in their long-term battle with the PRI. As a result, even as the possibility of attracting noncore voters increased in the 1980s and 1990s, party elites typically preferred to maintain tight links to their loyal base. Despite some political learning that undoubtedly occurred, on average, early joiners did not change their preferences, and as late as 1999 their initial political socialization had deep effects on their party-building preferences.

Party elites who joined later, on the other hand, had fewer personal ties to their party's traditional core. They joined at a time when fairer competition gave the opposition a much higher chance of winning, and thus they tended to focus on the electoral advantages of expansion over loyal representation of the base.

Recruiting "Good Types": New Activist Quality over Quantity

In general, niche parties recruit new activists from their core constituencies and rely on allied feeder organizations in society to supply known "good types" who share the party's goals. Catchall parties instead recruit from groups that are under-represented in their activist corps as a way of making inroads into noncore constituencies.[9] Table 6.1 shows that early joiners, especially office-seekers, preferred activist quality over quantity, and therefore wanted to maintain high barriers to new recruitment. Why would they choose mechanisms that kept their parties small instead of inviting in as many participants as possible?

High barriers to affiliation served three purposes that early joiners endorsed. First, when the dominant party had huge resource advantages, opposition parties were extremely worried about losing activists to the incumbent. Historically, seemingly strong opposition labor movements, popular movements, and parties were partially or fully demobilized as their activists were bought off and their constituencies re-incorporated into the PRI (Hellman, 1983; Eckstein, 1977; Haber, 1997). Prud'homme argues that this concern was pervasive:

Cooptation by the Mexican government has constituted a permanent feature of its relationship with the opposition. The awareness of this risk is so acute in some opposition forces that they equate dialogue with the authorities with cooptation (1997: fn 3).

By making affiliation relatively more difficult, the challengers molded identities that differentiated them from the dominant party and encouraged only the most committed activists to join. Presumably these more committed participants would be less vulnerable to cooptation.

Second, restricting affiliation to committed activists ensured that those who joined were high quality. When the challengers lacked the resources to communicate with voters through the mass media, they were forced to do face-to-face campaigning. Passionate proselytizers were viewed as more persuasive than unconvinced employees at getting voters to gamble on a lesser-known opposition party that could offer a vision of the future but not the instant patronage payoffs of the PRI.

Finally, high barriers to affiliation helped protect the precious few resources that opposition parties could generate for their members. Activists paid high opportunity costs for joining the opposition over the

---

[9] Media- and candidate-centered campaigns may be more successful at targeting noncore constituencies than grassroots organizing by activists. However, activists still play an important role in transmitting information between voters and candidates, and they help put a human face on the parties they represent. These functions may be particularly important for small and relatively unknown parties.

184   *Why Dominant Parties Lose*

incumbent. Since the challengers could not afford to lower the asymmetric costs of activism for large enough groups in society to facilitate broad recruitment, they used restricted resources to reward commitment. In this way they could increase the dedication of a handful of activists who were otherwise willing to pay the high costs of joining the opposition.

Restricting membership made less sense as the PRI's advantages declined. Instead of struggling to survive, opposition parties now needed to compete for the support of the average voter. A tight-knit and insulated activist corps would push them in the opposite direction toward their traditional (and small) bases. Later joiners wanted to avoid this fate by lowering barriers to affiliation and maximizing new activist recruitment. Rather than high-quality political evangelicals who would create new converts by transforming voters' worldviews, later joiners sought activists who would serve as campaign workers en masse. They wanted canvassers who would go door-to-door, legions to put up posters and paint slogans, and members to turnout at marches and fill plazas. These worker-bee activists would be part-time helpers closer to the low-level volunteer activists in the United States (Aldrich, 1983, 1995), and their actions would be directed less at creating converts to the partisan cause than to maximizing the vote.

Communication: Grassroots versus Media-Centered Campaigns

The modern electoral campaigns of catchall parties are waged primarily in the mass media. They are capital-intensive efforts that rely on sleek, professional, and image-oriented advertisement that often focus on candidate attributes. Niche parties instead mount labor-intensive campaigns that rely on socially embedded local party units with dedicated activists who spread the party's message door-to-door and in the streets. Table 6.1 shows that early joiners in Mexico's opposition parties endorsed a niche-oriented grassroots strategy. Why would they choose a slower and more arduous route for party building that would limit their appeals?

In Mexico, the opposition did not have access to the mass media before the late 1980s and did not get substantial air time until the run-up to the 1997 mid-term elections (see Chapter 3). The media was not technically unavailable; rather, the opposition was priced out of the advertising market. As a result, they were forced to communicate with the electorate essentially one voter at a time by establishing and maintaining a local presence. On the ground, opposition parties looked like social movements with dense localized networks in some areas and shallow to no presence in others.

Even as the mass media became more available to the opposition parties after the mid-1990s, early joiners remained more committed to grassroots communication with voters. This was especially true in the PRD where many older-style party elites had dedicated their lives to consciousness raising and local organization building. However, even in the PAN, the equivalent notion of civic education had encouraged the older generation of activists to become deeply embedded in their communities and active in conservative social organizations with partisan bias. Newer joiners were not uncommitted to these groups and to winning hearts and minds through base-level work, but they were more likely to recognize the advantages of mass advertising to achieve the more limited goal of winning votes.

Dominant Party Advantages and Opposition Party-Building Preferences: A Statistical Analysis

If the party-building strategies of early and later joiners are logical given the peculiarities of opposition party building in Mexico's dominant party system, can we predict the preferences of individual party elites based on changes in dominant party advantages over time? I use the Party Building Index (rescaled from 0 to 1) as the dependent variable and construct OLS regression models to account for the variation in responses. My main interest is whether the PRI's resource advantages at the time party elites initially joined the opposition still affected their party-building preferences in 1999, even when controlling for a host of demographic variables. As in Chapter 5, I measure the incumbent's resource advantages with the percent of GDP produced by state-owned enterprises, matched to each elite activist's initial year of affiliation. I expect that new office-seekers will respond to changing conditions more than new message-seekers. This hypothesis follows the logic developed in earlier chapters that the existing political conditions at the time elite activists first joined the opposition had durable effects on their party-building preferences. As a test, I again construct a faux longitudinal analysis in which the dependent variable – the Party Building Index – was measured in 1999 only but the explanatory variables relate to the prior political conditions that existed when each respondent first joined the opposition. This specification makes for an extremely conservative test that is significantly biased against my

186   *Why Dominant Parties Lose*

TABLE 6.2. *OLS Regression Models of Party Elites' Party-Building Preferences*

	PRD		PAN	
Variable	Coeff	Std Err	Coeff	Std Err
Resources*Office-seeker	0.01**	0.00	0.01**	0.00
Resources*Message-seeker	0.01	0.01	0.00	0.00
Type (0 = message, 1 = office)	0.01	0.17	−0.06**	0.03
Age	0.00	0.00	0.00	0.00
Religiosity	0.02**	0.01	0.01	0.01
Gender (0 = male, 1 = female)	0.10**	0.05	0.04*	0.02
Education	0.01	0.02	−0.02*	0.01
Position in party (0 = activist; 1 = leader)	−0.10	0.10	0.07*	0.04
Constant	0.23	0.20	0.62***	0.07
r^2		.11		.08
Number of cases		118		437

Entries are unstandardized coefficients.
*** $p < .01$; ** $p < .05$; * $p < .1$
Source: Mexico Party Personnel Surveys.

hypothesis. If party elites updated their preferences to reflect new conditions, then the effects of initial conditions on their party-building preferences would have been washed away by the time of the surveys.

Results are shown in Table 6.2. I parsed the PRI's resource advantages variable by party elite type so that the coefficients for office-seekers and message-seekers appear separately. The coefficient for Office-seekers*Resources is statistically significant and positive for both the PAN and PRD, indicating that as the incumbent's advantages rose, opposition elites preferred more niche party-building strategies, and as the playing field leveled, newer office-seekers opted for catchall strategies. Message-seekers, as expected, were unaffected by changes in the competitive environment because they are more interested in spreading their party's message than in winning office. The control variables generally have inconsistent effects across the parties.

An easy way to interpret the results of these models is to generate trended predicted values for elites' party-building preferences according to their year of initial affiliation with the opposition. To create the simulations in Figure 6.3, I hold all variables at their mean or mode, except the PRI's resource advantages which I allow to vary using their real value by year. As a result, the simulation reproduces the political conditions that a prospective party elite would have experienced when she decided to join the opposition.

Constrained to the Core

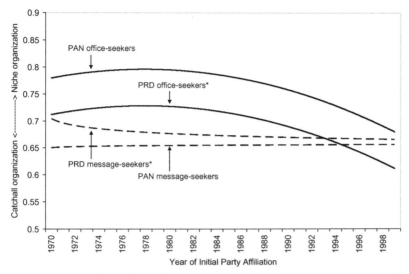

FIGURE 6.3. Party Elites' Party-Building Preferences (trends from model predictions).
*PRD elites before 1989 refer to those who joined a party or partisan organization of the independent left and remained active in the PRD once it formed.
Source: Mexico Party Personnel Surveys.

The figure shows that early joining office-seekers continued to endorse deep links to core constituencies in 1999, years after the opportunity for expansion made targeting new constituencies an electorally profitable strategy. The later an office-seeker joined, the more she supported expanding into new constituencies. The differences between office-seekers and message-seekers also played out as predicted. Early joining office-seekers were more niche-oriented than their message-seeker counterparts; however, as the partisan playing field leveled, new office-seekers became more interested in catchall strategies than did new message-seekers.

FROM PREFERENCES TO PRACTICES: BUILDING OPPOSITION PARTY ORGANIZATIONS

Party elites' failure to coordinate on the most efficient organizational form for expansion may be surprising, but did intra-party differences have meaningful effects on the actual structure of party organizations and their modes of expansion? First, I discuss the norms and procedures that niche-oriented early joiners structured into their parties and then I show how these structures limited expansion.

Designing Organizational Norms and Procedures

One of the key ways that early joiners created niche parties was to differentiate themselves from the incumbent by imposing high barriers to affiliation and advancement. To this end, both the PAN and the PRD established institutes to recruit and train new activists, funded executive level secretaries to track membership, and instituted formal and informal procedures designed to recruit "good types" from known core constituencies who were ideologically pure.

From its beginnings in 1939, the PAN considered itself as a party of "excellent minorities" where membership was restricted to ideologically compatible activists of high quality. Founding party president Manuel Gómez Morín viewed the PRI's sectoral organizations as inimical to democracy and the free expression of individual preferences. As a result, the PAN eschewed relationships with social organizations and relied exclusively on individual affiliation. This decision essentially limited the PAN to a minority base because the PRI's sectors included the major social groups of the early and mid-20th century. Ensuring that this minority was "high quality" required strict control over affiliation. Until 1996, prospective members had to be sponsored by an existing activist in good standing and then get approval from both the local party as well as the National Members' Registry that was controlled by the 20–30-member National Executive Committee. The committee also determined whether a recruit met the standard of having "an honest way of life,"[10] and it seemed in no hurry to add new members as it sometimes delayed affiliation decisions for up to a year (Mizrahi, 2003). Activists were also required to pass an exam on the party's history and basic principles that typically required taking a preparation course. The exam helped train new recruits but it also ensured that members were ideologically like-minded, committed to the cause, and literate with at least some formal education. According to Mizrahi, these safeguards "demonstrate the party's reluctance to include a heterogeneous and ideologically diverse population in its ranks" (2003: 56).

The PAN's high barriers to affiliation became a point of pride. One story was repeated by the party president and others during in-depth interviews. I was told of a high-level member of the PRI who defected and wanted to run as a PAN candidate. However, because he had not gone through the standard approval process, he was not allowed to affiliate with the party or run for office under its label, even though party leaders thought that

---

[10] PAN statutes, Article 8.

he could win. Eventually, he did meet the requirements, rose to a position in the National Political Council and, according to one national leader, "became one of the foremost authorities on the party's doctrine" (author interviews, 1999). This story typifies how many PAN leaders think about the relationship between the party and potential activists: the party molds them more than they mold the party.

The concern over ideological dilution ran so deep that members were willing to sacrifice electoral victories for purity. When the Mexico Party Personnel Surveys asked whether they would prefer to move their party to the center at the risk of mimicking their competitors or differentiate the PAN ideologically at the risk of losing elections, over 60% chose the latter. This emphasis on party identity seems almost fantastical from the perspective of theory that expects parties to act as rational vote maximizers.

In sum, the PAN functioned as a niche-oriented club in which membership was strictly limited. Mizrahi (2003) reached the same conclusion based on her extensive interviews of PAN personnel throughout the country. She refers to the PAN as a sectarian party and writes that it "institutionalized a set of internal rules designed to preserve its central ideological principles and safeguard it against political opportunists ... [these] rules restrain the growth of party militants, curtail the party's flexibility to respond effectively to a changing and more demanding electorate, and hinder the PAN's entrenchment among broader sections of the population" (2003: 52).

The parties of the independent left and the PRD approached the question of affiliation differently, but they ended up with strikingly similar results. Unlike the PAN, these parties did not impose formal barriers to affiliation; however, they all had strict informal barriers. Parties of the independent left were based on dissident labor organizations, peasant groups, and radical intellectual clubs (see Chapter 3). In sharp contrast to the PAN, individual affiliation in the left was almost unknown and advancement without the support of an organized social group was practically impossible.

The group basis of intra-party politics on the left migrated into the PRD when it formed in 1989. Formally, the PRD had an open affiliation procedure designed to incorporate broad segments of civil society. Party leaders hoped that low formal barriers would help expand on Cuauhtémoc Cárdenas' huge appeal in his 1988 presidential campaign and that they would be able to ride this wave of opposition sentiment to the presidency in the following election. Yet despite formal openness, recruitment was *de facto* regulated by factions comprising partisan groups, social

190   *Why Dominant Parties Lose*

movements, and nongovernmental organizations. These groups dominated to such an extent that according to one disgruntled ex-activist,

There are more than a few who have tried to affiliate with the PRD as simple citizens and have had to give up after coming up against the barrier of hermetic and sectarian groups that demonstrated little appreciation for individual activism (Sánchez, 1999: 100).

Based on in-depth interviews, I counted 22 important intra-party factions, known as *corrientes*, between the party's founding in 1989 and 2000. Sánchez (1999: 79–87) reports more than 30. These factions tended to be highly fluid, but ever-present. Early national factions such as Trisecta and Six Pack brought together pre-existing parties and partisan organizations of the independent left from 1989 to about 1992. In advance of the 1994 presidential elections, most groups coalesced into two mega-factions: the intellectually oriented Arcoíris[11] and the social movement-oriented Corriente de Izquierda Democrática (CID).[12] Following the 1994 elections, these mega-factions broke apart and new ones formed around each of the major PRD personalities. Nevertheless, these smaller personalist factions still had deep roots that traveled from national leadership to base-level organizations. As one example, internal documents show that candidates for the party presidency in Mexico City in 1998 measured their pre-electoral force exclusively by the local social and partisan organizations that supported them rather than by head-counts, polls, or prior internal election results.

Membership in base-level social and partisan groups and in the broader factions that coordinated them at the state and national levels served as the analytical equivalent to formal barriers to entry in the PAN. Factions operated as filters to ensure that only recruits who were known to share the party's ideological line played a role in local leadership and party conventions. According to Augustín Guerrero Castillo, then President of the PRD in the Federal District, "The *corrientes* are responsible for most of the growth of the party. Without their structure, there are no activists, because every activist belongs to a *corriente*" (cited in Sánchez, 1999: 100).

---

[11] Arcoíris included Porfirio Muñoz Ledo from the Democratic Current (CD), Jesús Ortega from the Revolutionary Workers Party (PRT), and Raúl Alvarez Garín and Marcos Rascón from the radical intellectual group Punto Crítico.

[12] The CID included Mario Saucedo from the Revolutionary National Civic Association (ACNR), Paco Saucedo from the massive Mexico City poor people's movement the Asamblea de Barrios, Carlos Imaz from the Coordinator of University Students (CEU), and René Bejerano and Dolores Padierna from the Popular Union New Tenochitlán (UPNT), another important poor people's movement in Mexico City.

How Organizational Design Limited Expansion

Whether formally or informally, both the PAN and PRD created high barriers to affiliation. The PAN's focus on "excellent minorities" and the PRD's use of gatekeeper factions rooted in local socio-political groups limited recruitment to core constituencies. That was precisely the idea: challenger party organizations were initially designed to generate tightly knit activist corps that would help the parties survive when they had little chance of winning and their members paid high costs for participation. The parties' early organizational forms created a pattern of expansion that might be called "intensive" because it prioritized depth over breadth and recruitment from known feeder groups. In the aggregate, intensive expansion tends to create islands of activist support within geographic units and, as a result, expanding into new areas is a slow and arduous process that involves significant base-level work to convert citizens to the party's worldview. In contrast, catchall parties engage in "extensive" expansion that prioritizes breadth over depth and adds new activists from noncore constituencies at a higher rate. Extensive expansion may occur through grassroots work but is more likely to be the downstream result of campaigns waged in the media.

The political biographies of individual party elites represented in Figure 6.4 show that both the PAN and PRD relied heavily on nonparty feeder groups associated with their core constituencies to provide new activists at least until the 1990s. PAN elites who joined in the 1960s belonged to an average of more than five feeder organizations. Most important among these were professional organizations, conservative groups associated with the Catholic Church, and family values groups such as Padres de Familia. These data echo Mabry's (1973) excellent in-depth study of the PAN from the 1940s to the 1960s that emphasized the party's deep links to lay Church groups. The figure also shows a notable reduction in memberships the later an elite activist joined the PAN, and by 1999, new elites belonged to just 1.5 feeder organizations. Thus, although the PAN was significantly reliant on core constituencies to provide new activists for decades, it had broadened its recruitment sources substantially by the late 1990s.

A similar pattern of recruitment occurred in the PRD. Elites who joined parties and partisan organizations of the independent left in the 1960s were members of more than four nonparty feeder organizations. There is a slight increase in the 1970s, probably because the PRI's use of repression in that era forced many leftists underground (see Chapter 3). Almost

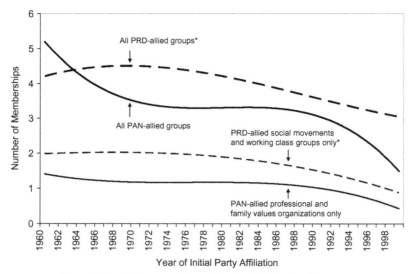

FIGURE 6.4. Party Elites' Nonparty Organizational Memberships.
*PRD elites before 1989 refer to those who joined a party or partisan organization of the independent left and remained active in the PRD once it formed.
Source: Mexico Party Personnel Surveys.

half of these nonparty memberships were working-class and neighborhood groups that formed the left's core support. By 1999, new elites held memberships in an average of just three allied organizations. Unlike in the PAN, the diversification of recruitment into the left occurred gradually after the 1977 electoral reform opened more space for party-based opposition. Overall, however, the PRD remained more reliant on specific feeder groups by the end of the period under study than did the PAN.

These dynamics of individual-level recruitment are also reflected in aggregate membership expansion across the country. Membership data help distinguish between niche and catchall forms of party organization in two ways. First, since niche parties erect high barriers to entry and limit affiliation to "good types," their activist corps may be small in absolute terms. Second, niche parties engage in "intensive" expansion by adding activists in areas where they already have support, whereas catchall parties do "extensive" expansion focused on noncore constituencies.

Figure 6.5 shows the PAN and PRD's overall membership and their Party Nationalization Score (PNS) scores.[13] The PNS, developed by Jones

---

[13] PAN membership data were supplied by Oscar Moya, Undersecretary of Organization and Director of the National Affiliation Registry. PRD membership were supplied by Dr. Carlos Wilson, Secretary of Organization.

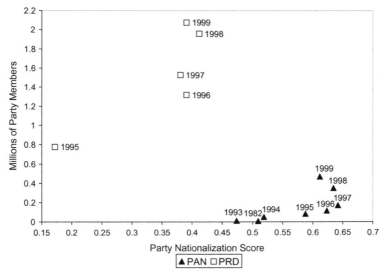

FIGURE 6.5. Party Membership and Geographic Concentration.
Sources: Author's calculations based on data from Registro Nacional de Miembros, PAN and Secretaría de Organización, PRD.

and Mainwaring (2003), measures how evenly spread a party is over geographic units. In this case, it measures the evenness of low-level activist presence across Mexico's 31 states and the Federal District.[14] A party that is spread evenly – regardless of the number of activists – receives a PNS score of one. A party that is maximally uneven receives a score closer to zero.

Looking just at overall membership on the vertical axis, one can see evidence of the PAN's priority for slow growth. Until the 1990s, it focused on attracting quality activists rather quantity. The party began in 1939 with 60 members. It did not reach 1,000 until 1958 and remained under 5,000 until 1980. From that point on, the number of active members approximately doubled every five years. Yet by 1994, it still had not reached 50,000 members. The next five years brought massive and consistent expansion, so that by 1999 the PAN claimed 472,387 members. Still, in a country with over 37 million voters, this represented a member-to-voter ratio of 1.26%. I compared this to 1999 density data for 59 first, second, and third-place-finishing parties in 20 European democracies gathered by Mair and Van Biezen (2001). In this list, the PAN would have ranked 17th, just above the mean of 1.2%. During this same time period, the PRI,

---

[14] Unlike the data on elite activists from the Mexico Party Personnel Surveys, membership rolls are dominated by low-level activists.

194 *Why Dominant Parties Lose*

which does not have a formal list of members, claimed over seven million activists, or a density score of 18.7%.[15] Based on these numbers, the PRI not only dwarfed the PAN, but it was far above the densest European party, Austria's OVP at 9.9%.

PRD membership data does not exist for the party's first six years, 1989–1995. Beginning in 1995, party records show almost 800,000 members. A year later, membership topped off at just below 1 million, and by 1999 it surpassed 2 million for a density score of 5.55%. These numbers fall far below the PRI but significantly surpass the PAN. They also place the PRD higher than all but three of Europe's parties. However, these data should be interpreted with caution. First, there were virtually no formal barriers to affiliation, and in-depth interviews suggest that many members register on the day of primary elections, almost as part of the voting process itself. As a result, the PRD's membership rolls include many who cannot really be counted as active contributors to the party. Second, during the earlier stages of party development, the majority of members came from the Federal District and the states of México and Michoacán. Total PRD membership minus these three states stood at only 70,000 in 1995, and this number was below the PAN's total membership of almost 85,000 in that year. The PRD only expanded significantly beyond its regional activist base after 1995.

The more interesting result comes from examining the relationship between PNS and overall membership by looking at the angle and direction of change over time in Figure 6.5. Movement from left to right indicates catchall growth because the party spreads into under-represented areas as it adds members. Movement from right to left indicates niche-oriented growth because the party becomes more geographically concentrated as it adds members. Perfect vertical movement indicates that the party reproduces its prior level of geographic concentration as it adds members.

Figure 6.5 shows that between 1982 and 1993, the PAN expanded by adding core members in states where it already had a presence. Even though it grew from 5,000 to 40,000 members in this period, the leftward movement indicates intensive growth through which the party actually became less nationalized and more niche-oriented. Membership increased sharply to over 120,000 between 1993 and 1996, and the rightward movement indicates catchall-style extensive expansion such that the party added activists in previously under-represented states. Expansion slowed again between 1996 and 1999; however, by this time the party

---

[15] Internal documents, PRI National Executive Committee (CEN).

was significantly larger and more nationalized than it had been two decades earlier.

Figure 6.5 also shows that the PRD experienced a dramatic leap in membership and increase in national coverage from 1995 to 1996. Subsequently, membership continued to soar, reaching a reported 2.1 million in 1999; however, coverage gains halted and the party expanded by adding members from underserved areas at the same rate as those from previously represented areas. Although the PRD came to dwarf the PAN in self-reported size, it sacrificed coverage. The PRD's highest PNS at 0.41 is lower than the PAN's lowest level of national coverage since 1980. Yet even at its 1999 PNS of 0.62, the PAN could not be considered a truly national party. Clearly both parties had difficulty expanding, a result that I argue derived from initial decisions to form niche-oriented organizations designed to protect the challenger parties' identities.

Case Studies of Opposition Party Building in Mexico City

What do the dynamics of opposition party building look like on the ground? In this section, I show that concrete experiences at the local level echo the processes documented with both individual-level data from the Mexico Party Personnel Surveys and aggregate data on party membership: both the PAN and PRD established strong ties to core constituencies in defined areas and then had difficulty expanding out of these niches to gain broader support.

The case studies focus on two boroughs in the Federal District of Mexico City: Miguel Hidalgo and Iztapalapa. Mexico City is important in its own right and as the political and economic center of the country. Its 40 federal electoral districts before the 1996 reforms and 30 after represent a meaningful proportion of the 300 single-member districts nationally, and its more than 5.5 million eligible voters make it the focus of presidential campaigns. In 1994, 37.5% of the three parties' campaign activities and fully 45% of the PRI's activities took place in the Federal District (Crespo, 1996: 181). The next largest proportion (just 5.9%) occurred in the State of Mexico that surrounds the Federal District, part of which is in the metropolitan zone. In addition, the incredible concentration of media in the Federal District creates an inevitable diffusion of information from city to national politics. For instance, citizens all over the country watched the 1997 mayoral elections unfold, and this created a positive coattails effect for the PRD.

No single state is representative of all of Mexico, and the Federal District's unique qualities distinguish it from other areas. In particular, the city

196   *Why Dominant Parties Lose*

was an historical hotbed of opposition political activity, in part because dissenters could organize more easily with limited resources in this densely populated area. The labor militancy of 1958, the student movements of 1968 and 1971, the emergence of leftist urban popular movements in the 1970s and their expansion after the 1985 earthquake all occurred in the city. In the 1982 and 1985 elections, when the Unified Mexican Socialist Party (PSUM) floundered nationwide with about 4% of the vote, it captured nearly 15% in the Federal District, and the available data for the contested 1988 presidential election show that Cárdenas won 45.5% of the citywide vote. The PAN's record in the Federal District before 1988 was even better: it won an average of over 30% of the vote in the 1960s and, after a dramatic dip in 1973, it rebounded to an average of over 20% from 1976 to the 1990s. Thus, the combination of high population density and a tradition of opposition voting may have made party expansion in the city more reliant on pre-existing organizations than elsewhere in the country.

In other ways, the Federal District looks similar to national politics. The PAN and PRD have met with different levels of success across the city's electoral districts, creating some areas of two-party competition between one challenger and the PRI, and some areas where all three parties compete. In broad strokes, this looks like the national distribution with PAN-PRI competition in the North, PRD-PRI competition in the South, and three-party competition in the Center.[16] Before 2000, the opposition parties did not compete head-to-head without the PRI anywhere in the Federal District.

Miguel Hidalgo and Iztapalapa were purposively selected for in-depth study to maximize variation in the patterns of party competition. As shown in Table 6.3, in the period under study, Miguel Hidalgo had three-party competition boroughwide, but one of its two federal electoral districts had PAN-PRI competition and the other had PRD-PRI competition. Iztapalapa had PRD-PRI competition. In all boroughs, like in Mexico in general, about 35–40% of voters consider themselves independents. All three parties competed vigorously for this large "floating" electorate, without which they could not win.

Miguel Hidalgo: Geographic Limits to Expansion
Miguel Hidalgo is home to almost 275,000 eligible voters. The borough includes the city's main park (Chapultepec) and the president's residence

---

[16] For work on the strategy implications of the varying number of parties subnationally, see Greene (2002a, 2008).

TABLE 6.3. *Borough Case Study Information*

Case	SES	Competitive Parties (1997)	Federal Election Returns (1997)			Party Identification (1999)			
			PAN	PRD	PRI	PAN	PRD	PRI	Indep.
Iztapalapa	Lower	PRD-PRI	12.9%	49.5%	25.4%	9.7%	20.0%	23.0%	44.0%
Miguel Hidalgo (District 5)	Lower	PRD-PRI	18.2%	42.2%	26.6%	15.4%	14.4%	21.7%	41.5%
Miguel Hidalgo (District 10)	Higher	PAN-PRI	28.3%	31.3%	29.3%				

Row totals for party identification do not add to 100% because "don't know" answers were excluded.

Sources: SES from INEGI, XI Censo General de Población y Vivienda, 1990; election returns from IFE, http://www.ife.org.mx; party identification from *Reforma* newspaper "Encuestas Delegacionales," 1999.

(Los Pinos). Bordering the park is the fashionable Polanco neighborhood and the elegant Lomas area. The borough also includes a working-class zone with giant public housing projects to the west and densely packed single-family homes and small apartment buildings to the east. Overall, Miguel Hidalgo has a somewhat higher standard of living than the city average, but it is geographically cleaved in two with the more prosperous Federal Electoral District 10 and the predominantly working-class District 5.

The PAN and PRD engaged in serious efforts to expand their vote shares in Miguel Hidalgo during the late 1990s. Both parties thought that it was important to win a plurality across the entire borough, not only because doing so would yield two congressional seats and add to the vote totals for mayor and for proportional representation seats in Congress, but because it would propel the party to the borough presidency. In the 1990s, the city underwent a political transformation from appointed to elected positions: the local legislature became fully independent in 1991, the mayor became an elected post in 1997, and borough presidents were first elected in 2000. The first borough presidency was coveted for its historical significance and because operatives thought it would secure their party's local power base well into the future.

But winning District 5 or 10 alone, even by a wide margin, would not be enough to win the borough presidency in three-party competition. Both parties needed to expand. In the 1997 federal elections, the PRD swept 29 of 30 districts and won the mayoral race. Nevertheless, it did better in working-class areas than in middle-class ones, and Miguel Hidalgo was no exception. Table 6.3 shows that in the richer District 10 it won 11% less than in the poorer District 5. The PAN experienced the inverse problem. It won 10% more in the richer District 10 than in the less prosperous District 5. The PRI vote was almost equal across the two districts. Local operatives from all parties thought that the PRD's performance in 1997 was especially strong due to Cárdenas' mayoral run, and in the next election they expected vigorous three-party competition in the borough at large, with PAN-PRI competition in District 10 and PRD-PRI competition in District 5. Thus, to win the borough, the PAN and PRD would need to expand where they lagged.

THE PRD: THE MIDDLE CLASS IS NOT IN THE STREETS. The PRD's presence in Miguel Hidalgo before 2000 owed almost entirely to a local leader named Javier Hidalgo and two community organizations that he helped create called the Neighborhood Defense Committees of Pensil and

Anahuac. Javier founded these groups following the 1985 earthquake that devastated large portions of Mexico City and left many working-class families homeless. An architect by training, he mobilized citizens to lobby the city and federal governments to rebuild damaged housing. These community groups joined with others from throughout the city to form the Unified Coordinating Committee of Earthquake Victims (CUD) which convinced the de la Madrid Administration to invest millions in housing reconstruction. By 1987, the government's reconstruction program was complete, but Javier and others saw the potential to maintain the budding movement. The CUD dissolved, but some of its members formed a citywide organization dedicated to public housing construction and urban service provision called the Assembly of Neighborhoods (AB) (see Cuéllar, 1993; Greene, 1997; Haber, 2006).

The symbol and sometime spokesperson of the AB was a comically out-of-shape superhero in a gleaming red and gold wrestler's outfit, complete with mask and cape, called *Superbarrio* Gómez. This self-styled "voice of the voiceless" began a run for the presidency in 1988, but quickly declined in favor of Cárdenas once he announced. The AB was a leading voice for the Cárdenas campaign and became a key pillar of PRD support in the city. The organization was so large that it could regularly turnout 5,000 or more people for marches, blockades, and street theater that often included staged wrestling matches between *Superbarrio* and some symbol of PRI power, complete with rigged officiating. Cárdenas did almost all of his neighborhood campaigning in *Superbarrio's Barriomóvil* until the mid-1990s, and he made the cartoonish red and yellow panel van a centerpiece of his image by standing on top of it rather than a stage as he celebrated his father's 1938 expropriation of the oil industry before massive crowds in the central plaza. For his part, Javier's organizing activities propelled him upward in the PRD, and to date he has been on the National Executive Committee, served as President of the National Political Council, been a two-term Federal District legislator, and a candidate for borough president.

Javier used his base in Pensil and Anahuac to expand the PRD's presence in the borough. In the typical style of neighborhood organizations, his groups staged meetings and marches, handed out flyers, hung banners, and painted logos on buildings. Activists canvassed the surrounding areas and slowly recruited new members, winning converts to the party's cause one at a time. They had little trouble expanding into the public housing projects where the PRI was once strong and they gained some support in

200 *Why Dominant Parties Lose*

demographically similar areas, but beyond that, expansion faltered. By 1999, the PRD had a presence in 80 neighborhoods, yet fully 40% of its 6,867 registered activists came from Anahuac (19.1%), Pensil (10.0%), and two geographically contiguous neighborhoods in District 5, Popotla (5.5%) and Tlaxpana (5.5%).[17] In the more prosperous District 10, it had a nontrivial number of activists only in Escandón (7.1%), Tacubaya (4.1%), and América (4.1%). Not coincidentally, these are the district's most working-class neighborhoods with many car repair shops and informal commerce in the streets.

By the run-up to the 2000 elections, the PRD had reached a plateau. It had recruited all it seemed able to from its core constituencies, and the community style of organization was no longer expanding its reach. Only 14.4% of the borough's voters identified with the PRD (see Table 6.3), and just 15.1% planned to vote for the party's congressional candidate. Javier put the problem this way:

I'm coming to the conclusion that the form of organization I have is not capable of expanding into District 10. It's a middle class area and people just do things differently there. I have tried everything, including personal door-to-door canvassing, and I'm lucky if I even get to the door before their guard dogs attack me! I just don't know how to expand the party in neighborhoods like Polanco (author interview, November 18, 1998).

The PRD in Miguel Hidalgo had reached the geographic limits of its expansion. It did the best where it could piggyback on pre-existing working-class organizations and it met with relative success in the rest of District 5 where it was favored by working-class demographics, but its niche-oriented intensive mode of expansion was poorly suited to cultivate support in prosperous District 10. The PRD could not become a catchall party capable of winning the entire borough unless it also incorporated a more modern party-building style that appealed to middle-class individuals not linked to politicized community groups. Indeed, in the 2000 race for borough president, Javier lost to his PAN rival, Arne Aus Den Ruthen, despite the PRD's decisive victory in the Mexico City mayor's race.

THE PAN: THE LOWER CLASS IS IN THE STREETS. The PAN in Miguel Hidalgo experienced similar expansion problems, but from the other side of the tracks. It has done well in the more prosperous District 10, but

[17] Author's calculations from membership data supplied by the Secretaría de Organización, PRD-DF.

its performance in the poorer District 5 has been lackluster (see Table 6.3).

In the run-up to the 2000 elections, Mauricio Candiani was the PAN's local leader. Mauricio was a young, energetic, and well-educated man who gave the impression of impending upward-mobility. He was quick to produce pamphlets, brochures, and flyers that he distributed throughout the borough. He also came well-armed with sample surveys and demographic analyses from census data produced by his staff in conjunction with the national party's research institute. PRD operatives rarely had such data and, when they did, they often dismissed them as less valid measures of public opinion than their own observation.

Before becoming borough party president, Mauricio was the PAN's District 10 president. There, middle-class constituents supported the party through a combination of individual affiliation and linkages to pre-existing residents' associations. (PAN operatives were quick to point out that they will not organize people into groups but will link to pre-existing ones.) These middle-class organizations were so unavailable to Javier in the PRD that he was not even sure if they existed. Mauricio found it relatively easy to organize campaign swings through this district, and his six paid staffers were sufficient to make preparations.

Party membership rolls from 1999 show that the PAN counted 1,133 registered activists in Miguel Hidalgo. This number reached barely one-sixth of the PRD's borough total. More importantly, the PAN suffered from a tremendous geographic imbalance: 76% of its activists were in District 10 and only 24% in District 5 – the inverse of the PRD's distribution.

When campaigning in District 10, Mauricio said that he primed the party's market-oriented economic policy message. He argued that diminishing the state's role in business would create new investment opportunities, increasing foreign trade would make more consumer goods available at better prices, and enhancing individual responsibility through, for example, privatizing pension funds, would reduce the tax burden. Mauricio found that these economically oriented campaign messages were especially important in District 10, not only because its residents are middle class, but also because the substantial Jewish population in the Polanco neighborhood is wary of the PAN's social conservatism and ties to the Catholic Church.

But the real battle is in expanding into District 5. "In lower class areas," Mauricio said, "I don't talk about the party's program. Instead, I talk about *gestión social*." *Gestión* involves championing citizens' needs or demands with the authorities. A party operative might help maneuver the bureaucracy to secure improved urban services, land titles, access to public programs, or the resolution of simple legal problems. *Gestión* is like constituency service, but it is routinely done by community leaders who are affiliated with social movements or political parties rather than by elected representatives alone. This was where the urban poor people's movements associated with the PRD excelled. But for Mauricio to do *gestión*, he first needed to convince residents to approach the PAN for assistance. He stated, almost pleadingly, "We need to give the party a face, let people know that we are their neighbors, and that we can be trusted." In other words, Mauricio needed activists for grassroots mobilizing. His six paid staffers were too few for the task, and attempts to canvass District 5 had all but failed. According to Mauricio,

It's natural that a party that recruits by personal contact and has middle class members will continue to recruit from the middle class. And this is a central problem that the party has. We need to expand our recruitment into the lower class. The only real way to do this is by canvassing door-to-door in the neighborhoods, having a presence in the street, and detecting potential leaders among the lower class and then encouraging them to join the party. But this is slow and difficult. I try to organize canvassing drives, but there are many local activists in the party who don't spend time in the streets. They don't know the lower class areas and they are afraid of them (author interview, July 26, 1999).

Without an organizational base or the ability to generate one in working-class neighborhoods, the PAN's vote share has been very sensitive to the personal appeal of its candidates. When the candidate has had broad appeal, as Fox did in 2000, the party has done well in lower-class areas. When the candidate has lacked broad appeal, the party has floundered and won only its core constituents. For instance, Carlos Castillo Peraza, the PAN's candidate for Federal District mayor in 1997, was tragically ineffective in generating lower-class support. His attempts to communicate with the poor included awkward non sequiturs and tasteless dirty jokes that even seemed to make him uncomfortable in the telling. As a result, the party lost convincingly, ceding all single- member districts throughout the city to the PRD except one – District 10 in Miguel Hidalgo. In fact, the 1997 campaign was so disastrous, that the PAN decided to reorganize in the Federal District. The new formula would create closer links with individual neighborhoods, and would particularly target lower-class areas for expansion. The borough of Iztapalapa was an important proving ground for this strategy.

Constrained to the Core

Iztapalapa: Islands and Bunkers

Iztapalapa is the most populous and one of the poorest boroughs in the Federal District. Its more than one million eligible voters – about 18% of the city's total – are divided into five federal electoral districts. Many homes in the borough are self-built, 20% do not have drainage, and 42% do not have access to public water service compared to 29% citywide. The borough's past encapsulates the history of urbanization, internal migration, and the *cacique* (political strongman) in Mexico. Families settled in Iztapalapa in waves that rippled out from the distant city center. As they did, they were often drawn into organizations of PRI-backed *caciques* that regulated access to urban services (public and private), building materials, and even land titles. If the government's political control reached down to the block level anywhere in Mexico, it was in Iztapalapa (Cornelius, 1975; Eckstein, 1977). Even in the 1990s after a dramatic increase in partisan competition, the PRI still controlled key organizations there including the large trash-pickers union (Guillermoprieto, 1994), the powerful local chapters of the National Confederation of Popular Organizations (CNOP), and the Territorial Movement (MT), as well as groups dedicated to neighborhood settlement and land invasions such as *Antorcha Popular* and those controlled by a shady figure known as *La Loba* (The She-Wolf).

Despite the long history of PRI control, the borough's size meant that neither the PAN nor the PRD could ignore it. All three parties campaigned vigorously there for the 1997 mayor's race and again in 2000 when federal representatives and the first elected borough president would be chosen. Prior elections typically showed PRI-PRD competition, with the PAN a distant third. Available official returns from the controversial 1988 election show that Cárdenas won over 50% boroughwide, almost 20% above his national average. Partly as a result, Iztapalapa became a principal target for PRONASOL, the Salinas Administration's (1988–1994) poverty alleviation program with pro-PRI bias described in Chapter 3. The program helped dent the PRD's support and opened space for the PAN to expand enough in the 1991 and 1994 elections to temporarily create local three-party competition. The PRD rebounded in 1997 with 49.5% of the vote to the PRI's 25.4% and the PAN's 12.9%, and in the 1999 officially nonpartisan elections for neighborhood representatives, PRD operatives claimed to have won 104 posts to the PRI's 45 and the PAN's lone victory.[18]

---

[18] I did not verify the 1999 results from other sources and the data should be treated with caution.

204   *Why Dominant Parties Lose*

In the run-up to the 2000 elections, all three parties made significant attempts to expand their support in Iztapalapa. The PRD saw the opportunity to solidify its base and generate a durable majority. The PRI sought to regain support that had drained away with the reduction in state resources. For the PAN, Iztapalapa was a testing ground for strategies to expand into working-class areas and improve on its dismal 1997 showing.

THE PRD: MAROONED. The PRD's support in Iztapalapa, like in Miguel Hidalgo, was built on pre-existing social movements and community organizations. Following the repression of the student movement in 1968 and 1971, some communist and socialist activists began organizing communities on the outskirts of Mexico City. One such group was the Revolutionary Popular Union – Emiliano Zapata (UPREZ). In 1980, the UPREZ was a major player in the National Coordinator of Urban Popular Movements (CONAMUP) that was linked to the opposition Unified Mexican Socialist Party (PSUM) and later to the Mexican Socialist Party (PMS), both of which were forerunners to the PRD. Other important support groups included the Assembly of Neighborhoods (AB) described in the prior section and the Civic Union of Iztapalapa (UCI).

However, the character of PRD-allied organizations in Iztapalapa differed from those in Miguel Hidalgo. Miguel Hidalgo is in the center of the city and contains older mixed-use neighborhoods with rental and owner-occupied housing as well as small businesses. Community groups there tend to establish a neighborhoodwide presence and incorporate multiple working-class interests. Iztapalapa, by contrast, has many large public interest housing projects that are physically separated from the rest of their neighborhoods. Many residents own their own homes, but typically they had to organize beforehand to claim land, secure political support to get housing constructed, and amass resources for a down-payment. This generated community organizations that are often more militant, tighter knit, homogeneous, and walled off from their surrounding neighborhood. Heated and sometimes violent territorial conflicts between PRD and PRI-affiliated organizations over land rights further stoked the militancy of some groups.

In Miguel Hidalgo, the presence of middle-class areas posed a programmatic challenge to the PRD's expansion. Iztapalapa's more homogenous working-class population should have been fertile ground for a consistent PRD majority. Yet its vote share bounced around in the 1990s and even after its convincing 1997 victory, identification with the PRD in 1999 was just 20% boroughwide (see Table 6.3). The PRD's allied organizations tended to create "islands" of support, and while these groups were very effective at mobilizing deep support in narrow slices of neighborhoods, they were much less effective at drawing in individual members from the surrounding neighborhood.

In 1999, PRD rolls showed 16,381 members in Iztapalapa. Unlike in Miguel Hidalgo, activists were more or less evenly distributed across the entire borough. However, within each district, membership concentrated where pre-existing social organizations were strong. As one example, District 22 had 2,501 members in 1999, fully 30% of which came from one public housing project called San Miguel Teotongo that was controlled by the UPREZ. On the PRD's group basis, borough party president Victor Hugo said,

There aren't many 'individual' members of the party here who affiliated without a prior affiliation with one of our organizations. People affiliate with the party because the leaders of their social organizations tell them to. This leads to a lot of activists, but of poor quality (author interview, July 14, 1999).

Victor won the local party presidency in a close election against ten other candidates. Each candidate was backed by specific community organizations that were linked to party factions at the state and national levels. Victor's support came from the UCI founded by Congressman René Arce while the second place candidate was backed by the UPREZ, and the third by organizations allied with the national Leftist Democratic Faction (CID). The election was so contentious that Victor thought he would be unable to run the party without support from the losing community organizations. In an interview in the party's beehive headquarters he said,

One of the biggest problems here is the institutionalization of social movements and community organizations in the party. These groups are powerful enough here that they threaten to leave the party and work alone unless they get their way (author interview, July 14, 1999).

The PRD appeared stifled in Iztapalapa. On the basis of demographics, the borough was ripe for a leftwing alternative, but the party was constrained by the passionate activism supplied by its allied social organizations. These groups created deep but narrow support and they forced a mode of intra-party politics that demanded close attention to factional battles and difficult power-sharing agreements. This inward orientation generated a vibrant party, but also a niche-oriented one that could

206 *Why Dominant Parties Lose*

not move beyond its core constituency to develop into a larger catchall competitor.

THE PAN: IN THE BUNKER. The PAN had almost no natural base of support in Iztapalapa, and it had no organizational presence there until 1997. The party's middle-class profile and free market appeals had little resonance with local residents. Further, its doctrine of individual as opposed to group affiliation fit poorly with the borough's long tradition of community organizing and *de facto* constrained it to minority status. Nevertheless, the PAN invested significant resources in Iztapalapa as part of its reorganization following the 1997 elections. The plan was to expand the party's organizational presence in working-class neighborhoods in order to diminish its reliance on notoriously volatile candidate-centered appeals. It hired 19 staffers and purchased a well-maintained building to serve as its headquarters. In sharp contrast to the choreographed chaos in the PRD's offices, the PAN's locale resembled a bunker. It was set back from the road and its only entrance was around the back, off an empty parking lot that was separated from the street by a car barricade. Inside, the staff seemed lonely in this large and quiet space.

The PAN's borough president in 1999 was Esperanza Gómez Mont. Previously, Esperanza was elected to the 1st Representative Assembly of the Federal District (ARDF) (1988–1991) and later appointed president of the middle-class Benito Juárez borough before it became an elected post. As borough president she was enormously popular and viewed as an effective leader. These were precisely the skills needed to launch the PAN in Iztapalapa. By 1999, the PAN counted 3,196 members in the borough, less than 20% of the PRD's total, and only 369 of these were active members who had completed the party's training course. To expand, the PAN planned to identify what it called "natural leaders" in each neighborhood and train them in the party's doctrine and style so that they could be "multipliers of the vote." At the same time, the party would need to shed its aloof image and become a party of service.

In one initiative, the PAN organized existing professional activists from across the city to give legal aid, limited health care, advice about home construction, and help in securing urban services to residents in Iztapalapa. These "Homogeneous Groups" of middle-class professionals would essentially perform the same *gestión social* functions that leaders of the PRI and PRD's social organizations did.

In a second initiative, the party launched a national program called Citizen Action and a citywide program called Citizen Promotion to carry out other acts of *gestión*. The national effort was led by Luisa María Calderón, a thoughtful anthropologist, member of the National Executive Committee, and sister of then party president Felipe Calderón (1996–1999). Following the PAN's poor performance against the left in 1988, the party decided that it needed to incorporate noncore constituencies. According to Luisa María,

> We realized that the lower class did not vote for the PAN. We decided that this was our main problem, and we needed to gain support among the lower class to expand. Citizen Action was a new idea. After 70 years of using theoretical and intellectual positions to convince the electorate, we decided to begin doing things *with* the electorate (author interview, July 26, 1999).

Yet the program remained anemic. By 1999 it ran some 300 projects that involved a maximum of 7,500 participants. Citizen Promotion in the Federal District reported running another 200–300 projects. To give a sense of the size of these efforts, the PRI reported about 16,000 projects in the Federal District alone in the same period (author interviews, 1999). Gabriela Gutiérrez, leader of the PAN's citywide effort, reported that

> *Gestión* is the primary way that the PAN can appeal to the lower class...but the party has been a little tentative with this strategy. We have not been able to work with key groups like informal street vendors because the PRI and PRD have already organized them. Also, if we did work with these groups, it would cause problems with our middle class small business support base in the Federal District. (author interview, May 7, 1999)

Before doing *gestión social*, the PAN needed to develop contacts in lower-class areas. Esperanza reported that the party was working hard to establish a neighborhood presence and had purchased eight small buildings for satellite headquarters throughout the borough. But it was not clear that these installations existed: when I asked to tour them, I was told that it was not safe and the buildings' addresses were not available. The PAN in Iztapalapa was in a bunker. It was unwilling to engage in organization-building through local community groups that dominated the borough and its operatives seemed afraid of the very constituents they were supposed to recruit as activists and voters.

The case studies presented in this section highlighted the difficulties of growing opposition party organizations at the local level. The PRD's close association with pre-existing social organizations in working-class neighborhoods limited its expansion to core constituencies that were defined by neighborhood in Miguel Hidalgo and by "islands" within neighborhoods in Iztapalapa. It had trouble drawing in unorganized working-class voters and seemed lost when it came to middle-class individuals who were neither organized in politicized associations nor particularly drawn to the party's statist and welfarist economic policy appeals. The PAN's much closer association with middle-class constituents gave it strength in neighborhoods populated by professionals, but its success in working-class areas was limited by its refusal to link with pre-existing social organizations, its skittishness about delivering services, and its sometimes Darwinian free market economic policy message. The PAN and PRD's appeals yielded core groups of voters that amounted to about 20% of the electorate. The limits of both parties left about 35–40% of the electorate unattached to any party during the 1990s. To catch more of these voters, the parties would have to find new formulas for expansion.

CONCLUSION

The PAN and PRD were constrained by their origins. Elite activists who joined challenger parties early on when the dominant party's resource advantages and use of repression were significant built niche organizations with tight links to core constituencies and high barriers to new activist affiliation. These organizational forms served a key purpose when they were created. They were an important ingredient in crafting opposition parties that were strictly distinguished from the dominant party and populated by hardcore activists who were more likely to remain active despite high costs and low benefits. At the same time, however, niche parties were small and had limited capacity to expand. When conditions conspired to make the PRI's advantages fall, challenger parties could have profitably transformed themselves into catchall competitors with broader and more centrist appeals. Nevertheless, their transition from niche to catchall was slow and halting in part because their organizations were poorly designed for innovation. As illustrated with national membership data and case studies from Mexico City, these organizational routines blocked the parties' ability to catch more activists and voters.

Niche-oriented party elites were both the heroes and the villains of opposition party development. On the one hand, they formed challenger parties when a strictly electoralist logic suggested that they should not. Further, they maintained these parties for decades under very inhospitable circumstances. Without them, challenger parties would never have gotten off the ground. But niche-oriented party elites also constrained their parties to less efficient positions once the dominant party's advantages declined and the fairer electoral market for votes yielded electoral rewards for centrism.

The PAN's presidential victory in the 2000 elections owes in large part to its ability to move beyond its traditional core constituency. Why and how it overcame intra-party rigidities – and whether these solutions are lasting – is the subject of Chapter 7.

7

Dominance Defeated

Voting Behavior in the 2000 Elections

To this point, this book has been about how the PRI used its advantages to defeat challengers and maintain the dominant party equilibrium during most of the 20th century. Even as free market economic restructuring progressively deprived the PRI of these advantages, dominance persisted because the dynamics of opposition party building created two key coordination problems for the challengers. First, the pattern of political recruitment yielded generational conflicts over strategy inside the opposition parties between relatively policy-extreme early joiners and more moderate later joiners. Second, since the PRI's advantages expelled challengers to the left and the right on economic policy issues, there were strong incentives not to coordinate their efforts against the incumbent even though they both wanted to defeat the PRI and transform Mexico into a fully competitive democracy.

Yet despite these problems, the PRI was eventually defeated. In the 2000 elections, Vicente Fox of the PAN won the presidency and became the first president to peacefully receive power from a political rival in Mexico's history. Why was an opposition party able to win in 2000 and why was that party the PAN instead of the PRD? This latter question is particularly intriguing because the austere economic conditions that turned voters away from the PRI resulted in part from the government's adoption of free market economic policies. At a time when left and center-left candidates began to win power in several Latin American countries, one might have expected the leftwing PRD to be in a better position than the rightwing PAN. Why did it turn out the other way around?

This chapter argues that the PRI lost because its declining advantages finally created a fair market for votes in 2000 that gave the challengers equal opportunities to compete for the average voter. It further argues that Fox won because he marshaled independent resources that allowed him to separate his campaign from the niche-oriented PAN and make an end-run around intra-party coordination problems. He then used his autonomy to craft a broad centrist message that focused on change and appealed beyond the party's traditional voters. By bypassing ideologically charged elites and making more centrist appeals to voters, Fox did what no opposition candidate ever had: he retained his party's core constituents while drawing in independents, centrists, and PRD defectors, all united by their desire for change. By contrast, the PRD's candidate, Cuauhtémoc Cárdenas, was constrained to his party's resources and made traditionally leftist appeals that did not resonate with the average voter.

The first section of this chapter shows that by the 2000 election, resource asymmetries between the PRI and the challengers had largely disappeared, and this created a fair market for votes for the first time. The second section draws on public opinion polls to argue that the opposition parties could win only if they formed an alliance or, if competing separately, one party managed to stand alone as the centrist pro-democracy option. The third section shows why, despite substantial incentives, the opposition alliance failed in 2000 and before. In the absence of interparty coordination, the candidates would have to overcome the persistent intra-party coordination problems that had limited their expansion. These problems were resolved through the fight over the nominations themselves. The fourth section shows why Fox won the PAN's nomination despite stiff resistance from party elites and why Cárdenas won the PRD's nomination even though he was clearly a losing candidate. The fifth section then describes the dynamics of the campaign to show how Fox yolked together a broad electoral coalition where Cárdenas and the PRI's Labastida failed. The final section before the conclusion brings the chapter's main elements together in a model of voting behavior using panel survey data.

EQUAL OPPORTUNITIES AND THE FAIR MARKET FOR VOTES IN 2000

By the run-up to the 2000 election, economic changes and election oversight mechanisms dramatically curtailed the PRI's access to illicit public resources. For the first time, this created equal opportunities for generating campaign finance and reduced both the quantity and effectiveness of the patronage resources that remained. Three changes gave rise to a fair electoral market for votes.

First, the political economy of single-party dominance eroded to the point that the PRI had run out of money for large-scale patronage politics. As developed in more detail in Chapter 3, the privatization of state-owned enterprises sharply reduced the size of the pie from which the PRI took liberal slices. By 2000, the government controlled just 5.5% of GDP, down from 22.3% 17 years earlier. This difference meant that US$153.7 billion less was being pumped through the government, thus depriving it of substantial resources that it could manipulate with a partisan logic. Government ownership fell so fast that in 2000 public holdings were just above half what they were (US$40.3 billion less) in the 1994 presidential election. In addition, the number of federal employees diminished from 2.71 million as late as 1992 (presumably it was much higher earlier) to just over 569,000 in 1999. As a result, the number of patronage jobs at the PRI's disposal fell and the PRI-controlled labor confederation (CTM) as well as the once powerful federal employees union (FSTSE) weakened dramatically. Even Salinas' stop-gap patronage system through the PRONASOL poverty-alleviation program came to an end as funding from privatization revenues slowed to a trickle. Overall, by 2000, the public trough that supplied the PRI's deep pockets had run shallow.

Second, as the PRI's access to illicit funds diminished, it increasingly consented to campaign finance regulations that involved legal public funding for all competitors and limits on private funding. The electoral code in place for the 2000 elections forbade contributions from government entities to political parties and reduced private contributions to just 0.5% of total party spending. The Federal Election Institute (IFE) now audited 100% of party receipts, up from just 16% in 1994. Combined with an increasingly free and investigative mass media and a Congress not controlled by the PRI, these measures helped root out and publicize the illicit use of public resources. Partly as a result, the president's secret budget also disappeared.

Finally, by the late 1990s a plural market for private campaign donations emerged for the first time. According to Lino Korrodi, Fox's long-time fundraiser, attempts to get private contributions in 1991 met with "total rejection." "Begging for money for an opposition candidate" he said, "was a sobering experience" and only a few of Fox's close friends gave money and then only in secret (Preston and Dillon, 2004: 480). But by 1997, when Fox declared his candidacy, Preston and Dillon (2004: 480–481) report that "for the first time Mexico's wealthiest men made

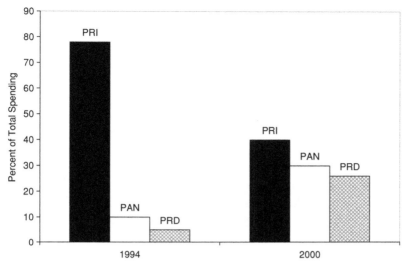

FIGURE 7.1. Reported Campaign Spending by Party, 1994 and 2000.
Source: Lujambio (2001).

important donations to an opposition presidential candidate," although they continued to do so in secret. Beginning in 1999, contributions came with such frequency that Korrodi stopped arranging candidate meetings for donations under US$300,000 (Preston and Dillon, 2004: 483).

Due to these three changes, reported campaign spending was far more equal across the parties than at any previous time. Figure 7.1 shows that in 2000 the PRI accounted for 40% of all reported spending, down from 78% in 1994. In 2000, the PAN accounted for 30% and the PRD 26%, up from just 10% and 5%, respectively, six years earlier. In addition, the PRI was the biggest spender in all municipalities before 2000, but in 2000 it outspent the challengers in just 46%.[1] Thus, even though resource asymmetries had fallen substantially before 1994, there was a dramatic leveling in 2000 compared to the prior presidential election just six years earlier.

Reported finances, however, do not tell the whole story. Despite measures to limit illicit funding, some opportunities to generate resources from the public budget remained. The civil service was still politically controlled, largely by the executive branch, and Arrellano and Guerrero

---

[1] The Federal Elections Institute (IFE) reports spending by electoral district. Greene, Klesner, and Lawson (2004) imputed values for the smaller municipalities using IFE mapping criteria.

(2000: fn 12) estimate that as late as 1997 there were some 20,000 employees "of confidence" that could be hired and fired for any reason. Several public sector unions remained powerful and unified as well. The massive oil workers union (STPRM) was tightly controlled by PRI politicians who used it to transfer US$147.2 million from the state-run oil company PEMEX to party coffers for the 2000 election (see Chapter 3 for details). The even larger public teachers union that runs employment in public education through a patronage-and-kickback system remained tightly controlled by then PRI insider Elba Esther Gordillo. Although local PRI offices and the party's affiliated sectoral organizations withered without the flow of public dollars, some leaders managed to capture enough resources to maintain powerful local organizations, including, for instance, *Antorcha Popular*, several informal sector workers groups, and the Trashpickers Union in Mexico City. Finally, some PRI governors manipulated fiscal decentralization in the 1990s to lock-in access to public resources. In Puebla, Manuel Bartlett (1993–1999) passed a state law that diverted federal funds away from cities, many of which were controlled by PAN mayors, to rural areas where the PRI was still politically strong. In Yucatán, Victor Cervera Pacheco used antipoverty and temporary employment programs to fund his patronage machine (Cornelius, 2004: 48). Yet with the exception of the massive illicit transfer from PEMEX to the PRI, there were no substantiated reports that the PRI abused public funds. Abuses likely still existed, but they were small enough to escape notice by the increasingly aggressive and investigative media.

IFE's auditing system was not a perfect deterrent either. The PAN spent more than the allowed limit in some districts and accepted prohibited foreign donations through the campaign vehicle Amigos de Fox. Amigos' full budget has never been revealed publicly, but the electoral court levied a US$56.4 million fine against the PAN and its coalition ally the Green Party (PVEM). If we take this as the actual amount of overspending, then it represents about 40% of what the PRI received through the PEMEX scandal. However, the very large number of television spots for Fox throughout the campaign suggests that Amigos spent much more. Although perverse, the PAN's use of illegal funds also represented a decrease in resource asymmetries. In the past, the PRI was the only party to raise illicit funds while the challengers were completely locked out of the fundraising market.

Finally, the increasing symmetry in campaign resources did not mean that patronage disappeared from partisan politics in 2000; rather, it potentially opened a plural patronage market. However, survey data shows that just 20.4% of voters received an exclusive gift from one of the parties in

Dominance Defeated   215

2000, 14.4% of which came from the PRI. Unfortunately, voters were not asked to describe the gifts, so they could have ranged from trivial booster buttons to foodstuffs to the portable washing machines doled out by the PRI governor of Yucatán state.[2] Overall, though, the flow of patronage fell far short of the "national reward and punishment system" of prior years and Cornelius concluded that "Old style machine politics have reached their limit in Mexico" (2004: 47–48).

Despite important abuses on the margins, resources were much more equal across parties than at any time in the past. Now the main opposition parties had sufficient funds to mount full-scale modern campaigns, stage candidate events throughout the country, buy media time, print and post campaign propaganda, hire campaign staff, and monitor voting on election day.[3] Overall, equalizing opportunities transformed what was a biased market for votes that favored the incumbent into a fair market where all parties could compete for voters' sympathies.

VOTERS AND PARTY STRATEGY OPTIONS IN THE 2000 ELECTIONS

Notwithstanding now fair elections, the PAN and PRD arrived at the start of the 2000 election campaign with a deficit. Polls in the late 1990s showed that the PRI had the solid support of about 36% of the electorate to the PAN's 20% and the PRD's 10%. About 34% of the electorate defined itself as independent. Thus, no party had a large enough core constituency to win outright, although the PRI had a substantial advantage even before the campaigns began. To win, the PAN and the PRD would have to retain their core voters, fight for independents, and perhaps even convince some of their rivals' core voters to defect.

The structure of competition dictated a limited set of workable strategies for accomplishing these goals. As discussed in prior chapters, Mexico's elections before 2000 were fought over two dimensions of partisan competition. One cleavage pitted those who preferred state-led economic

---

[2] Data are from the Mexico 2000 Panel Study (see footnote 15 for citation) and represent receipt of an exclusive gift from only one of the parties reported in any of the survey's four waves from February through July. I measured "exclusive" gifts with the idea that patronage only biases a voter in favor of one party if she does not receive a similar gift from another party. Nonexclusive gifts were given to 24% of voters with 18.8% coming from the PRI.

[3] While the challengers struggled to staff precinct committees with vote watchers in prior elections, in 2000, the PAN and PRD coalitions claimed to cover 85% and 73.5%, respectively, of the over 113,399 precincts throughout the country. See http://www.ife.org.mx.

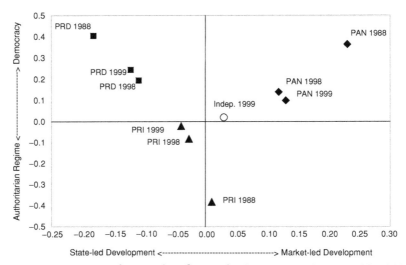

FIGURE 7.2. Location of Party Identifiers in the Competition Space, 1988–1999.
Note: Issue placements represent Z scores from factor analyses of issue items.
Sources: Gallup (IMOP) Poll 1988, LatinoBarometer 1998, and Zedillo Evaluation Survey (June 1999), *Reforma* newspaper. Issue items were matched as closely as possible across surveys.

development against those who wanted the market to lead. The other divided voters who preferred the status quo political regime from those who instead wanted a fully competitive democracy.

Figure 7.2 plots the relative positions of party identifiers and the mean location of independents in the competition space from 1988 to 1999. It shows that the large group of independents was, on average, quite centrist and that all three parties' identifiers became more centrist as their vote share expanded between 1988 and 1998.[4] These findings imply advantages to centrism; however, voter decisionmaking in two-dimensional spaces can be complicated. To the extent that issues matter, voters take into account the distance between their perception of the parties' issue stands and their personal preferences as well as the importance or salience they assign to each dimension.[5]

---

[4] Given what we know about the dynamics of expansion from Chapter 6, I suspect that most of the shift toward the center took place since the mid-1990s; however, appropriate survey data for this period were not available.

[5] For a discussion of theoretical models that demonstrate advantages to centrism for various assumptions about the competition space, see Chapter 1, "Supply-Side Approaches."

Unfortunately, the available surveys before 2000 do not contain the items needed to construct all these measures so I cannot directly represent the distribution of voters' salience-weighted preferences over the competition space. Magaloni (1996) provides an elegant workaround for this problem by examining opposition voters' possible preference orderings of the three parties. One group that I call "regime opposition voters" has preferences PAN>PRD>PRI or PRD>PAN>PRI (where ">" means preferred to). These voters prefer either challenger to the PRI, meaning that they may choose the opposition party they like less if they think it has a better chance of beating the PRI. We cannot place these voters in the competition space in Figure 7.2 with perfect accuracy, but we can say that they must be pro-democracy and that PRD regime voters lean left on economic issues whereas PAN regime voters lean right. A second group that I call "economic policy opposition voters" rank their preferences PAN>PRI>PRD or PRD>PRI>PAN where the PRI is always second. These voters must be on the right on economic policy if they prefer the PAN and on the left if they prefer the PRD. They may or may not favor democracy, but they are unlikely to be on the authoritarian side of the regime divide. The final group of "rigid opposition voters" is indifferent between the two parties they like least and have preferences PAN>PRI = PRD or PRD>PRI = PAN.[6] They are so extreme on economic issues that the other two parties appear similar from their vantage point.

Table 7.1 shows voters by type using a December 1998 *Reforma* newspaper national poll. It also shows PRI supporters that were either rigid pro-regime voters (PRI>PAN = PRD), left-leaners (PRI>PRD>PAN), or right-leaners (PRI>PAN>PRD). The beginning of 1999 was the virtual start of the 2000 campaign, so these data give a good sense of the conditions the parties faced when forming their strategies. The PRI had the clear advantage with 37.2% of the preferences. The PAN was much lower at 23.6%, and the PRD was a distant third at 18.3%. But there were also many votes that could be won by campaigning.

Some voters are more susceptible to campaign persuasion than others. Rigid voters were unlikely to defect but opposition parties had a chance to win independents as well as left- and right-leaning PRI identifiers by making centrist appeals that more closely resembled these voters' preferences. Regime opposition voters might also defect from the less to the

---

[6] Magaloni (1996) labels the three types "radical opposition," "ideological," and "rigid" voters.

TABLE 7.1. *Voter Types by Party Preference Orders, December 1998*

Voter Type	Preference Order	Percent of Voters	Approximate Issue Preference and Salience*	Best Strategy for Rival Opposition Party to Win each Voter Type
Rigid PAN	PAN>PRI=PRD	7.7	Right on economy, probably pro-democracy	None
Economic Policy PAN	PAN>PRI>PRD	6.7	Right on economy	PRD by moving center, but unlikely to work
Regime Opposition PAN	PAN>PRD>PRI	9.2	Very pro-democracy, lean right on economy	PRD by moving center to increase viability
PAN SUBTOTAL		**23.6**		
Rigid PRD	PRD>PRI=PAN	6.2	Left on economy, probably pro-democracy	None
Economic Policy PRD	PRD>PRI>PAN	4.1	Left on economy	PAN by moving center, but unlikely to work
Regime Opposition PRD	PRD>PAN>PRI	8.1	Very pro-democracy, lean left on economy	PAN by moving center to increase viability
PRD SUBTOTAL		**18.3**		
Right-leaning PRI	PRI>PAN>PRD	12.8	Authoritarian, right-leaning on economy	PAN by moving center
Left-leaning PRI	PRI>PRD>PAN	9.4	Authoritarian, left-leaning on economy	PRD by moving center
Rigid PRI	PRI>PAN=PRD	15.0	Very authoritarian	None
PRI SUBTOTAL		**37.2**		

Note: ">" means "preferred to" and "=" means "indifferent between"
* The more salient of the two dimensions is listed first.
Source: Zedillo Evaluation Survey, December 1998, *Reforma* newspaper.

more viable opposition candidate in order to beat the PRI. To gain their support, the challengers would have to square off against each other and try to convince voters of their viability. The best way to win this battle of perceptions – beyond the usual campaign bravado – was to actually win more support from other voters, which of course meant moving toward the center.

In addition to aligning their issue appeals with voters' preferences, candidates can try to enhance or prime the importance of particular issues (Riker, 1983; Johnston et al., 1992). Campaigning heavily on democracy might make voters re-weight their preferences and thus create more regime opposition voters. The PRI would be forced into the awkward position of either ignoring regime issues in its campaign or making pro-democracy statements that voters would probably not find credible. But priming democracy would not be sufficient on its own because the opposition parties would still have to fight each other for these regime opposition voters by moving toward the center.

The structure of competition thus yielded two options for the opposition to win in 2000. One was for the PAN and PRD to form an opposition alliance. They would likely win all regime opposition voters and the combination of a leftwing and rightwing party would essentially occupy the center, thus encouraging independents to swing in their favor. When added to each parties' rigid and economic policy voters, the opposition would likely carry the election. Without an alliance, the PAN and PRD's strategic challenge would be more complicated. They would have to fight each other for independents and regime opposition voters. This would mean moving toward the center but also making sure that the other challenger did not moderate. Without the alliance, the goal would be to stand alone as the centrist pro-democracy option.

WHY THE OPPOSITION ALLIANCE FAILED: CHANGE, BUT NOT AT ANY PRICE

Given their common goal of defeating the PRI and transforming Mexico into a fully competitive democracy, why did the challengers fail to form an opposition alliance historically and in 2000? Not only do challengers in dominant party authoritarian regimes have natural common cause against the incumbent, but with one exception, all these regimes use presidential formats that create what Linz and Valenzuela (1994) called "winner-take-all" politics. Since incumbents rarely need the support of small parties to govern as they often do in parliamentary systems, they

220 *Why Dominant Parties Lose*

TABLE 7.2. *Party Elites' and Voters' Support for the Opposition Alliance*

	Party Elites	Identified Voters
PAN	40.2	48.0
PRD	68.9	48.3
Independent Voters	—	39.0
All Voters	—	42.2

Entries are percentages.
Sources: Party elites from Mexico Party Personnel Surveys; voters from Zedillo Evaluation Survey, *Reforma* newspaper, December 1998.

freeze opposition parties out of the political debate, deny them positions in the administration, and retain virtually all of the state's resources. As a result, incentives for collaboration with the dominant party are typically lower and incentives for opposition cooperation are higher than they would be in parliamentary systems.

In addition to these constant historical incentives to coordinate against the PRI, circumstances surrounding the 2000 elections supplied even stronger short-term incentives.[7] Having stripped the PRI of its majority status in Congress for the first time in 1997, it seemed that together the challengers could win the presidency in 2000. In fact, the alliance appeared so natural that Shirk called it a "no brainer" (2005: 158).

Voters and party elites generally supported the alliance. Data from the Mexico Party Personnel Surveys in Table 7.2 shows that 40.2% of PAN elites and an overwhelming 68.9% of PRD elites wanted the alliance. This support was vital since a coalition would have to be approved by each party's National Assembly. Among voters, a December 1998 poll showed that almost half of PAN and PRD identifiers favored the alliance.[8] Support was lower among independents at 39%, but this group includes PRI sympathizers who probably preferred a divided opposition that would be easier to defeat. Other polls during 1999 showed that although Fox or

---

[7] Based on their simulations from 1988 presidential election returns, King, Tomz, and Wittenberg (2000: 358) conclude that "Hope of defeating the PRI, even under optimistic conditions, probably requires some kind of compromise between the two opposition parties."

[8] See *Reforma* newspaper's Zedillo Evaluation Survey, December 1998, N = 1200. A separate telephone poll found that 63% supported the alliance. See "Quieren mexicanos Alianza Opositora" *Reforma* September 28, 1999, N = 215. Since telephone polls usually have a partisan bias in Mexico, I use the lower estimate from the in-person poll.

Dominance Defeated

Cárdenas would lose to the PRI's candidate if they ran alone, the alliance was in a statistical dead heat with the PRI.[9]

Interest in the alliance was strong enough at both the elite and mass levels that, unlike in prior elections, PAN and PRD representatives sat down to hammer out an agreement. Although negotiations advanced further than most observers thought possible, the alliance failed to obtain. One possible reason is that election rules made inter-party alliances costly. Cross-party endorsements of presidential candidates alone were banned in 1993, so coalition partners are forced to agree on a full slate of candidates for all 628 legislative races. Coalitions must also produce a single electoral platform, and they receive the amount of public financing that corresponds to the largest partner alone rather than the sum of the members. This obviously provided disincentives for coordination in 2000; however, the barriers were not prohibitive since the PAN ultimately allied with the Green Party (PVEM) to create the Alliance for Change and the PRD allied with the Workers Party (PT), the Socialist Alliance Party (PAS), the Nationalist Society Party (PSN), and the Democratic Convergence Party (PCD) to from the Alliance for Mexico. Further, this argument gives no leverage in understanding why an opposition alliance failed before 1993.

Another explanation for the failed alliance highlights the inevitable need for either Cárdenas or Fox to resign his candidacy and rightly points out that neither was willing to do so. However, it is not clear whether their resistance owed to personal ambition alone or also to a rejection of each others' policy vision. Indeed, much of the negotiations dealt with policy questions and the difficulty of reconciling the parties' polarized platforms. At one point, the PRD announced that it had extracted a concession of "zero privatizations" of public enterprises, but the PAN ultimately rejected the idea and Fox announced his plan to privatize PEMEX and the electric utility.

Recognizing these historic differences, I argue that opposition coordination failed because PAN and PRD elites, and in particular early joiners, together with their core supporters in the electorate, were ideologically polarized on economic policy issues. If the parties were to challenge the PRI as a united front, they would have to iron out a compromise over numerous issues, including the role of the state and market forces in economic development in general and the specific fate of PEMEX and the electric utility; whether to prioritize economic growth or distribution and the

---

[9] Consulted at www.elector.com.mx/elecc2000/300899encuest.html.

222 *Why Dominant Parties Lose*

TABLE 7.3. *Opposition Voters' Support for the Opposition Alliance*

Type of Opposition Voter	PAN Supporters		PRD Supporters	
	Support for Alliance	Proportion of PAN Voters	Support for Alliance	Proportion of PRD Voters
Regime (ranks PRI third)	53.6	39.6	57.4	37.0
Economic Policy (ranks PRI second)	35.0	20.4	39.2	19.6
Rigid (ranks PRI & other opposition equally)	28.3	32.0	36.7	31.0

Entries are percentages.
Proportion of party voters columns do not add to 100 because a small proportion of voters had intransitive preferences and these respondents were excluded from the analysis.
Source: Zedillo Evaluation Survey, *Reforma* newspaper, December, 1998.

role of foreign capital flows in this process; the welfare responsibilities of the individual versus the state, especially regarding pensions; whether the public should pay for corporate losses that affect national economic health such as in the FOBAPROA banking scandal; and whether to thoroughly decentralize resource control or maintain a powerful central government that could direct resources for massive public projects such as poverty alleviation. Further, the coalition would have to endure for the entire six-year term and somehow divide responsibilities in a presidential system that was inappropriately designed for the task. Although some opposition voters and party elites downplayed these differences and favored beating the PRI by forming the alliance, the most ideologically polarized on the right and left staunchly opposed it. I show how this logic played out among voters and then among party elites.

Opposition Voters

Opposition voters differed in their support for the alliance based on their policy preferences and the importance they ascribed to democracy versus economic policy change. As above, the lack of detailed survey data on voters' issue preferences forces us to use their preference ordering of the parties as a shortcut. Table 7.3 shows that over 50% of regime opposition voters who prioritized democracy favored the alliance. Support is much

Dominance Defeated

223

TABLE 7.4. *Party Elites' Support for the Opposition Alliance by National Priority*

National Priority	PAN (Favor Alliance with PRD?)		PRD (Favor Alliance with PAN?)	
	Support for Alliance	Percent of PAN Elite	Support for Alliance	Percent of PRD Elite
Democracy	59.5	52.2	67.5	59.5
Economic Development or Social Justice	31.0	29.8	27.7	32.2

Entries are percentages.

Percent of party elites columns do not add to 100 because some respondents had intransitive preferences, and these cases were excluded from the analysis.

Source: Mexico Party Personnel Surveys.

lower, however, among economic policy voters. Only 35% of policy voters who identified with the PAN and 39.2% of policy voters who identified with the PRD favored the alliance. As we would expect, rigid opposition voters were the least supportive of the alliance at just 28.3% among PAN identifiers and 36.7% among PRD identifiers.

Table 7.3 also shows that the majority of the PAN and PRD electorates were either economic policy or rigid voters. Thus, if the parties allied, they would risk alienating their core constituencies. It was precisely these groups, cultivated by party elites, that had helped the challenger parties survive for decades when their chances of winning were vanishingly low. These loyalists viewed the alliance as a sell-out to a party that they perceived as diametrically opposed to their preferences.

Opposition Party Elites

Elites in the PAN and PRD had mixed incentives for supporting the alliance. On the one hand, a coalition seemed capable of winning the presidency and ending some seven decades of dominant party rule. On the other hand, economic policy differences divided the challengers and, as a result, allying may have alienated their core constituencies enough to make them stay home on election day. The alliance also threatened to dilute each party's independent identity that was forged over decades of struggle.

In the end, party elites split over the alliance much like their constituents did. Table 7.4 uses data from the Mexico Party Personnel Surveys to show that 59.5% of PAN elites who prioritized democracy endorsed the

224   *Why Dominant Parties Lose*

alliance, while only 31% of those who cared more about economic issues wanted it. The difference is even greater in the PRD. Some 67.5% of elites who prioritized democracy preferred the alliance but only 27.7% of those who prioritized other issues supported the alliance.[10]

To test whether these differences affected individual-level support for the alliance while controlling for other variables, I constructed a dependent variable from a four-fold rating of elites' personal support for the alliance (support strongly or weakly, oppose strongly or weakly). The main explanatory variables of interest were party elites' economic policy and regime preferences taken from the earlier analysis in Chapter 5. To capture the different weight that individuals applied to the two dimensions of partisan conflict, I used respondents' rankings of national priorities.[11] I then constructed salience-weighted economic policy and regime preferences. I further parsed these variables between office-seekers and message-seekers. The model also includes demographic variables as controls.

Results appear in Table 7.5. All variables had the predicted effects. The negative value for PAN office-seekers on the economic policy variable indicates that as these elites became more market oriented, they supported the alliance less. Similarly, the positive value for PRD elites means that as they favored statism more, they also supported the alliance less. The positive signs for regime preferences mean that support for democracy increased support for the alliance. The signs for party elite type indicate that office-seekers were more supportive of the alliance, presumably because it would increase the likelihood of winning.[12] The demographic variables, included as controls, had mixed and generally less important effects across the two parties.

The easiest way to appreciate the effects of party leaders' policy preferences is to look at simulations. Figure 7.3 shows predicted support for the opposition alliance by PAN and PRD office-seekers and message-seekers under four combinations of economic policy and regime preferences. To construct these simulations, I held all variables at their mean or mode, while setting the salience-weighted policy preferences to particular levels.

---

[10] The χ^2 test for support for the alliance across party elites with different national priorities was significant at the .1 level in both parties.

[11] Specifically, I weighted economic policy preference twice as much as regime preference for respondents who ranked economic development or social justice as the highest national priority. I used the reverse weighting for respondents who instead ranked democracy as the most important national priority.

[12] Since the Mexico Party Personnel Surveys were completed before candidate lists for legislative posts were settled, office-seekers in both parties likely thought they would get a nomination.

TABLE 7.5. *OLS Regression Models of National Party Leaders' Support for PAN-PRD Alliance in 2000*

Variable	PAN Coeff	PAN Std Err	PRD Coeff	PRD Std Err
Salience-weighted economic policy preference* Office-seeker	−0.92**	0.46	0.51**	0.25
Salience-weighted economic policy preference* Message-seeker	−0.10	0.41	0.65**	0.32
Salience-weighted regime preference	0.31*	0.18	0.36**	0.18
Gender (0 = male, 1 = female)	0.19	0.56	−0.53**	0.21
Age	−0.01	0.01	0.00	0.01
Education	0.33**	0.16	0.08	0.09
Religiosity	0.09	0.09	0.06	0.06
Type (0 = Message-seeker, 1 = Office-seeker)	1.04**	0.42	0.45*	0.30
Constant	−1.92*	1.14	−0.03	0.83
r^2	.18		.18	
Number of cases	111		139	

Entries are unstandardized coefficients.
*** p <.01; ** p <.05; * p <.1
Source: Mexico Party Personnel Surveys.

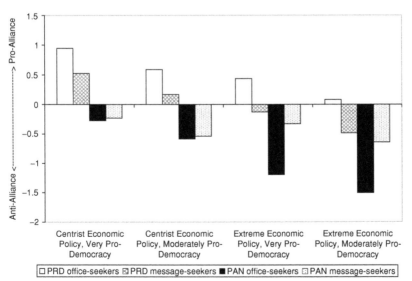

FIGURE 7.3. National Party Leaders' Predicted Support for PAN-PRD Alliance in 2000.

226 *Why Dominant Parties Lose*

The first finding is that PRD elites were generally more supportive of the alliance than PAN elites, but this could be an artifact of survey timing. Since samples were selected at party meetings, interviews were restricted to a pre-determined calendar. The PAN leadership survey was done in October 1998, before presidential candidates were formally nominated and when opinion polls showed the two challengers in a dead heat.[13] Given the uncertainty over which party would be stronger, PAN leaders may have preferred to wait and see before supporting the alliance. In contrast, the PRD leadership survey was completed in November 1999 when all three parties had nominated their candidates and polls showed Fox leading Cárdenas by a whopping 23%.[14] Many PRD elites must have realized that they were very unlikely to win the presidency and could extract more policy concessions by helping the PAN win than by losing and having no influence in the executive branch.

The second finding that jumps out of the figure is that elites who were centrist on economic policy and very pro-democracy favored the alliance much more than those who were extreme on economic policy and moderate on regime issues. The effect is large enough that even the group that favored the alliance most (PRD office-seekers) became virtually indifferent to it when policy preferences are changed. Shifting policy preferences also push PRD message-seekers from supportive to unsupportive and both types of PAN elites from marginally to staunchly against.

Economic policy extremism affected support for the alliance because it pushed opposition elites further from each other and, as polarization increased, PAN and PRD leaders' common interest in beating the PRI faded. As a result, substantial groups in each party saw the other challenger as their main rival, not the PRI. Some in the PRD routinely accused the PAN of collaborating with the government to marginalize the left in the 1970s and early 1980s, to steal the 1988 presidential election from Cárdenas, and to support an anti-nationalist political economy that favored the wealthy. Their counterparts in the PAN accused the PRD of advocating socialism, being derivative of the fiscally irresponsible and politically authoritarian PRI of the 1970s, and generally ignoring

---

[13] The LatinoBarometer 1998 poll that was in the field from November 14 to December 3 had vote intention by party tied between the PAN and PRD at just over 21% each. A December 1998 *Reforma* newspaper poll also had Fox and Cárdenas tied at about 22% regardless of the PRI's candidate.

[14] Mexico 2000 Panel Study, wave 1 in the field February 19–27. As early as March 1999, a *Reforma* newspaper poll showed that Fox beat Cárdenas by 11% whether the PRI's candidate was Labastida or Madrazo.

Mexico's economic realities in the era of global trade. The Mexico Party Personnel Surveys picked up these antagonisms by asking whether it would be worse for the country if the PRI or the other challenger party won in 2000. Among PAN elites, 23.9% chose the PRD as their main rival and 31.6% chose the PRI. In the PRD, 38% of elites thought of the PRI as their main rival and 17% worried more about the PAN. About 45% in both parties spontaneously responded that both of their rivals were equally bad for Mexico.

After months of trying to iron out a compromise, alliance negotiations stalled. Neither Cárdenas nor Fox was willing to give up his candidacy and their policy differences could not be resolved to satisfaction. In the absence of commitments for more protectionist economic policy – commitments the PAN was not willing to make – the PRD preferred to let the alliance crumble. As the negotiations fell apart, Cárdenas said that he wanted change, but not change at any price and that "a government of the PAN or a government of the PRI would represent the same step backwards for the country" (see Bruhn, 2004: 132). If he resigned, he said, it would allow the forces of "reaction and antipatriotism" to win (see Bruhn, 2005: 5–6). This sentiment ran so deep that just a few days after the election that finally ended PRI rule, some national level PRD elites privately confided that they wished the PRI had won instead of the PAN (author interviews, 2000).

Given such profound issue differences between the PAN and PRD – differences that emerged from the dynamics of opposition party building – Bruhn comments that "The failure of alliance negotiations is in some ways less surprising than the fact that they took place at all" (2004: 132). Behind the personal battle between Cárdenas and Fox lay deep divisions inside both opposition parties between moderate catchall players who generally supported the opposition alliance in order to win and comparatively extremist niche players who opposed it as a betrayal of their identity, decades of sacrifice, and the interests of their loyal constituents in the electorate. Without party leaders' full endorsement, it was virtually impossible to settle the complex negotiations for fusing the PAN and the PRD in the 2000 elections.

THE OPPOSITION'S DILEMMA: NOMINATING A CANDIDATE THAT COULD "WIN ELECTIONS WITHOUT LOSING THE PARTY"

After the opposition alliance failed, the PAN and PRD faced a difficult strategic situation. Electoral logic dictated that neither party's core support was sufficient to win the presidency. To expand, they would have to win regime opposition voters away from each other and win the large segment of independents in a three-way race with the PRI. The only way to accomplish both goals was to move toward the center on the issues. However, the logic of party representation dictated that campaigns should respond less to voters at large than to the preferences of party elites and their core supporters in the electorate.

This seemed like a true dilemma. A candidate who satisfied party elites would be too out of step with voters on the issues to win in the general election, but a candidate who responded to electoral logic would be considered unrepresentative of the party and, at worst, a traitor to its historic cause. Thus, a bad candidate could sail through the nomination process only to implode in the general election or a good candidate, if he squeaked through the nomination process, would be weakened by internal attacks and might not count with his party's full and energetic support in the general election. In the end, the PRD nominated a consummate insider – Cuauhtémoc Cárdenas – and the PAN chose an outsider with broad electoral appeal – Vicente Fox. Why then did Fox manage to win the nomination despite inevitable resistance from PAN elites and why did Cárdenas win the PRD's nomination given the serious doubt, if not clear conclusion, that he could not win the general election?

These outcomes are puzzling from the perspective of current nomination theory. Tsebelis (1990: Ch. 5) argues that British Labor Party activists committed political suicide in the 1970s and 1980s because they were extreme on the issues, controlled nominations, and played an iterated game with prospective candidates. Since nomination battles were periodic, activists preferred to lose a given election with an extremist candidate in order to signal that they would not accept moderation in the future. But, this logic only holds when the political prize is relatively small, like a single seat in parliament. In contrast, Mexico has a winner-take-all presidential system with an elongated six-year term. It seems very unlikely that nominators would prefer to lose and send a signal than win. From this perspective, Fox's nomination makes sense, but the PRD's political suicide with Cárdenas does not.

A second approach to nominations derives from May's (1973) influential work on intra-party relations in which activists are assumed to be radical on policy whereas both leaders and voters are assumed to be moderate. This implies that extremist candidates will win nominations controlled by activists (e.g., through a closed primary), but moderate candidates will win if leaders nominate. However, the dynamics of opposition party building in dominant party systems create comparatively radical leaders and more moderate activists, as demonstrated in previous chapters. From this perspective, it is easier to understand why the PRD's leaders committed political suicide, but not why the traditionally hierarchical PAN avoided it.

I argue that Fox made it through the PAN's nominating process because he raised independent resources and created a parallel party organization to promote his candidacy. As a result, he forced the PAN's leadership to accept electoral logic over the logic of party representation. In contrast, Cárdenas' deep moral authority appealed to PRD insiders and no outsider candidate with independent resources emerged on the left. As a result, the PRD bowed to the logic of party representation and followed the traditional nomination pattern that opposition parties on both the left and right had followed for decades.

The PRD's Political Suicide

Cárdenas was the consummate insider. As PRD founder, he was such a natural choice for the candidacy that a challenge from Porfirio Muñoz Ledo met with derision by other party leaders and the base. The Mexico Party Personnel Surveys, this time directed only at the highest level party leaders in the National Political Council, found that 84.6% endorsed Cárdenas and only 5.6% went for Muñoz Ledo. Thus, the more tightly linked a party elite was to the national party organization, the more he supported Cárdenas.

It was equally clear that Cárdenas had very little chance of winning independents and noncore constituencies in the general election. Although his candidacy had sparked broad national appeal in the 1988 elections, his 1994 showing left him with just 15% of the vote. His stint as Mexico City mayor beginning in 1997 was unremarkable and the PRD's strong performance in the 1997 midterm elections owed as much to effective leadership by party president Andrés Manuel López Obrador as it did to Cárdenas' mayoral run. So why did the PRD commit political suicide by nominating him?

PRD leaders rallied around Cárdenas because the perverse path of opposition party building in dominant party systems put a premium on moral authority rather than electoral popularity. Opposition parties were built by risk-takers who led when they had little hope of winning. Among these courageous activists, commitment to the cause helped build moral authority with one's peers. Moral authority might be thought of as the

230 *Why Dominant Parties Lose*

rough equivalent to martyrdom in hopeless revolutionary struggles. The more dedicated one was – often reflected in longevity of activism – the more he was revered as a natural leader. No one had more moral authority in the PRD than its founder. Thus, even though he was a two-time presidential loser, Cárdenas was perceived as the appropriate candidate. Defeated in internal polling and heckled by his co-partisans, Muñoz Ledo left the PRD as he charged that "Cárdenas is stuck in backwardness and dogmatism...He betrayed his friends who believe in a modern leftist party" (cited in Shirk, 2005: 147).

The PAN: Saving the Party from Itself

While Cárdenas was the natural candidate for the PRD, Fox faced a tough nomination battle. Much of the PAN's top leadership viewed Fox as a newcomer and dangerous outsider. He joined the party in 1987 after a career in the private sector that began as a delivery truck driver and ended as the President of Coca-Cola Mexico. Following a failed attempt to win the PRI's congressional nomination in 1984, he joined the PAN and won a Federal Deputy seat from his home state of Guanajuato in 1988. From the beginning, he taunted President Salinas in a series of biting personal attacks that embarrassed the PAN as it busily brokered deals with the PRI to exchange political support for electoral concessions at the state and local levels. In 1991, Fox campaigned for governor of Guanajuato and lost in what was widely viewed as a rigged election. In the negotiations that followed, PAN leadership accepted a deal that put long-time party insider Carlos Medina Placencia in office instead of Fox. This move caused such a rift between Fox and PAN leaders that he refused to campaign for the party's 1994 presidential candidate, Diego Fernández de Cevallos, and even came close to endorsing Cárdenas (Bruhn, 2004: 128).

Opposition to Fox inside the PAN was based as much on ideological disagreements as personal tensions. He was opposed by social conservatives for his equivocating position on abortion and because he was a single divorcee. Surprisingly, he was also questioned by fiscal conservatives who saw him, rightly or wrongly, as an irresponsible populist (Bruhn, 2004: 128) with ties to leftwing intellectuals including Jorge Castañeda and Adolfo Aguilar Zinser. Party stalwarts also noted his attempt to run under the PRI label and questioned his long-term commitment to the PAN. These insiders had substantial leverage because the 300 member National Council traditionally selected the party's presidential candidate.

Given elite opposition and rules that were stacked against him, how did Fox secure the nomination?

Fox leveraged the nomination out of a recalcitrant PAN because he began campaigning early and raised independent resources. He publicly announced his intention to run in July 1997, long before any of the parties made official nominations. He used his position as Governor of Guanajuato (1995–1999) to raise his public profile by campaigning for PAN candidates in other states while also campaigning for himself, and he made so many trips abroad to cultivate international support that his state legislature tried to restrict what the local newspapers portrayed as his Road Runner-like travels (Shirk, 2005: 124).

More importantly, Fox raised independent resources and extra-party support for his candidacy by creating Amigos de Fox. Amigos was a temporary campaign vehicle that is best described as a combination of Amway and an American political action committee. Each new member was asked to convince at least five friends to join, and every 70 members comprised one local unit. By February 2000, five months before the election, the organization had a reported 2 million members, more than four times the number of registered PAN activists.

Amigos de Fox had three pre-election goals. The first was to get small donations from a large number of citizens. With the decline in repression of opposition forces during the 1990s and the real sense that a challenger could win, individuals now felt freer to support challenger parties. Fox mined this new possibility by creating a vehicle for donations that was not directly regulated by campaign finance laws. As noted above, Amigos' fundraising has never been made public; however, Fox's marketing director Francisco Ortiz said that Amigos raised about US$16 million in the nomination campaign alone. For the general election, finance director Lino Korrodi implied that Amigos would contribute over US$28 million to the PAN, equal to more than 57% of the total spending permitted by law (Ortiz Pardo and Ortiz Pinchetti, 2000).

The second goal was to extend Fox's campaign beyond the PAN's loyal supporters. Early on he recognized that this group was too small to win the presidency, and in an October 1998 interview with the author, he calculated that the PAN could give him only about 20% of the electorate. The rest, he said, he would have to win through his campaign. Left to its own devices and resources, Fox was convinced that the PAN would fail. To win independents he needed a candidate-centered campaign unhampered by the party's traditionally rigid style or, as one member of Fox's campaign team confided, he "needed to save the PAN from the Panistas" (cited in Mizrahi, 2003: 145).

Amigos' final pre-election goal was to force the electoral logic of Fox's candidacy down the PAN's throat. His gamble paid off. Fox increased his name recognition from 18% in July 1997 to 70% by December 1998 (Bruhn, 2004: 130), and by June 1999 his favorability ratings were six points ahead of party insider and rival for the nomination, Fernández de Cevallos.

Fox's early and effective campaign for the nomination put party leaders in an awkward position. They recognized Fox's charisma and mushrooming popularity, but resisted electoral logic so much that the National Executive Committee met specifically to discuss how to block his nomination (Shirk, 2005: 125). If the party restricted nominating delegates to the 300 top-level party elites who traditionally chose the candidate, Fox might lose. But they ran the risk of appearing more authoritarian than both the PRD and the PRI that had opted for open primaries. On the other hand, if they opened the primary to registered PAN activists, Fox would win. The Mexico Party Personnel Surveys showed that 89.3% of delegates to the PAN's National Assembly supported Fox whereas only 8% supported Fernández de Cevallos. In fact, unlike in the PRD where support for Cárdenas-the-insider rose among higher-level party leaders, support for Fox-the-outsider increased the *less* tightly linked a respondent was to the national party. Fox was supported by 77% of party elites in a national-level post, 92% of those in a state or local position, and 95% of those without a formal position.

Immobilized by their rejection of Fox and their desire for a competitive candidate, the National Executive Committee tabled the nomination procedure until after the election of the new party president (Shirk, 2005: 126). In this race, pro-Fox delegates proved instrumental in helping Luis Felipe Bravo Mena beat Ricardo García Cervantes, a conservative stalwart deeply invested in the party's traditions (author interviews, 1998). Once Bravo Mena was installed, Fox's nomination was virtually assured. In an Extraordinary National Assembly in April 1999, leadership proposed and the delegates easily approved a primary that included all registered dues paying activists as well as registered sympathizers (*adherentes*). Fernández de Cevallos knew that he could not win the nomination under these circumstances and he bowed out, leaving Fox to run uncontested.

Left to its own devices, PAN leadership likely would have gone down the same path as the PRD by selecting an insider without broad electoral appeal. Shirk argues that Fox only squeaked through because

Dominance Defeated

TABLE 7.6. *Party Identification in February and Vote Choice in July*

Voted for...in July	Party ID in February			
	PRI	PAN	PRD	Independent
Labastida	70.8	8.0	14.3	24.4
Fox	24.3	86.7	22.4	59.8
Cárdenas	4.9	5.3	63.3	15.9

Entries are percentages.
Source: Mexico 2000 Panel Study, waves 1 and 4.

"Recognizing that PAN leaders were intent on protecting their control of the organization from the influence of the party's new pragmatic wing, Fox and his supporters created their own organizational apparatus, campaigned heavily outside the party and across ideological lines, and focused on running a candidate-centered, media-savvy campaign that largely ignored the PAN's programmatic agenda" (2005: 170). By the time of the nomination, the choice between a competitive Fox who was weakly attached to the PAN's identity and a losing Fernández de Cevallos who represented the party's core was so stark that nearly all of the PAN's top leadership acquiesced.

THE CAMPAIGNS, OR WHY FOX WON

The campaigns had a substantial effect on voting decisions. Data from the Mexico 2000 Panel Study[15] show that over 18% of the entire electorate defected from the party they identified with in February to vote for another party's candidate in July. When added to the large segment of independents, fully 45.5% of the electorate was up for grabs during the campaign. Table 7.6 shows that, in the end, Fox retained 86.7% of voters who identified with the PAN early in the campaign season while Labastida and Cárdenas kept just 70.8% and 63.3% of their party's supporters, respectively. Fox also extended his coalition by attracting more than 24% of PRI identifiers and over 22% of PRD identifiers. He dominated among independents too by pulling in almost 60%, compared to Labastida's 24.4%

---

[15] Participants in the Mexico 2000 Panel Study included (in alphabetical order): Miguel Basañez, Roderic Camp, Wayne Cornelius, Jorge Domínguez, Federico Estévez, Joseph Klesner, Chappell Lawson (Principal Investigator), Beatriz Magaloni, James McCann, Alejandro Moreno, Pablo Parás, and Alejandro Poiré. Funding for the study was provided by the National Science Foundation (SES-9905703) and *Reforma* newspaper.

and Cárdenas' 15.9%.[16] Thus, Fox accomplished what no opposition candidate ever had: he retained his party's loyal voters but also built on these minority constituencies to create a catchall coalition.

Why was Fox able to do this? How did he expand beyond the PAN's core supporters to draw in independents as well as PRD and PRI identifiers? How did he overcome the PAN's traditional rigidities that forced it to rely on its core voters? Why was Cárdenas limited to the PRD's loyal supporters and why did Labastida fail to recreate the PRI's traditionally broad electoral coalition?

The campaigns made different gambles about how voters would choose among the candidates. Labastida portrayed himself as a responsible centrist who represented a new and more democratic PRI. To win, he would have to retain as much of the PRI's eroding coalition as possible and draw in centrist independents by convincing them that the challengers represented a riskier version of change than he could offer. Cárdenas campaigned on economic nationalism and a more just distribution of resources, changes that he argued would go hand-in-hand with democracy. For him to win, he would have to convince non-PRD voters of the need for such deep economic policy change, while showing that the other two candidates represented the failed status quo. Fox also focused on change, but emphasized the need for turnover while making broad and often vague centrist economic policy appeals just as a successful opposition alliance would have. To beat the others, he would have to convince voters that he alone represented democratic change, that Cárdenas could not win, and that Labastida could not deliver on his promises. By eliminating Cárdenas and neutralizing Labastida's democratic credentials, Fox would not only retain the PAN's loyalists, he would also win regime opposition voters, independents, and even some right-leaning PRI identifiers. In the end, Fox's strategy prevailed because he accomplished four tasks that cast him as a centrist democratizer that could beat the PRI. I describe each task and then incorporate the relevant variables into a model of voting behavior.

Focusing on Democracy

Fox solidified his reformist credentials by campaigning heavily and effectively on the issue of democratic change that he defined as turnover. This

---

[16] Comparing vote choice in February, rather than party identification, and final reported vote in July yields almost exactly the same results.

emphasis was brilliantly summed up in the campaign's elegant slogan "ya" meaning "now" or "enough." "Ya" captured the idea that change was a long time in coming and that it was now finally the time to "throw the bums out." "Ya" appeared in almost all campaign slogans: "I want change NOW," "I want a better job NOW," "I want a safe place to play NOW." The slogan was easy to remember, catchy, and doubled as a hand-gesture with a "V" for victory that was turned into giant foam fingers for campaign rallies in cities and became what Preston and Dillon (2004: 491) called a "subversive signal of defiance of the PRI" that was subtly flashed to signal one's political sympathies. During the campaign, up to 75% of voters recognized it as Fox's slogan while a smaller proportion correctly assigned Cárdenas and Labastida to their slogans.[17] Finally, when the PAN formed an alliance with the small Green Party (PVEM) for the elections, the coalition was called "Alliance for Change." Cárdenas tried to tarnish Fox's democratic credentials by accusing the PAN of collaboration with ex-President Salinas, who was by then a reviled figure. Yet, as Bruhn (2004: 133) points out, the PAN's initial willingness to forge an opposition alliance with the PRD reinforced its democratic credentials and helped erase its collaborationist image.

Fox also attempted to prime the importance of democracy in order to increase the number of regime opposition voters. His campaign argued that Mexico's biggest problems – crime, poor public services, poverty, corruption, and crony capitalism that led to economic inefficiency and stalled growth – were symptoms of the lack of rotation in government. Voters should demand democracy, Fox said, like politicians from the left and the right who had stood up to the PRI over decades of struggle, including socialist party founder Heberto Castillo, Rosario Ibarra who spearheaded a mother's of the disappeared movement in the 1970s, and Salvador Nava, the enigmatic opposition leader in San Luis Potosí state.

Priming the democracy issue may have had a small but important effect. Just three weeks before the July election, 12.5% of respondents to the panel survey said that democracy was the country's most important problem when compared to other issues, and this represented a 2.3% increase from February.[18] Among those who reprioritized during the campaign,

---

[17] Data from the Mexico 2000 Panel Study shows that in wave 1 (February), 50% correctly identified Fox with his slogan, 40% identified Labastida's, and just 13% identified Cárdenas'. By wave 3 (June), identification of Fox's slogan was up to 75%, Labastida's to 69%, and Cárdenas' to 57%.

[18] These data are from open-ended responses to the Mexico 2000 Panel Study grouped into three categories. Economic problems included unemployment, salaries, inflation, poverty,

236 *Why Dominant Parties Lose*

24% identified with the PAN at the outset, but 52% voted for Fox in the end. Thus, priming may have increased Fox's vote share by 1.2%. While not in and of itself a silver bullet, this strategy may have paid off in an election that many observers thought would break within about five points between the winner and first loser.

Countering the PRI's Reformist Campaign

Fox's second task was to neutralize the image of a new and democratic PRI and convince voters that only an opposition candidate could bring change. To do so, Fox referred to Labastida as "the candidate of more of the same" while he compared his own goals to the heroic deeds of Nelson Mandela and Lech Walesa. Labastida's democratic credentials initially appeared stronger than those of prior PRI candidates because he won in the party's first ever primary; however, his rival for the nomination, Roberto Madrazo, set the stage for Fox by pounding Labastida for months as the "official candidate" who was tapped by outgoing President Zedillo in traditional authoritarian style using *el dedazo*. Madrazo's ingenious slogan employed a very colloquial meaning of his name to suggest that voters should "*Dale un Madrazo al Dedazo*" which loosely translates as "Down with the Finger Tap." During one period of the campaign, Labastida tried to distance himself from the PRI and claimed that he would force democracy on his party's authoritarian hardliners. Fox responded by calling him weak in the most unflattering sense: he referred to him as "*La vestida*" meaning "the transvestite." At the same time, Fox capitalized on his own tall and robust physique, classic mustache, cowboy boots, and deep confident voice to project the prototypical image of Mexican machismo and give the impression that he could tame the PRI hardliners. He also used aggressive campaign antics and advertising. PRI stalwarts were known as dinosaurs, so at some campaign events Fox taunted and then crushed a miniature dinosaur toy to uproarious cheers from the crowd. Finally, in one poster, the Fox campaign showed mug shots of past presidents awkwardly pasted to an austere stone wall as if convicts, with one blank space and the caption "Space reserved for the old face of the new PRI... We're ready to wake up from this collective nightmare" (Ortiz, 2002: 38).

and "the economy." Democracy included corruption and lack of good government. Crime included public security, kidnapping, and narcotrafficking. I did not use exit-poll data because self-reports about why voters chose a particular candidate may overemphasize particular issues.

Unsurprisingly, voters considered the PRI to be less democratic than the PAN and PRD. A March 1999 poll showed that 43.2% of respondents considered the PRI to be "authoritarian," whereas about one-quarter thought that this label applied to the PAN or PRD.[19] The PRI probably would have been considered more authoritarian than its rivals even without Fox's campaign tactics; however, his aggressive advertising and help from PRI-insider Madrazo may have helped counter the PRI's attempts to transform its image.

Winning Pro-Democracy Regime Opposition Voters from Cárdenas

Fox's third task was to convince voters that Cárdenas could not win, and thus a vote for Cárdenas was a "wasted" opposition vote. Having primed democracy, Fox could have easily sent regime opposition voters to Cárdenas and helped the PRI "divide and conquer." As early as the spring of 1998 Fox was aware of this dynamic and said, "I have to beat Cárdenas. If Cárdenas and I split the vote, the PRI wins" (Preston and Dillon, 2004: 489). To take regime opposition voters away from Cárdenas, he needed to convince voters that he had the better chance of beating the PRI. The best way to do this was to actually move ahead in the polls and, as described above, making centrist appeals that could attract independents and moderate PRI supporters was a key strategy for expanding the vote.

Cárdenas unwittingly helped Fox stand alone in the center by running a noncentrist campaign that mainly appealed to the PRD's core constituents. Like Fox, Cárdenas focused on the issue of change, but he criticized the PAN's emphasis on turnover as unsubstantial. Instead, Cárdenas argued for what he said was real change: a shift in economic policy that would not only maintain government ownership over PEMEX and the electric utility, but would actively use the government to redistribute the fruits of development and provide a social safety net for millions whose incomes crashed with economic crisis and the transition to free trade. He declared that his campaign would not be "frivolous like in the United States, but rather it [would] go into deeper issues" (see Shirk, 2005: 157) and he characterized it as "a more profound struggle to rescue the sovereignty of our country and to fulfill the demands of the Mexican people" (see Bruhn, 2000: 5). Bruhn concludes that "The PRD put its money on a programmatic polarization that relied on economic distinctions" (2004:

---

[19] *Reforma* newspaper Zedillo Evaluation Survey, March 1999.

143) and notes that the party's "Electoral Strategy 2000" lists economic issues as its top two priorities while subordinating democracy to fourth place (2000: 11).

By focusing on economic issues, Cárdenas tried to tap the well of resentment that PRD insiders were certain existed among voters. Like the Mexican left for decades, PRD leaders believed that objective conditions of poverty and inequality – conditions that were exacerbated by the crippling economic crises of 1982 and 1994 and made apparent by the FOBAPROA banking scandal – would fuel the left's vote. They believed so firmly in their own ability to divine the pulse of the people that they criticized surveys as frivolous and refused to consult them on many occasions.[20] (In contrast, Fox's team used daily tracking polls and in-depth monthly sample surveys.) As it turned out, the PRD was right in the sense that over half the electorate thought that economic problems including poverty, unemployment, inflation, and low salaries were the main issues rather than democracy, and this proportion remained virtually unchanged through the campaign.[21] But the voters were much more centrist on economic issues than Cárdenas and PRD leaders thought. As a result, Cárdenas' emphasis on leftwing economic policy constrained him to the PRD's core constituents, left Fox virtually alone to campaign on the democracy issue, and thus helped Fox win the battle of perceptions over which candidate could beat the PRI.

Fox also won the battle of perceptions because voters came to perceive him as more competent than Cárdenas. Fox's career path, from laborer to company director made him seem capable of operating in the cutthroat business world and deal effectively with the Mexico's most important economic partner, the United States. As Governor of Guanajuato, he aggressively advertised his innovations and successes. Cárdenas, on the other hand, portrayed himself as a tireless, if dour, champion of the people with a deep sense of social justice that motivated his public life. As Mayor of the Federal District of Mexico City (1997–1999), he refused to publicize his achievements and often repeated that his was an administration of action, not advertising.

While voters may have held Cárdenas in high regard as a person, they saw Fox as a more capable president. Using data from the June wave of the Mexico 2000 Panel Study, I constructed a Candidate Competence Index made up of voters' assessments of the candidates' ability to deal with three

---

[20] Cárdenas' 1994 campaign manager Adolfo Aguilar Zinser made the same complaint (Aguilar Zinser, 1995).

[21] Based on analysis of the Mexico 2000 Panel Survey. See footnote 18.

Dominance Defeated

pressing problems – the economy, crime, and public education. The index runs from 0 to 1, where lower scores are associated with higher competence. Voters placed Labastida at 0.324, Fox at 0.327, and Cárdenas at 0.428, indicating that Cárdenas was considered less competent overall than his two rivals whose ratings were virtually the same.[22]

Cárdenas' campaign style also put him at a disadvantage. While Fox waged an intensive media campaign in the style of a catchall party that Shirk refers to as "Americanized," Cárdenas campaigned in the style of a niche party and argued that "television dilutes politics in favor of spectacle" (see Bruhn, 2000: 18). For decades, the left had campaigned in the streets using rallies, marches, and face-to-face contact with voters. But although creating passionate converts was important for a challenger party under siege in years past, the grassroots strategy was tremendously ineffective at maximizing votes. According to Bruhn, "The PRD in particular seemed obsessed with an indiscriminate preference for grassroots campaigning" (2004: 147). It equated full plazas with full ballot boxes and the intensity of rally participants with turnout. Continuing with this strategy in 2000, Cárdenas wanted to visit each of the 300 electoral districts during the campaign, and in the end he made it to 220. While Cárdenas filled plazas, Fox racked up ratings points by carefully segmenting the electoral market, crafting 65 different commercials to target specific audiences (Ortiz, 2002: 13), and aggressively seeking out free coverage from local news in the most densely populated media markets.

Cárdenas' sober, noncentrist, issue-based, and grassroots-oriented campaign ultimately failed to convince voters that he could beat the PRI when compared to Fox's high energy and media-savvy campaign that focused on a theme that united more than it divided – "ya." Table 7.7 shows that, overall, voters thought that Fox had a 35.2% chance of winning, compared to Cárdenas' 22.8%. Labastida came in higher at 41.7%, but in historical context, this was actually quite low.[23] For nearly seven decades the PRI was thought of as "the only game in town" and all major political actors assumed it would win. Thus, giving the PRI candidate less than a 50% chance represented a major change in attitudes. Not surprisingly, partisans of each party thought that their candidate had the highest

---

[22] Differences between Cárdenas and the others were statistically significant at the .001 level. Differences between Fox and Labastida were statistically indistinguishable for voters in general, but among independents, PAN identifiers, and PRD identifiers, Fox was considered more competent, and these differences were significant at the .05 level.

[23] Following Magaloni and Poiré's (2004b) suggestion, I constrained the combined probability ratings for the three candidates to 1. So if a voter rated Labastida at .80, Fox at .80, and Cárdenas at .40, the scores were recalculated as .40, .40, and .20, respectively.

240 *Why Dominant Parties Lose*

TABLE 7.7. *Voters' Assessments of the Candidates' Probability of Winning*

Party ID	Labastida Probability	Cárdenas Probability	Fox Probability
PRI	51.6	19.2	30.2
PAN	33.2	21.7	44.6
PRD	26.3	40.3	33.1
Other	54.4	31.4	14.2
Independent	40.9	22.9	35.9
Mean	41.7	22.8	35.2

Entries are percentages.
Source: Mexico 2000 Panel Study, wave 2 (April/May).

probability of winning. But, importantly, PRD voters perceived that Fox had the second highest probability whereas Cárdenas came in third among PAN voters. This implies that while PRD regime opposition voters might strategically choose Fox to beat the PRI, PAN regime opposition voters were much less likely to choose Cárdenas because they assumed he would lose.

Claiming the Political Center

Fox's final task was to draw in independents and right-leaning PRI supporters. He did this by crafting a broad centrist campaign that downplayed specific economic policy issues and instead made general promises, including achieving 7% economic growth, tackling poverty, creating employment opportunities, and solving the Chiapas problem. He referred to "economic humanism" but never really defined it. When he was not vague, he played the role of the Sphinx, showing different faces to different constituents. For instance, he opposed privatizing PEMEX in public events in Mexico, but supported it in private international meetings with businessmen.

Despite his vague promises on a number of issues, Fox was generally perceived as a centrist in the sense that voters perceived him as closest to their issue preferences. Data from the 2000 Panel Study in Table 7.8 show the mean distance between voters' self-placement on three central issues in the campaign – economic privatization, democracy, and crime – and their perceptions of the candidates' stands. Independents and minor party identifiers perceived Fox as closest to them. Unsurprisingly, identifiers with the major parties lined up with their party's candidate; however PRD identifiers saw Fox as the second closest. Like assessments of the challengers' chances of winning, this further suggested that PRD regime opposition voters might strategically vote for Fox to defeat the PRI.

TABLE 7.8. *Mean Distance between Voter Self-Placement and Perception of Candidate Location on Key Campaign Issues*

| | Mean Distance from Voters to Perceived Candidate Positions in July | | | | | | | | |
| | Fighting Crime | | | Electric Utility Privatization | | | Political Reform | | |
Party ID in February	Labastida	Fox	Cárdenas	Labastida	Fox	Cárdenas	Labastida	Fox	Cárdenas
PRI	**2.71**	3.29	3.35	**2.54**	3.92	3.20	**2.54**	2.88	3.01
PAN	3.72	**2.30**	3.47	3.44	**2.53**	3.13	2.81	**2.35**	2.96
PRD	4.19	2.99	**2.39**	3.58	3.82	**2.69**	3.76	2.93	**2.54**
Other	7.67	**2.00**	2.67	4.67	**1.67**	2.00	4.33	**1.00**	5.67
Independent	3.34	**2.82**	3.09	3.29	**3.20**	3.22	2.85	**2.50**	2.72

Entries are linear distances. Shortest distances appear in bold.
Source: Mexico 2000 Panel Study, wave 1 and 4.

242   *Why Dominant Parties Lose*

TABLE 7.9. *Mean Distance between Voter Self-Placement and Perception of Candidate Location on the Left-Right Scale*

	PRI	PAN	PRD	Labastida	Fox	Cárdenas
All Voters						
February	3.02	3.32	3.91	–	–	–
April	2.96	3.21	3.92	2.98	3.08	3.91
June	3.06	3.04	3.58	3.05	3.00	3.49
July (post-election)	3.29	3.18	3.97	3.23	3.10	3.98
Independents						
February	3.33	3.05	3.61	–	–	–
April	3.41	2.87	3.68	3.38	2.82	3.50
June	3.21	2.70	3.21	3.04	2.62	3.10
July (post-election)	3.25	2.71	3.77	3.21	2.64	3.77

Entries are the absolute value of mean linear distances between each voter's personal preference on the 10-point left-right ideology scale and their perception of the parties' and candidates' locations on this same scale. Shortest distances appear in bold.
Source: Mexico 2000 Panel Study, wave 1 and 4.

Fox also knew that independents were repelled by the parties in general, so he actively distanced himself from the PAN to reinforce his centrist credentials. Noting that the PAN's official color is blue, Shirk writes that Fox had an acute "political fashion sense... donning a seemingly endless supply of denim duds and chambray shirts at practically every public appearance. Fox's penchant for blue apparel, however, was about the extent of his party-based appeals" (2005: 154). He hired a campaign team that excluded the party's top leadership and he used a headhunter to recommend a campaign manager rather than bring on a party insider with deep moral authority. He also relied on independent resources and grassroots mobilizing by Amigos de Fox more than the PAN. Unlike Cárdenas, Fox was not restricted to party resources that would have constrained his movement away from the PAN's old guard and its core voters. Still, Fox gambled on a risky strategy, since he could ill afford to lose the PAN's core voters.

Voters not only perceived Fox as the closest to their issue preferences, they also thought of him as more centrist than the PAN. Unfortunately, issue assessments for both candidates and parties were not available; however, the Mexico 2000 Panel Study did measure comparative assessments on a ten-point left-right ideology scale. Table 7.9 shows mean distances between voters' own positions and their perceptions of both the candidates' and the parties' positions. The data show that voters saw Fox as closer to them than the party. This implies that had Fox not run an

Dominance Defeated 243

independent campaign, he would have been perceived as less centrist. In fact, to the extent that the PAN appeared centrist, it probably benefited from Fox's issue-perception coattails. By comparison, Cárdenas was tied to the PRD's traditional appeals and both he and his party were perceived as very out of step with voters' preferences. Other data help confirm Fox's supra-party appeal. Of those who reported choosing their candidate due to his party affiliation, only 12.5% voted for Fox whereas 50% chose Labastida, and 37.5% chose Cárdenas. Table 7.9 also provides a more general confirmation of what we learned by looking at specific issue questions. Although independents always considered Fox as the most representative of their interests, voters in general came to perceive him as the closest candidate overall by the end of the campaign, implying that Fox's center-seeking strategy worked.

Before moving on, we need to consider the possibility that Fox's perceived proximity to the voters may not have resulted from voters' independent assessments of their own political concerns and the candidates' stands. If something else was responsible for these perceptions of closeness, then it would cut against the grain of my argument that Fox won in part because he moved toward the center. One possibility is that voters' sense of proximity resulted from projection effects where voters choose a candidate for nonissue reasons and then project their own issue preferences onto the candidates in an effort to reduce cognitive dissonance (Brody and Page, 1972; Conover and Feldman, 1989). Projection can be a "false consensus effect" where a voter directly aligns her policy preference with her perception of her preferred candidate's stand, or it can be due to "assimilation" or "contrast" effects where a voter draws closer to a candidate she likes or further from a candidate she dislikes.

Panel data are uniquely suited to test for projection effects because they permit analysis of how voters' dispositions early in the campaign affected their subsequent assessments of the candidates' issue positions. I followed Conover and Feldman's (1989) suggested model to test for projection regarding the three candidates' stands on crime, economic privatization, and political reform.[24] Of the nine tests (not shown), there was minor

---

[24] The basic model tested was as follows:

$$C_{ijk(t)} = b_0 + b_1 C_{ijk(t-1)} + b_2 R_{ik(t-1)} + (b_3 R_{ik(t-1)} * Peval_{j(t-1)})$$
$$+ (b_4 R_{ik(t-1)} * Neval_{j(t-1)}) + \varepsilon$$

Where $C_{ijk(t)}$ is the position of candidate j on issue k as perceived by voter i at time t, $R_{ik(t-1)}$ is the position of voter i on issue k at time $t-1$, and $Peval_{j(t-1)}$ and $Neval_{j(t-1)}$ represent positive and negative evaluations of candidate j. The first term after the constant measures stability in voters' issue assessments of the candidates. The second term captures

244   *Why Dominant Parties Lose*

evidence of a false consensus effect for Fox's perceived position on crime only. In the eight other cases there were no projection effects.

The absence of projection rules out the major threat to issue voting; however, two remaining threats could not be tested for. First, voters may have taken cues about the candidates' issue positions from the media, but media content data that corresponded to each panel wave were not available. Second, the overall stability of issue positions was somewhat low for crime and privatization, and very low for political reform (McCann and Lawson, 2003). Voters' placements of the candidates may reflect garbage-can answers that were picked at random. Although it is likely that random-ness increases when campaigns are vague and information is costly as they arguably were in Mexico in 2000, Bartels (1986) argues that voters who are very uncertain about candidates' positions typically do not answer issue questions on surveys, and thus should not be reflected in the data presented here. Thus, even though we cannot rule out all alternatives, it appears that issue positions may have played a role in 2000.

In sum, Fox ran a campaign focused on change that downplayed ideo-logical differences. He was able to claim the political center in part because his independent resources left him unhampered by the PAN and in part because Cárdenas vacated the center by pursuing a campaign focused on comparatively leftwing economic policies. Fox was further able to stand alone as the candidate of democracy because Labastida was a less credible democratizer and Cárdenas' economic policy focus made him less viable against the PRI. As a result, voters decided to choose Fox during the campaign and helped him yolk together a broad coalition. To show how all these elements came together in determining vote choice, the next section presents a statistical model.

A MODEL OF VOTING BEHAVIOR IN THE 2000 ELECTIONS

To analyze voters' decisions, I used data from the Mexico 2000 Panel Study to construct a model with five sets of explanatory variables.[25] The

---

"false consensus effects" where the voter infers that the candidate holds positions close to her own. The third and fourth terms capture "assimilation" and "contrast" effects where voters consider candidates they like to be closer to them and those they dislike to be further. If any of the variables other than the voters' prior assessments of candidate positions reach statistical significance, then projection is present.

[25] I measured vote choice (the dependent variable) using vote reports collected July 7–16, just 5–12 days after the election. Voters typically over-report choosing the winner, but the alternative was to use pre-election vote intentions collected almost one month before

first set includes vote choice in February. These variables should go a long way toward accounting for final vote choice just five months later; however, as shown in Table 7.6, the campaigns had a substantial impact on voters' decisions. In particular, voters abandoned Cárdenas while Labastida and especially Fox drew in their competitors' partisans. As a result, other variables must be at work.

The second set of variables concerns vote mobilization and includes whether a voter received a gift from the PRI or was visited by operatives from any of the three parties during the campaign. These variables test for the effects of machine politics (the patronage variable) and the activist network (the canvassing variables). Yet given the dramatic reduction in the PRI's patronage resources and its focus on the media campaign, the effects of these variables on voting behavior should be small to none.[26]

The third set of variables tap voters' assessments of Cárdenas' probability of winning the election, using data from late April/early May. Prospective probability assessments underlie strategic voting (Cox, 1997). In particular, voters who supported Cárdenas in February but thought that he had a low probability of victory should have been more likely to defect to another candidate. Who they defected to depended on their own stands on the issues. For regime opposition voters, democracy was more important so they should have defected to Fox. Economic policy voters should have defected to Labastida instead.

The fourth set of variables captures candidate representativeness. I construct measures of the salience-weighted issue distance from each voter to each candidate summed across the issues of crime, privatization, and political reform. These variables were created by assigning voters the following utility function:

$$U_{ij} = \sum_k -\alpha_{ik} |x_{ik} - C_{jk}|$$

This function states that voter i has utility for candidate j based on the distance between voter i's own position on issue k (x_{ik}) and her perception of candidate j's position on issue k (C_{jk}). This issue distance is

election day under the clearly fallacious assumption that no one changed their vote choice during the final month. In fact, 16.1% of the electorate switched vote choice from waves 3 to 4, 59.5% of whom switched to Fox. Discounting voters who already identified with the PAN in wave 3 or were independent, 25.7% of switchers came from other parties and may have falsely reported their vote choice. Thus, if Fox won zero votes from PRI and PRD identifiers in the last month of the campaign, then post-electoral vote reports mis-specify a maximum or 4.1% of scores on the dependent variable.

[26] These variables may affect turnout, but that is not the focus of this model.

then discounted by the salience that voter i ascribes to issue k (α_{ik} where $\sum \alpha_k = 1$). To compute salience, the issue that the voter considered the most important was weighted by one-half and the two less important issues were each weighted by one-fourth. If none of the three issues was considered priority, then all three were weighted equally at one-third. These salience-weighted distances were summed across all three issues to come up with a single number that describes how much voter i likes candidate j on all k issues. Operationalizing positional issues this way correctly captures the intent behind formal models of proximity voting.

The effects of issue proximity should be greater on voters who pay more attention to the campaigns. Those who pay less attention should be less able to identify the candidates' positions and less sensitive to shifts in those positions during the campaign. To test this prediction, I interacted the issue distance measures with a Campaign Attention Index that combines voters' self-reports of campaign attentiveness, frequency of talking about politics, and whether they followed the news on television, over radio, or in the newspaper.

The final set of variables measures voters' perceptions of the candidates' competence to deal with economic problems, crime, and public education. I combined the three competence ratings into a single additive index with a range from 0 to 1 for each of the three candidates where higher scores are associated with less competence. Competence should play a comparatively larger role in voters' assessments when campaigns are policy consensual or vague as many analysts thought Mexico's campaigns were in 2000.

I estimated the model using multinomial logit.[27] Results appear in Table 7.10. Creating substantively interpretable findings from the model requires us to transform the coefficients reported above and take account of the uncertainty that surrounds each one. Table 7.11 presents the baseline predicted probability of supporting each candidate for a voter who was undecided in February while all other variables were set at their mean

---

[27] Alvarez and Nagler (1998) argue that multinomial probit (MNP) should be used to examine vote choice in multiparty elections since, unlike multinomial logit (MNL), MNP does not assume that choices are independent across alternatives (the IIA assumption). As a result, MNP should produce better estimates; however, Dow and Endersby (2004) argue that MNP models are often weakly identified and return coefficients and standard errors that are indistinguishable from MNL unless the analysis has a very large number of observations. In addition, they argue that the problems associated with IIA are exaggerated and may not obtain when elections feature a stable number of competitors as they did in Mexico in 2000.

Dominance Defeated

TABLE 7.10. *Multinomial Logistic Regression Model of Vote Choice, 2000*

Variable	Vote for Cárdenas		Vote for Labastida	
	Coeff	Std Err	Coeff	Std Err
Issue distance to Labastida*Attention to campaign, w4	0.50	1.48	−1.38	1.31
Issue distance to Fox*Attention to campaign, w4	3.74**	1.73	4.37**	1.50
Issue distance to Cárdenas*Attention to campaign, w4	−3.28*	1.96	−0.89	1.68
Competence rating Labastida, w2	0.16	1.07	−1.68**	0.88
Competence rating Fox, w2	2.84**	1.35	1.85**	1.02
Competence rating Cárdenas, w2	−3.03**	1.27	−1.73*	0.96
Probability Cárdenas wins, w2	3.27*	2.04	−3.46**	1.73
Gift from PRI, w1-4	0.14	1.14	−0.13	0.82
Visit from PAN, w1-4	−3.64	9.81	−1.48	1.49
Visit from PRD, w1-4	2.93*	1.76	0.62	1.57
Visit from PRI, w1-4	0.44	1.03	0.56	0.89
Initial Vote intention for Labastida, w1	−0.19	0.86	1.55**	0.68
Initial Vote intention for Fox, w1	−2.24**	0.92	−2.71**	0.89
Initial Vote intention for Cárdenas, w1	0.70	0.92	0.23	0.87
Constant	−1.44	1.21	0.86	0.96

Vote for Fox is the excluded category
N = 277; LR chi^2(28) = 252.99; Prob>chi^2 = 0.0000
Log likelihood = −139.12; Pseudo r^2 = 0.48
*** p <.01; ** p <.05; * p <.1
Source: Mexico 2000 Panel Study, waves 1-4.

or mode.[28] These predictions – 14.6% for Cárdenas, 39.8% for Labastida, and 45.6% for Fox – come close to the actual outcome of the election. We can use these predictions as a baseline for examining the effects of the explanatory variables on vote choice.

Table 7.12 shows the effect of shifting each explanatory variable from its empirical minimum to maximum while holding other variables constant. Five findings emerge. First, vote choice in February was a good

---

[28] I used Clarify software for all post-estimation predictions (Tomz, Wittenberg, and King, 2001).

248   *Why Dominant Parties Lose*

TABLE 7.11. *Predicted Probabilities of Vote Choice for an Undecided Voter (Baseline Model)*

Candidate	Mean Probability	Standard Error	95% Confidence Interval	
Cárdenas	.1457	.059	.056	.290
Labastida	.3981	.088	.237	.576
Fox	.4562	.091	.293	.634

TABLE 7.12. *Predicted Effect of Explanatory Variables on Vote Choice (First Differences)*

Variable	Change in the Probability of Voting for Candidate		
	Cárdenas	Labastida	Fox
Vote intention for Labastida, w1	0.1090	**0.1384**	*0.1415*
Vote intention for Fox, w1	0.1083	0.1308	**0.1399**
Vote intention for Cárdenas, w1	0.1449	0.1699	0.1727
Issue distance to Labastida*Attention to campaign, w4	0.1293	−0.2204	0.0911
Issue distance to Fox*Attention to campaign, w4	0.1401	**0.3804**	**−0.5204**
Issue distance to Cárdenas*Attention to campaign, w4	**−0.2181**	−0.0353	0.2534
Competence rating Labastida, w2	0.1100	**−0.3167**	0.2067
Competence rating Fox, w2	0.2931	0.1538	**−0.4469**
Competence rating Cárdenas, w2	*−0.3164*	−0.1402	**0.4566**
Probability Cárdenas wins, w2	**0.6285**	**−0.5097**	*−0.2188*
Visit from PAN operative, w1-4	−0.1842	−0.1179	0.3022
Visit from PRD operative, w1-4	0.4445	−0.1370	−0.3075
Visit from PRI operative, w1-4	0.0419	0.0886	−0.1305
Gift from PRI, w1-4	0.0624	−0.0393	−0.0231

Bold indicates significant at the .05 level. Italics indicate significant at the .10 level.
Note: Competence rating scale is reversed. Higher scores are associated with less competence.

but incomplete predictor of final vote choice in July for Labastida and Fox; however, it played almost no role for Cárdenas. This indicates that when other variables are taken into account, voters had no particular unexplained attachments to Cárdenas and that many voters who supported him toward the beginning of the campaign defected by the end. It also indicates that campaign dynamics had a large effect on all three candidates' final vote shares. Second, voters' assessments of Cárdenas'

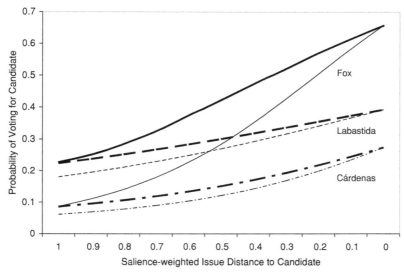

FIGURE 7.4. Effects of Issue Distance and Campaign Information on Candidate Choice (low information voters in bold lines; high information voters in thin lines).

chances of winning had a large effect on his vote share. When Cárdenas' initial supporters thought he could win, they stuck by him, but when they expected him to lose, they abandoned him for Labastida or Fox. Third, there is virtually no evidence of mobilized voting. Voters who received a gift from the PRI or a visit from an operative from the PAN or PRI were no more likely to vote for that party's candidate. There is a marginal but substantively small negative effect for Cárdenas when voters were visited by a PAN operative. This may reflect Fox's attempt to convince PRD voters that Cárdenas could not win, but there were so few visits overall that this hardly mattered. Fourth, issue distance mattered a great deal for Fox, somewhat for Cárdenas, and not at all for Labastida. This implies that Labastida was more constrained to PRI identifiers while Fox and Cárdenas could use their issue positions to attract or repel voters. Finally, competence ratings were important for all three candidates. Below, I examine issue distance, prospective probability assessments, and competence in more detail.

Figure 7.4 presents the effects of issue proximity on the predicted probability of supporting each candidate. Issue distance had a huge effect on the probability of supporting Fox, and there were substantial differences between informed voters (the thin lines) and uninformed voters (the thick lines). Both groups had almost a 66% probability of voting for Fox when they completely agreed with him on the issues. When an uninformed voter completely disagreed with him, her likelihood of voting for him dropped all the way to 22.7%. For informed voters who presumably cared more about representativeness, maximum disagreement with Fox dropped the probability of voting for him to 8.7%, equal to the likelihood of voting for Cárdenas. This implies that, as we would expect, voters who were very far on the left or decidedly opposed to democratic turnover were very unlikely to vote for Fox. It also indicates that Fox was able to draw in a lot of voters not identified with the PAN by moving closer to them on the issues. Thus, Fox likely would have done much worse in the election had he not minimized his issue distance to the voters by consciously moving toward the center.

Issue distance had no distinguishable effect on support for Labastida. As shown in Table 7.12 and implied by the shallow slope of the Labastida curve in Figure 7.4, voters who completely agreed with Labastida on the issues were no more likely to support him than those who completely disagreed. This is a dramatic indication of how reliant Labastida was on PRI identifiers who chose him essentially through no fault of his own. Additionally, this finding shows that Labastida was utterly unable to extend his electoral coalition with issue appeals.

Issue proximity had a small but statistically significant effect on the likelihood of supporting Cárdenas. Voters who completely agreed with him on the issues were 21.8% more likely to choose him than voters who completely disagreed with his stand. There were virtually no differences between voters who paid a lot or a little attention to the campaign. These findings imply that although Cárdenas' issue positions may have alienated some voters, there were other factors that drove his vote share down.

Assessments of Cárdenas' viability played a large role in sending voters away from him between February and July. The simulation in Figure 7.5 shows clearly that as voters lost faith in his chances, they became much more likely to defect. However, who they defected to depended on their own issue preferences. For the purposes of this simulation, I defined PRD regime opposition voters as those who planned to vote for Cárdenas in February, were maximally distant from Labastida on the issues, and minimally and equally distant from Cárdenas and Fox on the issues. All other variables were set at their mean or mode. In the figure, the solid lines show that these regime opposition voters were very likely to defect to Fox in order to defeat Labastida as they thought Cárdenas' chances declined. A voter who thought that Cárdenas was a sure winner had only a 27.7% probability of defecting to Fox. But if she saw Cárdenas as a sure loser,

Dominance Defeated

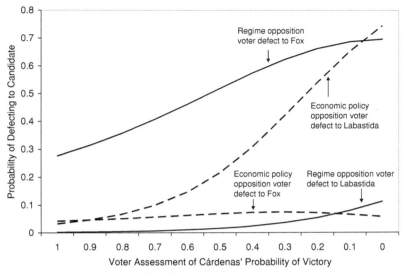

FIGURE 7.5. Probability of Defecting from Cárdenas.

that probability rose to 69.7%. At the same time, the chance that a regime opposition voter would defect to Labastida never rose above 11.4%.

The pattern of defection flips when considering a PRD economic policy supporter, defined here as a voter who supported Cárdenas in February and was close to him on the issues. Unlike regime opposition voters, these economic policy voters were closer to Labastida than they were to Fox on the issues.[29] The results, shown with the dashed lines, demonstrate that an economic policy voter who thought Cárdenas was a sure winner tended to stick with him and had only a 3.3% chance of defecting to Labastida. But as she thought Cárdenas would lose, her desire to prevent Fox from winning kicked in and she defected to Labastida with 74.6% probability. At the same time, there was very little chance (a maximum of 7.6%) that she would defect to Fox since he was further on the issues. The simulation does not show rigid PRD voters because they stuck with Cárdenas no matter how they assessed his chances.

These findings show that Cárdenas' supporters made strategic decisions as the election neared and his chances dwindled. Fox campaigned heavily on the "wasted vote" logic and appears to have convinced regime opposition voters who wanted to prevent a PRI victory that he was their

---

[29] Specifically, Cárdenas' issue distance was set at .15 (about half the mean), Labastida's at its mean of .26, and Fox at the maximum distance at 1.

252 *Why Dominant Parties Lose*

best choice. However, Labastida benefited from PRD economic policy voters who left Cárdenas to prevent a Fox victory.

Why was Cárdenas considered less viable? The major reason was that while Fox consciously moved toward the center and primed the democracy issue in order to maximize his appeal, Cárdenas' message of leftwing economic policy change increased his distance to the average voter. Yet, the final nail in Cárdenas' coffin came from voters' perceptions of his competence. Voters thought of Labastida and Fox as equally competent on average, but they thought that Cárdenas would have more trouble dealing with the major problems of the day. Interestingly, although high competence ratings helped all the candidates individually, when Cárdenas received a low rating, Fox benefited but not Labastida. Since there is a modest correlation between competence ratings for Fox and Cárdenas, voters may have identified them as substitutes for something they would have in common if they won – dealing with a defeated PRI and all the bureaucratic inertia that would likely remain. On this score, Fox's campaign may have made him appear much more capable. His "cowboy" attitude, harsh criticism of Labastida's toughness, and campaign antics like crushing toy dinosaurs may have convinced voters that he could deal with the regime's remnants whereas Cárdenas' sober statesmanlike style was less convincing on this issue.

On average, there were no differences between voters' competence ratings of Labastida and Fox. Although there is a mild correlation between Labastida's ratings and retrospective evaluations of the Zedillo Administration, there is no particular evidence that Fox won because he was considered a better administrator than Labastida. He won because his centrist campaign succeeded in moving beyond the PAN's core constituency and drawing in enough independents to match Labastida's large following of PRI faithful. In addition, Fox crucially benefited from PRD defectors who wanted to beat the PRI and thought that Cárdenas could not win. Fox could not have done this had he not campaigned as a centrist who was primarily interested in democratic change and had few strong ties to the PAN's minority following of the past.

CONCLUSION

Declining resource advantages made the PRI more vulnerable to defeat throughout the 1990s. However, coordination problems both within and between the opposition parties limited their ability to expand. They remained largely constrained to their core constituencies and were unable

Dominance Defeated   253

to attract the support of centrists and independents. Further, because neither opposition party seemed substantially more viable than the other in elections throughout the 1990s, they typically split the group of regime opposition voters who sought to defeat the PRI.

The 2000 elections were different for two reasons. First, illicit public resources were less available to the PRI than ever before. Government ownership of economic assets declined so rapidly that in 2000 public enterprise accounted for just 5.5% of GDP, almost half of what it was during the previous presidential election, and almost one-fifth of its share of the economy at its height 17 years earlier. At the same time, the electoral code used for 2000 made the parties more reliant on legal public funding by explicitly forbidding contributions from government entities and sharply reducing the limit on private contributions. Although illicit campaign funding remained, it fell far short of the PRI's wholesale use of public funds for partisan purposes in prior years.

Second, the 2000 elections were different because of Fox. Unlike Cárdenas, Fox was not organically tied to his party and thus was more capable of making broad centrist appeals even when they conflicted with the preferences of his party's elites. In order to win the nomination, however, Fox had to build his candidacy as an outsider. In particular, he needed to raise independent resources, a feat that his team ably accomplished through Amigos de Fox. These resources, although not always legal, essentially erased the remaining resource gap between the PRI and the PAN and allowed Fox to mount a full-scale modern campaign that used the mass media and armies of canvassers to disseminate information about the candidate. Fox also tapped into voters' desire for change. At the same time, Cárdenas ran a losing campaign focused on economic policy issues that only attracted the PRD's loyal minority of voters on the left. Finally, since voters did not view Labastida as a credible force for democracy, Fox managed to stand alone as the centrist pro-democracy candidate. This allowed him to bring together a "coalition for change" that included PAN identifiers, independents, PRI defectors who were centrists, and PRD defectors who were regime opposition voters.

After generations of PRI dominance, Fox found a path to victory. Although his victory was dramatic, it was substantially more mundane than episodes of democratization in other authoritarian regimes in South America and the former Soviet Union. First, Fox's victory was not so much a triumph of ideas as it was the triumph of a well-crafted moderate campaign. Fox won as a sensible centrist, not as a radical revolutionary. Second, unlike his political heroes, Lech Walesa and Nelson Mandela, Fox was not a great man of history who dealt a death blow to authoritarian incumbents. Rather, he was a well-groomed candidate with independent economic power who capped off decades of painstaking opposition party building by thousands of unsung and largely unremembered heroes. In the end, Fox could not have won without the PAN and the PAN could not have won without Fox.

8

Extending the Argument to Italy, Japan, Malaysia, and Taiwan

Mexico was just one of 16 dominant party systems, albeit the longest lasting to date. Other dominant parties have existed in Asia, Europe, and Africa. To this point, I have shown that the predictions derived from my resource theory of dominance hold up when tested with an abundance of quantitative and qualitative data about Mexico under PRI dominance during most of the 20th century. I have also shown that my explanation performs better than existing approaches that either overpredict or underpredict opposition party formation and success. But how generalizable is the theory? Can it account for single-party dominance in other countries with different cultural norms and political institutions? Does it make sense both for presidential systems like Mexico and for parliamentary ones? Do the dynamics of partisan competition that sustain the dominant party equilibrium result from particular electoral systems? Can the theory be extended not only to account for dominant party persistence in other authoritarian regimes but also to understand the dynamics of dominant party rule where the surrounding regime is democratic?

In this chapter, I show that my resource theory of dominance is surprisingly generalizable and that the unique features of dominance mute the effects of other variables thought to affect partisan dynamics. I do this by examining the dynamics of dominant party rule and opposition party building in Taiwan, Malaysia, Japan, and Italy. In extending the argument to these cases, I have two goals. First, I want to show that country-specific theories of dominance are often insufficient when viewed in cross-national perspective. Second, I want to use the four cases as what Skocpol and Somers (1980) called "parallel demonstration of theory" by showing that my argument correctly predicts the key characteristics of partisan competition in these systems. I try to construct "complete" analytic narratives of partisan dynamics to test multiple implications of my argument and convince the reader that I have not selected only the data that support my theory.

CHALLENGES IN COMPARING DOMINANT PARTY SYSTEMS

Making comparisons among dominant party systems poses an interesting methodological challenge associated with the number of cases and available data, and an interesting conceptual challenge associated with the differences between single-party dominance in authoritarian and democratic regimes. Before turning to the country cases, I discuss these challenges.

Methodological Challenges and Case Selection

There are currently not enough comparable data on incumbents' resource advantages to facilitate time-series cross-sectional statistical analysis,[1] and there are too few country cases of dominance to test a meaningful cross-sectional model. At the same time, there are too many cases to examine all of them in detail (sometimes referred to as a "medium N").[2] As a result, I chose four cases for in-depth analysis. I purposively selected cases that allow me to rule out alternative hypotheses (although the cross-national quantitative analysis in Chapter 1 was dedicated to this task as well). Case selection was also restricted by the available literature. There was not sufficient descriptive literature to score the variables of interest for many of the smaller countries (Bahamas, Gambia, Trinidad and Tobago), and although dropping these cases may bias my results, there was no avoiding it.

The in-depth comparison of four cases helps me to make six arguments. First, I analyze three cases from Asia and one from Europe, along with the

[1] Data on state-owned enterprises are surprisingly spotty across countries and time periods. Neither the World Bank nor the International Monetary Fund routinely collects data on state ownership – an astounding fact given the emphasis on privatization in recent decades. One possible reason is that incumbents may prefer not to "open the books" if they would show misuse of public funds. A second possible reason is that the definition of a state-owned enterprise varies considerably across countries and analysts have not overcome these measurement problems. The economic data presented in this chapter come from a variety of secondary sources but, for the reasons above, they should be taken with some caution.

[2] I do use cross-national statistical tests to assess rival hypotheses in Chapter 1 and below.

Mexico case, to show that single-party dominance is not a regional or cultural phenomenon. In particular, neither the hierarchy associated with Catholicism, the conformism associated with Confucianism, nor the obedience to authority associated with Islam are necessary causes of single-party dominance. Second, I chose two cases from the developing world (Malaysia and Taiwan) and two cases from the developed world (Italy and Japan) to illustrate that levels of economic development are not, in and of themselves, primary explanations for dominance. Third, I chose two cases where the dominant party lost definitively (Italy and Taiwan), one case where it remains in power (Malaysia), and one case (Japan) where scholars debate whether the LDP's 10 months out of power in 1993 really constitutes the end of single-party dominance. This comparison helps show that differences in the explanatory variables associated with my theory do in fact account for cross-case variation in dominant party persistence. Fourth, I included one presidential system like Mexico (Taiwan after 1996) and three parliamentary systems to show that dominance is compatible with both government formats.

Fifth, I chose countries that used different electoral formulas to show that institutions alone cannot account for dominance. Malaysia and Mexico before 1965 used plurality winner single-member districts. For theoretical reasons developed in Chapter 1, this system should have encouraged opposition parties to contest the moderate policy space and create a two-party system rather than single-party dominance, but it did not. Taiwan and Japan before 1993 used multi-member districts with the single nontransferable vote that should advantage large parties and encourage small ones to compete at the margins (Cox, 1997); however, it does not explain why one party was large to begin with. Japan after 1993 and Mexico after 1977 used a two-tiered compensatory system that eventually had 300 plurality winner single-member districts in the first tier and 200 seats elected through larger multi-member districts and a party list vote in the second tier. Italy before 1993 used a similar two-tier system, but one that included an optional preference vote for up to three candidates. Thus, single-party dominance was compatible with a variety of electoral systems ranging from ones that typically advantage large parties to those that typically do not.[3]

---

[3] While some electoral systems give incentives for divergent equilibria (Cox, 1990), as discussed in Chapter 1, "Supply-Side Approaches," these results cannot explain why one party is dominant nor can they explain the degree of opposition party extremism that sustains the dominant party equilibrium.

The Conceptual Challenge: Comparing Single-Party Dominance in Authoritarian and Democratic Regimes

The cross-national comparisons also help me make a final argument. I selected two cases that, like Mexico, are dominant party authoritarian regimes (DPARs) – Taiwan and Malaysia – and two cases that are dominant party democratic regimes (DPDRs) – Japan and Italy. It would be especially surprising if a theory that can account for the former cases can also account for the latter. Although my main interest is in generalizing to other DPARs, I think that my theory sheds light on the DPDRs as well. I expect that some readers will find the comparison of the two types controversial since scholars usually strictly distinguish between authoritarian and democratic regimes. However, I argue that the differences between DPARs – a subset of competitive authoritarian regimes, not fully closed authoritarian regimes – and DPDRs are somewhat smaller than might initially be expected, and that these differences are easily incorporated as explanatory variables in determining the persistence of single-party dominance.

DPDRs, or what Pempel (1990) called "uncommon democracies," qualify as dominant party systems because they satisfy the criteria developed in Chapter 1, including the power and longevity thresholds. Clear examples include India under Congress (1952–1977), Israel under Mapai/Labor Alignment (1949–1977), Italy under the DC (1946–1992), Japan under the LDP (1955–1993), Bahamas under the PLP (1967–1992), Luxembourg under the PCS (1980–), Sweden under the SAP (1936–1976), and Trinidad and Tobago under the PNM (1956–1986). South Africa's National Party (1953–1994) may also qualify. Although the broader political regime was clearly authoritarian because blacks were defined out of the national political community and brutally persecuted, it bears asking why the NP was able to maintain dominance among whites who were eligible voters.

While DPARs and DPDRs both have genuine elections, DPDRs do not use authoritarian controls and instead ensure all the surrounding freedoms commensurate with democracy as well as the clean operation of electoral institutions. As a result, elections not only pass the threshold of meaningfulness as defined previously, but are also at least minimally free.[4]

---

[4] There is also some question in the literature about whether DPDRs can be considered democracies since they do not have turnover. For instance, Pempel (1990: 7), writing on Japan, Sweden, Israel, and Italy states, "Such a situation [of dominance] requires either a rethinking of whether one-party dominant regimes can be democratic, or a rethinking of many existing notions about the links between elections, democracy, and alternations

Extending the Argument to Italy, Japan, Malaysia, and Taiwan 259

This difference led Sartori (1976) to bracket what he referred to as "hegemonic party" systems from "predominant" ones. In hegemonic systems, "The hegemonic party neither allows for a formal nor a de facto competition for power...Not only does alternation not occur in fact; it *cannot* occur, since the possibility of a rotation in power is not even envisaged" (1976: 230) and electoral fraud prohibits opposition victories (1976: 194). In contrast, in the predominant systems, there is fair competition and "equality of opportunities" between the incumbent and challengers such that the incumbent could lose at any moment (1976: 194–196). I disagree with this typology for two reasons. First, Sartori understates the meaningfulness of elections in DPARs. As discussed in Chapter 2, DPARs typically do not need fraud because they leverage their resource advantages to virtually win elections before election day. Incumbents in DPARs may attempt fraud when elections are predicted to be close, but even then the uncertainty associated with stealing elections means that no one knows *ex ante* whether fraud will be successful. Electoral competition in DPARs is genuine and even though it is severely biased, opposition forces expect that they have some positive, albeit very small, probability of winning. Second, Sartori overstates the fairness of elections in DPDRs. Country experts make it clear that at least in Italy and Japan (as shown below) and probably in India and Israel, the opposition did not have equality of opportunities because the incumbent had exclusive access to the resources of the state that it used to outspend challengers at every turn and bribe voters with patronage goods. As a result, elections were far from fair.

Thus, DPARs and DPDRs both have regular and at least meaningful elections where all opposition forces are allowed to form parties and compete for all elected posts, but incumbents win control of the executive and legislature for decades. I argue that these similarities are sufficient that we should expand the contrast space for my theory to include both DPARs and DPDRs. Clearly, there are differences in the scores on the relevant explanatory variables across cases and over time. In particular, although incumbents in both DPARs and DPDRs enjoy resource advantages, DPARs alone benefit from authoritarian tools. These tools include the threat of repression that substantially raises the costs of participating in the opposition far beyond the high opportunity costs paid by challengers in DPDRs and the potential for electoral fraud that leads

---

in government" (also see Richardson, 1997). Similarly, Przeworski et al. (2000: 23–28) struggle with the question of alternation and find ad hoc ways to code some dominant party systems as democracies and others as authoritarian.

opposition actors to discount their probability of victory. These differences are real, systematic, and significant, but the job of comparative analysis is to discover the effects of these differences rather than to avoid broader theorizing by splitting cases into ever smaller categories. Taking variations in the explanatory variables into account actually avoids what Sartori (1970) called "conceptual stretching." Stretching occurs when scholars, more often working in the large-N tradition, lump unlike cases together without attention to differences in explanatory variables. As a result, the relationships they discover are potentially spurious. In contrast, I compare a small number of cases with detailed attention to differences in the constellation of explanatory variables that contribute to the similar outcome.

Observable Implications of My Resource Theory for Other Dominant Party Systems

If my resource theory of dominance travels well to other contexts beyond Mexico, then we should observe at least the three main implications of the theoretical argument developed in Chapter 2. First, opposition parties should be niche-oriented competitors during the incumbent's long tenure in power, even when spatial and electoral-system dynamics should have encouraged them to compete as catchall competitors. Challenger parties should have made comparatively noncentrist policy appeals or focused on noncentral partisan cleavages. As a result, the opposition parties should have attracted only a narrow slice of the electorate and been unable to defeat the incumbent individually. Second, there should have been multiple opposition parties that would not coordinate against the incumbent in large part due to their ideological differences. Finally, in both DPARs and DPDRs, the incumbent should have benefited from dramatic resource advantages that biased voters in its favor, and its rule should only have been threatened when access to resources diminished. In DPARs alone, the incumbent should also have relied on the threat or use of repression, and the decrease in repression should also be associated with the increasing size and competitive viability of opposition parties; however, repression should have been employed as a secondary tool. I also developed a set of fine-grained hypotheses about elite activist recruitment in Chapter 4. Testing these implications requires very detailed data on intra-party politics that are not available for challengers in most countries; however, when data are available, I show that my predictions about generational differences inside the opposition parties over strategy options hold true.

Extending the Argument to Italy, Japan, Malaysia, and Taiwan 261

EXTENDING THE ARGUMENT TO OTHER DOMINANT PARTY AUTHORITARIAN REGIMES

In this section, I extend my argument to account for dominant party persistence in Malaysia and its failure in Taiwan using existing case studies, economic data, and public opinion data where available.

Taiwan: Authoritarian Dominance Defeated

Taiwan's Kuomintang (KMT) was dominant from the time the party's elites arrived on the island from mainland China in 1949 until its loss of the presidency in 2000; however, until 1987, Taiwan was under martial law, opposition parties were legally banned, and dissidence was met with violent repression (Liu, 1999: 67–68). As a result, I classify Taiwan until 1987 as a fully closed authoritarian one-party regime. Once martial law was lifted and opposition parties were allowed to register, competition became meaningful, as defined in Chapter 1. Thus, from 1987 to 2000, I classify Taiwan as a dominant party authoritarian regime. During this period, the repression of opposition forces declined continuously. As one measure, the Freedom House civil rights score was at five in 1987 (where seven is the most repressive) and fell to one (equal to the United States) by 2000.

During the period of KMT dominance, the two main opposition parties remained niche-oriented competitors. According to Rigger, the opposition Democratic Progressive Party (DPP) "emphasized ideological and symbolic politics which limited its appeal to Taiwan's pragmatic, conservative majority" (2001b: 946) and kept it geographically restricted in scope (Liu, 1999: 73). Chu argues that the DPP's "sluggish growth in partisan support" was due to "its ideological rigidity and its organizational weakness" (2001: 277) and that it was "too ideological to become a majority party without significant further internal evolution" (2001: 195). Even though the DPP initially cast itself as a pan-KMT opposition, it quickly chose to emphasize ethnic politics in order to mobilize native Taiwanese voters and their interest in independence (Liu, 1999: 71). These appeals "tapped a deep vein of dissatisfaction in Taiwanese society" (Rigger, 2001b: 952); however, it was a losing electoral strategy because "Ethnic politics solidified the DPP's core, but eventually drove away pro-democracy Mainlanders who came to see it as an anti-Mainlander party, and also nervous moderates who viewed its positions on cross-strait and national identity issues as provocative and risky" (Rigger, 2001b: 951). On the opposite pole, the opposition New Party (NP) aligned itself with Mainlanders and campaigned on unification as its primary appeal (Tien and Cheng, 1999; Liu, 1999).

The KMT, in contrast, maintained a moderate centrist position on unification that placed it between the pro-independence DPP and the pro-unification NP. Chu argues that "By taking an ambiguous centrist position on the predominant cleavage dimensions and an eclectic, pragmatic posture on socioeconomic issues, the KMT was able to retain its broad appeal to all classes and social groups" (2001: 281). A 1995 public opinion survey showed that respondents were normally distributed over the independence issue (see Liu, 1999), and an analysis of these data demonstrates that KMT identifiers were centrist whereas DPP and NP identifiers were spread to the right and left.[5] The challengers' polarization "allows the KMT to define the DPP's advocacy of independence as a threat to security while criticizing the NP's proactive stand on unification as a potential sellout of Taiwanese interests to the Beijing regime" (Tien and Cheng, 1999: 39; also see Chu, 2001: 278). As a result of their niche-oriented profiles before 2000, the DPP was unable to win more than about one-third of the vote and typically won just one-quarter in genuine elections. The NP fared even worse at about 14% in its best showing.

Why did the dominant party equilibrium obtain in Taiwan? An institutional argument would focus on two effects of the single nontransferable vote (SNTV) system for the legislative Yuan. SNTV is thought to advantage large parties that can maximize cross-district efficiency in the number of nominees by engineering strategic withdrawals of weak candidates (Cox, 1996).[6] But this argument cannot account for why one party was significantly larger than the others to begin with. In addition, this approach ultimately rests on the claim that the incumbent's resource advantages allowed it to follow a more efficient nominating strategy (Cox, 1996, 1997). Under certain assumptions about voting behavior, SNTV

[5] The median KMT identifier was centrist and favored "maintain status quo, wait for developments;" the median DPP identifier was on the left and supported a position between "move towards independence" and "maintain status quo permanently;" and the median NP identifier was on the right and favored "move toward unification."

[6] The SNTV system distributes seats to the top M vote-getters where M is district magnitude. As a result, candidates have individual incentives to maximize their personal vote. Party central committees have incentives to distribute the party's votes across the maximum number of nominees without wasting votes on candidates under the minimum seat-winning threshold. This requires nominating the optimal number of candidates and encouraging weaker candidates to withdraw, typically by offering them alternative positions or payoffs (Cox, 1996, 1997).

also encourages parties to carve out specific niches with comparatively noncentrist appeals (i.e., a dispersed equilibrium) (Cox, 1990: 921); however, as shown in Chapter 1, the relevant models predict that the center party typically loses and thus cannot easily account for single-party dominance by the centrist KMT. Below, I argue that the SNTV system did play an important role, but for other reasons. It made the KMT more vulnerable than dominant parties in other systems to relatively smaller decreases in its resource advantages over challengers. Another alternative argument is that sluggish economic growth turned voters away from the KMT. However, this argument runs into two problems. First, although GDP growth in the late 1990s lagged as a result of the Asian financial crisis, it never fell below 4.4% in the worst year and was at a strong 5.8% in 2000 when the KMT was defeated. Second, data presented in Chapter 1 show that fully 51% of citizens who were the *most* dissatisfied with the KMT's performance in office still planned to vote for it. Thus, retrospective evaluations were not the main drivers of the KMT's electoral fortunes.

Like in Mexico's PRI, the KMT had tremendous resource advantages that made elections manifestly unfair and gave challengers very little chance of winning. Chu writes that the KMT controlled a "huge financial empire" (2001: 285) yielding US$4 billion in net assets for the party in 1995 and a total value of about US$16 billion (Tien, 1997: 147). By 2000, estimates put the KMT's total asset value much lower at US$6.7 billion (Lin, 2000; also see Chu, 2001: 285), and by 2001 it had dropped precipitously to US$2.6 billion (Rigger, 2001b: 950). Despite this decrease over time, the KMT was far richer than its rivals. Rigger writes that the DPP, in contrast, "has long suffered extreme economic straits. Until 1997, the party relied on individual donations for most of its income; it labored under a burden of chronic debt and financial shortfall" (2001b: 950) and "at one point it was only saved from bankruptcy by a personal donation from the party president" (Ferdinand, 1998: 190). In 2000 the DPP's assets totaled US$900,000 (Rigger, 2001b: 950), still far below the KMT's resources.

These resource asymmetries between the incumbent and challengers were so massive that Rigger argues that "As long as the KMT was in power, it was impossible for the DPP (or any other party) to compete with the Kuomintang machine on its own terms. Only the KMT was in a position to deploy the political and economic resources of the state to support a pervasive system of patronage networks ... Although direct manipulation of elections through fraud is rare in Taiwan today, politicians and

264   *Why Dominant Parties Lose*

local factions affiliated with the KMT control networks capable of mobilizing millions of votes" (2001b: 949; also see Huang and Yu, 1999: 87;
Chu, 2001: 269). The KMT's "tremendous financial, organizational and
ideological resources" (Chu, 2001: 269) allowed it to dramatically outspend competitors (Solinger, 2001: 36) and "kept the opposition at a
disadvantage, limiting its ability to convey its message to the electorate"
(Cotton, 1997: 100). Resource asymmetries also affected recruitment into
the opposition much in the way they did in Mexico and other dominant party systems. According to Liu, "Since [opposition] party membership does not provide supporters with any material benefit, only activists
and the politically committed are keen to join" (1999: 73; also see Chu,
2001: 289).

The KMT's advantages derived from two sources: its ability to convert
public resources into partisan goods and its own enterprises. The party
traditionally engaged in "the clandestine transfer of government funds to
the KMT's coffers" (Kuo, 2000: 12; also see Tien, 1997: 148). It could do
so because the party made all administrative and judicial appointments
in the central government (Rigger, 2001b: 950), and the politically controlled and quiescent public bureaucracy failed to act as a gatekeeper to
the illicit use of public funds. The KMT's control, like the PRI's, was so
secure that it could virtually force bureaucrats to work for the party during
campaign seasons. Eyton states that "Taiwan's civil service is supposed
to be politically neutral. In practice, for most of the past half-century,
ascending the ranks of the civil service was as much dependent on one's
status as a member of the then-ruling Kuomintang (KMT) party as it was
on any administrative ability. Indeed the boundaries between the civil service and the KMT party organization were so hazy that officials would
regularly and repeatedly hop between the two" (2002: 1; also see Rigger,
2001b: 950). The civil service was so thoroughly politicized that once
the DPP won in 2000, it needed to "dissolve the partisan allegiance of
state bureaucrats and military officers, and redress the gross asymmetry
in resources between the KMT and other parties" (Chu, 2001: 268).

The KMT, like Malaysia's UMNO and Israel's Labor Party, also benefited from very large conglomerates that were owned by the party itself,
"including a complex web of party-run or party-invested enterprises, a
major television network, newspapers, and leading radio stations" (Chu,
2001: 269) as well as "a number of lucrative firms in hitherto highly protected financial and upstream petrochemical sectors" (Tien and Cheng,
1999: 40; also see Xu, 1997; Kuo, 2000) with assets that accounted
for 30% of GNP (Fields, 1998: 1). The KMT used "state-owned and

Extending the Argument to Italy, Japan, Malaysia, and Taiwan 265

party-owned capital for development, patronage, and regime and campaign financing" (Fields 1998: 1).

The particular strength and size of the KMT's businesses owe in part to Taiwan's unique history. Whereas other dominant parties grew out of state-building experiences inside a single national territory, the KMT was previously organized under Chiang kai-Shek on Mainland China before it lost the civil war to Mao's forces and fled to Taiwan. As a result, the KMT had substantial assets and even some party-affiliated businesses that it brought to Taiwan. In addition, once on Taiwan, the party took over the many industries that were created under Japanese colonial rule. Some of these businesses became property of the state while others were transferred directly to the KMT. From that point on, in fact, there were substantial similarities between KMT-owned and state-owned enterprises. Both were in protected and strategic sectors of the economy and both benefited from monopoly government contracts, special licensing, and privileges over private capital in development policy goals (Fields, 1998: 5–7; Kuo, 2000: 12).

Yet after decades, the KMT's resource base was threatened in the late 1990s for two reasons. First, like in Mexico and other dominant party systems, the privatization of state-owned enterprises decreased the state's resources and thus distanced the KMT from a source of patronage (Fields, 1998: 1–2; Kuo, 2000). Between 1987 when martial law was lifted and 2000 when the KMT lost, state-owned enterprises fell from more than 7% of GDP to just 5%. This almost 29% reduction was in fact quite substantial since it accounted for a loss of over US$5.7 billion in public ownership.[7] At the same time, government participation in gross fixed capital formation fell by 20% and most of this decrease came from the privatization of state-owned enterprises.[8] This reduction deprived the federal government of substantial assets and large numbers of jobs that could have been used for patronage purposes. Second, along with privatization, the KMT's businesses came under more pressure for efficiency gains to compete in increasingly open domestic markets and internationally. As a result, these firms were transformed from protected organizations that could be milked as cash cows for patronage into competitive ones in which managers more strictly controlled budgets (Fields, 1998).

---

[7] Author's calculations using data from Taiwan Ministry of Economic Affairs http://www. moea.gov.tw/ and average year 2000 exchange rate from http://www.x-rates.com/d/TWD/ USD/hist2000.html.

[8] Taiwan Ministry of Economic Affairs, http://www.moea.gov.tw/.

As fiscal pressure on the KMT mounted, it sought funding from two new sources. First, like Mexico's PRI, the KMT turned to legal public funding. In 1997, it instituted a system of limited public party financing with regulations designed to advantage the KMT by linking compensation to electoral performance.[9] The law also included new but amazingly weak regulations for campaign contributions and spending that only apply to the 28-day official campaign period (Manikas and Thornton, 2003: 331). Outside that period there are no limits on contributions or expenditures, and there are no audits at any time. Second, the KMT increasingly used local political bosses that were associated with organized crime to bring in the vote. But by relying on this illicit funding known as "black gold politics," the party made its public image vulnerable to attack in Taiwan's now free media environment (Chu, 2001: 274), and several of these bosses were caught in embarrassing corruption scandals in the 1990s.

Although the KMT's resource advantages declined less than in other dominant party systems where the incumbent eventually lost, even small decreases had more consequential effects in Taiwan due to the SNTV system for legislative elections. This system makes races highly candidate-centered and puts a premium on cultivating secure local clienteles since it pits candidates from the same party against each other (Carey and Shugart, 1995). SNTV tends to raise campaign costs for individual politicians because voters in each district can play politicians off each other in demanding constituency service. The system also raises costs for party central committees since maximizing efficiency in the number of nominees across districts requires them to convince weaker politicians not to run, typically by offering side payments (Cox, 1997). High campaign costs coupled with all-against-all competition also encourage politicians to develop independent resources that help them compete against their co-partisans as well as politicians from other parties. But these independent resources also make candidates less dependent on central party committees and make dominant parties in SNTV systems more susceptible to defections of powerful politicians. Thus, Taiwan's KMT was more threatened by a comparatively smaller reduction in its access to resources than dominant parties in other systems.

---

[9] Presidential candidates that win more than one-third of the votes gained by the winner and legislative candidates that win more than three-quarters of the votes required to win a legislative seat can apply for small reimbursements. Parties that surpass the 5% threshold also receive compensation proportionate to the number of votes they win. See Article 45-1 through 45-3 of Taiwan's Public Officials Election and Recall Law available at http://www.cec.gov.tw.

Extending the Argument to Italy, Japan, Malaysia, and Taiwan 267

These factors played an important role in the KMT's loss in the 2000 presidential elections to the DPP's Chen Shui-bian. Tien argues that "the decline in clientelism helps explain the decline in KMT support" (1997: 147). More specifically, resource vulnerability interacted with elite rivalries to cause a split in the KMT. The split caused conflict in the party's patronage machine and dramatically increased the uncertainty about how well it would operate. These problems were exacerbated by embarrassing scandals associated with the KMT's increasing reliance on organized crime for party finance. At the same time, the opposition DPP's access to resources increased enough to permit a full-scale national campaign (Rigger, 2001b).

In 2000, the KMT suffered from elite rivalries that were difficult to resolve given that the electoral system promoted politicians with independent resources. The front-running candidates for the KMT's presidential nomination were Lien Chan who the party's chairman supported and James Soong who the chairman adamantly opposed. Soong suggested a party primary, but the chairman opted for a more restricted nomination process that ensured Lien's victory. Soong was offered the vice-presidency as a consolation prize, but at 57 he may have calculated that he would be too old to run for president if Lien served two terms (Diamond, 2001: 67). Thus, given his ambitions, Soong had no place to go but outside the party. High-level defections from dominant parties are relatively rare in general; however, the KMT's decline in resources made it more vulnerable to defections in the late 1990s. Soong had served as governor of Taiwan province (1994–1998) where he "worked brilliantly to develop his own political power base by cultivating direct ties to grassroots constituencies and cementing patron/client bonds with local bosses" (Diamond, 2001: 56). Thus, Soong had independent resources and personal popularity that he could use in a presidential run, and he bolted to run as an independent.

The presidential election now had three candidates, and it revolved around two main partisan cleavages: unification versus independence and democratizing political reform versus the status quo regime. As in Mexico's three-way presidential race in 2000, Taiwan's candidates were aware that the trailing candidate could be "dumped" by strategic voters who wanted to defeat the frontrunner (Diamond, 2001: 54–55). These considerations informed campaign strategies that ended up helping the DPP's Chen. Early in the campaign season, Soong led in the opinion polls (Diamond, 2001: 61). Lien and the KMT launched a smear campaign against him by claiming that he was intimately tied to "black gold" politics and could not deliver political reform with stability. The strategy worked, and

268   *Why Dominant Parties Lose*

Soong's popularity fell; however, the episode also highlighted Lien's own and seemingly larger reliance on "black gold." In a massive campaign blunder, Lien confirmed his detractors' criticisms by appearing in public with two of the country's most notorious mobsters (Diamond, 2001: 63). Thus, Lien was smeared by the same charges he leveled against Soong, leaving the opposition DPP's Chen as the only credible reform candidate.

Second, the split between Soong and Lien created uncertainty in the KMT's patronage machine. According to Diamond, "Many of the local bosses who had reliably produced for the KMT in previous elections used KMT money to reward Soong supporters in 2000" and, taking advantage of this confusion, "Many of the bosses simply pocketed the large sums they were given to distribute as expressions of 'gratitude' to individual voters" (2001: 63). Overall then, "The KMT machine was in disarray" (Diamond, 2001: 67).

Finally, Chen's reformist credentials might not have mattered much had the DPP's doggedly pro-independence image not moderated. In prior elections, independence versus unification had been the main partisan cleavage and the average voter viewed the DPP as too strongly supportive of independence and overly identified with ethnic Taiwanese against Mainlander interests. Chen managed to overcome related battles inside the DPP and instead ran a much more centrist campaign than prior DPP candidates (Rigger, 2001a; Diamond, 2001: 69). Like Fox in Mexico, Chen managed to moderate on the main partisan cleavage, prime the regime change, and stand alone as the reformist candidate.

On election day, KMT voters split between Lien, the official candidate and Soong, the renegade. The now acceptable and reformist Chen benefited and won the election with 39.3% of the vote. Had the campaigns developed differently or had the KMT machine remained unified, there is little question that the KMT would have won. Lien came away with 23.1% of the vote and Soong with 36.8%, less than three points below the winner. Thus, the peculiarities of the electoral system and the particular issues surrounding the 2000 campaigns made relatively smaller decreases in the KMT's resource advantages more consequential and helped the KMT lose at lower levels of resource symmetry between incumbent and opposition than in Mexico and other dominant party systems.

Malaysia: Persistent Authoritarian Dominance

In Malaysia, the United Malays National Organization (UMNO) became the dominant political force beginning in 1959, and since 1974 it has been

Extending the Argument to Italy, Japan, Malaysia, and Taiwan 269

the senior partner in a governing coalition called the Barisan Nasional (BN). From 1957 when Malaysia gained independence from Britain until 1971, the country experienced political instability and the authorities even imposed emergency rule, closing the national legislature from 1969 to 1971. Thus, I code Malaysia as a fully closed authoritarian regime before 1971. After that date, emergency rule was lifted, the legislature was re-opened, and regular and meaningful elections have been held. According to Crouch, elections were "contested vigorously by opposition parties... [and], therefore, were meaningful contests even if the outcome for the BN was never seriously in doubt" (1996: 56). He further states that, "Malaysian elections have not been characterized by widespread fraudulent practices such as ballot-box stuffing or blatant physical pressure on voters, and there has been no serious legal barriers to parties wishing to contest – with the exception of the Communist Party (CPM) and the Labour Party, which the government believed had been infiltrated by communists" (Crouch, 1996: 57; also see Case, 2001: 49). Data also show that the number of detentions under the Internal Security Act, the government's main tool for repressing political dissidents, fell progressively from its peak in the early 1970s to the 1990s (Munro-Kua, 1996: 146). Consequently, I code Malaysia since 1971 as a dominant party authoritarian regime.[10] To be clear, the government has used targeted and episodic repression against opposition activists (Munro-Kua, 1996: Chs. 4 and 6; Crouch, 1996: 31); however, repression was never so heavy-handed that it discouraged the opposition from participating in electoral politics (Case, 2001: 49).

As in other dominant party systems, opposition parties have remained niche-oriented competitors while the dominant UMNO has a more catchall character. Ethnic divisions between Malays, Chinese, and Indians form the main partisan cleavage, and Crouch (1996: 236–237) argues that this cleavage was reinforced by racial, linguistic, cultural, and class divisions.[11] UMNO relies heavily on the support of ethnic Malays, but it also wins votes from about half the Chinese community and a portion of the Indian community (Gomez, 2002: 83; Crouch, 1996: 30), making it into a catchall organization. At the same time, "the opposition was

---

[10] The first post-1969 elections under dominant party rule occurred in 1974. Crouch (1996) refers to Malaysia as a "semi-authoritarian system," Means (1996) calls it a "soft-authoritarian regime," and Case (2001) calls it a "pseudo-democracy."

[11] My spatial approach to the dominant party equilibrium works when parties are based on ethnicity if these divisions map onto policy divides, as Crouch (1996) argues they do in Malaysia.

divided into competing parties based on ethnic identity" (Crouch, 1996: 30). Specifically, the DAP aligned itself with the urban Chinese community and the PAS with the mostly rural Islamists, representing themselves as organic defenders of these groups (Crouch, 1996: 30, 73, 82). Even though these primarily ethnic appeals meant that "Opposition parties have always maintained solid if limited bases of support...The essential problem has been that, in order to mobilize votes in a communal society, the parties have had to stress communal issues that by their very nature appeal only to one community" (Crouch, 1996: 64). Malaysia's demographic structure forces single ethnicity parties to remain relatively small. Whereas Malays and Bumiputeras that are aligned with UMNO account for about 60% of the population, Chinese and Indians, about half of which are aligned with the opposition, account for 24% and 7% of the population, respectively.

In carving out these solid but narrow bases of support, the challengers established relatively extreme positions on the issues. The PAS has been UMNO's most powerful challenger in recent years, but it in particular seeks to establish Islamic law nationally and did so in one state where it won power. Crouch also argues that the PAS's leaders are hardliners who openly admire the Iranian Revolution of 1979 (Crouch, 1996: 67–68). The DAP, on the other hand, has traditionally campaigned for the political and economic rights of non-Malays, but has only won about half of the Chinese community on election day. Thus, whereas the opposition parties are comparatively radical proponents of individual ethnic or religious groups, UMNO mobilizes from across various groups and stands as a comparatively moderate and centrist catchall party.

Despite their common interest in defeating the incumbent, the challengers' polarization on ethnic and religious issues kept them from coordinating against the UMNO/BN (Crouch, 1996: 30). The opposition parties did not manage to create a coalition until 1990, and even then it was short lived. Importantly, the coalition emerged at a time when Malaysia was in economic trouble and following an important wave of privatizations that limited the state's ability to distribute patronage (Singh, 2000: 35). The coalition expanded the opposition's combined vote to 46.6%, some 5–10% above its historic draw, yet it was unable to unseat the UMNO/BN. Singh argues that although the DAP "agreed to downplay its controversial 'Malaysian Malaysia' proposal [and] the PAS diluted its intention of establishing an Islamic state...The main reason for failure was that the opposition forces were unable to bridge the ideological chasm that

Extending the Argument to Italy, Japan, Malaysia, and Taiwan 271

separated them" (2000: 34–35).[12] The main opposition parties unified again in 1999 as the Barisan Alternatif (BA) and won 40.2% of the vote but failed to unseat UMNO/BN with 56.6%. In the subsequent election in 2004, UMNO/BN reasserted its dominance with 63.9% of the vote. Chua (2001) agrees that the opposition coalition's main problem concerned the component parties' comparative ideological extremism. In particular, he states that "If BA is to succeed in unseating UMNO, PAS must tone down its desire for an Islamic Malaysia. It must contest UMNO for the moderate political discursive space, project itself as reasonable about religion, win the hearts and minds of the Malay middle class, overcome the skepticism of the Chinese and Indian electorates, and gain the support of ideologically multiracial organizations and activists" (2001: 142–143).

Why have the opposition parties limited themselves to narrow slices of the electorate by appealing only to individual ethnic groups or religious communities in Malaysia's multi-ethnic society? Why have they refused to follow a pan-ethnic catchall strategy like the UMNO/BN or coordinate successfully to mirror such a strategy with a centrist opposition coalition? This puzzle is even more surprising because Malaysia, like Mexico before 1965, uses a single-member district plurality electoral formula that gives incentives for opposition parties to coordinate and contest UMNO for the average voter.

As in other dominant party systems, UMNO benefited from resource advantages that essentially selected the types of politicians and voters willing to oppose the incumbent. UMNO's advantages allowed it to control the "moderate discursive space" and ensure that only those who were highly opposed to the status quo on policy would form independent challenger parties. But of course such parties appealed too narrowly to generate broad support.

UMNO's access to resources derived from its control over a large public sector, party-owned businesses that operated in protected sectors, and collusive relationships with big business that was forced to operate in a state-dominated economy. Malaysia's large public sector emerged as a political response to two things. First, as in other developing countries, the state played a vital role in accumulating and directing capital for industrial development in the context of a weak domestic capitalist class (Gerschenkron, 1962). Second, public sector growth was a political

---

[12] Note that the DAP's "Malaysian Malaysia" campaign signified increasing the influence of the Chinese ethnic community at the expense of ethnic Malays.

272 *Why Dominant Parties Lose*

response to race riots that plunged Malaysia into social chaos in 1969. Initially the government increased authoritarian controls but UMNO politicians decided that full authoritarianism was not a viable long-term solution to ethnic rivalries. Instead they embarked on an ambitious plan to transfer wealth from the economically dominant Chinese population to ethnic Malays. Over the next two decades, the National Economic Plan (NEP) expanded Malay ownership of corporate equity from just 2.4% of the national total in 1970 to 20.3% in 1990. Over the same period, ownership by foreign residents reduced from 63.3% to 25.1% (Munro-Kua, 1996: 164).

Instituting the NEP required the state to acquire massive economic holdings. The government gained businesses in cement, rubber, shipping, hotels, telecommunications, electricity, oil, and gas, among others, and engaged in ambitious long-term planning through successive five-year Malaysia Plans. From 1971 to 1975, the plan included public development expenditure of 11.2% of GNP, rising to 14.6% for the 1976–1980 period. Even as late as 1991–1995 when many developing countries were drastically diminishing the state's involvement in the economy, public development expenditure in Malaysia still accounted for 14.8% of GNP, and a similar level was forecast for 1996–2000.[13] Public investment also remained steady at about 13% of GDP in the mid-1990s (Bouton and Sumlinski, 2000: 51).

As the state's role in the economy expanded, so too did the size of the public bureaucracy designed to administer it. Figures were not available for the 1970s; however, public sector employment stood at 607,000 in 1981 and rose to 801,700 by 2000, a 32.1% increase.[14] Ethnic Malays were recruited into the civil service, often straight out of university, and encouraged to participate in UMNO at the same time (Crouch, 1996: 133). In 1957, 56% of government service employees (excluding police and military) were ethnic Malays. By 1990, that proportion had risen to 66%, over-representing Malays compared to their population share (author's calculations based on Munro-Kua, 1996: 156–157). The politicization of the public bureaucracy was sufficient that, as in other dominant party systems, "Government machinery at the local level was regularly mobilized during election campaigns" (Crouch, 1996: 62). Case similarly

---

[13] See *Sixth Malaysia Plan, 1991–1995*. Kuala Lumpur: National Printing Department, 1991.

[14] For 1981 figure, see Ramanadham (1995: 137); for 2000 figure, see ILO, http://www.ilo.org.

Extending the Argument to Italy, Japan, Malaysia, and Taiwan 273

argues that "Malay civil servants are dependent on government largesse and thus a potent UMNO constituency" and during elections, "The government makes uninhibited use of state facilities and government workers" (2001: 48, 50).

The combination of a large state and a politically quiescent public bureaucracy gave UMNO substantial control over resources that it could deploy for partisan purposes. Crouch argues that "One consequence of the huge expansion of the public sector was a decline in accountability and increased scope for the misuse of public funds" (1996: 202). Chua further states that "This plan [the NEP] not only opened up opportunities for UMNO to enrich itself through proxy companies, but also created a political economy characterized by corruption and cronyism or, in the words of the UMNO government, 'handouts' for the favored. (In this sense, the UMNO-dominated government recalls the KMT's position in Taiwan's economy)" (2001: 139). Similarly, Gomez argues that the relationship between state and society transformed under the NEP: "the party's hegemony allowed it access to state rents that could be disbursed to develop a powerful party base. Since UMNO had actively encouraged Malays to develop a 'subsidy mentality' and to view the state as protector of their interests, the distinction between patronage and NEP implementation became increasingly blurred" (2002: 86).

The economic dominance of the state also meant that private business owners became reliant on UMNO politicians. Malay businessmen regularly sought government protection and "non-Malay business faced increasing competition from the growing state sector and regularly experienced difficulties in obtaining licenses, permits, and contracts. Often Chinese businesspeople were forced to accept Malay partners who made little contribution to management but whose contacts with UMNO facilitated dealings with the government" (Crouch, 1996: 238–239). Thus, as in other dominant party systems, including at least Mexico and Italy, the state's major role in the economy transformed the private business community into a willing supporter of the UMNO-led government.

Like in Taiwan, the incumbent also owned businesses that benefited from state protection (Gomez, 1991, 1994). According to Chua, "Both UMNO and the KMT had amassed great wealth through their proxy companies and used the largesse of the state, under-girded by national economic growth, to gain legitimacy and popular support" (2001: 141). This control has led to "money politics" that Gomez says "includes, among other things, favoritism, conflicts of interest, and nepotism in the award of state-created rents, securing votes during federal and party elections by disbursing current and future material benefits, and the direct and indirect interference of political parties or influential politicians in the corporate sector" (2002: 83). Teh argues that "money, gifts, and contracts [were used] to 'buy' supporters or voters" (2002: 338; also see Chua, 2001: 134). The number of enterprises owned by party-affiliated politicians even expanded in the 1980s and 1990s as the state privatized public enterprises. Gomez states that "Some party officials and businessmen linked to UMNO benefited from highly leveraged buyouts [of public companies] with financial support from state-owned banks" (2002: 93).

These monopoly rents from various sources allowed UMNO to dramatically outspend its competitors during and between elections. In particular, the party used public monies to distribute patronage and substantially bias voters in its favor. Gomez argues that UMNO "had control over and access to the state apparatus [and could] wield these economic resources as a mechanism of exchange and patronage" (1994: 6). It did so through "UMNO's vast patronage machinery that has been pivotal in enabling the party to win and maintain electoral support" (Gomez, 1994: 290; also see Gomez, 2002: 107). Thus, the governing coalition "had a crucial advantage over the opposition parties because they could offer access to special favors and opportunities. In contrast, identification with the opposition meant denial of the benefits associated with the patronage network" (Crouch, 1996: 240).

Analysts who focus on economic performance legitimacy and retrospective voting as causes of dominant-party persistence might have expected UMNO to lose after the 1997 Asian economic crisis. In 1998, GDP fell by 7.5%, inflation nearly doubled, and the external debt reached a five-year high. Despite a crisis much worse than in other dominant party systems in which incumbents lost, UMNO has remained in power. There are at least two compelling reasons for its continued dominance. First, even though the economy as a whole suffered and UMNO resources declined somewhat, the government remained centrally involved and even briefly increased its share of investment. Although other countries affected by the crisis adopted IMF-prescribed adjustment policies that included privatization, Malaysia staunchly resisted this logic. Since major businesses remained public and the NEP also stayed in effect, the balance of public versus private resources remained virtually unchanged and large groups of voters still rely on UMNO for jobs and the material resources it provides in exchange for political support. Due to its continued privileged access to public resources, UMNO has maintained its catchall coalition and forestalled elite defection.

A second reason for continued dominance is that UMNO under Mahathir became more rather than less repressive by using the Internal Security Act (ISA) to selectively prosecute political dissidents.[15] Although the number of detentions fell to a low of 68 in 1989 (Munro-Kua, 1996: 146), it rose precipitously to over 230 in just one incident in 1998[16] and in 2000, protesters against trials of opposition leaders were dispersed by riot police using water cannons and tear gas, and opposition newspapers were swept off the streets.[17] According to Kua Kia Soong, director of the Malaysian human rights organization SUARAM, "The ISA has been kept in use all this time mainly because it is a very convenient tool at the disposal of the ruling coalition."[18] Similarly, the Asian Human Rights Commission reports that "When we look at every wave of ISA arrests and detentions since 1960, we can see a clear pattern of its use whenever the ruling coalition faces a crisis."[19] Overall, it appears that authoritarian rule is hardening to compensate for UMNO's mild decrease in resources. Due to this confluence, we cannot know for certain whether resources or repression are more important in sustaining UMNO dominance; however, the variation in repression over time suggests that, as in other dominant party authoritarian regimes, coercion is employed as a secondary tool when resource advantages wane. If the use of repression expands in the future, Malaysia will likely transition back to a fully closed authoritarian regime. If the use of repression declines to prior levels, then I expect that UMNO's continued dominance will depend on its ability to maintain state involvement in the economy and divert public resources for partisan use.

EXTENDING THE ARGUMENT TO DOMINANT PARTY DEMOCRATIC REGIMES

In this section, I show how my argument helps account for dominant party durability and failure in dominant party democratic regimes. Case studies

[15] Amnesty International Malaysia Report 2004, http://web.amnesty.org/report2004/mys-summary-eng.

[16] Asia Human Rights Commission Urgent Appeal, "Malaysia: ISA Detentions and More than 230 Detained for 'Illegal Assembly'" October 26, 1998. http://www.ahrchk.net/ua/mainfile.php/1998/48/

[17] Polity IV Country Report 2003: Malaysia, http://www.cidcm.umd.edu/inscr/polity/Mal1.htm.

[18] Baradan Kuppusamy, "Malaysia's Security Blanket" *Asia Times*, August 6, 2005, http://www.atimes.com/atimes/Southeast_Asia/GH06Ae01.html

[19] Asian Human Rights Commission Human Rights Solidarity, http://www.hrsolidarity.net/mainfile.php/1999vol09no12/1959/

indicate that the dominant party equilibrium existed in DPDRs much like in DPARs. For instance, challengers to India's catchall Congress Party were smaller noncentrist parties with minority appeals that would not coordinate against the incumbent (Riker, 1976; Chhibber, 2001; Chandra, 2004), and thus allowed the Congress Party to sustain power for 25 years. Laver and Schofield (1990) and Tarrow (1990: 317) similarly argue that Italy's Christian Democrats captured the pivot, spread challengers to the right and left, and remained dominant for 35 years. Arian and Barnes write that in both Israel and Italy, opposition parties were "likely to behave like sectarian, group-specific parties" (1974: 610; also see Shalev, 1990: 84, 92–99). Even challengers to Japan's LDP – usually considered a rightwing party (but see Inoguchi, 1990: 212) – formed as small and fragmented parties that appealed to particular core constituencies (Scheiner, 2006; Richardson, 2001: 145; Ware, 1996: 58), thus allowing the LDP to rule for 38 years.

Like in DPARs, incumbents in these "uncommon democracies" (Pempel, 1990) benefit from dramatic resource advantages that they use to outspend challengers and bribe voters. Unlike in DPARs, they do not have authoritarian tools at their disposal; however, they benefit from institutional and political environments that discourage opposition coordination more than in DPARs. Whereas almost all DPARs have presidential systems, all DPDRs use parliamentary formats that allow small opposition parties to voice their concerns in floor debates and even play important roles in policymaking when the dominant party does not reach a majority by itself.[20] When coupled with permissive electoral systems, parliamentarism should create more small opposition parties, increase the likelihood that these parties are formed by defectors from the dominant party rather than by outsiders, and increase incentives for the dominant party to buy challenger party support in parliament. Thus, the electoral system and government format in DPDRs provide some disincentives for opposition coordination (but see Christensen, 2000). Political conditions provide further disincentives. Unlike in DPARs, the absence of repression and other authoritarian controls in DPARs diminish the likelihood that a unifying theme emerges that could rally opposition forces with different policy goals against the incumbent. As a result, challenger parties that are polarized to the left and the right do not have a common grievance

---

[20] The importance of small parties does not contradict the definition of dominance developed in Chapter 1 in which the dominant party must participate for any viable government coalition to form.

Extending the Argument to Italy, Japan, Malaysia, and Taiwan 277

against the incumbent that could fuel an alliance (Riker, 1976; Laver and Schofield, 1990; Tarrow, 1990: 317; Cox, 1997). Yet, as shown in Chapter 1, existing arguments do not specify how dominant parties successfully expel challengers from the most efficient positions where they could have at least matched the incumbent's vote share, thus ending single-party dominance.

Perhaps, following the logic of existing alternative arguments described earlier, DPDRs just happen to have less voter demand for opposition parties or more restrictive electoral formulas that diminish the effective number of parties. However, reproducing the cross-national quantitative tests of alternative hypotheses in Chapter 1 by comparing DPDRs rather than DPARs to all fully competitive democracies also finds that there is no statistically significant difference in the level of ethno-linguistic fractionalization – a common proxy for social cleavages – in 1961 or in 1985 and no difference in the mean district magnitude for lower house elections. Yet DPDRs had, on average, almost 0.5 fewer effective parties than their fully democratic counterparts. Thus, in DPDRs, like in DPARs, dominant parties persist and opposition parties fail despite enough social cleavages, permissive electoral institutions, and sufficient ideological space for the opposition to occupy.[21] In this section, I show how my resource theory better explains dominant party persistence and failure in Italy and Japan.

Japan: Persistent Democratic Dominance

Japan's Liberal Democratic Party (LDP) formed as a merger between the Liberal Party and the Democratic Party in 1955 and maintained dominance until 1993 when it was ousted by a broad coalition of opposition parties. However, the opposition government lasted less than one year before the LDP returned to power in 1994. Although some authors argue that LDP dominance has ended (Curtis, 1999: 40), others treat Japan as a case of continuing single-party dominance (Hrebenar, 2000: 2; Scheiner, 2006). My main interest is in the period of unbroken LDP dominance before 1993, although continued dominance after 1994 is instructive since it has occurred under different electoral rules.

The literature on single-party dominance in Japan focuses on three types of explanations. First, some analysts note that the LDP won a majority of seats in parliament with only a plurality of the popular vote and argue that malapportionment advantaged the incumbent by giving more

---

[21] See Chapter 1 for an extended discussion of alternative theories.

seats to rural districts where it was strong. Although true, this explanation begs the question of why opposition parties were unable to make inroads into LDP rural strongholds over the long term. Second, others argue that the SNTV electoral system advantaged the incumbent as in Taiwan; however, the LDP dominated under the multimember system in place after 1994 as well. As noted above, this argument also ultimately rests on the claim that the incumbent's resource advantages allowed it to follow a more efficient nominating strategy (Cox, 1996, 1997). A third set of explanations focuses on problems inside the opposition parties, including low-quality candidates, party leaders that were relatively less interested in winning elections, and ideological rigidity (see Christensen, 2000 for a summary). I argue that all of these characteristics are the downstream result of the LDP's resource advantages and thus fit nicely within my explanation. I agree with Scheiner when he states that "Clientelism plays front and center in the Japanese political system, and clientelism lies at the core of Japanese opposition failure" (2006: 64).

Like in Mexico and other dominant party systems, the incumbent's resource advantages forced challengers to organize as niche-oriented parties that either made comparatively noncentrist policy appeals on the main partisan cleavages or focused on less salient cleavages. Due in part to their ideological differences, the challengers were unable to coordinate effectively against the incumbent. That this argument works in Japan is especially surprising for two reasons. First, many analysts consider the LDP to be a rightwing party. Since its main competitors were arrayed to its left, the challengers could have coordinated as a connected coalition. Second, Scheiner argues that at least since the 1990s when the country experienced a prolonged period of economic decline, the LDP was "not popular" (2006: 1). Thus, one would expect voters to "throw the bums out." How could an unpopular rightwing party maintain long-term dominance?

As in other dominant party systems, Japan's main opposition parties were niche-oriented competitors that appealed to narrow slices of the electorate. The Japanese Communist Party (JCP) initially followed a militant Stalinist revolutionary line in the 1950s. As a result, its vote share dropped from about 10% to just 2% (Muramatsu and Krauss, 1990: 299) and its membership plummeted (Berton, 2000: 270). It eventually became a parliamentary opposition in the 1960s and 1970s, and thus recuperated its former vote share; however, even then it clung to "scientific socialism" in the Perestroika era, rejected capitalism, derided the socialist party's "rightward degeneration," and warned against the rise

Extending the Argument to Italy, Japan, Malaysia, and Taiwan 279

of "Japanese fascism" (Berton, 2000: 264–265). Consequently, both its vote share and its membership stagnated until the late 1980s and then declined in the 1990s (Berton, 2000: 270).

The Japanese Socialist Party (JSP) was also niche-oriented, at least through the 1980s. Kitschelt argues that the socialists self-destructed because "The JSP remained an intellectual's party inspired by different brands of extreme antiparliamentary and anticapitalist radicalism and never made it out of its political ivory tower" (1994: 294). Otake similarly argues that unlike its socialist counterparts in Western Europe that reformed, the JSP "remained a fundamentalist opposition party with respect to program" (1990: 129). He states that, in the middle of an affluent society, "the party relied on Marxist terminology and analysis...against what it called the 'reactionary, fascist LDP government'" (1990: 129), and that it "failed to make major policy adjustments, even though the electorate continually showed itself more and more hostile to JSP proposals" (1990: 131). As a result, Otake argues that "the party's electoral fortunes dropped steadily" (1990: 131, 159) because, much like in opposition parties in other dominant party systems, "efforts by 'revisionists' to adapt the party's program to the preferences of average Japanese voters foundered until 1986 on the resistance by leftists" (1990: 132) whose support was based on the party's traditional core constituencies that provided the party with financing, campaign workers, and candidates (1990: 155, 157, 158; also see Curtis, 1988).

The Clean Government Party (CGP) or Komeito emerged in 1964 from the Buddhist lay organization, Soka Gakkai. Soka Gakkai is a proselytizing organization for the fundamentalist Orthodox Nichiren Sect of Buddhism that believes all other religions are heresy and has been characterized as intolerant and exclusive (White, 1970: 21–22). As a result, Komeito is a highly disciplined organization with a well-defined core constituency and a clear programmatic agenda. Even though it is centrist on the main partisan cleavage, the public identifies it as more focused on less salient issues associated with religion and culture. Nonbelievers worry about Soka Gakkai's commitment to the core values of Japanese democracy, and this has limited Komeito's expansion. The party typically wins about 8–10% of the seats in lower house elections, but its vote has been characterized as "inelastic" and nearly half the public views it as "fanatical" (Hrebenar, 2000: 170, 179). Somewhat like Mexico's PAN before the 1980s, Komeito tried to mobilize support on a noncentral partisan cleavage and was thus distrusted by many voters as unrepresentative of their interests.

Japan's very different opposition parties found it almost impossible to form alliances for national elections that "often focus on foreign policy or ideological issues" (Christensen, 2000: 75). Even though the SNTV electoral system provided some disincentives for opposition coordination at the elite level, Christensen argues that the stable environment for small parties that allowed them to calculate the costs and benefits of cooperation as well as their secure and overlapping bases of support provided incentives in favor of coordination (2000: 65). Yet coordination was rare in part due to deep-seated ideological differences between the parties.

The socialist JSP was the largest opposition party and it pivoted between the communist JCP to the left and Komeito to the right. If substantial opposition coordination were to emerge, it would have to include the Socialists. However, the JSP was internally divided between a radical faction that leaned to the left and a moderate faction that leaned to the right. As one or the other faction gained more power over time, the ascendant faction tried to cobble together an alliance with its favored partner, only to be pulled back, formally or informally, by the other faction.

The Socialists and Communists attempted their first national level alliance for the 1971 elections. Before that date, the Communists were considered too radical and out of touch with the average voter to be a helpful ally. But moderation during the 1960s made them a more attractive partner. Nevertheless, as talks opened, the JSP's right-leaning faction opposed the alliance on ideological grounds and threatened to defect (Christensen, 2000: 85, 92). Later alliance negotiations with Komeito foundered because it expected the Socialists to moderate (Christensen, 2000: 86). Even though the alliance went through formally, it failed in practice because Socialist activists and some leaders refused to coordinate efforts with the centrists (Christensen, 2000: 87, 90–91). A new attempt in 1974 led to similar results (Christensen, 2000: 93–95). By 1977, radicals in the Socialist Party gained dominance again and tried another alliance with the Communists for the upper house elections of that year. But it too failed in practice as socialist activists on the ground did not institute the agreement (Christensen, 2000: 97). By 1980, moderates had beaten back the radicals' advance due in part to the moderation of the party's most important support unions (Christensen, 2000: 99–100). An attempted alliance with Komeito for the 1980 double elections failed miserably as divisions in the Socialist camp doomed its electoral performance. In fact, the opposition did so poorly that Komeito decided that an opposition alliance could not defeat the LDP and it should instead try to join the LDP-led coalition in the government (Christensen, 2000: 103, 114). In sum, Christensen argues that "Ideology clearly matters, and it has hampered efforts by the opposition to take power from the LDP or to reduce LDP influence" (2000: 160).

Even though the opposition remained uncoordinated, how could a right-leaning LDP still hold the broad center? Although analysts agree that it is a rightwing party, they also characterize it as a broad coalition of all major social groups. Muramatsu and Krauss argue that the LDP "has been very flexible in responding to social change by pragmatically meeting, at least somewhat, the demands of a wide range of social groups when it has had to, thus making itself into a 'catch-almost-all' party" (1990: 303). The LDP was also able to "co-opt the issues of the opposition and dampen their negative impact on the party" (1990: 301; also see Inoguchi, 1990: 193), much like the Mexican PRI's firefighting strategy described in Chapter 3. Inoguchi similarly describes the LDP as a catchall party that, paradoxically, "solidly holds the Downsian center, unlike some of the other rightwing parties" (1990: 212; also see Scheiner, 2006: 168, 172). I argue that the LDP, like other dominant parties, was able to hold the broad center even when it did not offer centrist policies and simultaneously force challengers to carve out smaller electoral niches because it benefited from dramatic resource advantages that it used to attract voters with material benefits.

Unlike in Mexico, there is no evidence that the LDP illicitly transferred funds from public enterprises to party coffers, although it sometimes funded public projects and then took kickbacks from businesses that were awarded bids (Schlesinger, 1997; Scheiner, 2006: 72–73). Instead, it generated resource advantages over the opposition in two ways. First, it used its control over the public policy apparatus to distribute pork, subsidies, tax breaks, licenses, contracts, price supports, loans, and economic protection against foreign competition to particular electoral districts or constituents based purely on political considerations (Curtis, 1971; Calder, 1988; Woodall, 1996; Richardson, 1997; Pempel, 1998). Curtis argues that "the Liberal Democratic Party has energetically used the government purse to reward its supporters, to cultivate new support, and to reorder the government's policy priorities" (1988: 46; also see Muramatsu and Krauss, 1990: 298). Similarly, Inoguchi states that "The LDP often made timely, client-targeted, and thus, on the whole, effective use of its public policy tools, aided by its hold over the bureaucracy" (1990: 225). As a result, Scheiner argues that public works spending is the best tracer of clientelist behavior in Japan (2006: 86). Since postwar Japan needed huge amounts of reconstruction and the large hinterland needed

282   *Why Dominant Parties Lose*

substantial infrastructural investment, LDP politicians could continually exchange pork in the form of local collective goods for votes (Woodall, 1996). Schlesinger (1997), for instance, paints a vivid portrait of Kakuei Tanaka, Japan's most successful "Shadow Shogun" politician, who ruled the LDP machine for decades by his effective use of public funds.

Second, as in other dominant party systems, LDP control over public policy meant that private business could prosper under state protection by colluding with the incumbent. As a result, businesses donated both openly and illegally in massive amounts to the LDP and its individual candidates (Curtis, 1988: 161–164). According to Scheiner, "The LDP was able to use the resources of the state – especially in the form of subsidies and funding of projects in areas such as construction – to encourage particular regions to support the party. This resource edge was doubly advantageous for the LDP because it also encouraged donors to contribute money to LDP candidates, who, if victorious could continue distributing state resources" (2006: 2). Hrebenar reports that "The primary source of party funds during the First Party System [1955–1993] was 'corporate Japan.' During the 1970s, Japanese business gave an officially reported total of about 9 billion per year to the LDP" and this amount is just the "tip of the iceberg" (2000: 69). Hrebenar also documents the multiple backdoor methods that the LDP used to raise funds and underreport expenditures while skirting campaign finance laws (2000: 69–73).

The LDP could manipulate public policy so consistently and effectively because it managed to subordinate Japan's powerful bureaucracy (Muramatsu and Krauss, 1990: 296; Inoguchi, 1990; Richardson, 1997: 3–4; Christensen, 2000: 22–23). Although Johnson (1982) characterized the bureaucracy as independent and capable of resisting political logic, and Campbell (1989) argues that the LDP did not manipulate the macroeconomy in substantial ways, other analysts make it clear that at least as far as domestic pork was concerned, the LDP managed to use the public budget for its partisan goals. Curtis writes that "Bureaucrats had nothing to gain and potentially a great deal to lose by adopting a posture of openly challenging the LDP...The LDP was the only game in town insofar as political power was concerned, and the bureaucracy responded accordingly" (1999: 62). Case studies suggest that Japan's public bureaucracy was not nearly as politicized as were its counterparts in other dominant party systems; however, bureaucrats did not block the LDP's often quite targeted use of the public budget to award contracts to particular businesses and to benefit particular constituencies.

Extending the Argument to Italy, Japan, Malaysia, and Taiwan 283

The dominant party distributed patronage to voters in two ways. First, it doled out massive amounts of pork, as described above. Pork is not traditionally viewed as a form of clientelism because it is virtually impossible to monitor individual-level voting in exchange for local public goods (see Kitschelt, 2000); however, Scheiner argues that "collective monitoring" in Japan involves "parties monitoring the extent to which particular interest groups or geographic regions support them through donations, campaigning, political quiescence, or a substantial number of votes" (2006: 71). He concludes that pork can be "highly targetable" and that "collective monitoring can be quite precise" (2006: 71–74; also see Curtis, 1971).

Second, the LDP also had a method of distributing patronage to individual voters through candidate-support organizations called *kōenkai*. Politicians invest up to US$1 million to maintain these groups in their districts (Christensen, 2000: 10), and they may contain many tens of thousands of members (Scheiner, 2006: 71). According to Curtis, *kōenkai* members "turn to it for various favors and services much as Americans turned to the urban party machine in its heyday earlier in the century. It is this doing of a great variety of favors for the electorate that imposes the greatest demands on the *kōenkai* staff's time and the politician's purse" (1971: 145). Scheiner explains that "In exchange, *kōenkai* members are expected to vote for the candidate, campaign on the candidate's behalf, and provide the names of additional people whom the *kōenkai* can contact to ask to support the candidate" (2006: 71).

Resource advantages benefit the LDP even more than they would other dominant parties because campaign laws restrict opposition parties' ability to substitute labor for capital. According to Hrebenar, opposition parties like "Komeito and the JCP raise less money but have the best grassroots organization in the nation" (2000: 69). Yet the "straight-jacket campaign activities restrictions law" (2000: 38) that is "the most restrictive in the democratic world" (2000: 50) means that "almost every type of campaign activity that would involve the voter in any but the most superficial way was prohibited. In particular, door-to-door campaigning, signature drives, polling, providing food or drink, mass meetings, parades, unscheduled speeches, multiple campaign vehicles, and candidate-produced literature are illegal in contemporary Japanese campaigns. Instead, a candidate's contacts with his or her potential voters must, by law, be channeled through a limited number of government-produced postcards, posters placed on official signboards, a maximum of five government paid newspaper ads of specific size and content, several television and radio announcements, a number of joint speech meetings, and government-financed handbills and brochures" (2000: 50–51).[22] As a result, the opposition parties have trouble expanding and cannot attract the independent voters that now account for more than half of the electorate (Scheiner, 2006). While cash-rich *kōenkai* attract members for the LDP quite easily, "The opposition parties enter into a downward spiral of organizational reliance. They rely on organizations to get the vote out and win elections, but these organizational ties and restrictions on direct appeals hinder their efforts to persuade floating [i.e., independent] voters. In a self-fulfilling prophecy, the organizational ties of the party further weaken the party's efforts to expand its appeal beyond its core of organizational voters" (Christensen, 2000: 185).

In sum, the LDP's resource advantages forced challengers to form as niche-oriented parties with clear support constituencies in the electorate that they secured through solid but narrowly based organizations. In one sense, the LDP's advantages gave it even more electoral power than other dominant parties. While in other systems the incumbent was positioned between the challenger parties and expelled them to the left and the right, the LDP's advantages were sufficient to keep a rightwing party in power and force the challengers to form away from the center.

The period of uninterrupted LDP dominance came to an end in 1993 when powerful party members defected and formed new parties. Like in Taiwan, the SNTV system gave individually successful politicians their own independent resources that the party could not control. As a result, ambitious elites that could not win by remaining inside the dominant party had reasons to defect when they thought that they could get support from the existing opposition. The incentives for defection were particularly high in Japan in 1993 because politicians knew that they would likely take enough parliamentary seats with them to defeat the LDP (Reed and Scheiner, 2003). Importantly, however, the LDP was not as thoroughly defeated as ousted dominant parties in presidential systems. As a result, the LDP was able to retain many of its funding sources, and after less than one year in the opposition, it once again became dominant.[23]

---

[22] Obviously, the parties routinely violate these restrictions and the LDP gets away with more violations than its opponents (Hrebenar, 2000: 53; Curtis, 1988: 111). Even when the parties campaign strictly within the letter of the law, incumbents are advantaged because challengers have difficulty generating name recognition with such limited contact with the voters.

[23] In 1994, Japan adopted a new mixed-member electoral system that, like Mexico's, features 300 single-member districts and 200 proportional representation seats elected in

Italy: Democratic Dominance Defeated

The Christian Democratic Party (DC) dominated Italian politics beginning in 1945. It temporarily ceded the prime ministership to its coalition partners for two relatively brief periods in the 1980s, but regained it until 1992 when it lost definitively and the postwar party system disintegrated. I am primarily concerned with the period of unbroken dominance that lasted until 1982; however, prominent analysts think DC dominance lasted until 1992 (Golden, 2004), and their arguments about the period of elongated dominance support mine. In particular, Spotts and Wieser argue that the DC remained dominant after 1982 because the parliamentary format allowed it to "retain a majority of cabinet positions and ultimate control of the government" (1986: 15), in particular because it controlled the key ministries "that wield influence or a lot of patronage" (1986: 16).

The postwar Italian public was deeply divided between a secular and socialist or communist left and a Catholic right that was more pro-capital but not entirely anti-labor (Farneti, 1985: 10–15; Zuckerman, 1979: 90–91). Given this bimodal distribution of voter preferences, how did a right-leaning party manage to establish and maintain dominance? One explanation is that the DC, backed by the United States, used a campaign of fear of communism to rally all religious and nonleft forces (Warner, 1998). But this argument fails to explain why dominance from the left occurred in other countries with similar voter preference distributions but without the extreme fear of communism. Similarly, some argue that the DC lost once the end of the Cold War removed the communist threat, but country experts Guzzini (1994) and Golden (2004) provide compelling arguments against this thesis.

Other forces helped the DC expand its vote share beyond its policy appeals to create a multiclass alliance (della Porta and Vannucci, 1999: 96; Spotts and Wieser, 1986: 20, 39) that Sartori (1976: 138) characterizes as catchall. Most analysts agree that what Tarrow called a "system of pluralist patronage" (1990: 318) was the key to the DC's breadth (LaPalombara, 1964; Shefter, 1977b; di Palma, 1980: 152; Hine, 1987: 84). Zuckerman argues that unlike the communist party that was primarily limited to Marxist sympathizers, the DC was able to expand beyond

---

multimember districts. The reassertion of LDP dominance clearly indicates that the electoral system itself does not cause single-party dominance. At the same time, Japan's new opposition parties are much more centrist, less ideological, and less niche oriented in general than their pre-1993 counterparts (see Scheiner, 2006).

286 *Why Dominant Parties Lose*

its programmatic identifiers (1979: 91, 105) and win about 30–40% of its vote through patronage (1979: 91).[24] Warner states that "The DC was able to become a broad center-right party largely because DC leaders moved beyond vague programmatic appeals to use patronage" (1998: 572). Similarly, Golden argues that "The massive system of political patronage" was used for "enlarging the party's aggregate vote share while protecting the incumbency advantage of individual legislators" (2000: 10). Finally, Rimanelli characterizes the DC arrangement as a "widespread patronage system (to lock-in the vote) so pervasive and greedy that in the end it consumed the entire politico-economic system" (1999: 26).

The DC's center-right policy stance plus patronage not only drew in broader constituencies, but also made the party into the coalitional fulcrum of Italian politics (Laver and Schofield, 1990: 80; Castles and Mair, 1984: 85). Sartori refers to Italy under the DC as a classic case of polarized pluralism that featured a centrist catchall party or coalition flanked by relatively extremist parties to the left and the right that engaged in ideologically oriented centrifugal or center-fleeing competition (1976: 132–140). The DC, together with the ideologically vague social democrats (PSDI), Liberals (PLI), and Republicans (PRI) formed the centrist governing coalition (albeit with shifting alliances), while the Italian Communist Party (PCI) flanked it to the left and the neo-fascist Italian Socialist Movement (MSI) flanked it to the right.

The opposition MSI was a niche party that made specialized appeals to a narrow slice of the Italian electorate. It was an "anemic reincarnation of Fascism" that stood for Mussolini's ideals, including extreme social conservatism, a strong central government, nationalism, and a strong role for the armed forces in politics. It never formally recognized Italy's constitution and held existing political institutions in disdain. The MSI's most extreme elements even endorsed armed revolution, although the more moderate (yet still fascist!) faction continually gained force in the 1980s (Spotts and Wieser, 1986: 96–99). As a result of this radicalism, the MSI never won more than 8.7% of the vote in parliamentary elections from 1948 to 1992 and typically won about 5%.

Unlike the unsuccessful MSI, the PCI typically polled at about 25% of the vote in parliamentary elections in the postwar period and reached as high as 34.4% in 1976. Compared to other communist parties around the

---

[24] Before 1993, Italy used a proportional representation electoral system with an optional preference vote for up to three specific candidates. Zuckerman (1979) takes preference voting as a proxy for patronage voting.

Extending the Argument to Italy, Japan, Malaysia, and Taiwan 287

world and to other opposition parties in dominant party systems, it was fantastically successful. There are three compelling explanations for this comparative success. First, the PCI was reasonably popular because there was a substantial group of voters that preferred leftwing policies, and the party gained legitimacy by successfully identifying itself with resistance to fascism. Second, the PCI was financed by the Soviet Union until the 1980s and therefore was not as poor as challengers in other dominant party systems that typically relied exclusively on (very limited) domestic sources of funding. Finally, the parliamentary format encouraged the DC to create broad governing coalitions, much like Japan's LDP. Tolerating and buying off challengers was often cheaper than risking increased partisan polarization that could lead to political instability and even the breakdown of democracy, as it had in several South American countries. The parliamentary format thus gave the PCI more influence in government and encouraged some private donors to contribute to the party in exchange for favors. In presidential dominant party systems, challengers were typically locked out of this type of clientelist exchange. Yet despite trading on its influence in some areas of the country, the PCI remained fundamentally a programmatic party with niche-oriented appeals and could not expand beyond its natural support among leftists whereas the DC was highly clientelist and catchall in character.

All of these factors made the PCI less impoverished and more moderate than many communist parties and many challengers to dominant parties. But while it formally gave up on violent revolution and began to oppose Soviet expansionism in 1968 for its invasion of Czechoslovakia, its degree of moderation before the late 1970s can be overstated. Sartori (1976: 142) argues that it acted as an obstructionist party of "negative integration." Despite some work that characterizes the PCI as truly centrist (Tarrow, 1975), elite and mass opinion research supports the conclusion that it was comparatively radical and out of step with the average voter until at least the mid-1970s. On the mass side, Barnes and Pierce (1971: 6) show that voters placed the PCI furthest to the left at 12 on a scale that runs from 1 (left) to 100 (right). By comparison, voters placed the DC just right of center at 55 and the fascist MSI at 78, a position less far to the right than the PCI was to the left. On the elite side, Putnam writes that "Italian communist politicians are radical, programmatic, and ideologically committed Marxists" (1975: 209) with the "zeal of missionaries." They are "no mere social democrats" (1975: 182) even though they are clearly not revolutionaries (1975: 204). Putnam's 1968 surveys show that whereas DC and PSI politicians were quite centrist and accepting of the

288   *Why Dominant Parties Lose*

existing socio-economic system, some 85% of PCI politicians rejected the system completely or substantially (1971: 667). A similar pattern emerged with respect to the existing political system (1971: 668). Only 5% of PCI national councilors thought that extremist positions should be avoided in political controversies, compared to 55% of the noncommunist left and 82% of other parties' councilors (Putnam, 1975: 181).

Like in Mexico's opposition parties, there is evidence that the fine-grained generational differences predicted by my resource theory of dominance obtained inside the PCI. Older members had more partisan hostility and a more rigid ideological style than younger ones, and this finding holds true across age categories (Putnam, 1971: 674), at least until the mid-1970s, after which comparable research was unavailable.[25] The older generation had been socialized in the early postwar period when DC dominance was strongest and the PCI was a "closed party" (Hellman, 1975: 87). For these politicians, it made little sense to join an opposition party with a low chance of winning unless they were highly opposed to the status quo on policy. Younger politicians entered the opposition when the DC's power had declined somewhat. According to Putnam, "The younger Communist cohort shows strikingly lower levels of partisan hostility, political and social distrust, and resistance to compromise" (1975: 213 fn 25). Once the DC needed coalition partners to sustain its rule, opposition parties had the option to bandwagon in support of the government. Much like Japan's resource-seeking opposition, the Italian opposition went for it.

Why were the challenger parties sufficiently unattractive to the average Italian voter that the DC was able to maintain long-term dominance? I argue that the system of "pluralist patronage" was key and that the DC gained access to such large amounts of patronage by politicizing the resources of the state. Spotts and Wieser describe Italian politics thusly:

One of Italy's unique features is the existence of a vast sector of public and semipublic bodies that dominate virtually every area of national life: organizations as disparate as giant industries and banks, welfare and charitable agencies, [and] radio and television... These bodies are collectively so important they comprise what is known as the sottogoverno, "subgovernment"... the sottogoverno

---

[25] Tarrow (1975) argues that the youth movement that swept Italy in the late 1960s subsequently brought more radicals into the PCI, suggesting that the trend Putnam (1971) observed did not continue. Tarrow's finding presents a more complicated picture but actually supports my argument because my theory predicts that moderates should not join the opposition unless and until the incumbent's resource advantages decline. They had not by the early 1970s that Tarrow writes about.

Extending the Argument to Italy, Japan, Malaysia, and Taiwan   289

has been turned into a reservoir of partisan power, funds, and jobs without equal in any other Western democracy [that] are parceled out by the parties in a process that has come to be called lottizzazione, 'allotment.' The party loyalists who are placed in key positions in turn command enormous amounts of patronage. They award contracts for the construction of buildings, highways, and factories; they grant bank loans, pensions, and promotions; they allot franchises, financial subsidies, and jobs. And they do it strictly on the basis of partisanry...This exploitation of the sottogoverno by means of lottizzazione for the sake of clientelism through the granting of patronage is the lifeblood of the political system. Hence the general rule of Italian politics: Patronage tends to entrench in power and absolute patronage entrenches absolutely (1986: 6).

The authors summarize the source of DC dominance as "*sottogoverno* + party control = political power" (1986: 140).

The DC used the state to generate patronage goods in three ways. First, it distributed funds from infrastructure investment projects to loyal constituents. Even during the postwar economic boom, the South remained underdeveloped compared to the more dynamic and internationalized North. To address these regional disparities, the DC created a massive development fund called the Cassa per il Mezzogiorno that was administered by the central government. LaPalombara cites a bureaucrat who "notes that the Cassa per il Mezzogiorno has become a gigantic patronage organization which employs people and awards development contracts strictly on the basis of political considerations" (1964: 344). Tarrow argues that the DC engaged in the "manipulation of blocs of votes through the allocation of economic development projects from the state" (1967: 331) and Golden concurs that the Cassa "was aimed specifically and deliberately at expanding the bases for the DC's political patronage" (2000: 13).

Second, the DC dramatically expanded the state's involvement in business and industry. The largest of the state's companies is the Institute for Industrial Reconstruction (IRI) that was established in 1933 to bail out companies that failed in the wake of the worldwide depression. In the mid-1980s, it had become Europe's largest corporation and held a controlling interest in most of the country's metalworks, shipping, aircraft and airlines, telecommunications, electronics, engineering, Alfa Romeo, radio and television, the autostrade, the nation's three largest banks, and even many hotels (Zuckerman, 1979: 83). In the postwar period, the government also established the National Corporation for Hydrocarbons (ENI) that controlled the Italian Gas and Oil Company (AGIP), most nuclear energy and chemical production, and some textile firms, making it the world's ninth largest firm in the mid-1980s. Two other state companies, EFIM and GEPI, were dedicated to bailing out ailing firms. The government also controlled all major commercial and savings banks as well as special credit institutions, accounting for about 80% of banking facilities and "therefore holds nearly complete control over the country's investment funds" (Spotts and Wieser, 1986: 139). Finally, the government controlled the social security agency that had a 1983 budget equal to 21% of GNP. All told, there were about 60,000 state-owned enterprises (Zuckerman, 1979: 83) that accounted for about one-third of the country's total sales, more than one-fourth of industrial employment, and over one-half of total fixed investment (Spotts and Wieser, 1986: 129, 136–137). Yet, "Even the raw data do not fully convey the weight and influence of Italy's public corporations. The state industries and banks occupy the heights of economic power ... Some Western states have large public sectors but none has such a breadth of economic power with such a depth of national influence" (Spotts and Wieser, 1986: 140). If the DC could gain access to these resources, it would have a virtually unlimited supply of campaign funds.

Third, the DC used the public bureaucracy itself as a source of patronage jobs for supporters. The dramatic growth of the public sector in the postwar period increased the public bureaucracy from less than about 8% of the total labor force before the war to 22.3% in 1981 (Pignatelli, 1985: 166, 170), and about half of the 4 million public employees in 1990 were in central ministries (Golden, 2000: 14). Zuckerman (1979: 83) reports that particularly sensitive positions in the bureaucracy and ones that controlled resources were reserved for DC loyalists. Spotts and Wieser explain that access to public sector jobs required DC membership "for virtually every appointment, including secretaries, messengers, and clerks" (1986: 144). Warner reports that one Neapolitan said, "I became a DC member because they said to me: 'If you don't become a party member, you can't find work'" (1998: 578).

The DC had access to the resources of the state because it exerted political control over the public bureaucracy. Spotts and Wieser argue that "The civil service and its operations have been shamelessly politicized" (1986: 130) and LaPalombara writes that the DC "is in a very strong position to corrupt the bureaucracy because those bureaucrats who do not cooperate with the party – and therefore with the groups that have power within it – have little hope in general of making a career" (1964: 326). Golden explains that even though the public bureaucracy was supposed to be neutral and nonpartisan, "Civil service regulations were regularly evaded in order to construct a public bureaucracy in which appointments were based on partisan patronage rather than on professional expertise" (2000: 2). Temporary appointments were permitted without review and could be made permanent through collective legislation that sometimes affected hundreds of thousands of employees, noncivil servants could be attached to higher echelons in the public administration, exam results were fixed, and promotions were based on political connections rather than merit (Golden, 2000: 15–18). Between 1973 and 1990, about 60% of the public bureaucracy had not taken merit exams and "By the 1980s, the bulk of appointment to the public sector was taking place in clear violation of the spirit of civil service regulations even if in nominal conformity to legal requirements" (Golden, 2000: 17; also see della Porta and Vannucci, 1999: 137).

Most importantly, the parastatal sector was exempt from civil service regulations, allowing the DC to colonize it for political purposes. By the end of the 1960s, all presidents and vice-presidents of the IRI, all non-technical leaders of the ENI except one, and eight of 10 managers of other important public corporations were DC members, as were the vast majority of lower level employees (Zuckerman, 1979: 84; also see Spotts and Wieser, 1986: 141). Since the bureaucracy was very hierarchically organized, even a small number of top managers could effectively control resources, appointments, and promotions.

Massive resources flowed from public enterprises to the DC's campaign war chests. Until 1974, contributions from government agencies to political parties were legal. Yet even after the law went into effect, the DC used its political clout to divert public resources. In 1977, *Il Mondo* estimated that the DC had received about $100 million in illicit campaign financing from public corporations. A 1984 investigation found that almost $200 million had been funneled from the IRI to the DC. Another source estimated that about 6.5 trillion lire a year was involved in kickbacks associated with public works contracts and illegal party financing between 1982 and 1992 (*Economist*, 3/20/93, p. 69). In several other cases, high-level public figures denounced the illicit use of public funds to carry out DC campaigns. Finally, DC campaigns were also funded by public banks that made hundreds of million of dollars of unsecured loans (Spotts and Wieser, 1986: 145).

The postwar expansion and partisan use of state-owned enterprises through the public bureaucracy was part of the DC's strategy to reinforce its political dominance. Naturally, the government's involvement in the economy was partly a product of the need to accumulate capital for national economic expansion in the context of late development

(Gerschenkron, 1962), and partly the result of a Keynesian compromise between labor and capital that created an extensive welfare state. Nevertheless, the politicization and use of public resources obeyed a purely partisan logic designed to lock-in incumbency advantages that did not occur in other late developers and in other European nations with large welfare states but without dominant parties. In particular, the DC had two incentives for generating a reliable resource stream by penetrating the state and diverting its funds for partisan use. First, the party initially relied on the Church for resources; however, in order to expand its vote share and construct a broader multiclass alliance it sought to become independent (Kalyvas, 1996). Second, although the DC won an outright majority in the 1948 elections, it fell to a plurality in 1953. Securing resource advantages could stop this electoral slide. Thus, beginning in the 1950s, "Under [Prime Minister] Fanfani's guidance they [the DC] conceived the idea of constructing a power based outside of government. In the public enterprises and other agencies they saw a potential empire that could provide great political and financial riches" (Spotts and Wieser, 1986: 141). By the middle of the decade, the DC had completed "the annexation of the state economic sector" (Spotts and Wieser, 1986: 24), yielding a virtually bottomless chest of illicit resources for DC partisan advantage.

Nevertheless, after decades of dominance, the DC's electoral power diminished during the 1980s and its rule came to a definitive end in 1992. Unlike in other dominant party systems where existing challenger parties eventually unseated the incumbent, in Italy the DC's loss was accompanied by the virtual disintegration of the "first republic." The change was so dramatic that Mershon and Pasquino (1995) refer to it as a "regime change." The most proximate cause for this wholesale electoral realignment was voters' disgust over a series of high-profile influence-peddling scandals that involved large numbers of politicians, businesses, public enterprises, and mafia bosses. These scandals, collectively known as *tangentopoli*, exposed a web of shady deals that involved political favors, kickbacks, and episodes of shocking violence. However, the scandals were the result of prior changes that threw Italy's previously stable system of patronage politics into disequilibrium.

Until the 1980s, the DC benefited from dramatic financial advantages over the opposition through its near-monopoly access to public resources. However, in the 1980s, pressure from foreign competitors and partners in the European Union to meet macro-economic targets forced a reduction of public investment and government involvement in economic activity

Extending the Argument to Italy, Japan, Malaysia, and Taiwan 293

generally retracted. This pressure led to three changes that threatened the DC's resource base.

First, investment in the South through the Cassa per il Mezzogiorno that the DC used to distribute patronage fell by a factor of six, from as much as 1.7% of GDP in 1972 to just 0.3% of GDP in 1988. This change deprived the government of about 15 billion lire in 1988 prices that it could have used for public investment.[26] Grants and subsidies from the central government to the South also decreased sharply by 30% during this period.[27] Another central government tool for southern economic development that operated with a patronage bias was the state-owned GEPI that purchased ailing private firms. Over time, GEPI's holdings included a disproportionate number from the South, yet it largely failed to turn these businesses around. Amidst other economic pressures in the 1980s, GEPI's holdings were diminished (Locke, 1995: 63). The retrenchment of the government's development role in the South reduced the DC's ability to generate votes from its most secure bastion of support.

Second, state-owned enterprises became so inefficient, in part because they were run with a political rather than a business logic, that many were in chronic debt. The situation became sufficiently untenable that, despite DC resistance to privatization, some state-owned enterprises were sold off beginning in 1985. In 33 deals, six commercial banks and holding companies, the Alitalia airline, telecommunications, construction, manufacturing, steelworks, investment, and food products companies were transferred in whole or in part to the private sector (Bortolotti, 2005: 51, 59). Overall, between 1978 and 1991, state-owned enterprises fell from almost 7% of GDP to just above 5%.[28] As a result of these reductions, the public enterprise workforce decreased by over 150,000 employees between 1976 and 1987.[29] Data were not available for the period from 1987 to 1992, but because many more public businesses were transferred to the private sector during this period than in the prior one, it is likely that there were even larger reductions in the workforce. Bortolotti estimates

---

[26] Data on the Cassa per il Mezzogiorno come from Kostoris, 1993: 80. Data on GDP in current lire are from *OECD Economic Surveys: Italy*, various years. Calculations by the author.

[27] Grants and subsidies data come from Kostoris, 1993: 92. GDP growth rate data are from World Bank, *World Development Indicators*. http://0-devdata.worldbank.org.

[28] World Bank, *Bureaucrats in Business: The Economics and Politics of Government Ownership Dataset*, available at http://econ.worldbank.org.

[29] Author's calculations based on Kostoris, 1993: 136.

that the overall contribution of state-owned enterprises to value added, employment, and fixed capital formation decreased by about 20% from the late 1970s to the early 1990s (2005: 48). Overall, these reductions, like the decreasing outlays for development projects in the South, deprived the DC of some of the resources it used to buy political support.

Although privatizations were important, they played a smaller role in threatening the DC's resource base than similar processes did in Mexico, and in fact most privatization in Italy occurred after the DC lost power following the 1992 elections. Part of the reason is that DC politicians staunchly opposed privatization because "Public means patronage" and "most politicians, and virtually all members of la classe politica, remain deeply suspicious of privatization...a huge public sector, with all the patronage that goes with it, has allowed the Christian Democrats to build a base for themselves outside the Roman Catholic church. This has consolidated their grip on power. It has meant that, when private companies run into trouble, the state steps in to take them over, 'saving' jobs, winning clients, placing friends and adding to future sources of political contributions" (*Economist*, 5/26/90, p. 13).

Third, domestic business had always been an important source for campaign finance in a system that della Porta and Vannucci refer to as a long-term contract for protection (2000: 3) that involved "practically all the large industrial firms" (Bruno and Segreto, 1996: 666 cited in Golden, 2004: 1246). But as these businesses came under increasing pressure to compete in the emerging European Community and public companies doled out fewer contracts in protected areas, private firms had incentives to defect from the patronage for protection bargain. Golden argues that "A commitment to profit-making in a European scale, then, shifted Italian businesses into a position of opposition to rather than collusion with the DC-led regime" (2000: 25) and it was "the withdrawal of big business from the system of corruption and patronage that catalyzed the collapse of the postwar political regime" (2000: 25).

In the 1992 elections, the DC won less than 30% of the vote for the first time in the postwar period and thus "weakened the main government party enough to allow the judiciary to proceed with what turned into massive investigations into widespread criminal wrongdoing by Italy's postwar political elite, especially politicians from the parties of the government" (Golden, 2004: 1239). These so-called "clean hands" investigations were "triggered by the concomitant financial crisis of the state, its parties, and major Italian industries which undermined the major actors' ability to uphold their clientelistic system" (Guzzini, 1994: 1). As a result, the judiciary lifted the legal immunity under which members of parliament had operated for decades, and this "generated a cascade of confessions, investigations, removal of immunity, and prosecutions which toppled the postwar regime" (Golden, 2000: 25). As his government fell, Prime Minister Craxi boldly confronted the judiciary, the businessmen in the court's galley, and the public by declaring that "Everybody knew . . . What needs to be said, and which in any case everyone knows, is that the greater part of political funding is irregular and illegal" (cited in della Porta and Vannucci, 2000: 2).

CONCLUSION

This chapter extended the resource theory of dominance beyond Mexico to other dominant party systems in Asia and Europe. Despite major differences among these systems in their level of economic development, cultural heritage, government format, electoral formula, and relevant historical period, all of these countries evidenced the dominant party equilibrium. This equilibrium involved a catchall incumbent that held the political center and niche-oriented opposition parties that were either relatively extremist on the main partisan dimensions of competition or campaigned on less salient issues. I argued that this pattern can be explained primarily by the incumbent party's resource advantages that allowed it to distribute material benefits to supporters. At the same time, opposition parties were resource poor and this left them at a competitive disadvantage because it forced them to rely on programmatic or ideological appeals to attract their candidates and activists as well as their voters.

The source and distribution method of politicized resources varied somewhat across dominant party systems, but in all cases, the incumbent party used the economic power of the state to generate advantages. In at least Mexico, Malaysia, Taiwan, and Italy, state-owned enterprises served as cash cows that could be mined for partisan purposes, both by transferring resources illicitly to the dominant party's coffers and by providing jobs and contracts to supporters. In most cases the public bureaucracy was also used to campaign for the dominant party and the administrative resources of the state were transformed into partisan goods. In all cases under study, but particularly in Japan and Italy, the incumbent used development policies to target resources to particular constituencies based on partisan political logic. Given the specificity of the targeting, Scheiner (2006) on Japan and Golden (2004) on Italy argue that this type of pork should be thought of as patronage. In all the cases reviewed, the state's deep involvement in the economy also encouraged private business to contribute to the incumbent party in exchange for protected markets and/or government contracts. Overall, dominant parties used the economic power of the state to reinforce their advantage. When privatization diminished the state's economic role, incumbents in all the cases increasingly turned to a combination of private financing, illicit funds from organized crime, and, in Mexico and Taiwan, legal public financing largely designed to help the incumbent. In some cases, these new funding sources became centerpieces of political corruption scandals that helped turn voters against the incumbent. Yet it is important to bear in mind that these scandals were the downstream result of changing economic conditions that encouraged incumbents to seek new revenue streams. Thus, in all cases, when more of the economy fell into private hands, dominant parties' resource bases were threatened and their electoral positions eroded. The one holdout remains Malaysia where the dominant party has not lost. In this case, the state remains deeply involved in economic development and UMNO has resisted important aspects of the Washington consensus on economic privatization and marketization. Barring other exogenous shocks that shake the dominant party, until and unless privatization diminishes the state's role or legal restrictions effectively stop the incumbent from using public resources for partisan advantage, I expect that it will remain dominant.

9

Conclusions and Implications

Dominant party systems present two major puzzles. If dominant party advantages are overwhelming, then why do opposition parties form at all? On the other hand, if opposition parties compete in genuine elections, then why does single-party dominance persist? Despite the predictions of existing theory, 16 countries on four continents had dominant parties during the 20th century and, by century's end, 11 had transformed into fully competitive democracies with turnover.

This book offered a theory to explain both equilibrium dominance and its breakdown; that is, a theory to account for both stable long-term single-party dominance *and* the incumbent party's eventual loss at the polls. I argued that hyper-incumbency advantages deeply affect partisan competition and help sustain dominance. In particular, dominant parties' monopoly or near monopoly access to public resources allows them to outspend challengers at every turn, saturate the media, pay armies of canvassers, blanket the national territory with their logo, and generally speak to voters through a megaphone while opposition parties speak with a whisper. Most importantly, dominant parties' hyper-incumbency advantages allow them to bribe voters with patronage goods. Dominant parties also raise the costs of participating in the opposition by imposing opportunity costs for not joining the incumbent and, in some systems, by targeting repression against opposition forces when patronage fails.

Identifying that dominant parties use resources and sometimes use repression to sustain their rule is not particularly surprising or innovative; however, prior research has been largely descriptive and has not incorporated these elements into a complete theory of single-party dominance. One of my argument's main contributions is to link the political economy of single-party dominance – a large state sector and a politically quiescent public bureaucracy – to opposition party failure by specifying the mechanisms that translate these macro-causes into micro-effects on the dynamics of political recruitment.[1] As part of this argument, I crafted new formal theories that take incumbency advantages seriously. I showed that disadvantaged opposition parties have a lower chance of winning no matter what strategies they pursue. Yet unlike existing theories that predict that no challenger party should form in the presence of identifiable incumbency advantages, I show how policy incentives can motivate working for a losing cause. Since the electoral competition game is biased, the only citizens willing to form opposition parties are those who disagree sharply with the status quo policies offered by the incumbent party. Further, the only citizens willing to volunteer as candidates and activists, enduring high personal costs and reaping low traditional benefits, are those who value expressing support for such an anti-status quo cause. The benefit of partisan expression lies not in winning office or receiving a paycheck, but in working hard to transform fellow citizens' views about politics. But the only people willing to participate in a risky and likely failing party that offers little more than a soapbox to stand on to announce their views are those who disagree with the dominant party so vehemently that they simply cannot remain quiet.

This approach yields a theory of dominance because it shows how the dynamics of political recruitment generate a relatively centrist and catchall dominant party populated by careerists and comparatively noncentrist challenger parties made up of anti-status quo personnel. Riker (1976) first identified the importance of noncentrist challenger parties in sustaining single-party dominance, but he did not supply a full theory. In particular, he did not propose the mechanism that leads opposition parties to adopt relatively extreme positions that are electorally inefficient. This outcome is especially puzzling in the presence of institutional and spatial incentives to moderate that obtained in a number of dominant party systems. By incorporating the effects of asymmetric resources and costs of participation into partisan competition, I offer one way to complete Riker's approach and fashion a fully specified theory of single-party dominance. I showed how this theory helps explain the empirical dynamics of party competition in Mexico over time (Chapter 3) as well as the

---

[1] Scheiner's (2006) excellent study on Japan argues that centralized governments with patronage lead to local opposition party failure. As discussed in earlier chapters, I agree with and build on his insightful argument.

individual-level process of party affiliation (Chapter 5). I also showed in Chapter 8 that my theory accounts for partisan dynamics in other dominant party systems, both where the surrounding regime is authoritarian (Malaysia and Taiwan) and where it is democratic (Italy and Japan).

This theory also has implications for the study of Mexico and politics in its now fully competitive democracy, the formation and development of resource-poor parties that emanate from society, and for the study of hybrid or competitive authoritarian regimes. I use the remainder of the conclusion to discuss these implications.

MEXICO'S PAST AND FUTURE POLITICS

Mexico has played a somewhat awkward role in the comparative politics literature. Some of the most nuanced treatments have viewed Mexico as a *sui generis* case and avoided or downplayed direct comparisons with other countries (Camp, 2003; Cornelius and Craig, 1991; Hellman, 1983; Smith, 1979). Others who do put Mexico in comparative perspective have moved in one of two directions. In the 1950s and early 1960s, Mexico was often compared to the United States as a peculiar variant of democracy without turnover (Fitzgibbon, 1951: 519; Cline, 1962: 149–156, 173; Scott, 1964: 146). In the late 1960s and 1970s, scholars began to pay more attention to repression and the deficiencies in partisan contestation, and some compared it to the fully closed military authoritarian regimes in South America (Brandenburg, 1964: 3–7; González Casanova, 1965; Kaufman Purcell, 1973: 29; Reyna and Weinert, 1977). More recent research by scholars who use dichotomous regime classifications (i.e., all regimes are labeled authoritarian or democratic) such as Przeworski and colleagues (2000) and Boix (2003) also lump Mexico in with fully closed authoritarian regimes such as China under Communist Party rule and Chile under dictatorship. But neither comparison captures the characteristics of Mexico's hybrid regime under the PRI. Instead, it seemed as though scholars often exaggerated Mexico's democratic or authoritarian characteristics to make it fit with other easily identifiable cases, and they looked close to home by comparing Mexico to its northern or southern neighbors.

I have argued that Mexico under the PRI should be thought of as a dominant party authoritarian regime that combined meaningful but unfair competition with selective and episodic repression of opposition forces. It was neither fully authoritarian nor fully democratic, but contained elements of each. Far from making it a unique case, Mexico shared these characteristics with a broader set of dominant party systems that are far flung across the globe. Rather than mirroring other countries in Latin America, Mexico's politics under the PRI looked much more like Malaysia under UMNO and Taiwan under the KMT. It even shared important characteristics with Japan under the LDP and Italy under the DC, although these dominant party democratic regimes clearly lacked the repressive tools of their authoritarian counterparts. Thus, for some purposes, region may be a misleading starting point for comparison, and instead scholars should look more broadly across time and space to find the appropriate comparison set.

Making large-N comparisons between dominant party systems and fully competitive democracies with turnover helped show that single-party dominance is not primarily due to insufficient voter demand, restrictive electoral institutions, or the absence of sufficient ideological space for the challengers to occupy. It is also not linked to a country's level of socio-economic development or equality. Making comparisons among a handful of country cases further helped show that dominant party persistence is not due to country or regionally specific factors and does not owe to religion or culture. Rather, I used an in-depth study of Mexico and comparisons to other instances of single-party dominance to show the critical importance of hyper-incumbency advantages that derive from dominant parties' politicization of public resources.

My resource theory of single-party dominance gives distinctive leverage on four central questions in the study of Mexico's past politics. First, I showed why opposition parties failed during decades of PRI dominance despite meaningful elections. PRI advantages distorted opposition party recruitment, organization, and strategies so significantly as to make challenger parties undercompetitive at the polls. Second, I showed that opposition forces failed to coordinate against the PRI despite their common interest in democracy because the dynamics of recruitment into the opposition generated parties that were polarized over economic policy between a statist left and a market-oriented right. Third, I showed that the PRI survived despite massive voter rejection of its performance following the 1982 economic crisis not only or perhaps even primarily because of electoral fraud, but due to disagreement within each opposition party over strategic position-taking. Even though later joiners endorsed centrist strategies, early joiners in both the PAN and PRD were policy extremists who built niche-oriented organizations that helped their parties survive during the lean years but were too rigid to permit strategic innovation once opportunities opened toward the center of the competition space.

Finally, I showed that Vicente Fox of the PAN won the presidency in 2000 and ended PRI rule because he was able to raise independent resources, make an end-run around his party's entrenched organization, and mount a campaign that emphasized change in government while making centrist albeit sometimes vague economic policy statements. Voters responded by overcoming the coordination problems that opposition party elites could not: They defected from the PRD's Cárdenas and voted for Fox.

The origin and evolution of opposition parties also has implications for Mexico's future politics, including the number of competitive parties, legislative politics and social choice outcomes, and political representation.

Barring dramatic changes to the electoral system, Mexico will continue to have at least three main political parties. Until generational change creates leadership turnover in the PAN and PRD, the hardcore of partisan elites on the left and right will not easily give up on their policy beliefs nor will they likely create broader alliances since they perceive that such moves would water down their parties' hard-won identities. Reactions against entrenched party leaders may lead factions to break away from the PAN and PRD to form their own parties; however, neither existing party will likely disappear over the medium term, and therefore we are unlikely to see a system with less than three major parties.

These dynamics also mean that the PRI is unlikely to disappear. For those who viewed Mexico under the PRI as a fully authoritarian regime, this result should be surprising. With the onset of free and fair elections, incumbent parties in constitutionally or *de facto* one-party regimes tend to lose quickly and decisively, even if, like Eastern European communist parties, they are re-born as reformists several election cycles later (Grzymala-Busse, 2002). In contrast, the PRI has remained largely intact and it has continued to be a major electoral force now six years after it lost the presidency. The PRI's staying power is partly due to PAN and PRD's failures. The formerly opposition parties' inability to transform themselves into moderate parties that compete at the center on economic policy has ceded space for the PRI to portray itself as a responsible option that splits the difference between its leftwing and rightwing competitors. Clearly, the PRI's future success depends on a number of factors: It must live down its reputation as an authoritarian party, solidify rules for the selection of candidates and leaders in the absence of presidential interference, overcome the rigidities associated with its atrophied sectoral organizations, and settle factional disputes. If these obstacles can be overcome, the PAN's and PRD's failure to "squeeze" the PRI's vote share by moderating puts the

302 *Why Dominant Parties Lose*

former dominant party in a surprisingly competitive position (see Greene, 2008).

As a result of three-party competition that includes the still polarized PAN and PRD, congressional gridlock of major policy initiatives will remain a daunting possibility. The two formerly opposition parties are disciplined (Weldon, 2004) and rarely vote together on major economic policy issues. Decades of deep-seated tension, even outright hatred, means that their coordination on important noneconomic issues is also relatively infrequent. As a result, the PRI is often the pivot in Congress, and no matter which party controls the executive branch, the success or failure of ordinary legislation will depend on its votes. However, since it is less likely that the PRI plus one of the other two major parties will control the supermajority necessary to pass constitutional amendments, some of the most pressing and long-lasting reforms may continue to founder.

The dynamics of opposition party building that led to parties with relatively strong programmatic commitments have some surprisingly negative implications for political representation. The PAN's and PRD's deep but narrow ties to the electorate have left 35–40% of voters as self-identified independents. As a result, we are likely to see continued tension between the parties and their presidential candidates. Unlike in other countries with presidential systems where party organizations tend to downplay program and support center-seeking strategies (Samuels, 2002: 470–471), the PAN and PRD have continued to place a stronger emphasis than we might expect on representing their core constituencies. This will continue to encourage candidates to make risky end runs around their party organizations and mount independent campaigns dedicated to drawing in independents, much like the Fox campaign did in 2000. Campaigns in this mold would leave successful candidates with unclear mandates and little responsibility to their parties. Such an outcome is not at all surprising in other Latin American democracies where loose ties between candidates and their parties have permitted dramatic policy swings such as "neoliberalism by surprise" (see Stokes, 2001; Levitsky, 2003); however, it is more surprising in Mexico where the opposition parties took pains to craft and protect their distinct programmatic identities that are now, ironically, under threat due to their own success.

Thus, Mexico provides somewhat of a cautionary tale that reaches similar conclusions to existing literature on the crisis of representation in Latin America, but for different reasons. Country experts throughout the region and Brazilianists in particular have raised concerns about excessively weak parties that underlie "inchoate" party systems (Mainwaring, 1999). These arguments tend to suggest that parties provide too

Conclusions and Implications

little ideological structure to give voters meaningful choices and too little discipline to constrain their candidates or guide voting in Congress. The implied remedy would be to cultivate more responsible and programmatically oriented parties. But in Mexico, the PAN and PRD's rigidity, not their weakness, has encouraged candidates to circumvent their own parties in the attempt to catch more voters. If parties in other Latin American countries are underinstitutionalized, then the PAN and PRD exhibit at least one element of overinstitutionalization – their ideological commitments have inhibited expansion. Paradoxically, these different paths may lead to the same end, one that requires Mexico's former opposition parties to engage in a difficult re-evaluation about the preferred balance between their hard-won historical identities and their desire to win elections.

PARTY DEVELOPMENT

My resource theory of single-party dominance also has implications for the study of externally mobilized parties that emanate from society rather than from legislators who are already inside government. In addition to challengers to dominant parties, external parties emerge regularly in established party systems, including third parties in the United States as well as Green parties, radical right parties, and a substantial number of the 261 new parties that formed in Western Europe between World War II and the 1990s (see Hug, 2001: 80). Despite their existence, we lack a convincing and complete theory about why these parties form and how they develop. Existing work on new party entry tells important parts of the story by looking at the amount of available ideological "space" to propose new policies (Palfrey, 1984) and the reactions of existing parties (Hug, 2001; Meguid, 2005); however, like the original Downsian model of party competition and existing theoretical extensions, these approaches ignore the question of resources. I have shown that differential resource endowments are a crucial variable because disadvantaged parties may experience limited success even when electoral institutions are permissive and there is sufficient voter demand and ideological space.

The effects of asymmetric resources are clearest among challengers to dominant parties because opposition parties in these systems are especially resource deprived and thus provide a limiting case.[2] Such challengers are locked out of access to the resources of the state and private donors are

[2] One could further argue that opposition parties in presidential dominant party systems are the most resource deprived while the incentives described in Chapter 8 give challengers in parliamentary systems somewhat more access to resources.

unlikely to fund them since doing so cannot buy much influence in government and runs the risk of retribution from the incumbent. Although less striking, externally mobilized parties in fully competitive democracies also face quite important barriers to resource mobilization, especially when *de facto* cartels among the established parties fund themselves from the public trough (Katz and Mair, 1995). Paying attention to how these parties generate resources from society may shed light on the dynamics of recruitment, the character of their organizations, and their often inefficient electoral strategies.

Resource-poor parties face particular problems of political recruitment. They have such a low chance of winning that they cannot provide potential joiners with instrumental benefits for their participation over the short term. Their low resources also rule out the solution suggested by Olson (1971) and Tullock (1971) to offer material side-payments such as a paycheck or an in-kind grant. As a result, resource-poor parties typically rely on volunteers to serve as both candidates and activists rather than the paid professional party personnel found in most parties with resources. But these volunteers still need reasons to participate in a high-cost activity that is unlikely to succeed. In the absence of some alternative incentive to overcome the collective action problem, theory leads us to believe that potential dissent will fail to become actual dissent and new parties will not form at all. Since they obviously do form, we need a framework that helps understand why. I argue that one solution is found in the value of expressive benefits that come from working hard for an esteemed cause. Citizens with strong views about public policy value the opportunity to express these views publicly, and opposition parties offer them a platform from which to speak. By making such a platform available, party founders essentially craft these incentives out of thin air and make them selectively accessible to those who participate. Expressive benefits may be powerful enough to help opposition parties recruit members – albeit members with strongly held anti-status quo views – even when the incentives highlighted in standard party theory suggest that potential participants should simply abstain from politics.

This argument takes issue with the notion that politicians only care about winning office. Competing to win is the exclusive incentive that underlies ambition theory (Schlesinger, 1966) and has dominated the study of parties for the past 40 years. Adding expressive benefits might also be considered a challenge to orthodox rational choice approaches; however, it does not move outside the rational choice framework since prospective candidates and activists in my model still explicitly weigh the costs and benefits of participation. Rather, my research implies that extending the rational choice approach to externally mobilized parties that are organized by citizens rather than by office-holders and to political contexts beyond the fully competitive democracies requires sensitive study of the actors on the ground to get their utility functions right.

Adding expressive benefits to participation endows parties with meaningful identities that merit, in the minds of candidates and activists, hard work, sacrifice, and dedication. Resource-poor outsider parties are likely to protect these identities by erecting formal or informal barriers to new recruitment predicated on the idea that participants should be "good types" capable of representing the cause. For the same reason, "moral authority" gained through blood, sweat, and tears, rather than popularity, charisma, or electability is the currency that wins leadership posts and candidacies. Thus, while competitive parties with resources tend to open to society to recruit broadly, resource-poor outsider parties tend to turn inward to survive. The risk of such an approach to party building, however, is that externally mobilized parties may become club-like organizations with insular identities and narrow followings.

The dynamics of recruitment into resource-poor parties – due in large part to the role of expressive benefits – generate strikingly different intra-party dynamics than predicted by existing theory. I showed that elite activists' policy extremism over the long-term depended on the level of the challengers' disadvantages at the time of their initial affiliation with the opposition. If these disadvantages decline more or less linearly over time as they did in Mexico, then generational differences will produce early joiners with comparatively extreme policy preferences and later joiners with more moderate preferences.

The existence of relatively radical leaders and moderate activists is the opposite of the prediction made by the best-known approach to intra-party politics. Following insights by Hirschman (1970), May's (1973) "special law of curvilinear disparities" theorized that leaders are vote maximizers that want to reflect voters' preferences to win elections whereas lower-level activists participate for ideological reasons and therefore hold more radical preferences. For this to occur, either moderates must be selected for advancement or activists must undergo a psychological transformation as they rise (Kitschelt, 1989b). However plausible this theory may be for the fully competitive democracies, it does not hold for challengers to dominant parties. The effects of initial socialization were so powerful among party elites in Mexico that their early extremism was immune to both the psychological attractiveness of winning through moderation and to learning as political conditions opened opportunities to win more votes by moderating. As a result, the implications of May's "law" for the relationship between party organizations and competitiveness are turned on their head. If he were correct, such that activists with power would turn their parties into principled losers, then a party dictator would be the recipe for success. But challengers to dominant parties are principled by design. Thus, the more hierarchical they are, the more they will remain "constrained to the core" while party democracy may instead enhance the prospects for expansion.

Finally, if leaders maintain control and pull their parties away from the center even in the presence of incentives to moderate, their strategies will not only diminish their competitiveness but they will also affect social choice outcomes. Unless a center party has an outright majority, then congressional coalitions will pass legislation that is skewed to the left or right. There is obviously nothing normatively problematic about this situation; however, it does imply more shifts in social choice outcomes than the optimistic Downsian view of democracy suggests. Downs (1957) and scores of subsequent theorists have argued that, for a wide variety of partisan configurations, the act of competition itself would encourage politicians to mute their principles in favor of sober interests by adopting the centrist policies preferred by the core of voters, and this would produce stable public policies over time. But this outcome is predicated on politicians wanting to win at all cost. If they value partisan expression instead, then even in the presence of incentives to moderate, social choice outcomes may be difficult to reach and unstable over time.

Regimes and Regime Change

My argument yields four insights about regimes and regime change. First, I show that incumbents can maintain the dominant party equilibrium in competitive party systems without overarching reliance on heavy-handed electoral fraud or bone-crushing repression. The dynamics of long-term electoral dominance are subtler. Incumbents may use resource advantages to cause deep distortions in the electoral market for votes. In so doing, they condition the type of opposition parties that form, making them into electorally weak niche parties that issue comparatively extreme policy statements. As a result, unfair competition means that dominant parties virtually win elections before election day. Authoritarian tools can play important secondary roles when other pre-election mechanisms fail; however, if incumbents value the legitimacy that comes from meaningful

Conclusions and Implications

electoral competition, then they must use these tools delicately since too much force can drive opposition forces away from party politics and toward social movements or revolutionary organizations. If this happens, dominant party rule breaks down into fully closed authoritarian one-party rule without challengers.

Second, my argument has implications for the relationship between the economic role of the state and the concentration of political power. I showed that incumbents survive by transforming public resources into partisan goods. This implies that dominant parties have incentives to grow the state and maintain a politically quiescent public bureaucracy. It is not that a large public sector creates dominance since there are of course many economies with large public sectors that do not have dominant parties. Rather, single-party dominance cannot long survive without access to a steady stream of resources, and one of the most reliable streams comes from public coffers.

This further implies that the political economy of dominance will be easier to maintain when incumbents are not pressured to liberalize their economies. Partly for this reason, dominant party systems were more plentiful in the period before the 1980s when import-substitution industrialization and, in some cases autarky, protected national economies. Increasing domestic and international pressures over the last 30 years have led to a shift toward free markets in several cases, and the accompanying sell-off of state-owned enterprises has threatened dominant parties by diminishing their access to public resources. Malaysia provides a useful contrasting case because UMNO was able to resist these pressures and single-party dominance has been sustained.

The relationship between resource monopoly and political monopoly has long been recognized in the study of fully closed authoritarian regimes. Nowhere was this affinity clearer than in the communist world, about which Dahl argued, "a centrally directed command economy ... provide[s] political leaders with such powerful resources for persuasion, manipulation, and coercion as to make democracy extremely unlikely in the long term" (1992: 82; also see Schumpeter, 1947). Work on the rentier state has similarly argued that fully closed authoritarian regimes resist democratizing pressure more successfully when they have access to rents from oil or other minerals (Chaudhry, 1997; Ross, 2001).

However, these insights have not been generalized to dominant party authoritarian regimes or the broader category of competitive authoritarian regimes. I argue that resource concentration and in particular incumbents' ability to politicize the resources of the state are key variables

308   *Why Dominant Parties Lose*

in studying regime dynamics in competitive authoritarian regimes, not just in fully closed authoritarian regimes. Incumbent dominant parties with large politicized states at their disposal can use patronage to distort the electoral market for votes so much that they dampen the long-term democratizing pressures from socio-economic modernization. For this reason, cross-national neo-modernization studies that measure overall societal wealth with GDP per capita (Przeworski et al., 2000; Boix and Stokes, 2003) or the distribution of wealth with the GINI coefficient (Boix, 2003)[3] incorrectly predict that most dominant party authoritarian regimes should be democracies. Where dominant parties transform the state from a neutral actor into their own piggy bank, the *balance* between the public and private sectors is even more important than standard modernization measures for explaining the stability of dominant party rule and its breakdown.[4]

Third, I argue that policy disagreement is an important but underappreciated element in stalled transitions to democracy in authoritarian regimes that permit party competition. These transitions do not occur through elite pacts that open the way for founding elections. Rather, since the electoral arena remains open in competitive authoritarianism, transitions to fully competitive democracy rest on building opposition party electoral capacity. Still, one of the most puzzling observations about competitive authoritarian regimes in general and dominant party authoritarian regimes in particular is their persistence even when a majority of voters rate the incumbent's performance negatively. At these times, opposition coordination seems like an obvious strategy (Howard and Roessler, 2006), yet coordination almost always fails. I argue that elite coordination failure results from ideological differences that become structured into the opposition through the process of political recruitment. An important implication is that the regime cleavage – the exclusive focus of current literature on transitions to democracy – that presumably unites challengers against authoritarian incumbents is not the only force, and in some cases not even the primary force in determining the geometry of cooperation. Rather, traditional cleavages like economic development policy in Mexico, ethnicity in Malaysia, and relations with China in Taiwan divide challenger parties and often doom coordination. In these cases, dominant party rule may

---

[3] As Ross (2001: 330) points out, Przeworski et al. simply drop cases where fuel exports in 1984–1986 accounted for more than half of total exports (2000: 77 fn 2).

[4] Incumbents may be able to create collusive relationships with business partners, but these partners are less controllable than public sector bureaucrats and may defect to fund challenger parties under certain conditions.

be prolonged because opposition parties prefer a centrist authoritarian incumbent to remain in power rather than coordinate with a challenger whose policies they despise.

Finally, my argument yields some general policy implications for actors interested in promoting democracy in dominant party systems. In order to level the playing field and diminish hyper-incumbency advantages, such actors should press for third-party or international financial audits of state-owned enterprises, prohibitions against party-owned businesses and financial donations from government agencies to parties, civil service professionalization, and electoral management bodies with oversight and sanctioning powers, including regular audits of the parties' revenues and expenditures. None of these are quick fixes, but all avenues should help limit the discretionary power of dominant parties to politicize the resources of the state and spend them for partisan advantage. To the extent that unchecked access to public resources can be restrained, the numerous incumbents around the world that would like to develop their own dominant parties may fail to consolidate long-term control.

References

Abramson, Paul, John Aldrich, and David Rohde (1994) *Change and Continuity in the 1992 Elections*. Washington, DC: CQ Press.

Adams, James (1999) "Policy Divergence in Multicandidate Probabilistic Spatial Voting" *Public Choice* 100: 103–122.

Adams, James, Samuel Merrill III, and Bernard Grofman (2005) *A Unified Theory of Party Competition*. New York: Cambridge University Press.

Aguilar Zinser, Adolfo (1995) *Vamos a ganar! La pugna de Cuauhtémoc Cárdenas por el poder*. Mexico City: Oceano.

Aldrich, John (1983) "A Downsian Spatial Model with Party Activism" *American Political Science Review* 77, 4: 974–990.

Aldrich, John (1993) "Rational Choice and Turnout" *American Journal of Political Science* 37, 1: 246–278.

Aldrich, John (1995) *Why Parties? The Origin and Transformation of Political Parties in America*. Chicago: University of Chicago Press.

Aldrich John and William Bianco (1992) "A Game-Theoretic Model of Party Affiliation of Candidates and Office Holders" *Mathematical and Computer Modeling* 16, 8–9: 103–116.

Alesina Alberto and Stephen Spear (1988) "An Overlapping Generations Model of Electoral Competition" *Journal of Public Economics* 37, 3: 359–79.

Alvarez, R. Michael and Jonathan Nagler (1998) "When Politics and Model Collide: Estimating Models of Multiparty Elections" *American Journal of Political Science* 42, 1 (June): 55–96.

Alves, Maria Helena (1985) *State and Opposition in Military Brazil*. Austin: University of Texas Press.

Ames, Barry (1970) "Bases of Support for Mexico's Dominant Party" *American Political Science Review* 64, 1: 153–167.

Arian, Alan and Samuel Barnes (1974) "The Dominant Party System: A Neglected Model of Democratic Stability" *Journal of Politics* 36, 3 (August): 592–614.

312 References

Arredondo Ramírez, Pablo, Gilberto Fregoso Peralta, and Raúl Trejo Delabre (1991) *Así se calló el sistema: Comunicación y elecciones en 1988*. Guadalajara: University of Guadalajara.

Arrellano, David and Juan Pablo Guerrero (2000) "Stalled Administrative Reform of the Mexican State" in B. Schneider and B. Heredia (eds.) *Reinventing Leviathan: The Political Economy of Administrative Reform in Developing Countries*. Miami: North-South Center Press.

Arriola, Carlos (1988) *Los empresarios y el estado, 1970–1982*. Mexico City: Porrúa.

Arriola, Carlos (1994) *Ensayos sobre el PAN*. Mexico: Porrúa.

Aspe, Pedro (1993) *Economic Transformation the Mexican Way*. Cambridge: MIT Press.

Bailey, John (1988) *Governing Mexico: The Statecraft of Crisis Management*. New York: St. Martin's Press.

Banks, Jeffrey and Roderick Kiewiet (1989) "Explaining Patterns of Candidate Competition in Congressional Elections" *American Journal of Political Science* 33, 4: 997–1015.

Barnes, Samuel and Roy Pierce (1971) "Public Opinion and Political Preference in France and Italy" *Midwest Journal of Political Science* 15, 4: 643–660.

Bartels, Larry (1986) "Issue Voting Under Uncertainty: An Empirical Test" *American Journal of Political Science* 30, 4 (November): 709–728.

Bartra, Roger (1987) *La jaula de la melancolía: identidad y metamorfosis del mexicano*. Mexico: Grijalbo.

Bartra, Roger (1989) "Changes in Political Culture: The Crisis of Nationalism" in W. Cornelius, J. Gentleman, and P. Smith (eds.) *Mexico's Alternative Political Futures*. La Jolla: Center for U.S.-Mexican Studies.

Basáñez, Miguel (1983) *La lucha por la hegemonía en México, 1968–1980*. Mexico City: Siglo Veintiuno.

Basáñez, Miguel (1996) *El pulso de los sexenios: 20 años de crisis en México*. Mexico City: Siglo Veintiuno.

Beck, Thorsten, George Clarke, Alberto Groff, Philip Keefer, and Patrick Walsh (2001) "New Tools in Comparative Political Economy: The Database of Political Institutions" *World Bank Economic Review* 15 (February): 165–176.

Berton, Peter (2000) "Japanese Communist Party: The 'Lovable' Party" in R. Hrebenar *Japan's New Party System*. Boulder: Westview Press.

Besley, Timothy and Steven Coate (1997) "An Economic Model of Representative Democracy" *Quarterly Journal of Economics* 112, 1: 85–114.

Blondel, Jean (1972) *Comparing Political Systems*. New York: Praeger.

Boix, Carles (1998) *Political Parties, Growth and Equality*. New York: Cambridge University Press.

Boix, Carles (2003) *Democracy and Redistribution*. New York: Cambridge University Press.

Boix, Carles and Susan Stokes (2003) "Endogenous Democratization" *World Politics* 55, 4 (July): 517–549.

Borjas Benavente, Adriana (2003) *Partido de la Revolución Democrática: Estructura, organización interna y desempeño público, 1989–2003*. Mexico City: Gernika.

References 313

Bortolotti, Bernardo (2005) "Italy's Privatization Process and its Implications for China" Fondazione Eni Enrico Mattei Working Paper No. 118, Milan, Italy.

Bouton, Lawrence and Mariusz Sumlinski (2000) "Trends in Private Investment in Developing Countries" *International Finance Corporation Paper 41.* Washington, DC: World Bank.

Brandenburg, Frank (1956) *Mexico: An Experiment in One-Party Democracy.* Philadelphia: University of Pennsylvania.

Brandenburg, Frank (1964) *The Making of Modern Mexico.* Englewood Cliffs, NJ: Prentice Hall.

Brody, David and Benjamin Page (1972) "Comment: The Assessment of Policy Voting" *American Political Science Review* 66, 2 (June): 450–458.

Brooker, Paul (2000) *Non-Democratic Regimes: Theory, Government and Politics.* New York: St. Martin's Press.

Brownlee, Jason (2005) "Ruling Parties and Durable Authoritarianism" Working Paper No. 23, Center on Democracy, Development, and the Rule of Law, Stanford University.

Bruhn, Kathleen (1996) "Social Spending and Political Support: The 'Lessons' of the National Solidarity Program in Mexico" *Comparative Politics* 28, 2: 151–177.

Bruhn, Kathleen (1997) *Taking on Goliath: The Emergence of a New Left Party and the Struggle for Democracy in Mexico.* University Park: Pennsylvania State University Press.

Bruhn, Kathleen (2000) "The Importance of Being Cuauhtémoc: The 2000 Presidential Campaign of the PRD." University of California, Santa Barbara, mimeo.

Bruhn, Kathleen (2001) "Party Ideological Placement and the Left-Right Cleavage: A Reassessment from the South." University of California, Santa Barbara, mimeo.

Bruhn, Kathleen (2004) "The Making of the Mexican President 2000: Parties, Candidates, and Campaign Strategy" in J. Domínguez and C. Lawson (eds.) *Mexico's Pivotal Democratic Election.* Stanford: Stanford University Press.

Bruhn, Kathleen and Kenneth F. Greene (2007) "Elite Polarization Meets Mass Moderation in Mexico's 2006 Elections" *PS: Political Science and Politics* 40, 1 (January): 33–37.

Bruno, Giovanni and Luciano Segreto (1996) "Finanza e industria in Italia, 1963–1995" in F. Barbagallo (ed.) *L'Italia nella crisi mondiale: L'ultimo ventennio. Storia dell'Italia repubblicana Vol. 3, No. 1. Economia e società.* Turin, Italy: Einaudi.

Buendía, Jorge (2004) "The Changing Mexican Voter, 1991–2000" in K. Middlebrook (ed.) *Dilemmas of Political Change in Mexico.* London: Institute of Latin American Studies, University of London.

Cain, Bruce, John Ferejohn, and Morris Fiorina (1987) *The Personal Vote: Constituency Service and Electoral Independence.* New York: Cambridge University Press.

Calder, Kent (1988) *Crisis and Compensation: Public Policy and Political Stability in Japan.* Princeton: Princeton University Press.

314   *References*

Camp, Roderic (1995) *Political Recruitment across Two Centuries: Mexico, 1884–1991*. Austin: University of Texas Press.

Camp, Roderic (2003) *Politics in Mexico*. 4th ed. Oxford: Oxford University Press.

Campbell, John (1989) "Democracy and Bureaucracy in Japan" in T. Ishida and E. Krauss (eds.) *Democracy in Japan*. Pittsburgh: University of Pittsburgh Press.

Carey, John and Mathew Shugart (1995) "Incentives to Cultivate a Personal Vote: A Rank Ordering of Electoral Formulas" *Electoral Studies* 14, 4: 417–439.

Carothers, Thomas (2002) "The End of the Transition Paradigm" *Journal of Democracy* 13, 1: 5–21.

Carr, Barry (1985) *Mexican Communism, 1968–1983: Eurocommunism in the Americas?* La Jolla: Center for U.S.-Mexican Studies.

Carr, Barry (1992) *Marxism and Communism in Twentieth-Century Mexico*. Lincoln: University of Nebraska Press.

Case, William (2001) "Malaysia's Resilient Pseudodemocracy" *Journal of Democracy* 12, 1: 43–57.

Castañeda, Jorge (2000) *Perpetuating Power: How Mexican Presidents Were Chosen*. New York: The New Press.

Castles, Francis and Peter Mair (1984) "Left-Right Political Scales: Some Expert Judgments" *European Journal of Political Research* 12, 83–88.

Centeno, Miguel (1994) *Democracy within Reason: Technocratic Revolution in Mexico*. University Park: Pennsylvania State University Press.

Chand, Vikram (2001) *Mexico's Political Awakening*. Notre Dame: University of Notre Dame Press.

Chandra, Kanchan (2004) *Why Ethnic Parties Succeed*. New York: Cambridge University Press.

Charlesworth, James (1948) "Is Our Two-Party System Natural?" *Annals of the American Academy of Political and Social Science* 259: 1–9.

Chaudhry, Kiren (1997) *The Price of Wealth: Economies and Institutions in the Middle East*. Ithaca: Cornell University Press.

Cheng, Tun-jen (2001) "One-Party Hegemony and Democratic Transition: Comparing Mexico, Taiwan and Turkey." Paper prepared for presentation at Conference on The Rise of the DPP and PAN in Taiwan and Mexico, Duke University, January 26–27.

Chhibber, Pradeep (2001) *Democracy without Associations*. Ann Arbor: University of Michigan Press.

Chong, Dennis (1991) *Collective Action and the Civil Rights Movement*. Chicago: University of Chicago Press.

Chong, Dennis (2000) *Rational Lives: Norms and Values in Politics and Society*. Chicago: University of Chicago Press.

Christensen, Ray (2000) *Ending the LDP Hegemony: Party Cooperation in Japan*. Honolulu: University of Hawaii Press.

Chu, Yun-han (2001) "The Legacy of One-Party Hegemony in Taiwan" in L. Diamond and R. Gunther (eds.) *Political Parties and Democracy*. Baltimore: Johns Hopkins University Press.

Chua, Huat Beng (2001) "Defeat of the KMT: Implications for One-Party Quasi-Democratic Regimes in Southeast Asia" in M. Alagappa (ed.) *Taiwan's*

Presidential Politics: Democratization and Cross-Strait Relations in the Twenty-First Century. New York: M. E. Sharpe.

Clark, Peter and James Wilson (1961) "Incentive Systems: A Theory of Organizations" *Administrative Studies Quarterly* 6: 129–166.

Cline, Howard (1962) *Mexico: Revolution to Evolution, 1940–1960*. London: Oxford University Press.

Coleman, James (1960) "The Politics of Sub-Saharan Africa" in G. Almond and J. Coleman (eds.) *The Politics of Developing Areas*. Princeton: Princeton University Press.

Collier, Ruth Berins and David Collier (1991) *Shaping the Political Arena*. Princeton: Princeton University Press.

Collier, Ruth Berins (1992) *The Contradictory Alliance: State-Labor Relations and Regime Change in Mexico*. Berkeley: International and Area Studies, University of California.

Conover, Pamela Johnston and Stanley Feldman (1989) "Candidate Perception in an Ambiguous World: Campaigns, Cues, and Inference Processes" *American Journal of Political Science* 33, 4 (November): 912–940.

Cornelius, Wayne (1975) *Politics and the Migrant Poor in Mexico City*. Stanford: Stanford University Press.

Cornelius, Wayne (2004) "Mobilized Voting in the 2000 Elections: The Changing Efficacy of Vote Buying and Coercion in Mexican Electoral Politics" in J. Domínguez and C. Lawson (eds.) *Mexico's Pivotal Democratic Election*. Stanford: Stanford University Press.

Cornelius, Wayne and Ann Craig (1991) *The Mexican Political System in Transition*. Monograph 35, Center for U.S.-Mexican Studies.

Cotton, James (1997) "East Asian Democracy: Progress and Limits" in L. Diamond, M. Plattner, Y. Chu, and H. Tien (eds.) *Consolidating the Third Wave Democracies*. Baltimore: Johns Hopkins University Press.

Coulon, Christian (1990) "Senegal: The Development and Fragility of Semidemocracy" in L. Diamond, J. Linz, and S. M. Lipset (eds.) *Politics in Developing Countries: Comparing Experiences with Democracy*. Boulder: Lynne Rienner.

Cover, Albert and Bruce Brumberg (1982) "Baby Books and Ballots: The Impact of Congressional Mail on Constituent Opinion" *American Political Science Review* 76, 2: 347–359.

Cox, Gary (1987) "The Uncovered Set and the Core" *American Journal of Political Science* 31, 2: 408–422.

Cox, Gary (1990) "Centripetal and Centrifugal Incentives in Electoral Systems" *American Journal of Political Science* 34, 4 (November): 903–935.

Cox, Gary (1996) "Is the Single Nontransferable Vote Superproportional: Evidence from Japan and Taiwan" *American Journal of Political Science* 40, 3 (August): 740–755.

Cox, Gary (1997) *Making Votes Count*. New York: Cambridge University Press.

Crespo, José Antonio (1996) *Votar en los estados: Análisis comparado de las legislaciones electorales estatales en México*. Mexico City: Fundación Friedrich Naumann.

316 References

Cross, John (1998) *Informal Politics: Street Vendors and the State in Mexico City*. Stanford: Stanford University Press.

Crouch, Harold (1996) *Government and Society in Malaysia*. Ithaca: Cornell University Press.

Cuéllar Vázquez, Angélica (1993) *La noche es de ustedes, el amanecer es nuestro: Asamblea de Barrios y Superbarrio Gómez en la Ciudad de México*. Mexico City: National Autonomous University of Mexico.

Curtis, Gerald (1971) *Election Campaigning, Japanese Style*. New York: Columbia University Press.

Curtis, Gerald (1988) *The Japanese Way of Politics*. New York: Columbia University Press.

Curtis, Gerald (1999) *The Japanese Logic of Politics*. New York: Columbia University Press.

Dahl, Robert (1992) "Why Free Markets Are Not Enough" *Journal of Democracy* 3, 3 (July): 82–89.

Davis, Otto, Melvin Hinich, and Peter Ordeshook (1970) "An Expository Development of a Mathematical Model of the Electoral Process" *American Political Science Review* 64: 426–448.

de Palma, André, Gap-Seon Hong, and Jean-Francoise Thisse (1990) "Equilibria in Multi-Party Competition under Uncertainty" *Social Choice and Welfare* 7: 247–259.

della Porta, Donatella and Alberto Vannucci (1999) *Corrupt Exchanges: Actors, Resources, and Mechanisms of Political Corruption*. New York: Aldine and Gruyter.

della Porta, Donatella and Alberto Vannucci (2000) "Corruption and Political Financing in Italy" Transparency International Workshop on Corruption and Political Financing. http://www.transparency.org/working_papers/country/italy_paper.html

Deininger, Klaus and Lyn Squire (1996) "A New Data Set Measuring Income Inequality" *World Bank Economic Review* 10, 3: 565–591.

di Palma, Giuseppe (1980) "The Available State: Problems of Reform" in P. Lange and S. Tarrow (eds.) *Italy in Transition*. London: Frank Cass.

Diamond, Larry (2001) "Anatomy of an Electoral Earthquake: How the KMT Lost and the DPP Won the 2000 Presidential Election" in M. Alagappa (ed.) *Taiwan's Presidential Politics*. Armonk, NY: M. E. Sharpe.

Diamond, Larry (2002) "Thinking about Hybrid Regimes" *Journal of Democracy* 13, 2 (April): 21–35.

Diaw, Aminata and Mamadou Diouf (1998) "The Senegalese Opposition and its Quest for Power" in A. Olukoshi (ed.) *The Politics of Opposition in Contemporary Africa*. Stockholm: Uppsala.

Díaz-Cayeros, Alberto (1997) "Asignación política de recursos en el federalismo mexicano: Incentivos y restricciones" *Perfiles Latinoamericanos* 6, 10: 35–74.

Díaz-Cayeros, Alberto, Federico Estévez, Beatriz Magaloni (2001) "A Portfolio Diversification Model of Electoral Investment: Competition and Policy Choice in Mexico's PRONASOL, 1989–1994" American Political Science Association Annual Meeting, San Francisco, August 30–September 2.

Dillon, Samuel (2000) "Mexico's Ruling Party Accused of Diverting Public Money" *New York Times*, March 27, 2000: A6.

Domínguez, Jorge and James McCann (1996) *Democratizing Mexico: Public Opinion and Electoral Choices*. Baltimore: Johns Hopkins University Press.

Dow, Jay and James Endersby (2004) "Multinomial Probit and Multinomial Logit: A Comparison of Choice Models for Voting Research" *Electoral Studies* 23: 107–122.

Downs, Anthony (1957) *An Economic Theory of Democracy*. New York: Harper and Row.

Dresser, Denise (1991) *Neopopulist Solutions to Neoliberal Problems: Mexico's National Solidarity Program*. La Jolla: Center for U.S.-Mexican Studies.

Duverger, Maurice (1954) *Political Parties: Their Organization and Activity in the Modern State*. Translated by Barbara and Robert North. New York: Wiley.

Ebenstein, William (1945) "Public Administration in Mexico" *Public Administration Review* 5, 2 (Spring): 102–112.

Eckstein, Susan (1977) *The Poverty of Revolution: The State and the Urban Poor in Mexico*. Princeton: Princeton University Press.

Eisenstadt, Shmuel and Luis Roniger (1981) "The Study of Patron-Client Relations and Recent Developments in Sociological Theory" in S. N. Eisenstadt and René Lémarchand (eds.), *Political clientelism, Patronage, and Development*. Beverly Hills: Sage.

Eisenstadt, Todd (1999) "Electoral Justice in Mexico: From Oxymoron to Legal Norm in Less Than a Decade," *Third International Congress on Electoral Law*, National Autonomous University of Mexico, UNAM-IIJ, Mexico City.

Eisenstadt, Todd (2004) *Courting Democracy in Mexico: Party Strategies and Electoral Institutions*. New York: Cambridge University Press.

Enelow, James and Melvin Hinich (1982) "Nonspatial Candidate Characteristics and Electoral Competition" *Journal of Politics* 44: 115–130.

Epstein, Leon (1986) *Political Parties in the American Mold*. Madison: University of Wisconsin Press.

Esping-Andersen, Gøsta (1985) *Politics against Markets: The Social Democratic Road to Power*. Princeton: Princeton University Press.

Esping-Andersen, Gøsta (1990) "Single-Party Dominance in Sweden: The Saga of Social Democracy" in T. J. Pempel (ed.) *Uncommon Democracies: The One-Party Dominant Regimes*. Ithaca: Cornell University Press.

Eyton, Laurence (2002) "Taiwan opposition shoots itself in the foot" *Asia Times*, June 29. http://www.atimes.com/china/DF29Ad01.html.

Farneti, Paolo (1985) *The Italian Party System, 1945–1980*. New York: St. Martin's Press.

Feddersen Timothy, Itai Sened, and Stephen Wright (1990) "Rational Voting and Candidate Entry under Plurality Rule" *American Journal of Political Science* 34, 4: 1005–1016.

Féher, Ferenc, Agnes Heller, and Gyorgy Markus (1983) *Dictatorship over Needs*. London: Basil Blackwell.

Ferdinand, Peter (1998) "Party Funding and Political Corruption in East Asia: The Cases of Japan, South Korea and Taiwan" in R. Austin and M. Tjernström (eds.)

318 *References*

Funding of Political Parties and Election Campaigns. Stockholm: International Institute for Democracy and Electoral Assistance.

Fields, Karl (1998) "KMT, Inc. Party Capitalism in a Developmental State" JPRI Working Paper No. 47 (June).

Fiorina, Morris (1981) *Retrospective Voting in American National Elections.* New Haven: Yale University Press.

Fischer, Bernhard, Egbert Gerken, and Ulrich Hiemenz (1982) *Growth, Employment, and Trade in an Industrializing Economy: A Quantitative Analysis of Mexican Development Policies.* Tubingen: J. C. B. Mohr.

Fish, Steven (1995) *Democracy from Scratch: Opposition and Regime in the New Russian Revolution.* Princeton: Princeton University Press.

Fitzgibbon, Russell (1951) "Measurement of Latin-American Political Phenomena: A Statistical Experiment" *American Political Science Review* 45, 2 (June): 517–523.

Garretón, Manuel Antonio (1989) *The Chilean Political Process.* Boston: Unwin Hyman.

Garrido, Luis Javier (1987) "Un partido sin militantes" in S. Loaeza and R. Segovia (eds.) *La vida política mexicana en la crisis.* Mexico City: El Colegio de México.

Geddes, Barbara (1994) *Politician's Dilemma: Building State Capacity in Latin America.* Berkeley: University of California Press.

Geddes, Barbara (1999a) "What Do We Know About Democratization After Twenty Years?" *Annual Review of Political Science* 2: 115–144.

Geddes, Barbara (1999b) "Authoritarian Breakdown: Empirical Test of a Game Theoretic Argument" American Political Science Association, Atlanta, September 2–5.

Geddes, Barbara (2003) *Paradigms and Sand Castles: Theory Building and Research Design in Comparative Politics.* Ann Arbor: University of Michigan Press.

Gerschenkron, Alexander (1962) *Economic Backwardness in Historical Perspective.* Cambridge, MA: Harvard University Press.

Givens, Terri (2005) *Voting Radical Right in Western Europe.* New York: Cambridge University Press.

Golden, Miriam (2000) "Political Patronage, Bureaucracy and Corruption in Postwar Italy." Working Paper without number. Russell Sage Foundation.

Golden, Miriam (2004) "International Economic Sources of Regime Change: How European Integration Undermined Italy's Postwar Party System" *Comparative Political Studies* 37, 10 (December): 1238–1274.

Gomez, Edmund (1991) *Money Politics in the Barisan Nasional.* Kuala Lumpur: Forum.

Gomez, Edmund (1994) *Political Business: Corporate Involvement in Malaysian Political Parties.* Cairns: James Cook University Press.

Gomez, Edmund (2002) "Political Business in Malaysia: Party Factionalism, Corporate Development, and Economic Crisis" in E. Gomez (ed.) *Political Business in Asia.* New York: Routledge.

Gómez, Leopoldo and John Bailey (1990) "La transición política y los dilemas del PRI" *Foro Internacional* 31, 1: 57–87.

González Casanova, Pablo (1965) *La democracia en México*. Mexico City: Era.

Goodliffe, Jay (2001) "The Effect of War Chests on Challenger Entry in U.S. House Elections" *American Journal of Political Science* 45, 4: 830–844.

Green, Donald and Jonathan Krasno (1988) "Salvation for the Spendthrift Incumbent: Reestimating the Effects of Campaign Spending in House Elections" *American Journal of Political Science* 32, 4: 884–907.

Greenberg, Joseph and Kenneth Shepsle (1987) "The Effects of Electoral Rewards in Multiparty Competition with Entry" *American Political Science Review* 81: 525–537.

Greene, Kenneth F. (1997) "Complejidad, cohesión y longevidad en un movimiento urbano popular: La Asamblea de Barrios de la Ciudad de México" in S. Zermeño (ed.) *Movimientos sociales e identidades colectivas en México*. Mexico City: UNAM-IIS.

Greene, Kenneth F. (2002a) "Opposition Party Strategy and Spatial Competition in Dominant Party Regimes: A Theory and the Case of Mexico" *Comparative Political Studies* 35, 7 (September): 755–783.

Greene, Kenneth F. (2002b) *Defeating Dominance: Opposition Party Building and Democratization in Mexico*. Unpublished Ph.D. Dissertation, Department of Political Science, University of California, Berkeley.

Greene, Kenneth F. (2008) "Dominant Party Strategy and Democratization" *American Journal of Political Science* 52, 1 (January) 2008: 16–31.

Greene, Kenneth F., Joseph Klesner, and Chappell Lawson (2004) "How to Win a Mexican Election (Legally): Campaign Effects in a New Democracy" Latin American Studies Association, Las Vegas, Nevada, October 7–9.

Grindle, Merilee (1977) *Bureaucrats, Politicians, and Peasants in Mexico: A Case Study in Public Policy*. Berkeley: University of California Press.

Groseclose, Tim (2001) "A Model of Candidate Location When One Candidate Has a Valence Advantage" *American Journal of Political Science* 45, 4 (October): 862–886.

Grzymala-Busse, Anna (2002) *Redeeming the Communist Past: The Regeneration of Communist Parties in East Central Europe*. Cambridge: Cambridge University Press.

Guillermoprieto, Alma (1994) *The Heart that Bleeds: Latin America Now*. New York: Knopf.

Guzzini, Stefano (1994) "The Implosion of Clientelistic Italy in the 1990s" Working Paper No. 94/12, European University Institute, Florence, Italy.

Haber, Paul (1997) "¡Vamos por la dignidad de Durango! Un estudio del poder sociopolítico" in S. Zermeño (ed.) *Movimientos sociales e identidades colectivas en México*. Mexico City: UNAM-IIS.

Haber, Paul (2006) *Power from Experience: Urban Popular Movements in Late Twentieth-Century Mexico*. University Park: Pennsylvania State University Press.

Haggard, Stephan and Robert Kaufman (1995) *The Political Economy of Democratic Transitions*. Princeton: Princeton University Press.

Hartz, Louis (1955) *The Liberal Tradition in America: An Interpretation of American Political Thought Since the Revolution*. New York: Harcourt Brace.

Hechter, Michael (1987) *Principles of Group Solidarity*. Berkeley: University of California Press.

Hellman, Judith Adler (1983) *Mexico in Crisis*. 2nd ed. New York: Holmes and Meier.

Hellman Judith Adler (1994) "Mexican Popular Movements, Clientelism, and the Process of Democratization." *Latin American Perspectives* 21, 2: 124–142.

Hellman, Stephen (1975) "Generational Differences in the Bureaucratic Elite of Italian Communist Provincial Federations" *Canadian Journal of Political Science* 1: 82–106.

Hine, David (1987) "Italy: Parties and Government under Pressure" in A. Ware (ed.) *Political Parties*. London: Blackwell.

Hinich, Melvin and Michael Munger (1997) *Analytical Politics*. New York: Cambridge University Press.

Hirschman, Albert (1970) *Exit, Voice, and Loyalty: Responses to Declines of Firms, Organizations, and States*. Cambridge: Harvard University Press.

Holm, John (1987) "Elections in Botswana: Institutionalization of a New System of Legitimacy" in F. M. Hayward (ed.) *Elections in Independent Africa*. Boulder: Westview Press.

Howard, Marc and Phillip Roessler (2006) "Liberalizing Electoral Outcomes in Competitive Authoritarian Regimes" *American Journal of Political Science* 50, 2 (April): 365–381.

Hrebenar, Ronald (2000) *Japan's New Party System*. Boulder: Westview Press.

Hsieh, John Fuh-sheng, Dean Lacy, and Emerson Niou (1998) "Retrospective and prospective voting in a one-party-dominant democracy: Taiwan's 1996 presidential election" *Public Choice* 97: 383–399.

Huang, Teh-fu and Ching-shin Yu (1999) "Developing a Party System and Democratic Consolidation" in S. Tsang and H. Tien (eds.) *Democratization in Taiwan: Implications for China*. New York: St. Martin's Press.

Hug, Simon (2001) *Altering Party Systems*. Ann Arbor: University of Michigan Press.

Huntington, Samuel (1970) "Social and Institutional Dynamics of One-Party Systems" in S. Huntington and C. Moore (eds.) *Authoritarian Politics in Modern Society: The Dynamics of Established One-Party Dominant Systems*. New York: Basic Books.

Huntington, Samuel and Clement Moore (1970) "Conclusion: Authoritarianism, Democracy, and One-Party Politics" in S. Huntington and C. Moore (eds.) *Authoritarian Politics in Modern Society: The Dynamics of Established One-Party Dominant Systems*. New York: Basic Books.

Inoguchi, Takashi (1990) "The Political Economy of Conservative Resurgence under Recession: Public Policies and Political Support in Japan, 1977–1983" in T. J. Pempel (ed.) *Uncommon Democracies: The One-Party Dominant Regimes*. Ithaca: Cornell University Press.

Jackson, John (1999) "Electoral Competition with Endogenous Activists" American Political Science Association Annual Meeting, Atlanta, Georgia, September 2–5.

Jacobson, Gary (1980) *Money in Congressional Politics*. New Haven: Yale University Press.

References

Jacobson, Gary and Samuel Kernell (1981) *Strategy and Choice in Congressional Elections*. New Haven: Yale University Press.

Johnson, Chalmers (1982) *MITI and the Japanese Miracle: The Growth of Industrial Policy, 1925–1975*. Stanford: Stanford University Press.

Johnson, Kenneth (1965) "Ideological Correlates of Right Wing Political Alienation in Mexico" *American Political Science Review* 59, 3 (September): 656–664.

Johnson, Kenneth (1978) *Mexican Democracy: A Critical View*. New York: Praeger.

Johnston, Richard, André Blais, Henry Brady, and Jean Crête (1992) *Letting the People Decide: Dynamics of a Canadian Election*. Stanford: Stanford University Press.

Jones, Mark and Scott Mainwaring (2003) "The Nationalization of Parties and Party Systems: An Empirical Measure and an Application to the Americas" *Party Politics* 9 (March): 139–166.

Jowitt, Kenneth (1992) *New World Disorder: The Leninist Extinction*. Berkeley: University of California Press.

Kalyvas, Stathis (1996) *The Rise of Christian Democracy in Europe*. Ithaca: Cornell University Press.

Karl, Terry (1986) "Imposing Consent? Electoralism vs. Democratization in El Salvador" in P. Drake and E. Silva (eds.) *Elections in Latin America*. La Jolla: Institute of Latin American Studies, University of California, San Diego.

Karl, Terry and Philippe Schmitter (1991) "What Democracy Is ... And Is Not" *Journal of Democracy* 2 (Summer): 75–89.

Katz, Richard and Peter Mair (1995) "Changing Models of Party Organization and Party Democracy: The Emergence of the Cartel Party" *Party Politics* 1, 1: 5–28.

Kaufman Purcell, Susan (1973) "Decision-Making in an Authoritarian Regime: Theoretical Implications from a Mexican Case Study" in *World Politics* 26, 1 (October): 28–54.

Kessler, Timothy (1999) *Global Capital and National Politics: Reforming Mexico's Financial System*. Westport: Praeger.

Key, V. O. (1964a) *Southern Politics in State and Nation*. New York: Knopf.

Key, V. O. (1964b) *Politics, Parties, and Pressure Groups*. New York: Crowell.

Key, V. O. (1966) *The Responsible Electorate: Rationality in Presidential Voting, 1936–1960*. Cambridge: Belknap Press of Harvard University Press.

King, Gary, Robert Keohane, and Sidney Verba (1994) *Designing Social Inquiry*. Princeton: Princeton University Press.

King, Gary, Michael Tomz, and Jason Wittenberg (2000) "Making the Most of Statistical Analyses: Improving Interpretation and Presentation" *American Journal of Political Science* 44, 2 (April): 347–61.

Kirchheimer, Otto (1966) "The Transformation of West European Party Systems" in J. LaPalambara and M. Weiner (eds.) *Political Parties and Political Development*. Princeton: Princeton University Press.

Kitschelt, Herbert (1989a) *The Logics of Party Formation: Ecological Politics in Belgium and West Germany*. Ithaca: Cornell University Press.

Kitschelt, Herbert (1989b) "The Internal Politics of Parties: The Law of Curvilinear Disparity Revisited" *Political Studies* 37, 3: 400–421.

Kitschelt, Herbert (1990) *Beyond the European Left: Ideology and Political Action in the Belgian Ecology Parties*. Durham: Duke University Press.

Kitschelt, Herbert (1994) *The Transformation of European Social Democracy*. New York: Cambridge University Press.

Kitschelt, Herbert (1995) *The Radical Right in Western Europe*. Ann Arbor: University of Michigan Press.

Kitschelt, Herbert (2000) "Linkages between Citizens and Politicians in Democratic Polities" *Comparative Political Studies* 33, 6/7 (August/September): 845–879.

Kitschelt, Herbert and Steve Wilkinson (eds.) (2007) *Patrons, Clients and Policies: Patterns of Democratic Accountability and Political Competition*. Cambridge: Cambridge University Press.

Klesner, Joseph (1994) "Realignment or Dealignment? Consequences of Economic Crisis and Restructuring for the Mexican Party System" in M. Cook, K. Middlebrook, and J. Molinar (eds.) *Politics of Economic Restructuring: State–Society Relations and Regime Change in Mexico*. La Jolla: Center for U.S.–Mexican Studies.

Klesner, Joseph (1997) "Electoral Reform in Mexico's Hegemonic Party System: Perpetuation of Privilege or Democratic Advance?" American Political Science Association Annual Meeting, Washington, DC, August 28–31.

Kollman, Kenneth, John Miller, and Scott Page (1992) "Adaptive Parties in Spatial Elections" *American Political Science Review* 86, 4: 929–937.

Kostoris, Fiorella (1993) *Italy: The Sheltered Economy*. Oxford: Oxford University Press.

Krauze, Enrique (1997) *Mexico, Biography of Power: A History of Modern Mexico, 1810–1996*, Translated by Hank Heifetz. New York: HarperCollins.

Kuo, Chengtian (2000) "New Financial Politics in Taiwan, Thailand, and Malaysia," Department of Political Science, National Chengchi University, http://www.la.utexas.edu/research/cgots/ accessed 9/2305.

Kuran, Timur (1991) "Now out of Never: The Element of Surprise in the East European Revolution of 1989" *World Politics* 44 (October): 7–48.

Laakso, Markku and Rein Taagapera (1979) "Effective Number of Parties: A Measure with Application to West Europe" *Comparative Political Studies* 12: 3–27.

Langston, Joy (2001) "Why Rules Matter: Changes in Candidate Selection in Mexico's PRI, 1988–2000" *Journal of Latin American Studies* 33: 485–511.

LaPalombara, Joseph (1964) *Interest Groups in Italian Politics*. Princeton: Princeton University Press.

Laver, Michael and Norman Schofield (1990) *Multiparty Government*. Oxford: Oxford University Press.

Lawson, Chappell (2002) *Building the Fourth Estate: Democratization and the Rise of a Free Press in Mexico*. Berkeley: University of California Press.

Lawson, Chappell (2004) "Television Coverage, Vote Choice, and the 2000 Campaign" in J. Domínguez and C. Lawson (eds.) *Mexico's Pivotal Democratic Election*. Stanford: Stanford University Press.

Lehoucq, Fabrice (2003) "Electoral Fraud: Causes, Types, and Consequences" *Annual Review of Political Science* 6: 233–256.

References

Levite, Ariel and Sydney Tarrow (1983) "The Legitimation of Excluded Parties in Dominant Party Systems: A Comparison of Israel and Italy" *Comparative Politics* 15, 3 (April): 295–327.

Levitsky, Steven (2003) *Transforming Labor-Based Parties in Latin America: Argentine Peronism in Comparative Perspective.* New York: Cambridge University Press.

Levitsky, Steven and Lucan Way (2002) "The Rise of Competitive Authoritarianism" *Journal of Democracy* 13, 2: 51–65.

Levitsky, Steven and Lucan Way (2006) "Competitive Authoritarianism: The Origins and Evolution of Hybrid Regimes after the Cold War." Unpublished manuscript of chapters 1 and 2, Harvard University and University of Toronto.

Levitt, Steven and Catherine Wolfram (1997) "Decomposing the Sources of Incumbency Advantage in the U.S. House" *Legislative Studies Quarterly* 22: 45–60.

Lichbach, Mark (1996) *The Cooperator's Dilemma.* Ann Arbor: University of Michigan Press.

Lichbach, Mark (1998) *The Rebel's Dilemma.* Ann Arbor: University of Michigan Press.

Lin, Oliver (2000) "Lien wants KMT assets put in trust" *Taipei Times*, January 3: A1.

Lin, Tse-min, James Enelow, and Han Dorussen (1999) "Equilibrium in Multi-candidate Probabilistic Voting" *Public Choice* 98: 59–82.

Lin, Tse-min (2007) "The 'Minumum-Sum Point' as a Solution Concept in Spatial Voting" Paper presented at the Midwest Political Science Association meeting, Chicago IL, April 12–15.

Linz, Juan and Arturo Valenzuela (eds.) (1994) *The Failure of Presidential Democracy.* Baltimore: Johns Hopkins University Press.

Lipset, Seymour Martin (ed.) (1998) *Democracy in Europe and the Americas.* Washington, DC: Congressional Quarterly.

Lipset, Seymour Martin and Stein Rokkan (1967) "Cleavage Structures, Party Systems, and Voter Alignments: An Introduction" in S. M. Lipset and S. Rokkan (eds.) *Party Systems and Voter Alignments: Cross–National Perspectives.* New York: Free Press.

Lipson, Leslie (1953) "The Two–Party System in British Politics" *American Political Science Review* 47: 337–358.

Liu, I-chou (1999) "The Development of the Opposition" in S. Tsang and H. Tien (eds.) *Democratization in Taiwan: Implications for China.* New York: St. Martin's Press.

Loaeza, Soledad (1999) *El Partido Acción Nacional, la larga marcha, 1939–1994: Oposición leal y partido de protesta.* Mexico City: Fonda de Cultura Económica.

Locke, Richard (1995) *Remaking the Italian Economy.* Ithaca: Cornell University Press.

Londregan, John and Tom Romer (1993) "Polarization, Incumbency and the Personal Vote" in W. Barnett, M. Hinich and N. Schofield (eds.) *Political Economy: Institutions, Competition and Representation.* New York: Cambridge University Press.

324   *References*

Lujambio, Alonso (2000) *El poder compartido: Un ensayo sobre la democratización mexicana*. Mexico City: Oceano.

Lujambio, Alonso (2001) "Dinero y democratización: El financiamiento y la fiscalización de los partidos políticos en la transición mexicana a la democracia, 1988–2000." International Seminar on Money and Electoral Competition: Challenges for Democracy, Federal Elections Institute, Mexico City, June 5–8.

Lustig, Nora (1992) *Mexico: the Remaking of an Economy*. Washington, DC: The Brookings Institution.

Mabry, Donald (1973) *Mexico's Acción Nacional: A Catholic Alternative to Revolution*. Syracuse: Syracuse University Press.

MacLeod, Dag (2004) *Downsizing the State: Privatization and the Limits of Neoliberal Reform in Mexico*. University Park: Pennsylvania State University Press.

Magaloni, Beatriz (1996) "Dominancia de partido y dilemas duvergerianos en las elecciones federales de 1994" *Política y Gobierno* 3, 2: 281–326.

Magaloni, Beatriz (1997) *The Dynamics Of Dominant Party Decline: The Mexican Transition To Multipartyism*. Unpublished Ph.D. Dissertation, Department of Political Science, Duke University.

Magaloni, Beatriz (2006) *Voting for Autocracy: Hegemonic Party Survival and its Demise in Mexico*. New York: Cambridge University Press.

Magaloni, Beatriz and Alejandro Poiré (2004a) "The Issues, the Vote, and the Mandate for Change" in J. Domínguez and C. Lawson (eds.) *Mexico's Pivotal Democratic Election*. Stanford: Stanford University Press.

Magaloni, Beatriz and Alejandro Poiré (2004b) "Strategic Coordination in the 2004 Mexican Presidential Race" in J. Domínguez and C. Lawson (eds.) *Mexico's Pivotal Democratic Election*. Stanford: Stanford University Press.

Magar, Eric and Juan Molinar Horcasitas (1995) "Medios de comunicación y democracia" in J. Alcocer (ed.) *Elecciones, diálogo y reforma en México, 1994, Volume 2*. Mexico City: Nuevo Horizonte.

Mainwaring, Scott (1999) *Rethinking Party Systems in the Third Wave of Democratization: The Case of Brazil*. Stanford: Stanford University Press.

Mair, Peter and Ingrid Van Biezen (2001) "Party Membership in Twenty European Democracies, 1980–2000" *Party Politics* 7, 1: 5–21.

Manikas, Peter and Laura Thornton (2003) *Political Parties in Asia: Promoting Reform and Combating Corruption in Eight Countries*. Washington, DC: National Democratic Institute.

Martínez Valle, Adolfo (1995) *El Partido Acción Nacional: Una historia política, 1939–1976*. Unpublished B.A. thesis, Department of Political Science, Autonomous Technological Institute of Mexico (ITAM), Mexico City.

Martínez Verdugo, Arnoldo (1985) *Historia del comunismo en México*. Mexico City: Grijalbo.

Martínez, Omar (2002) "Datos duros sobre monitoreos de coberturas electorales" http://www.cem.itesm.mx/dacs/buendia/rmc/rmc63/omartinez.html, accessed 10/10/02.

May, John (1973) "Opinion Structures and Political Parties: The Special Law of Curvilinear Disparity" *Political Studies* 21: 135–151.

Mayhew, David (1974) *Congress: The Electoral Connection.* New Haven: Yale University Press.

McCann, James and Chappell Lawson. 2003. "An Electorate Adrift? Public Opinion and the Quality of Democracy in Mexico" *Latin American Research Review* 38, 3 (October): 60–81.

McDonald, Ronald (1971) *Party Systems and Elections in Latin America.* Chicago: Markham.

McKelvey, Richard (1986) "Covering, Dominance, and Institution–Free Properties of Social Choice" *American Journal of Political Science* 30, 2: 283–314.

Means, Gordon Paul (1996) "Soft Authoritarianism in Malaysia and Singapore" *Journal of Democracy* 7, 4 (October): 103–117.

Meguid, Bonnie (2005) "Competition between Unequals: The Role of Mainstream Party Strategy in Niche Party Success" *American Political Science Review* 99, 3 (August): 347–359.

Merino, Mauricio (1996) "De la lealtad individual a la responsabilidad pública" *Revista de Administración Pública* 91: 5–18.

Mershon, Carol and Gianfranco Pasquino (eds.) (1995) *Italian Politics: Ending the First Republic.* Boulder: Westview Press.

Middlebrook, Kevin (1986) "Political Liberalization in an Authoritarian Regime: The Case of Mexico" in G. O'Donnell, P. Schmitter, and L. Whitehead (eds.). *Transitions from Authoritarian Rule: Latin America.* Baltimore: Johns Hopkins University Press.

Middlebrook, Kevin (1995) *The Paradox of Revolution: Labor, The State, and Authoritarianism in Mexico.* Baltimore: The Johns Hopkins University Press.

Miller, Warren and Donald Stokes (1963) "Constituency influence in Congress" *American Political Science Review* 57 (March): 45–56.

Miller, Warren and Kent Jennings (1986) *Parties in Transition: A Longitudinal Study of Party Elites and Party Supporters.* New York: Russell Sage Foundation.

Mizrahi, Yemile (1998) "The Costs of Electoral Success: The Partido Acción Nacional in Mexico" in M. Serrano (ed.). *Governing Mexico: Political Parties and Elections.* London: Institute of Latin American Studies.

Mizrahi, Yemile (2003) *From Martyrdom to Power: The Partido Acción Nacional in Mexico.* Notre Dame: University of Notre Dame Press.

Moctezuma Barragán, Esteban and Andrés Roemer (2001) *A New Public Management in Mexico.* Burlington: Ashgate.

Moe, Terry (1980) The Organization of Interests: Incentives and the Internal Dynamics of Political Interest Groups. Chicago: University of Chicago Press.

Molinar Horcasitas, Juan (1991) *El tiempo de la legitimidad.* Mexico City: Cal y Arena.

Molinar Horcasitas, Juan (2001) "Las elecciones de 1997 en México: Evaluación del sistema de partidos y la reforma electoral en materia de regulación financiera." Conference on Political Parties and Elections, Federal Elections Institute (IFE), Mexico City. http://www.trife.gob.mx/wcongreso/molinarc.html.

Molinar Horcasitas, Juan and Jeffrey Weldon (1994) "Electoral Determinants and Consequences of National Solidarity" in W. Cornelius, A. Craig, and J. Fox (eds.) *Transforming State–Society Relations in Mexico: The National Solidarity Strategy*. La Jolla: Center for U.S.–Mexican Studies.

Moreno, Alejandro (1999) "Ideología y voto: Dimensiones de competencia política en México en los noventa" *Política y Gobierno* 6, 1: 45–81.

Moreno, Alejandro (2003) *El votante mexicano: Democracia, actitudes políticas y conducta electoral*. Mexico City: Fonda de Cultura Económica.

Munro-Kua, Anne (1996) *Authoritarian Populism in Malaysia*. London: MacMillan.

Muramatsu, Michio and Ellis Krauss (1990) "The Dominant Party and Social Coalitions in Japan" in T. J. Pempel (ed.) *Uncommon Democracies: The One-Party Dominant Regimes*. Ithaca: Cornell University Press.

Needler, Martin (1971) *Politics and Society in Mexico*. Albuquerque: University of New Mexico Press.

Niou, Emerson and Peter Ordeshook (1992) "A Game Theoretic Analysis of the Republic of China's Emerging Electoral System" *International Political Science Review* 13, 1: 59–79.

O'Donnell, Guillermo and Philippe Schmitter (1986) *Transitions from Authoritarian Rule: Tentative Conclusions about Uncertain Democracies*. Baltimore: Johns Hopkins University Press.

Olson, Mancur (1971) *The Logic of Collective Action: Public Goods and the Theory of Groups*. Cambridge: Harvard University Press.

Olukoshi, Adebayo (1998) "Introduction" in A. Adebayo (ed.) *The Politics of Opposition in Contemporary Africa*. Uppsala: Nordiska Afrikainstitutet.

Oppenheimer, Andrés (1996) *Bordering on Chaos: Guerrillas, Stockbrokers, Politicians, and Mexico's Road to Prosperity*. Boston: Little, Brown.

Ortiz Pardo, Francisco and Francisco Ortiz Pinchetti (2000) "La meta: 20 millones de votos" *Proceso* 1215 (February 13): 12–24.

Ortiz, Francisco (2002) *Comprender a la gente: Por qué ganó Fox*. Mexico City: Nuevo Siglo.

Osborne, Martin and Al Slivinski (1996) "A Model of Political Competition with Citizen–Candidates" *Quarterly Journal of Economics* 111, 1: 65–96.

Osei-Hwedie, Bertha (2001) "The Political Opposition in Botswana: The Politics of Factionalism and Fragmentation" *Transformation* 45: 57–77.

Otake, Hideo (1990) "Defense Controversies and One–Party Dominance: The Opposition in Japan and West Germany" in T. J. Pempel (ed.) *Uncommon Democracies: The One–Party Dominant Regimes*. Ithaca: Cornell University Press.

Padgett, Leon (1976) *The Mexican Political System*, 2d ed. Boston: Houghton Mifflin.

Palfrey, Thomas (1984) "Spatial Equilibrium with Entry" *Review of Economic Studies* 51, 1: 139–156.

Panebianco, Angelo (1988) *Political Parties: Organization and Power*. New York: Cambridge University Press.

Pempel, T. J. (1990) "Introduction. Uncommon Democracies: The One-Party Dominant Regimes" in T. J. Pempel (ed.) *Uncommon Democracies: The One-Party Dominant Regimes*. Ithaca: Cornell University Press.

Pempel, T. J. (1998) *Regime Shift: Comparative Dynamics of the Japanese Political Economy*. Ithaca: Cornell University Press.

Pignatelli, Andrea (1985) "Italy: The Development of a Late Developing State" in R. Rose (ed.) *Public Employment in Western Nations*. New York: Cambridge University Press.

Poiré, Alejandro (1999) "Retrospective Voting, Partisanship, and Loyalty in Presidential Elections: 1994" in J. Domínguez and A. Poiré (eds.) *Toward Mexico's Democratization*. New York: Routledge.

Pomper, Gerald (1992) *Passions and Interests: Political Party Concepts of American Democracy*. Lawrence: University Press of Kansas.

Prescott, Edward and Michael Visscher (1977) "Sequential Location among Firms with Foresight" *Bell Journal of Economics* 8: 378–393.

Preston, Julia and Samuel Dillon (2004) *Opening Mexico*. New York: Farrar, Straus and Giroux.

Prud'homme, Jean-Francois (1997) "El PRD: Su vida interna y sus elecciones estratégicas." Working Paper No. 39. División de Estudios Políticos, Centro de Investigación y Docencia Económicas (CIDE), Mexico City.

Przeworski, Adam and John Sprague (1986) *Paper Stones: A History of Electoral Socialism*. Chicago: University of Chicago Press.

Przeworski, Adam, Michael Alvarez, José Cheibub, and Fernando Limongi (2000) *Democracy and Development*. New York: Cambridge University Press.

Putnam, Robert (1971) "Studying Elite Political Culture: The Case of 'Ideology'" *American Political Science Review* 65, 3 (September): 651–681.

Putnam, Robert (1975) "The Italian Communist Politician" in D. Blackmer and S. Tarrow (eds.) *Communism in Italy and France*. Princeton: Princeton University Press.

Rahim, Lily (2001) "The Political Agenda Underpinning Economic Policy Formulation in Singapore's Authoritarian Developmental State" in U. Johannen and J. Gomez (eds.) *Democratic Transitions in Asia*. Singapore: Select Publishing.

Ramanadham, V. V. (ed.) (1995) *Privatization and Equity*. New York: Routledge.

Ramírez Saiz, Juan Manuel (1986) *El movimiento urbano popular en México*. Mexico, D.F.: Siglo Veintiuno.

Reed, Steven and Ethan Scheiner (2003) "Electoral Incentives and Policy Preferences: Mixed Motives Behind Party Defections in Japan" *British Journal of Political Science* 33: 469–490.

Reveles Vásquez, Francisco (1996) *El proceso de institucionalización organizativa del Partido Acción Nacional, 1984–1995*. Unpublished Ph.D. Dissertation, Faculty of Political Science, National Autonomous University of Mexico.

Reyna, José Luis and Richard Weinert (eds.) (1977) *Authoritarianism in Mexico*. Philadelphia: Institute for the Study of Human Issues, Inter-American Politics Series.

Richardson, Bradley (1997) *Japanese Democracy: Power, Coordination, and Performance*. New Haven: Yale University Press.

Richardson, Bradley (2001) "Japan's '1955 System' and Beyond" in L. Diamond and R. Gunther (eds.) *Political Parties and Democracy*. Baltimore: Johns Hopkins University Press.

Rigger, Shelley (2001a) *From Opposition to Power: Taiwan's Democratic Progressive Party*. Boulder: Lynne Rienner.

Rigger, Shelley (2001b) "The Democratic Progressive Party in 2000: Obstacles and Opportunities" *China Quarterly* 168: 944–959.

328 *References*

Riker, William (1976) "The Number of Political Parties: A Reexamination of Duverger's Law" *Comparative Politics* 9, 1: 93–106.

Riker, William (1983) "Political Theory and the Art of Heresthetics" in A. Finifter (ed.) *Political Science: The State of the Discipline*. Washington, DC: American Political Science Association.

Rimanelli, Marco (1999) *Comparative Democratization and Peaceful Change in Single-Party-Dominant Countries*. New York: St. Martin's Press.

Rivera Ríos, Miguel Angel (1986) *Crisis y reorganización del capitalismo mexicano, 1960–1985*. Mexico City: Ediciones Era.

Rocha Menocal, Alina (2001) "Do Old Habits Die Hard? A Statistical Exploration of the Politicization of Progresa, Mexico's Latest Federal Poverty-Alleviation Programme, under the Zedillo Administration" *Journal of Latin American Studies* 33, 51: 513–558.

Rodríguez Araujo, Octavio and Carlos Sirvent (2005) *Instituciones electorales y partidos polítocs en México*. Mexico City: Jorale.

Roeder, Philip (2001) "Ethnolinguistic Fractionalization (ELF) Indices, 1961 and 1985." http//:weber.ucsd.edu \ ~proeder \ elf.htm, accessed December 10, 2003.

Rogozinski, Jacques (1993) *La privatización de empresas paraestatales*. Mexico City: Fondo de Cultura Económica.

Rohde, David (1979) "Risk-bearing and Progressive Ambition: The Case of the United States House of Representatives" *American Journal of Political Science* 23 (February), 1–26.

Rosenstone, Steve, Roy Behr, and Edward Lazarus (1984) *Third Parties in America*. Princeton: Princeton University Press.

Ross, Michael (2001) "Does Oil Hinder Democracy?" *World Politics* 53, 3 (April): 325–361.

Saldierna, Georgina (1999) "Dar prioridad al frente nacional progresista, pide López Obrador" *La Jornada*, (January 18): 3.

Salinas, Carlos (1994) "Sexto Informe de Gobierno, Anexo Estadístico" Mexico City: Poder Ejecutivo Federal.

Samuels, David (2002) "Presidentialized Parties: The Separation of Power and Party Organization and Behavior" *Comparative Political Studies* 35, 4 (May): 461–483.

Sánchez, Marco Aurelio (1999) *PRD, la elite en crisis: Problemas organizativos, indeterminación ideológica y deficiencias programáticas*. Mexico City: Plaza y Valdés.

Sanderson, Steven (1981) *Agrarian Populism and the Mexican State*. Berkeley: University of California Press.

Sartori, Giovanni (1968) "The Sociology of Parties: A Critical Review" in O. Stammer (ed.) *Party Systems, Party Organizations, and the Politics of New Masses*. Berlin: Institute for Political Science, Free University of Berlin.

Sartori, Giovanni (1976) *Parties and Party Systems: A Framework for Analysis*. New York: Cambridge University Press.

Schattschneider, E. E. (1942) *Party Government*. New York: Rinehart.

Schedler, Andreas (2002) "The Menu of Manipulation" *Journal of Democracy* 13, 2 (April): 36–50.

References

329

Schedler, Andreas (2005) "From Electoral Authoritarianism to Democratic Consolidation" in R. Crandall, G. Paz, and R. Roett (eds.) *Mexico's Democracy at Work*. Boulder: Lynne Rienner.

Scheiner, Ethan (2006) *Democracy without Competition: Opposition Failure in a One-Party Dominant State*. New York: Cambridge University Press.

Schlesinger, Jacob (1997) *Shadow Shoguns: The Rise and Fall of Japan's Political Machine*. Stanford: Stanford University Press.

Schlesinger, Joseph (1966) *Ambition and Politics: Political Careers in the United States*. Chicago: Rand McNally.

Schlesinger, Joseph (1991) *Political Parties and the Winning of Office*. Ann Arbor: University of Michigan Press.

Schmitt, Karl (1970) *Communism in Mexico*. Austin: University of Texas Press.

Schumpeter, Joseph (1947) *Capitalism, Socialism, and Democracy*. New York: Harper.

Scott, Robert (1964) *Mexican Government in Transition*. Urbana: University of Illinois Press.

Semo, Enrique (2003) *La búsqueda, 1. La izquierda mexicana en los albores del siglo X*. Mexico City: Oceano.

Shadlen, Ken (2004) *Democratization without Representation: The Politics of Small Industry in Mexico*. University Park: Pennsylvania State University Press.

Shalev, Michael (1990) "The Political Economy of Labor-Party Dominance and Decline in Israel" in T. J. Pempel (ed.) *Uncommon Democracies: The One-Party Dominant Regimes*. Ithaca: Cornell University Press.

Shefter, Martin (1977a) "Patronage and its Opponents: A Theory and Some European Cases," Cornell University Western Societies Program Occasional Paper No. 8.

Shefter, Martin (1977b) "Party and Patronage: Germany, England, and Italy" *Politics and Society* 7: 403–451.

Shefter, Martin (1994) *Political Parties and the State: The American Historical Experience*. Princeton: Princeton University Press.

Shirk, David (2005) *Mexico's New Politics: The PAN and Democratic Change*. Boulder: Lynne Rienner.

Shvetsova, Olga (1995) *Design of Political Institutions in Divided Societies*. Unpublished Ph.D. Dissertation, Department of Political Science, California Institute of Technology.

Singh, Hari (2000) "Opposition Politics and the 1999 Malaysian Elections" *Trends in Malaysia: Election Assessment* 1 (January): 33–38.

Skocpol, Theda and Margaret Somers (1980) "The Uses of Comparative History in Macrosocial Inquiry" *Comparative Studies in Society and History* 22: 174–197.

Smith, Benjamin (2005) "Life of the Party: The Origins of Regime Breakdown and Persistence under Single-Party Rule" *World Politics* 57 (April): 421–451.

Smith, Peter H. (1979) *Labyrinths of Power: Political Recruitment in Twentieth-Century Mexico*. Princeton: Princeton University Press.

Smith, Peter H. (1989) "The 1988 Presidential Succession in Historical Perspective" in W. Cornelius, J. Gentleman, and P. Smith (eds.) *Mexico's Alternative Political Futures*. La Jolla: Center for U.S.-Mexican Studies.

330 *References*

Snyder, James (1994) "Safe Seats, Marginal Seats, and Party Platforms: The Logic of Platform Differentiation" *Economics and Politics* 6: 201–214.

Snyder, Richard (2001) *Politics after Neoliberalism: Reregulation in Mexico.* New York: Cambridge University Press.

Solinger, Debra (2001) "Ending One-Party Dominance: Korea, Taiwan, Mexico" *Journal of Democracy* 12, 1: 30–42.

Spotts, Frederic and Theodor Wieser (1986) *Italy: A Difficult Democracy.* New York: Cambridge University Press.

Stokes, Susan (2001) *Mandates and Democracy: Neoliberalism by Surprise in Latin America.* New York: Cambridge University Press.

Stokes, Susan (2007) "Political Clientelism" in C. Boix and S. Stokes (ed.) *Handbook of Comparative Politics.* Oxford: Oxford University Press.

Stone, Walter, Sandy Maisel, and Cherie Maestas (2004) "Quality Counts: Extending the Strategic Politician Model of Incumbent Deterrence" *American Journal of Political Science* 48, 3 (July): 479–495.

Taagapera, Rein and Matthew Shugart (1991) *Seats and Votes: The Effects and Determinants of Electoral Systems.* New Haven: Yale University Press.

Tarrow, Sidney (1967) *Peasant Communism in Southern Italy.* New Haven: Yale University Press.

Tarrow, Sidney (1990) "Maintaining Hegemony in Italy: 'The Softer they Rise, the Slower they Fall!'" in T. J. Pempel (ed.) *Uncommon Democracies: The One-Party Dominant Regimes.* Ithaca: Cornell University Press.

Tarrow, Sydney (1994) *Power in Movement.* New York: Cambridge University Press.

Teh, Yik Koon (2002) "Money Politics in Malaysia" *Journal of Contemporary Asia* 32, 3: 338–345.

Tien, Hung-mao (1997) "Taiwan's Transformation" in L. Diamond, M. Plattner, Y. Chu, and H. Tien (eds.) *Consolidating the Third Wave Democracies.* Baltimore: Johns Hopkins University Press.

Tien, Hung-mao and Tun-jen Cheng (1999) "Crafting Democratic Institutions" in S. Tsang and H. Tien (eds.) *Democratization in Taiwan: Implications for China.* New York: St. Martin's Press.

Tomz, Michael, Jason Wittenberg, and Gary King (2001) "CLARIFY: Software for Interpreting and Presenting Statistical Results" http://gking.harvard.edu/clarify/

Trejo, Guillermo and Claudio Jones (1998) "Political Dilemmas of Welfare Reform: Poverty and Inequality in Mexico" in S. Purcell and L. Rubio (eds.), *Mexico under Zedillo.* Boulder: Lynne Rienner.

Trejo Delabre, Raúl (2000) "Procesos electorales y medios de comunicación" Federal Elections Institute, Mexico City. http://www.raultrejo.tripod.com/ensayosmedios/ProcesoselectoralesymediosIFEmayo00ppt, accessed 12/7/05.

Tsebelis, George (1990) *Nested Games: Rational Choice in Comparative Politics.* Berkeley: University of California Press.

Tucker, Robert (1961) "Towards a Comparative Politics of Movement-Regimes" *American Political Science Review* 55, 2 (June): 281–289.

Tucker, Robert (1965) "The Dictator and Totalitarianism" *World Politics* 17, 4: 555–583.

Tullock, Gordon (1971) "The Paradox of Revolution" *Public Choice* 11 (Fall): 89–99.

Van de Walle, Nicolas (2002) "Africa's Range of Regimes" *Journal of Democracy* 13, 2 (April): 66–80.

Van de Walle, Nicolas (2006) "Tipping Games: When Do Opposition Parties Coalesce?" in A. Schedler (ed.) *Electoral Authoritarianism*. Boulder: Lynne Rienner.

Van de Walle, Nicolas and Kimberly Butler (1999) "Political Parties and Party Systems in Africa's Illiberal Democracies" *Cambridge Review of International Affairs* 12, 1: 14–28.

Ware, Alan (1996) *Political Parties and Party Systems*. New York: Oxford University Press.

Warner, Carolyn (1998) "Getting out the Vote with Patronage and Threat: The French and Italian Christian Democratic Parties, 1945–1958" *Journal of Interdisciplinary History* 28, 4: 553–582.

Weiner, Robert (2003) *Anti-competition in 'Competitive' Party Systems*. Unpublished Ph.D. Dissertation, Department of Political Science, University of California, Berkeley.

Weldon, Jeffrey (2004) "Changing Patterns of Executive-Legislative Relations in Mexico" in J. Middlebrook (ed.) *Dilemmas of Political Change in Mexico*. London: Institute of Latin American Studies, University of London.

White, James (1970) *The Sokagakkai and Mass Society*. Stanford: Stanford University Press.

Wittman, Donald (1983) "Candidate Motivation: A Synthesis of Alternative Theories" *American Political Science Review* 77, 1: 142–157.

Woodall, Brian (1996) *Japan under Construction: Corruption, Politics, and Public Works*. Berkeley: University of California Press.

World Bank, World Development Report 2000–2001. Washington, DC: World Bank.

Xu, Dianqing (1997) "The KMT Party's Enterprises in Taiwan" *Modern Asian Studies* 31, 2: 399–413.

Zaller, John (1998) "Politicians as Prize Fighters: Electoral Selection and Incumbency Advantage" in J. Geer (ed.) *Politicians and Party Politics*. New York: Palgrave Macmillan.

Zarembo, Alan (2001) "Truth and Consequences" *Newsweek International* (December 10): 40.

Zermeño, Sergio (1982) "De Echeverría a de la Madrid: Las clases altas y el estado mexicano en la batalla por la hegemonía. Washington, DC: Wilson Center, Working Paper 118.

Zolberg, Aristide (1966) *Creating Political Order: The Party-States of West Africa*. Chicago: Rand McNally.

Zuckerman, Alan (1979) *The Politics of Faction: Christian Democratic Rule in Italy*. New Haven: Yale University Press.

Index

Abramson, Paul, 19, 174
Abreu, Jogin, 27
activists, 141, 184. *See also* party elites
Adams, James, 26, 50, 52, 54, 65
Aguilar Zinser, Adolfo, 230, 238
Aldrich, John, 11, 121, 122, 129, 133, 136, 159, 184
Alemán, Miguel, 74, 79–81
Alliance for Change, 221
Almazán, Juan Andreu, 78
Alvarez, R. Michael, 246
Alves, Maria Helena Moreira, 44
Ames, Barry, 46
Amigos de Fox, 114, 214, 231–32, 242, 253
Angola, 13
Antorcha Popular, 203, 214
Arap Moi, Daniel, 7
Arce, René, 205
Argentina, 83
Arian, Alan, 10, 16, 46, 276
Arredondo Ramírez, Pablo, 110
Arrellano, David, 99, 100, 213
Arriola, Carlos, 9, 87–90, 166
Aspe, Pedro, 101–3, 105
Assembly of Neighborhoods (AB), 199, 204
Authentic Revolutionary Party of Mexico (PARM), Mexico, 94

authoritarian regimes. *See* fully closed authoritarian regimes; one-party regimes
authoritarian tools, 14, 15, 34, 57–59, 259, 306. *See also* electoral fraud; *individual country cases*; repression
Avila Camacho, Manuel, 74, 77, 79

Bahamas, 256
Bailey, John, 46, 80, 85
bank nationalization, Mexico, 92
Bank Savings Protection Fund (FOBAPROA), Mexico, 112, 222, 238
Banquet, the, Mexico, 105
Barisan Alternatif (BA), Malaysia, 271
Barisan Nasional (BN), Malaysia, 37, 269. *See also* United Malays National Organization (UMNO)
Barnes, Samuel, 10, 16, 46, 276, 287
Bartels, Larry, 244
Bartlett, Manuel, 214
Bartra, Roger, 45, 73
Basañez, Miguel, 88, 89, 173, 233
BDP. *See* Botswana Democratic Party

333

Beck, Thorsten, 15, 18, 23, 24
Bejerano, René, 190
Berton, Peter, 278, 279
Besley, Timothy, 130
Bianco, William, 11, 121, 133
biased party competition. *See* dominant party resource advantages; party competition, spatial theories of; patronage; repression
black-gold politics, Taiwan, 266, 268
Blondel, Jean, 10, 15, 16
BNF. *See* Botswana National Front
Boix, Carles, 12, 22, 158, 299, 308
Borjas Benavente, Adriana Leticia, 9, 154
Bortolotti, Bernardo, 293
Botswana, 17, 22, 37
Botswana Congress Party (BCP), 38
Botswana Democratic Party (BDP), 17, 38
Botswana National Front (BNF), 37
Bouton, Lawrence, 272
Brandenburg, Frank, 4, 76, 299
Bravo Mena, Luis Felipe, 232
Brazil, 44, 85, 104, 302
Brody, David, 243
Brooker, Paul, 10, 44
Brownlee, Jason, 62
Bruhn, Kathleen, 8, 9, 73, 74, 81, 86, 93, 94, 106, 107, 144, 152, 154, 160, 177, 227, 230, 232, 235, 237, 239
Bruno, Giovanni, 294
Buendía, Jorge, 20, 174
bureaucracy. *See* public bureaucracy
Business Coordinating Council (CCE), Mexico, 88, 89
Butler, Kimberly, 15

cacique, 203
Calder, Kent, 281
Calderón Hinojosa, Felipe, 124
Calderón, Luisa María, 207
camarillas, 99. *See also* Institutional Revolutionary Party (PRI)
Cameroon, 13
Camp, Roderic Ai, 99, 233, 299

campaign finance. *See also* dominant party resource advantages; patronage
in Mexico, 107–14, 149, 212, 231
equality of, 213, 215
government donations, 111
illegal funds, 113, 114, 213
and party competitiveness, 107
private donations, 111, 212
in Taiwan, 266, 268
campaign restrictions, Japan, 283
campaigns. *See* Cárdenas Solorzano, C.; Fox, V.; Labastida, F.
Campbell, John, 282
Candiani, Mauricio, 201, 202
Cárdenas Solorzano, Cuauhtémoc, 7, 93, 95, 154, 189, 196, 198, 199, 203, 211, 221–53 *passim*, 301
campaign strategy of, 234, 253
campaign style of, 239
centrism of, 240–44
competence ratings of, 238, 252
defection from, 245, 249, 251
electoral coalition of, 233
nomination of in 2000, 229–30, 267
noncentrism of, 252
viability assessments of, 250, 252
voter defection from, 240
Cárdenas, Lázaro, 73–94 *passim*
Carey, John, 61, 266
Carothers, Thomas, 14
Carr, Barry, 9, 79–82, 85–87, 152
Case, William, 269, 272
Cassa per il Mezzogiorno, Italy, 289, 293
Castañeda, Jorge, 7, 94, 95, 230
Castillo Peraza, Carlos, 202
Castillo, Heberto, 84, 235
Castles, Francis, 286
catchall parties. *See also individual party names*
definition of, 37
extensive expansion of, 191
organizational profile of, 179
recruitment style of, 183
voter communication style of, 184

Catholic Church, 111, 191
CD, Mexico. *See* Democratic Current
Centeno, Miguel Angel, 101, 106
Cervera Pacheco, Victor, 214
Chand, Vikram, 9
Chandra, Kanchan, 276
Charlesworth, James, 18
charro, 79. *See also* authoritarian
    tools
Chaudhry, Kiren, 307
Chen, Shui-bian, 267, 268
Cheng, Tun-jen, 10, 45, 262, 264
Chhibber, Pradeep, 276
Chile, 7, 44, 87, 104, 134, 299
Chong, Dennis, 122–24
Christensen, Ray, 276, 278, 280,
    282–84
Christian Democratic Party (DC),
    Italy, 276, 285, 300. *See also*
    dominant party systems;
    dominant party democratic
    regimes (DPDRs)
  alternative arguments for
    dominance, 285
  as catchall party, 285
  end of dominance, 294
  parliamentarism and dominance,
    287
  resource advantages, 285, 288
    control of public bureaucracy by,
      290–91
    decline of, 292–94
    origin of, 289–91
    types of, 289–91, 294
Chu, Yun-han, 38, 45, 122, 261–64,
    266
Chua, Huat Beng, 37, 38, 271, 273,
    274
Civic Alliance, Mexico, 111
Civic Union of Iztapalapa (UCI),
    Mexico, 204
civil service. *See* public bureaucracy
Clark, Peter, 123, 125
cleavages. *See* partisan cleavages
clientelism. *See also* patronage
  as compared to patronage, 40
  in Italy, 289
  in Japan, 278, 281, 283

in Taiwan, 267
public goods taregting and, 283
Cline, Howard, 4, 299
CNC. *See* National Campesino
    Confederation, Mexico
CNOP. *See* National Confederation of
    Popular Organizations
Coate, Steven, 130
Coleman, James, 15
Collier, David, 45, 76, 77, 80
Collier, Ruth Berins, 45, 76, 77, 80,
    91
Colosio, Luis Donaldo, 105
command economy, 307
competitive authoritarianism, 11, 14,
    15, 307, 308
conceptual stretching, 260
Conchello, José Angel, 87, 165
Confederation of Industrial Business
    Chambers (CONCAMIN),
    Mexico, 89
Confederation of Mexican Workers
    (CTM), 75, 77, 100, 104, 105,
    212
Congress Party, India, 258, 276
congressional gridlock, Mexico, 8,
    302
Conover, Pamela Johnston, 243
Coordinator of University Students
    (CEU), Mexico, 190
Cornelius, Wayne, 50, 72, 81, 98, 102,
    111, 203, 214, 215, 233, 299
costs of participation. *See* opportunity
    costs; party elites; repression
Côte d'Ivoire, 13
Cotton, James, 122, 264
Coulon, Christian, 37
Cox, Gary, 11, 15, 16, 18, 23–26, 48,
    52, 62, 70, 121, 127, 133, 177,
    245, 257, 262, 263, 266, 277,
    278
Craig, Ann, 50, 72, 81, 98, 102, 299
Crespo, José Antonio, 195
Cristero Rebellion, 76
  Mexico, 78
Cross, John, 104
Crouch, Harold, 45, 50, 269, 270,
    272–74

CTM. *See* Confederation of Mexican Workers
Cuéllar, Angélica, 199
Curtis, Gerald, 277, 279, 281–84

Dalton, Matt, 97, 156
DAP. *See* Democratic Action Party, Malaysia
Davis, Otto, 48
DC. *See* Christian Democratic Party, Italy
de la Madrid, Miguel, 91, 166, 199
de Palma, André, 26, 177
debt crisis. *See* economic crisis, in Mexico
dedazo, 77, 236
Deininger, Klaus, 22
della Porta, Donatella, 285, 291, 294, 295
Democratic Action Party (DAP), Malaysia, 38, 270
Democratic Current (CD), Mexico, 93, 154, 190
Democratic Mexican Party (PDM), 86
Democratic Progressive Party (DPP), Taiwan, 38, 261–63, 267, 268
democratization. *See* transitions to democracy
di Palma, Guiseppe, 285
Diamond, Larry, 14, 267, 268
Diaw, Aminata, 20, 37
Díaz-Cayeros, Alberto, 106
Dillon, Samuel, 98, 99, 212, 235, 237
dinosaurs, 236. *See also* Institutional Revolutionary Party (PRI)
Diouf, Mamadou, 20, 37
doctrinarios, 166. *See also* National Action Party (PAN)
dominant parties. *See also* dominant party systems
  centrism of, 45, 309
  defection from, 61–62
  legitimacy of, 10, 46
  origins of, 10
  and turnout, 46
dominant party authoritarian regimes (DPARs), 14, 16, 258, 261–76,

307. *See also individual party names and countries*
dominant party democratic regimes (DPDRs), 258, 259, 275–95. *See also individual party names and countries*
dominant party equilibrium, 16, 306
  in Botswana, 37
  formal model of, 47–59
  in Italy, 285–88
  in Japan, 278–81
  in Malaysia, 37, 268–71
  in Mexico, 37, 71, 72
  in Senegal, 37
  in Taiwan, 38, 261–62
dominant party resource advantages, 5–6, 298, 306. *See also individual party names;* patronage
  control of public bureaucracy, 41
  effects on political parties, 39
  measurement of, 149–50
  and probability of victory, 47–52
  types of, 39–42
dominant party systems. *See also* dominant parties; dominant party authoritarian regimes (DPARs); dominant party democratic regimes (DPDRs); *individual party names and countries;* resource theory of single-party dominance
  authoritarian tools and, 34, 42–45
  case selection for comparison, 256
  compared to fully competitive democracies, 17
  compared to predominant party systems, 259
  cultural theory of, 10, 257
  definition of, 12–16
  dominant party's policy appeals and, 45–47
  DPARs compared to DPDRs, 258–60
  economic crisis and, 21
  examples of, 16, 37, 258
  existing theories of, 10, 17–27, 257

institutional theory and, 22–24, 257
in Italy, 284–95
in Japan, 277–84
in Malaysia, 37, 268–75
modernization theory and, 21–22, 257
neutral models and, 24–26
non-neutral models and, 26–27
opposition coordination in, 308
opposition party types in, 35–38
parliamentary systems, 15, 220, 257, 276
patronage. *See* patronage
presidential systems, 15, 219, 257, 302
proto-dominant party systems, 14
rational choice theory and, 24–27
regime classification, 12
regional dominance, 17
repression. *See* repression
resource advantages. *See* dominant party resource advantages; resource theory of single-party dominance
retrospective voting theory and, 19–21, 308
role of the state in, 22, 149, 307
social cleavages theory and, 18–19
in Taiwan, 38, 261–68
Domínguez, Jorge, 95, 143, 144, 160, 173, 174, 176, 177, 233
Dow, Jay, 246
Downs, Anthony, 48, 178, 306
DPARs. *See* dominant party authoritarian regimes
DPDR. *See* dominant party democratic regimes
DPP. *See* Democratic Progressive Party, Taiwan
Dresser, Denise, 106
Duverger, Maurice, 10, 16, 22
Duverger's Law, 22, 23

Eastern Europe, 301
Ebenstein, William, 100
Echeverría, Luis, 74, 84, 85, 87–89, 165

Eckstein, Susan, 183, 203
economic crisis, 174
effects on party elites' policy preferences, 159
in Malaysia, 274
in Mexico, 8, 74, 89–91, 94, 102, 115, 166, 173
effective number of parties, 17–19
Egypt, 13, 62
Eisenstadt, Shmuel, 50, 158
Eisenstadt, Todd, 7, 59, 95
ejidos, 80
elections
fraud. *See* electoral, fraud
in Italy, 285, 292, 294
in Japan, 277, 284
in Malaysia, 269
in Mexico, 2. *See also* Cárdenas Solorzano, C.; Fox, V.; Labastida, F.
1976, 86, 89, 165
1988, 7, 93, 95, 196, 203
2000, 210–54
fairness of, 150, 210–15
freeness of, 71
meaningfulness of, 2, 71
other elections, 91, 94, 195, 198, 200, 202, 203
in Taiwan, 2000, 266–68
meaningful competition, 13, 14, 259, 269
electoral authoritarianism, 14. *See also* competitive authoritarianism
electoral fraud, 14, 15, 34, 35, 42, 259, 300, 306
with certainty, 42
compared to resource advantages, 43, 58
effects on opposition parties, 42, 58
evidence of, 43
in Kenya, 13
in Malaysia, 269
in Mexico, 4, 7, 72, 73, 86, 91–95, 174
requirements for success of, 43
in Taiwan, 263
with uncertainty, 14, 43

electoral law
in Japan, 283
in Mexico, 86, 98, 107–14, 165, 168
electoral management bodies, 41, 309
electoral system
effect of district magnitude, 22–24
in Italy, 257
in Japan, 257, 278, 285
in Malaysia, 24, 257, 271
in Mexico, 24, 177, 257, 271
single nontransferable vote (SNTV), 262, 266, 278, 280, 284
in Taiwan, 24, 257
electoral-professional parties, 37
elite activists. *See* party elites
Endersby, James, 246
Epstein, Leon, 4, 52, 60, 121
equilibrium dominance. *See* dominant party equilibrium
Estévez, Federico, 106, 233
ethno-linguistic fractionalization, 18
European Manifestos Project, 73, 144
European Union, 292
expressive incentives. *See* party elites
externally mobilized parties, 11, 122, 303
extremism, definition of, 33

Farneti, Paolo, 285
FDN. *See* National Democratic Front, Mexico
Feddersen, Timothy, 24, 48
Federal Elections Institute (IFE), Mexico, 110, 113, 114, 212–14
Federal Electoral Tribunal (TRIFE), Mexico, 114
Federation of Public Sector Unions (FSTSE), Mexico, 100, 104, 212
Féher, Ferenc, 44
Feldman, Stanley, 243
FEP. *See* People's Front Party, Mexico
Ferdinand, Peter, 122, 263
Fernández de Cevallos, Diego, 230, 232, 233
Fields, Karl, 264, 265
Fiorina, Morris, 20, 174

firefighting strategy, 73, 75, 95, 114, 159. *See also* Institutional Revolutionary Party (PRI)
Fischer, Bernhard, 77
Fish, M. Steven, 44
Fitzgibbon, Russell, 4, 299
FOBAPROA, *See* Bank Savings Protection Fund
Fox, Vicente, 2, 29, 38, 97, 114, 202, 210–53 *passim*, 268, 301, 302, 325, 326
Amigos de Fox. See Amigos de Fox
campaign strategy of, 234–43, 253
campaign style of, 239
centrism of, 240–44, 252, 253
competence ratings of, 238, 252
distance from PAN, 242, 253
electoral coalition of, 211, 233
independent resources of, 229, 231
nomination battle in 2000, 230–33, 267
Freedom House scores, 44, 96–97, 261
FSTSE. *See* Federation of Public Sector Unions
Fuentes-Berain, Rossana, 27
fully closed authoritarian regimes, 307, 308
as compared to dominant party systems, 134
as compared to Mexico, 96
definition of, 4
examples of, 13
fully competitive democracies, 304

Gabon, 13
Gambia, 16, 256
García Cervantes, Ricardo, 232
Garretón, Manuel Antonio, 44
Garrido, Luis Javier, 80
Geddes, Barbara, 16, 21, 98, 105, 120
Gerken, Egbert, 77
Gerschenkron, Alexander, 271, 292
gestión social, 201, 202, 207
Gibney, Mark, 97, 156
Givens, Terri, 11, 122
Golden, Miriam, 285, 286, 289–91, 294, 295

Gómez Mont, Esperanza, 206, 207
Gómez Morín, Manuel, 188
Gomez, Edmund, 122, 269, 273, 274
Gómez, Leopoldo, 46
González Casanova, Pablo, 4, 88, 299
González Morfín, Efraín, 88
Gordillo, Elba Esther, 214
green parties, Western Europe, 41, 122, 303
Green Party (PVEM), Mexico, 114, 214, 221, 235
Greenberg, Joseph, 25
Greene, Kenneth F., 8, 10, 143, 196, 199, 213, 302
Grindle, Merilee, 99
Grofman, Bernard, 50, 52, 54, 65
Groseclose, Timothy, 50, 51, 57
Grzymala-Busse, Anna, 301
Guerrero Castillo, Augustín, 190
Guerrero, Juan Pablo, 99, 100, 213
Guillermoprieto, Alma, 203
Gutiérrez, Gabriela, 207
Guyana, 13
Guzzini, Stefano, 285, 294

Haber, Paul, 106, 183, 199
Haggard, Stephan, 21, 22, 159, 174
Hartz, Louis, 18
Hechter, Michael, 124
Heller, Agnes, 44
Hellman, Judith Adler, 45, 75, 81, 83, 85, 87, 93, 183, 299
Hellman, Stephen, 288
Hidalgo, Javier, 198–200
Hiemenz, Ulrich, 77
Hine, David, 285
Hinich, Melvin, 26, 48, 50
Hirschman, Albert O., 129, 130, 305
Holm, John, 38
Howard, Marc Morjé, 7, 62, 308
Hrebenar, Ronald, 277, 279, 282–84
Hsieh, John Fuh-sheng, 20, 21
Huang, Teh-fu, 264
Hug, Simon, 12, 303
Hugo, Victor, 205
Huntington, Samuel, 10, 45, 73

hyper-incumbency advantages, 39, 63, 98, 119, 297, 300, 309. *See also* dominant party resource advantages; *individual party names*; patronage

Ibarra, Rosario, 235
Ibarrola, Christlieb, 87
IFE. *See* Federal Elections Institute
Imaz, Carlos, 190
import-substitution industrialization (ISI), 101, 104, 307
inchoate party systems, 302
incumbency advantages, 39. *See also* hyper-incumbency advantages
independent left, Mexico, *See* Party of the Democratic Revolution (PRD), predecessors to
India, 258, 276
Indonesia, 13
informal sector, 92, 104, 214
Inoguchi, Takashi, 276, 281, 282
Institute for Industrial Reconstruction (IRI), Italy, 289
Institutional Revolutionary Party (PRI), Mexico, 16. *See also* dominant party systems; dominant party authoritarian regimes (DPARs)
authoritarian preceptions of, 237
authoritarian tools and, 72
candidate launch 2000, 140, 267
compared to other dominant parties, 255–96
defeat of in 2000, 44, 210, 267
historical relationship with opposition, 75–96 *passim*
identifiers, 215, 233, 248, 250
legitimacy of, 165
nomination politics in 2000, 232, 267
performance evaluations. *See* retrospective voting
policy position of, 72, 73. *See also* firefighting strategy
centrism, 73, 164
effects on party elites' policy preferences, 159

Index

Institutional Revolutionary Party
(*cont.*)
  shift to left, 75–77, 84–87
  shift to right, 77–82, 91–92
  post-democratization survival of, 8, 301
  as pragmatic party, 10, 46, 73
  predecessors to, 80
  prospective evaluations of, 21, 174
  recruitment into, 77, 138
  repression and, 75–97, 168. *See also* repression
  resource advantages, 34, 75–96 *passim*, 102, 185
    control of public bureaucracy, 99–101
    decline of, 105, 114, 173, 211–15
    origin of, 97–99, 101–107
    sectoral organizations, 75, 80, 104, 105, 188, 214
  voter dissatisfaction with. *See* retrospective voting
  voter identification with, 173
institutional theory, 22–24, 71, 72
interest groups, 124
Internal Security Act (ISA), Malaysia, 275
internally mobilized parties, 11
Islamic Party of Malaysia (PAS), 38, 270
Israel, 258, 264, 276
Italian Communist Party (PCI), 286–88
Italian Social Movement (MSI), 286
Italy under the DC, 255, 257–59, 276, 284–95, 300
Iztapalapa, Mexico City, 195, 196, 203–8

Jackson, John, 129, 130
Japan under the LDP, 255, 257–59, 276–84, 295, 300
Japanese Communist Party (JCP), 278, 280
Japanese Socialist Party (JSP), 279, 280
Jennings, Kent, 148
Johnson, Chalmers, 282

Johnson, Kenneth, 78, 83, 84
Johnston, Richard, 219
Jones, Claudio, 107
Jones, Mark, 192
Jowitt, Ken, 44, 45

Kalyvas, Stathis, 292
KANU. *See* Kenya African National Union
Karl, Terry, 11, 14
Katz, Richard, 304
Kaufman Purcell, Susan, 4, 299
Kaufman, Robert, 21, 22, 159, 174
Kenya, 7, 13
Kenya African National Union (KANU), 7
Keohane, Robert, 16
Kessler, Timothy, 85, 87, 106, 112
Key, V.O., 18, 20, 174
King, Gary, 16, 220, 247
Kirchheimer, Otto, 37
Kitschelt, Herbert, 11, 37, 50, 122, 129, 136, 158, 279, 283, 305
Klesner, Joseph, 86, 107, 176, 213, 233
KMT. *See* Kuomintang, Taiwan
kōenkai, Japan, 283
Kollman, Ken, 178
Komeito/Clean Government Party (CGP), Japan, 279, 280
Krauss, Ellis, 278, 281, 282
Krauze, Enrique, 1
Kuo, Chengtian, 264, 265
Kuomintang (KMT), Taiwan, 16, 38, 261, 264–65, 300. *See also* dominant party systems; dominant party authoritarian regimes (DPARs)
  as catchall party, 262
  centrism of, 262
  defection from, 267
  institutional argument for dominance, 262
  performance of, 263. *See also* retrospective voting
  prospective evaluations of, 21
  resource advantages, 263–64

control of public bureaucracy, 264
decline of, 265–67
origin of, 264–65
Kuran, Timur, 174

Laakso, Markku, 18
Labastida, Francisco, 211, 233, 235, 236, 239, 243–45, 247–52
campaign strategy of, 234, 253
competence ratings of, 239, 252
democratic credentials of, 236
electoral coalition of, 233
Lacy, Dean, 20, 21
land redistribution, Mexico, 77, 79, 85
Langston, Joy, 80
LaPalombara, Joseph, 285, 289, 290
Latin America
compared to Mexico, 7, 44, 87, 104, 299
rise of the left across, 210
Laver, Michael, 15, 62, 276, 277, 286
Law of curvilinear disparities, 228, 305
Lawson, Chappell, 94, 110, 176, 213, 233, 244
leaders. See party elites
Leftist Democratic Faction (CID), Mexico, 190, 205
Lehoucq, Fabrice, 43
Levite, Ariel, 10
Levitsky, Steven, 6, 11, 12, 14, 15, 48, 302
Liberal Democratic Party (LDP), Japan, 276, 277, 280, 300. See also dominant party systems; dominant party democratic regimes (DPDRs)
as catchall party, 281
end of dominance, 284
existing explanations for dominance, 277
resource advantages
control of public bureaucracy, 282
types of, 281–83
as rightwing party, 278

Liberal Mexican Party, 88
Liberation Theology, 84
Lichbach, Mark, 12, 122
Lien, Chan, 267, 268
Lin, Oliver, 263
Lin, Tse-min, 26, 177
Linz, Juan, 61, 219
Lipset, Seymour Martin, 18, 38
Lipson, Leslie, 18
Liu, I-chou, 261, 262, 264
Loaeza, Soledad, 9, 37, 77, 78, 87, 88, 166
Locke, Richard, 293
Lombardo Toledano, Vicente, 77
Londregan, John, 50
López Obrador, Andrés Manuel, 124, 229
López Portillo, José, 74, 86, 89, 90, 166
Lujambio, Alonso, 90, 91, 112, 213
Lustig, Nora, 85, 91, 102, 103

Mabry, Donald, 9, 76–79, 191
machine politics. See patronage
MacLeod, Dag, 101–4, 106, 107
Madagascar, 13
Madrazo, Roberto, 236, 237
Magaloni, Beatriz, 9, 20, 21, 62, 106, 143, 144, 174, 217, 233
Magar, Eric, 110
Mahathir, Mohammad, 275
Mainwaring, Scott, 193, 302
Mair, Peter, 193, 286, 304
Malaysia under UMNO, 16, 37, 50, 122, 255, 257, 258, 268–75, 295, 296, 300, 307, 308. See also United Malays National Organization (UMNO)
as dominant party authoritarian regime, 269
as fully closed authoritarian regime, 269
economic crisis, 274
National Economic Plan (NEP), 272–73
Mandela, Nelson, 236
Manikas, Peter, 266
Markus, Gyorgy, 44

Martínez, Omar, 110
Martínez Valle, Adolfo, 78, 87, 88
Martínez Verdugo, Arnoldo, 86, 152
mass media, 94, 184
May, John, 129, 130, 136, 148, 159, 228, 305
McCann, James, 95, 143, 144, 160, 173, 174, 176, 177, 233, 244
McDonald, Ronald, 15
McKelvey, Richard, 26
meaningful electoral competition. *See* elections
Means, Gordon Paul, 269
Medina Placencia, Carlos, 230
medium N analysis, 256
Meguid, Bonnie, 303
Merino, Mauricio, 100
Merrill III, Samuel, 50, 52, 54, 65
Mershon, Carol, 292
message-seekers. *See* party elites
Mexican Communist Party (PCM), 13, 80–82, 84–86, 92, 93, 152
  membership of, 80, 82
  registration of, 71, 80, 86
Mexican Democratic Party (PDM), 76
Mexican Employers' Association, 88
Mexican left. *See* Party of the Democratic Revolution (PRD), predecessors to
Mexican Revolution, 73, 76, 125
Mexican Revolutionary Party (PRM), 75, 80
Mexican Socialist Party (PMS), 86, 93, 152, 165, 204
Mexican Unified Socialist Party (PSUM), 86, 92, 93, 151, 152, 196, 204
Mexican Worker-Peasant Party (POCM), 82, 152
Mexican Workers Party (PMT), 84, 86, 152
Mexico Party Personnel Surveys
  description of, 27, 140–42
  sample sizes, 141
  stock versus flow, 142
Mexico under the PRI. *See also* dominant party resource

advantages; electoral fraud; National Action Party (PAN); Party of the Democratic Revolution (PRD); repression
  compared to fully closed authoritarian regimes, 7, 44, 134, 299
  in comparative perspective, 299
  as a democracy, 4, 72, 299
  as a dominant party authoritarian regime (DPAR), 299
  as a fully closed authoritarian regime, 4, 72, 299
  history of party competition, 75–96
Middlebrook, Kevin, 75, 79, 81, 83
Miguel Hidalgo, Mexico City, 195–202
Miller, John, 178
Miller, Warren, 148
Mizrahi, Yemile, 9, 78, 90, 124, 166, 188, 189, 232
MLN. *See* National Liberation Movement
Moctezuma Barragán, Esteban, 99, 100
modernization theory, 21–22, 71, 158, 308
Moe, Terry, 123, 124
Molinar, Juan, 13, 71, 80, 81, 106, 107, 110, 144
Moore, Clement, 10
moral authority, 175, 229, 305
Moreno, Alejandro, 27, 143, 174, 176, 233
Mozambique, 13
MRM. *See* Revolutionary Teacher's Movement
MRP. *See* People's Revolutionary Movement
MSI. *See* Italian Social Movement
MT. *See* Territorial Movement, Mexico
multi-method approach, 27
Munger, Michael, 26
Muñoz Ledo, Porfirio, 93, 154, 190, 229, 230
Munro-Kua, Anne, 269, 272, 275

Muramatsu, Michio, 278, 281, 282

NAFTA, 177
Nagler, Jonathan, 246
National Action Party (PAN), Mexico.
    See also Fox, V.; opposition
    parties; party elites
  activist recruitment, 182–84,
    188–89
  adherentes, 232
  Catholic Church and, 76, 77, 90,
    144
  Catholic humanism and, 77, 88,
    165
  as Christian Democratic party,
    87
  core constituency of, 37, 181–82,
    202, 206
  cost of participation in, 79
  economic liberals and, 76, 78, 90,
    165, 166
  existing descriptions of, 9
  extremism of, 164, 165, 177, 301
  feeder organizations, 191
  formation of, 76
  history of, 75–96 *passim*
  identifiers with, 177, 215, 223, 233,
    248
  limits of expansion, 202, 207
  membership, 192–95, 201, 206
  moderation of, 165, 166
  National Assembly, 141
  National Council, 150, 230
  National Executive Committee, 232
  as niche party, 37, 189
  nomination politics in 2000,
    227–33, 267
  organization of, 188–90
  platform of, 177
  prospective evaluations of, 174
  repression of, 78
  social conservatives and, 76, 88,
    165
National Autonomous University of
    Mexico (UNAM), 83
National Campesino Confederation
    (CNC), Mexico, 75, 104

National Chamber of Transformation
    Industries, Mexico, 89
National Confederation of Popular
    Organizations (CNOP),
    Mexico, 80, 81, 90, 104, 106,
    203
National Coordinator of Urban
    Popular Movements
    (CONAMUP), Mexico, 204
National Democratic Front (FDN),
    Mexico, 93, 94, 110, 154
National Economic Plan (NEP),
    Malaysia, 272–73
National Liberation Movement
    (MLN), Mexico, 152
National Reconstruction Cardenist
    Front Party (PFCRN), Mexico,
    94
National Revolutionary Party (PNR),
    Mexico, 75
National Solidarity Program
    (PRONASOL), Mexico, 94,
    106, 203, 212
National Workers' Union (UNT),
    Mexico, 105
Nationalist Society Party (PSN),
    Mexico, 221
Nava, Salvador, 235
Needler, Martin, 72
neopanistas, 166. *See* National Action
    Party (PAN), economic liberals
    and
New Party (NP), Taiwan, 262
niche parties, 175. *See also* opposition
    parties; *individual party names*
  definition of, 35
  intensive expansion, 191
  organizational profile, 179
  recruitment style, 182
  voter communication style,
    184
Niou, Emerson, 20, 21
nomination theory, 228–29
non-neutral entry models. *See* party
    competition, spatial theories of;
    resource theory of single-party
    dominance

O'Donnell, Guillermo, 11
office-seekers. *See* party elites
oil, 76, 90, 307. *See also* PEMEX
OIR-LM. *See* Revolutionary Leftist
    Organization-Proletarian Line
Olson, Mancur, 122, 304
Olukoshi, Adebayo, 20
one-party regimes, 26, 44, 301
OPEC, 91
Oppenheimer, Andrés, 105
opportunity costs, 60, 120, 131, 133,
    137, 148, 155, 183, 259,
    297
opposition alliance, Mexico, 219, 220,
    223–27
  failure of, 75, 221, 227
  negotiations over, 221, 227
opposition parties. *See also individual*
    party names
  collective action problem in, 62,
    122–24
  coordination failure, 62, 270,
    278–81, 308
  defection from dominant party and,
    61–62
  form of, 35, 37
  founder's problem, 53, 66–70
  information asymmetries and, 59
  in Italy, 286–88
  in Japan, 278–81
  in Malaysia, 269–71
  in Mexico. *See also* independent
    left; National Action Party
    (PAN); Party of the Democratic
    Revolution (PRD)
    candidates for executive office
    and, 302
    collective action problem in, 175,
    178, 210
    coordination failure between, 7,
    9, 147, 210, 300, *See also*
    opposition alliance
    historical opportunities for
    development, 73–96
    incentives for centrism, 176
    legality of, 71
    new parties in 1990s, 142
    as niche parties, 6, 71

opposition alliance. *See*
    opposition alliance
  organization of, 188–90
  party-building case studies,
    187–208
  poverty of, 102, 122, 184
  recruitment into, 182–84. *See*
    party elites
  repression of, 96–97
  strategy options in 2000, 215–19,
    267
moral authority and, 60, 175
party-building problems, 11, 59–63
path-dependency in, 62
policy motivations of, 52–55
poverty of, 122, 297
recruitment into. *See* party elites
spatial strategy of, 55–57, 60
in Taiwan, 261
in United States, 41
in Western Europe, 41
opposition party elites. *See* party
    elites
Ordeshook, Peter, 20, 48
Ortiz Pardo, Francisco, 231
Ortiz Pinchetti, Francisco, 231
Ortiz, Francisco, 231, 236, 239
Osborne, Martin, 25, 130
Osei-Hwedie, Bertha, 17, 38
Otake, Hideo, 279

Padgett, Leon, 45
Padierna, Dolores, 190
Page, Benjamin, 243
Page, Scott, 178
Palfrey, Thomas, 25, 303
PAN. *See* National Action Party
Panebianco, Angelo, 37, 124, 129
parallel demonstration of theory, 255
Parás, Pablo, 233
PARM. *See* Authentic Revolutionary
    Party of Mexico
partisan cleavages. *See also*
    retrospective voting; voters
  in Italy, 285
  in Japan, 281
  in Malaysia, 270
  in Mexico, 142–46, 215–19

in Taiwan, 261
party activists. *See* party elites
party affiliation. *See* party elites
Party Building Index, 179
party competition
  adaptive party theory, 177
  neutral models, 3, 7, 24–26, 48, 56, 71, 72, 176
  non-neutral models, 3, 26–27, 72. *See also* resource theory of single-party dominance
  and resource advantages, 303
  spatial theories of, 175, 303
Party of the Democratic Revolution (PRD), Mexico, 93. *See also* Cárdenas Solorzano, C.; opposition parties; party elites
  activist recruitment practices, 189–90
  core constituencies of, 37, 181–82
  defectors from PRI and, 152
  electoral performance in 1990s, 94
  existing descriptions of, 9
  expansion of, 38
  factions in, 190
  family tree, 152
  formation of, 94
  identifiers with, 177, 215, 223, 233, 248
  limits of expansion, 200, 205
  membership of, 192–95, 200, 205
  moderation of, 165, 166, 168
  National Convention of, 141
  National Political Councilors, 155
  as niche party, 37
  nomination politics in 2000, 227–33, 267
  organization of, 188–90
  platform of, 177
  predecessors to, 75–96 *passim*, 150–54, 165, 190
  prospective evaluations of, 174
  reliance on social movements, 200, 204
  repression of, 95. *See also* repression; party elites
party elites (leaders and activists)
  activists, definition of, 141

adverse selection into opposition parties, 149
careerism, 298
costs of participation, 43, 120, 133–35, 148, 155–56, 175
dominant party elites' centrism, 148
effects of probability of victory on, 148, 164
in Italy, 288
in Mexico
  cooptation of, 183
  generational conflicts, 175
  party-building preferences, 179–87
  perception of core constituencies, 181–82
  political associations and, 151
  quality of, 183
  year of affiliation, 150–55
in Taiwan, 264
message-seekers, 120, 126, 130, 148, 156
  affiliation decisions of, 131–37
  description of, 125–27
  empirics of party affiliation, 160–68
  measurement of, 156
  party-building preferences of, 179–89
  support for opposition alliance, 223–27
  utility functions of, 129–30
office-seekers, 120, 148, 156
  affiliation decisions of, 131–37
  description of, 125–27
  empirics of party affiliation, 160–68
  measurement of, 156
  party-building preferences of, 179–89
  support for opposition alliance, 223–27
  utility functions of, 127–29
opposition party founders, 124
party affiliation decisions, 59–62. *See also* party elites, costs of participation
  abstention from activism, 134

346 *Index*

party affiliation decisions (*cont.*)
  existing theories of, 120–23
  formal model of, 119–38
  incentives for, 5, 11, 52, 53,
    120–24, 128
  policy preferences and, 146
party personnel, defintion of, 141
policy preferences of
  hypotheses for, 147–48
  measurement of, 142–47
  office-seekers vs. message-seekers,
    125, 148, 157
  sincere preferences, 131–35
  statistical model of, 148–62
repression of. *See* repression
similarity of opposition candidates
  and activists, 59
socialization of, 149, 305
utility functions of, 129–30
party financing. *See* campaign finance
party identification. *See* voters
party leaders, 141. *See also* party elites
Party Nationalization Score, 192
party platforms, 144
party-owned businesses, 40, 264, 271,
  309
PAS. *See* Islamic Party of Malaysia
Pasquino, Gianfranco, 292
patronage. *See also* dominant party
    resource advantages; *individual
    party names*
  definition of, 40
  effects, compared to electoral fraud,
    58
  in Italy, 288–94
  in Japan, 281–83
  in Malaysia, 271–74
  marginal effects of by SES, 50
  in Mexico, 75–107 *passim*, 111,
    114, 173, 211–15, 245, 249
  modeling effects on party
    competition, 47–59
  modeling magnitude of, 64–66
  modernization and, 50
  networks for distribution, 49, 283
  origin of, 40–41
  in Taiwan, 263–66
  theoretical distribution of, 48

turnover and, 41
unavailability to opposition parties,
  48
voter response to, 49
PCI. *See* Italian Communist Party
PCM, Mexico. *See* Mexican
    Communist Party
PDM. *See* Mexican Democratic Party
PEMEX (Petróleos Mexicanos), 90,
  101, 221, 237, 240. *See also*
  oil
PEMEXgate, 113, 114, 214
Pempel, T.J., 10, 15, 16, 33, 258, 276,
  281
pendulum theory, 72, 73, 95. *See also*
    Institutional Revolutionary
    Party (PRI)
People's Action Party (PAP),
    Singapore, 16
People's Front Party (FEP), Mexico, 84
People's Progressive Party (PPP),
    Gambia, 16
People's Revolutionary Movement
    (MRP), Mexico, 152
PFCRN. *See* National Reconstruction
    Cardenist Front Party
Pierce, Roy, 287
Pignatelli, Andrea, 290
Plaza de Tlatelolco, 83
PMT. *See* Mexican Workers Party
PNR. *See* National Revolutionary
    Party, Mexico
POCM. *See* Mexican Worker-Peasant
    Party
Poiré, Alejandro, 176, 233
polarized pluralism, 23, 286
political economy of single-party
    dominance, 6, 34, 212, 297,
    307
political recruitment. *See* party elites
Pomper, Gerald, 124
Popular Defense Committee (CDP),
    Mexico, 106
Popular Front policy, 77
Popular Socialist Party (PPS), Mexico,
    82, 94, 152
Popular Union New Tenochitlán
    (UPNT), 190

populism, Mexico, 74–79
  conservative reaction to, 77–79
  neopopulism, 84–91
pork-barrel politics, 39
poverty-alleviation programs, Mexico, 107
PPS. *See* Popular Socialist Party
PRD. *See* Party of the Democratic Revolution
Prescott, Edward, 25
Preston, Julia, 98, 99, 212, 235, 237
PRI, Mexico. *See* Institutional Revolutionary Party (PRI), Mexico
priming of voters, 219, 235, 237
privatization. *See* state-owned enterprises
PRM. *See* Mexican Revolutionary Party
PRONASOL. *See* National Solidarity Program
PRT. *See* Revolutionary Workers Party
Prud'homme, Jean Francois, 183
Przeworski, Adam, 12–14, 16–18, 21, 22, 158, 259, 299, 308
PS. *See* Socialist Party, Senegal
PST. *See* Socialist Workers Party
PT. *See* Workers Party
public bureaucracy, political control of, 290–91, 307, 309. *See also* public sector; state-owned enterprises
  in Japan, 282
  in Malaysia, 272
  in Mexico, 85, 99–104, 213
  in Taiwan, 264
public sector. *See also* public bureaucracy; state-owned enterprises
  in Italy, 290
  in Malaysia, 271
  in Mexico, 85, 92, 212
Punto Crítico, 190
Putnam, Robert, 287, 288
PVEM. *See* Green Party, Mexico

radical rightwing parties, Western Europe, 122, 303

Rahim, Lily, 122
Ramanadham, V.V., 272
Ramírez Saiz, Juan Manuel, 92
rational choice theory, 24–27
rebel's dilemma, 12, 122
Reed, Steven, 284
rentier state, 307
repression, 57–59, 120, 133–35, 148, 155–56. *See also* authoritarian tools
  in dominant party authoritarian regimes, 44–45
  in Malaysia, 269, 272, 275
  in Mexico, 4, 72, 75, 78, 81, 83, 92, 95–97, 231
  in Taiwan, 261
  theoretical role of, 43
resource advantages. *See* dominant party resource advantages; patronage
resource theory of single-party dominance, 5–6, 34–59, 260
  adding authoritarian tools, 57–59
  comparative evidence for, 255–96
  formal model of, 47–59
  founder's problem, 66–70
  generalizability of, 255
  modeling patronage, 64–66
  political economy and, 6, 34, 212, 297, 307
  probability-maximizing party utility functions, 51
resource-poor parties, 303–306
retrospective voting. *See also* partisan cleavages; voters
  in Japan, 278
  in Mexico, 8, 9, 19, 20, 71, 72, 94, 166, 173, 174, 210, 252, 300
  in Senegal, 20
  in Taiwan, 20, 263
  in the United States, 19, 174
  theory of, 19–21, 175
Reveles Vásquez, Francisco, 88
Revolutionary Leftist Organization-Proletarian Line (OIR-LM), Mexico, 152

Revolutionary National Civic Association (ACNR), Mexico, 83, 190
revolutionary nationalism, Mexico, 73
Revolutionary Popular Union – Emiliano Zapata (UPREZ), Mexico, 204
Revolutionary Teacher's Movement (MRM), Mexico, 152
Revolutionary Workers Party (PRT), Mexico, 84, 86, 92, 93, 190
Reyes Heroles, Jesús, 86
Reyna, José Luis, 4, 45, 72, 299
Richardson, Bradley, 259, 276, 281, 282
Rigger, Shelley, 38, 261, 263, 264, 267, 268
Riker, William, 7, 8, 34, 57, 62, 219, 276, 277, 298
Rimanelli, Marco, 286
Rivera Ríos, Miguel Angel, 82
Rocha Menocal, Alina, 107
Rodríguez Araujo, Octavio, 13, 71, 86
Roeder, Philip, 18
Roemer, Andrés, 99, 100
Roessler, Phillip, 7, 62, 308
Rogozinski, Jacques, 106
Rohde, David, 11, 121
Rokkan, Stein, 18
Romer, Tom, 50
Roniger, Luis, 50, 158
Ross, Michael, 307, 308

Saldierna, Georgina, 124
Salinas de Gortari, Carlos, 7, 93–95, 103, 105, 106, 156, 166, 203, 212, 230, 235
Samuels, David, 302
Sánchez, Marco Aurelio, 9, 190
Sanderson, Steven, 101
Sartori, Giovanni, 10, 15, 16, 19, 23, 42, 259, 260, 285–87
Saucedo, Francisco, 190
Schattschneider, E.E., 124
Schedler, Andreas, 14, 45, 108
Scheiner, Ethan, 61, 276–78, 281–85, 295, 298

Schlesinger, Jacob, 281, 282
Schlesinger, Joseph, 11, 121, 124, 304
Schmitt, Karl, 71, 80–82, 84, 85
Schmitter, Philippe, 11
Schofield, Norman, 15, 62, 276, 277, 286
Schumpeter, Joseph, 14, 307
Scott, Robert, 4, 76, 299
secret budget, Mexico, 111
Secretary of the Interior, Mexico, 83, 86, 109
Secretary of the Treasury and Public Credit (SHCP), Mexico, 100
Segreto, Luciano, 294
selection bias, 16
Semo, Enrique, 81, 92
Sened, Itai, 24, 48
Senegal, 17, 37
Shadlen, Kenneth, 89
Shalev, Michael, 276
SHCP. See Secretary of the Treasury and Public Credit
Shefter, Martin, 11, 99, 122, 158, 285
Shepsle, Kenneth, 25
Shirk, David, 9, 78, 79, 87, 88, 165, 166, 220, 230–32, 237, 239, 242
Shugart, Mathew, 23, 61, 266
Shvetsova, Olga, 25
Singapore, 16, 22, 122
Singh, Hari, 38, 270
single-party dominance. See dominant parties; dominant party systems
Sirvent, Carlos, 13, 71, 86
Skocpol, Theda, 255
Slivinski, Al, 25, 130
Smith, Benjamin, 22
Smith, Peter H., 72, 99, 299
Snyder, James, 178
Snyder, Richard, 101
social choice, 306
social cleavages theory, 18–19, 71, 72
social movements, 92, 124. See also independent left; student protest

Socialist Alliance Party (PAS), Mexico, 221
Socialist Party (PS), Senegal, 17, 37
Socialist Workers Party (PST), Mexico, 151
sociological theory of party competition. *See* social cleavages theory
Soka Gakkai, 279
Solid South, 17
Solinger, Dorothy, 45, 122, 264
Somers, Margaret, 255
Soong, James, 267, 268, 275
sottogoverno, 289
Spotts, Frederic, 285, 286, 288, 290–92
Squire, Lyn, 22
state, economic role of, 149, 307. *See also* public bureaucracy; public sector; state-owned enterprises
state-owned enterprises, 6, 33, 40, 295, 307, 309
  in Italy, 289–90, 293, 294
  in Malaysia, 272
  in Mexico, 8, 98, 100, 105, 109, 149, 182
    compared to other countries, 104
    privatization of, 94, 106, 166, 173
    as proxy for resource advantages, 160, 185
    relationship between PRI and, 101
    size of, 85, 100–107, 111, 212
    types of, 101
  in Taiwan, 265
Stokes, Susan, 22, 48, 302, 308
STPRM, 214
strategic voting. *See* voters
student protest, 83, 85, 89. *See also* repression
Sumlinski, Mariusz, 272
Superbarrio Gómez, 199

Taagapera, Rein, 18, 23

Taiwan under the KMT, 16, 38, 122, 255, 257, 258, 261–68, 295, 296, 300, 308
  as dominant party authoritarian regime (DPAR), 261
  as fully closed authoritarian regime, 261
tangentopoli, Italy, 292
Tanzania, 13
Tarrow, Sidney, 10, 124, 276, 277, 285, 287–89
Teh, Yik Koon, 274
TELMEX, 101
TEPJF. *See* Federal Electoral Tribunal
Territorial Movement (MT), Mexico, 106
third parties, United States, 41, 303
Thornton, Laura, 266
threshold of representation, 24
Tien, Hung-mao, 262–64, 267
Tomz, Michael, 220, 247
transitions to democracy
  via elections, 2, 11, 301, 308
  from fully closed authoritarian regimes, 253
Trejo Delabre, Raúl, 110
Trejo, Guillermo, 107
Trinidad and Tobago, 256
Trisecta, 190
Tsebelis, George, 228
Tucker, Robert, 10, 44, 45
Tullock, Gordon, 122, 304
Tunisia, 13
turnover, 41, 98

UMNO. *See* United Malays National Organization
uncommon democracies. *See* dominant party democratic regimes (DPDRs)
Unified Coordinating Committee of Earthquake Victims (CUD), 199
Union for National Order (UNS), Mexico, 78
Union of Mexican Petroleum Workers (STPRM), 113

United Malays National Organization (UMNO), 16, 37, 38, 50, 268, 270, 296, 300, 307. *See also* dominant party systems; dominant party authoritarian regimes (DPARs)
  as catchall party, 269
  repression and, 275
  resource advantages
    control over public bureaucracy, 272
    decline of, 274
    origins of, 271–73
    types of, 271–74
United States, 41
UNS. *See* Union for National Order, Mexico
UNT. *See* National Workers' Union, Mexico

Valenzuela, Arturo, 61, 219
Vallejo, Demetrio, 84
Van Biezen, Ingrid, 193
Van de Walle, Nicolas, 7, 14, 15, 17, 62
Vannucci, Alberto, 285, 291, 294, 295
Vatican II Council, 88
Velázquez, Fidel, 77
Venezuela, 104
Verba, Sidney, 16
Visscher, Michael, 25
vote buying, 40, 75. *See also* patronage
voter dissatisfaction. *See* retrospective voting
voters. *See also* partisan cleavages; retrospective voting
  dealignment of, 19, 21, 173
  in Mexico
    campaign effects, 233, 245, 246, 248
    centrism of, 176
    economic policy opposition voters, 217, 219, 223, 251
    independents, 196, 208, 216, 219, 231, 233, 242
    issue voting, 177, 244–46, 249–50

    party identification. *See* PAN, PRI, PRD
    priorities of, 238
    projection, 243–44
    regime opposition voters, 217, 219, 222, 237
    rigid opposition voters, 217, 219, 223
    voting behavior in 2000, 244–54, 267
  retrospective voting. *See* retrospective voting
  strategic voting, 240, 245, 249, 252, 267

Walesa, Lech, 236
Ware, Alan, 16, 276
Warner, Carolyn, 285, 286, 290
Way, Lucan, 6, 11, 12, 14, 15
Weiner, Robert, 15, 61
Weinert, Richard, 4, 45, 72, 299
Weldon, Jeffrey, 106, 302
White, James, 279
Wieser, Theodor, 285, 286, 288, 290–92
Wilson, James Q., 123, 125, 192
Wittenberg, Jason, 220, 247
Wittman, Donald, 50, 56
Woodall, Brian, 281, 282
Workers Party (PT), Mexico, 106, 221
Wright, Stephen, 24, 48

Xu, Dianqing, 264

Yu, Ching-shin, 264

Zambia, 13
Zarembo, Alan, 83
Zedillo, Ernesto, 98, 107, 236, 252
Zermeño, Sergio, 89
Zimbabwe, 17
Zimbabwe Africa People's Union (ZAPU), 17
Zimbabwe African National Union (ZANU), 17
Zolberg, Aristide, 45
Zuckerman, Alan, 285, 286, 289–91